Praise for *Thriving in Graduate School*

"Over the years, higher education has been trying to encourage more students from historically marginalized backgrounds to attend graduate school, but education systems—especially grad school—aren't particularly built to be a welcoming and nurturing clime for such students. Dr. Shanok and Dr. Benedicto Elden's *Thriving in Graduate School: The Expert's Guide to Success and Wellness* is a big step in the right direction, as it explores common struggles faced by historically marginalized students—such as impostor syndrome, microaggressions, multicultural competence, and funding—and provides practical ways to help students not only succeed in graduate school but also do so while keeping their wellness. Graduate programs throughout the country should have a copy of this book to share with their students." —**E. J. R. David**, associate professor of psychology, University of Alaska Anchorage; author of *Brown Skin, White Minds: Filipino -/ American Postcolonial Psychology*, editor of *Internalized Oppression: The Psychology of Marginalized Groups*, and coauthor of *The Psychology of Oppression*

"In the midst of pandemic and austerity, swelling evidence of anxiety and depression, thrilling movements for racial and gender justice, and higher ed in free fall, *Thriving in Graduate School* offers a jazz of voices that will comfort, resonate, infuriate, and offer up brilliant strategies for moving through—with scholarly lust, activist passions, with babies, and partners (who do and don't get it); thriving amid and confronting racial microaggressions, homophobic texts, and neoliberalism; with rent overdue, some harassing faculty, a few amazing mentors, secretaries who are underpaid and hold the academic world together. In the midst you will find a lava-like fountain of academic purpose. Or at least the energy to write another three hundred words a day and care for yourself/selves. The essays in this book read like poetry for the almost PhD—some pieces will invite you to laugh, others to cry, a few to write nasty emails (that you won't necessarily send)—but on these pages, even in lock down, you will meet sisters and brothers and transgender colleagues who recognize and name the journey through an institution as oppressive as it can be liberating. Arielle F. Shanok and Nicole Benedicto Elden offer you a GPS for navigating the joyful and infuriating pathway to graduation and to remember your intellectual projects of desire and purpose. Brav@ to the editors and authors, and to the students who lay in bed wondering if it's worth it!" —**Michelle Fine**, Distinguished Professor of Critical Psychology, Women's Studies, American Studies, and Urban Education with a focus on social justice, CUNY Graduate Center; founding faculty member, Public Science Project

"*Thriving in Graduate School* is an outstanding volume that should be read by those applying to graduate school, those enrolled in graduate programs, faculty and administrators responsible to educate graduate students, and mental health professionals committed to providing psychological services to students. This volume brings together an incredibly diverse narrative of actual lived experiences, relevant research evidence that applies to a range of common graduate school experiences across a wide spectrum of academic programs as well as the diverse individual identities of students. Realistic and optimistic suggestions, or takeaways, are offered at the end of each chapter, about how to manage consequential relationships and the unique challenges of the graduate school journey." —**Robert Keisner**, PhD, professor of psychology; former director of the Clinical Psychology Doctoral Program, Long Island University, New York

"*Thriving in Graduate School: The Expert's Guide to Success and Wellness* is a refreshing book for graduate students. Through simple, engaging, and casual language, the authors demystify the experience of graduate work normalizing it and validating the tough experiences lived by students. Issues such as impostor syndrome, procrastination, and anxiety are presented in a candid way offering self-reflection exercises and wisdom tips to empower students to overcome these and other challenges. This book offers suggestions for students, faculty, administrators, and mental health providers in the support of graduate students. In this way, the authors offer a holistic approach that is easy to follow. This is a great book for first-generation graduate students. Last but not least, cultural diversity is addressed with great sensitivity. This is a great book not only for graduate students but all staff working in academic settings serving students." —**Dinelia Rosa**, PhD, director, Dean Hope Center of Educational & Psychological Services, Teachers College, Columbia University; former president, New York State Psychological Association; director of clinical training, TC Resilience Center for Veterans & Families; adjunct full professor, Teachers College Clinical Psychology program

"Dr. Shanok and Dr. Elden provide readers with a detailed description of the individual dynamics and external pressures encountered in graduate school with a how-to menu of techniques to cope with these challenges. Their suggestions and recommendations are relevant and useful not just for graduate students but for all those who have busy, demanding lives with complex choices about their careers."
—**N. Mendie Cohn**, clinical psychologist; former director, Clinical Psychology Internship Training Program, Kings County Hospital Center, Brooklyn, New York

Thriving in Graduate School

Thriving in Graduate School

The Expert's Guide to Success and Wellness

Edited by Arielle F. Shanok
and Nicole Benedicto Elden

ROWMAN & LITTLEFIELD
Lanham • Boulder • New York • London

Published by Rowman & Littlefield
An imprint of The Rowman & Littlefield Publishing Group, Inc.
4501 Forbes Boulevard, Suite 200, Lanham, Maryland 20706
www.rowman.com

6 Tinworth Street, London SE11 5AL, United Kingdom

British Library Cataloguing in Publication Information Available

Library of Congress Cataloging-in-Publication Data

Names: Shanok, Arielle F., 1976- editor. | Elden, Nicole Benedicto, 1971- editor.
Title: Thriving in graduate school : the expert's guide to success and wellness / edited by Arielle F. Shanok and Nicole Benedicto Elden.
Description: Lanham, Maryland : Rowman & Littlefield Publishing Group, 2021. | Includes bibliographical references and index. | Summary: "This book provides real-world examples and suggestions on how to succeed in graduate school from those with first-hand experience"—Provided by publisher.
Identifiers: LCCN 2020054172 (print) | LCCN 2020054173 (ebook) | ISBN 9781538133293 (cloth) | ISBN 9781538133309 (epub)
Subjects: LCSH: Universities and colleges—United States—Graduate work—Handbooks, manuals, etc. | Graduate students—United States—Handbooks, manuals, etc.
Classification: LCC LB2371.4 .T57 2021 (print) | LCC LB2371.4 (ebook) | DDC 378.1/55—dc23
LC record available at https://lccn.loc.gov/2020054172
LC ebook record available at https://lccn.loc.gov/2020054173

~

Contents

Acknowledgments

This book is dedicated to the three most important people in my life. To my partner, Kevin, who allowed me the safe space to stumble, to grow, to persevere, to thrive, and to rest. To my daughter, Ashleigh, whom I love so profoundly and whose compassionate, nurturing, and creative soul is such a light in this very imperfect world! Finally, to my departed Lola, my secure base. A Filipina warrior whose *tapang* and *lakas ng loob* continues beyond her death and courses through the veins of all who love her! I also want to acknowledge and thank all the graduate students, past and present, whose lived experiences mark every page of this book. And Arielle F. Shanok, my coconspirator, colleague, and dear friend, who has made this journey such a blessing!

Nicole Benedicto Elden, PsyD

This book is dedicated to my mom, Rebecca Shahmoon Shanok, a passionate, visionary, unrelenting fighter for social justice, and to my exuberant, inventive, devoted dad, Charles Shanok. Both of their lifelong love and encouragement gave me the imagination and confidence to embark on this book journey, and both of whom passed away during its writing. To my partner, Martin, whose enduring support has carried me through, and to Remy and Simon, who are at the center of our hearts and worlds. To my brother, Noah, his wife, Anya, and our extended family for their love and care. To the many resourceful, resilient gradu-ate students who have taught and inspired me over the past twelve years. To all of our wise, articulate contributors from whom I have learned so much. And to Nicole Benedicto Elden, whose partnership in this project made it a joy.

Arielle F. Shanok, PhD

~

Introduction

Editors' Love Letter to Graduate Students

Nicole Benedicto Elden and Arielle F. Shanok

Dear Graduate Students (and their loved ones),

With deep respect, we the editors, along with our chapter authors, write this book to you. We applaud your courage to embark on this adventure, admire your perseverance, and honor your journey. We recognize your diverse, intersecting identities and acknowledge the power structures within academia and broader society that can make the academic journey that much more challenging. We offer guidance on a vast array of grad school life topics to help you navigate wisely—this is the book we wish we had when we were in graduate school! Above all else, we encourage you to take care of yourself. We hope you will inhale the compassion that we intend to convey and laugh (and cry) with us about the absurdities you will face along the way. Your journey is unique but you are not alone.

Dear Faculty, Administrators, and Mental Health Professionals,

Thank you for caring about your students! We hope that through the personal vignettes shared within, we can sensitize you to the myriad experiences and intersectional identities of your graduate students. This book will help you to help them excel. At the end of each chapter is a

1

list of suggestions for supporting your students through the challenges that are raised in the chapter. While reading the chapters will bring the students' perspectives into clearer view, you don't need to read the chapters to be able to draw from the suggestions.

Research now documents what we all already knew: A staggeringly large percentage of grad students struggle and suffer. This book is written for grad students *and* the village of those supporting them because the better that we understand and empathize with the challenges students confront, the better equipped we are to help them thrive.

Yours most sincerely,
Arielle F. Shanok, PhD, and Nicole Benedicto Elden, PsyD

About the Editors and Authors:

Arielle and Nicole are clinical psychologists who run a graduate school counseling center serving a diverse community of doctoral and master's students in sciences, arts, and humanities. Every day, now for more than a decade, they sit with grad students collaboratively strategizing about how to overcome grad school challenges in order to thrive. Increasingly, they are also providing consultation to faculty and administrators on how to improve their programs. Arielle and Nicole are also recovering grad students—Arielle earned her doctorate in 2007 from Teachers College, Columbia University; Nicole earned hers in 2006 from Long Island University, CW Post. Furthermore, they are compassionate, patient, wise, and moderately funny human beings.

Each chapter is written by an expert on the chapter topic. Some, like the editors, are directors of graduate university departments. Most are psychologists—experts in helping people increase self-knowledge, build self-esteem and self-compassion, develop healthy relationships, and effectively pursue their dreams. Each was once a graduate student, and all have committed their careers to helping graduate students excel.

PART I

~

GETTING STARTED!

CHAPTER ONE

~

Welcome!

What You Need to
Know about Graduate School

Arielle F. Shanok

*Grad school is its own unique world with many unspoken rules. The
sooner that you can understand and acclimatize to your new surroundings, the faster you can channel your efforts in fruitful directions.*

Getting Oriented

Success is subjective in graduate school. You define what is of greatest
importance for your life journey. In your undergrad schooling, likely
good grades, some extracurricular activities, and graduating equaled
success. Here, you have a broader array of options. In addition to
coursework and student activities, you may have research, conferences,
and publications to think about. You are more likely to be teaching
and/or working in other capacities. You have specific skills to hone and
connections to make with peers and mentors in your field.

All the possibilities can be exciting *and* overwhelming. Since you
will likely not be able to do everything you want to do at the standard
you want to do it, you'll have to make choices. Listen to your internal
compass. *Your grad school goals will be your GPS.* You don't need to ace
every class to be an outstanding student. Your goals can dictate which
classes to give your all, how much time and energy to devote to research, teaching, networking, and so on. It's easy to become consumed

by the many arenas in which you are asked to perform—in written work, presentations, exams—and forget that you are attending grad school for you!

Identifying Your Goals

You may be coming to grad school with clarity on what you want to do professionally. Or, you may have no idea what you want to do and hope grad school will help you figure it out. Or somewhere in between. In any of the above cases, you can identify goals that are associated with your professional life journey. These will likely evolve over time. For example, if you have no idea what you want to do professionally, one initial goal might be to try out different roles to see which, if any, you like. Writing down your goals, revisiting them regularly, and, if appropriate, revising them during your time in grad school will help you choose from the abundant paths beckoning your attention.

Particularly if you're not sure what you want to do professionally, keep listening to what you enjoy (if anything) of the many activities you try in grad school. Perhaps you discover that you'd prefer to clean vomit than go into your lab, but you notice that teaching is energizing. This is important information. In most fields there are teaching jobs that don't require research. Maybe you feel your soul withering when you think of the long, isolated hours you would spend doing archival research and writing, but you notice that you enjoy group projects. This helps you know that you want to develop collaborations or work in settings where you would be part of a team. If you don't enjoy anything you do in grad school at all, but do enjoy other activities, you might consider shifting course.

Pay attention to your career-related daydreams. When you're spacing out on your commute or in the shower, what do you imagine that brings you pleasure? Are you accepting an award (looking supremely dapper, of course) for best advisor of the year applauded by dozens of appreciative advisees and admiring colleagues? You can learn from this that serving in a mentorship role is important to you. Perhaps you are parachuting into a remote mountainous region of India to study a rare plant species that could help to thwart future pandemics. This tells you that adventure and discovery with practical, health-promoting application appeal to you. So keep fantasizing! When you listen to your reverie, you can learn about what is meaningful and enlivening to you.

Big career questions aside for a moment, what else do you want from grad school? Lasting friendships? Role models? Fun exploring your new town or city? Having clarity on these goals will guide your choices about how you spend your time. Perhaps planning a night out or weekend picnic with your cohort isn't just procrastination.

The extrinsic rewards on your journey may be fewer than you expect. You will be lucky to find mentors and peers in your life who care. If you are used to being mobilized by praise from others, this may be an adjustment. Particularly during dissertation or thesis work, you may not get feedback for long stretches of time. Yet, the intrinsic reward for building a career that is fulfilling for you is a grand long-term gift to yourself. Like, you might actually *want* to get out of bed in the morning to go to work because you care about what you do. Until you adjust to the limited extrinsic rewards, it's perfectly acceptable to buy yourself a pack of stickers that say "well done" and "good job" and put them on your papers (or forehead) when appropriate.

Re-Examine Your Work Habits

Like success, where, when, and how you do your work are also less well defined in grad school. You will likely have more unscheduled spans of time with bigger projects to complete. How do you work most effectively? Do you rely on deadlines and pull all-nighters? You might be able to squeak by with this strategy during coursework. However, you will have to figure out a different approach for your thesis or dissertation. As one student who was working on her dissertation told me, "I'm a sprinter, but this is a marathon." Together we figured out how to turn her dissertation into a series of sprints. Knowing your strengths can help you find ways to leverage them in grad school. Similarly, knowing your pitfalls can help you avoid them. Yes, you may need to exit your apartment in order to escape the seductive lure of Netflix.

Where *do* you work best? Do you unleash your most potent productivity in a silent, sterile library or in the buzz and clatter of a neighborhood coffee shop? Do your frontal lobe neurons come ablaze alone in your bedroom or surrounded by a study group in the student lounge?

Does music help or hinder? If it helps, what genre for what kind of work? For most people, different tasks call for different measures.

What time of day are you the sharpest? Most likely to get into a flow? Experience the least pain and most pleasure doing work? That's your golden window. Myth holds that you are a more worthy human being if you happen to be a morning person. That's one model that may or may not be yours. When you can, build your schedule so that you can focus on your top priorities during your most fertile hours, whether they are six to eight a.m. or eleven p.m. to one a.m.

Speaking of scheduling, do you have a calendar system that helps you keep track of appointments and assignment due dates? If not, now is a good time to set one up. You might have to try out a few different strategies to see what works best for you. Is Google calendar with alarmed appointment reminders your cup of tea, or are you more of an old-fashioned pencil and paper calendar person? It is worthwhile to invest some time figuring this out. This will function as an extension of your brain and will reduce your three a.m. "Oh sh&$@% I forgot to . . . !!!" wakings.

Grad school is a balancing and juggling challenge, even for those of you who are skillful at time management. Figuring out when to do what so that your top priority tasks get done on time can sometimes feel like doing advanced calculus. We regularly underestimate the time that tasks take. Therefore, when you are planning out a task that you want to accomplish, add in some extra time. The very worst that will happen is that you'll finish early. We often beat ourselves up for not accomplishing things in our intended timeframe without realizing that our notions of time when we established the timeframe were not realistic.

Break tasks down into bite-size bits. When the task is well-defined and doable in one sitting, getting started is easier. Many of us find that small tasks such as "write outline for literature review section" or "write for a half hour starting where I left off" leave less room for interference by paralyzing perfectionistic thoughts. Avoid, for example, planning to spend your afternoon on the following to-do list item: "research and write (outstanding, original, publishable, award-winning) midterm paper." By the evening, you may find that you have a very clean house or in-depth knowledge of the *New York Times* travel section, but you are not likely to have made much progress on your paper. See more on procrastination and perfectionism in chapter 17, Taming the Tenacious Beast of Procrastination: Building a Bridge between Intention and Action, and specific strategies for writing in chapter 16, Getting the Writing Done: Completing Your Paper, Thesis, or Dissertation.

Be planful about your time and goals but remain flexible when more important demands come up. It is likely that during your time in graduate school at least one major life event will occur—marriage, divorce or major breakup, decision to come out, significant injury or illness, death of a loved one, giving birth. These will impact your progress. Check in with yourself regularly about what you need. Please exercise self-compassion when, for example, writing a paper two months or even eight months after a parent passed away. Accept that it's going to be harder and take longer than it would have if you weren't grieving. Even less-draining events can significantly derail us, like getting bed bugs or having a roommate in crisis. Having just endured the Covid-19 pandemic, a large-scale lesson in flexibility and adaptability, let the wisdom you likely gained guide you: Focus on what you can control and acknowledge that some things are outside of your control; and self-care is not optional.

Understand Your Inner Rule Book

If you are a human being, you have developed a set of rules to simplify the infinite choices we have of how to make sense of and behave in our daily lives. The rules are usually intended to decrease various kinds of pain and increase a range of benefits. Most of these rules are not fully conscious. A large number of them were developed in childhood and adolescence under circumstances much different from your current one.

Now that you are in grad school, take some time to examine what your rules are. Ask yourself which ones will serve you well here and which ones you might want to alter. For example, consider the following questions: What if you are sitting in class and don't understand what the professor is talking about? What does your rule book tell you about this? Are you, like many of us, likely to have a sinking sense of stupidity? If so, then you've identified a rule: If I don't understand something, I must be stupid. Rules often guide our actions. In this case, you might choose not to ask a question, because you'd think it could reveal your stupidity to others. If so, perhaps this inner rule is unhelp-ful. A more helpful one might be: I came to grad school to learn, so if I don't understand, I can ask. If you are confused, very likely others are too. They may perceive you as courageous or secure in your own intel-ligence to be bold enough to ask.

What if you get back a paper with comments from your professor that are mostly positive but include a few critical points? Are you likely to feel that you did poorly? Another common inner rule among grad students is: Anything short of perfect is failure. Yet, it is the job of professors to help you strengthen and sharpen your skills. If they are doing their jobs, you may be upset for the duration of your schooling because of their comments, which were actually intended to help you grow. Of course, some professors could use some schooling in giving critical feedback in a digestible manner. Their mode of giving feedback may be their own weakness.

What if you really do bomb something, like fail an exam? Would this mean something to you about your value as a human being? Would it color your belief in your capacity to succeed at anything? Many of us get knocked down by a failure because we generalize its significance rather than seeing it as one area we need to work on. As a first-year stu-dent told me while grieving about a failed quiz, "This [academic work] is the *one* thing I thought I was good at!" One way to help yourself up is to focus on what specific problem the failure identified and what you can do about it. Perhaps it means that you have a weak foundation of knowledge in the content area of the exam. The solution may be that you have to set aside more time to study the material. This may be the last thing you feel like doing, but it sure beats feeling like a colossal failure as a human being! Take a few days away from the material if you need a break. Then make a plan to get back at it.

If you are enterprising in grad school, you will experience rejections and failures. If you are courageous enough to submit your work for pub-lication, some submissions will be rejected. If you apply for grants, you will not get all of them. While feeling upset is a normal response, how you interpret the rejection will significantly impact how upset you get. Try to remind yourself that you were brave to try. If you have an inner rule that identifies rejections as learning opportunities, they will be less debilitating. Our brains actually grow from missteps.[1]

Take a moment to write down some of your inner rules that impact your graduate school experience. Then, write down matching aspiratory rules that will be more adaptive in graduate school. For example, current rule: "Anything short of perfection is failure." Aspired-to rule: "I'll do the best I can with the time and resources I have."

Each time a situation triggers one of your inner rules, bring to mind the aspired-to rule and try to internalize it a tiny bit. Repeat. Repeat. Repeat. Habits take time to change. Plus, if you believe that a particular rule keeps you safe in one way or another, it will be hard to let it go. Remind yourself that even the fact that you are noticing your inner rules is a step forward. Have patience and compassion for yourself as you make these important shifts that will likely improve your quality of life in grad school and beyond. If you find that your rules are too rigid, don't budge when you attempt to alter them, and significantly negatively impact your ability to function or your quality of life, it might be a useful time to seek out a counselor.

Another possible explanation for a failure on an exam or other high-pressure performance situation is performance anxiety. If you have the experience of knowing the material well but then going blank or freezing up during the exam, losing access to the knowledge you just had, you may be having a fight, flight, or freeze response to the testing environment. This means that you are having the kind of physiological response that prepared our prehistoric ancestors well when they had to confront predatory animals. Your body is gearing up for extraordinary exertion. Your limbs prepare to mobilize, areas of your midbrain become highly active, and your higher-order thinking takes a back seat.

For those of us living or attending school in dangerous neighborhoods, where people or traffic patterns are a physical threat, this response may still appropriately help you mobilize when crossing the street or commuting home at night. On exams, unfortunately, this may hinder your access to memory and complex thought. If you think that performance anxiety may be negatively impacting your performance or quality of life, reach out to a counselor about this specific issue. There are a number of strategies that can help. Chapter 3, So . . . It's Not Just Me? Coping with Stress and Anxiety in Graduate School, includes some of them.

Rejuvenate

In February of my second year of my doctoral program, I hit a low point. My qualifying exam was a few weeks away, a draft of my en route master's thesis was due before the exam, I was working three jobs and, as you can imagine, barely sleeping. I questioned whether the toll grad school was taking on my mental health was worth it. One night, staring bleary-eyed at my computer screen in anger and despair, I made a promise to myself. For the duration of my time in grad school, every week I would schedule some time for myself: From Friday night when I left work until Saturday at one p.m., I abided by two rules that I followed religiously: 1) I was not allowed to do any academic or job-related work and 2) I was not allowed to do anything I didn't feel like doing. I managed to keep these promises, which helped me survive and complete graduate school. For me, they operationalized self-care and self-respect.

You don't need to wait to hit a low point to set up protected time and space. What might your versions of this look like? What boundaries can you create to protect you from the relentless river of work? Having a time each night when you stop working might help, whether realistically that time is seven o'clock or midnight. For those with the luxury of having space to work at home outside of your bedroom, you may choose to maintain your bedroom as a sanctuary away from work.

A student I knew had an advisor who emailed her at all times of day and night asking her to complete tasks for her research fellowship. The student came to me because she felt "on edge all the time." We pieced together that her chronic low-grade anxiety was closely connected to her advisor's demands. The student recognized that she had an inner rule that said she had to respond right away. She wisely and courageously decided that each day she would set aside a two-hour period to address her advisor's requests, and that she would not read or reply to the emails outside of that time. Furthermore, she decided that Sunday was her day off from her advisor. She postponed checking her advisor's emails until Monday. To her relief, her advisor never complained. And she wrote her a strong recommendation letter.

If you feel you can take a day off per week, do it! If that feels like too much time, try for half a day. If you don't take some time away, your body will eventually demand it, either by getting sick or just by refusing to get off the couch. Plan some activities that access different parts of you than school does.

Before starting grad school, I worked as a park ranger. Most of my time was spent outdoors. During my first weeks of grad school, I frequently peered out my classroom windows bemoaning the glass and concrete separating me from the outdoors. After a few months, I forgot to miss the part of me that came alive when the wind hit my skin and the sky stretched all around me. When I felt like I was drowning my second year, I began craving the outdoors again. I planned a solo camping trip to the mountains over a long weekend in April. The unseasonably cold weather didn't stop me. I trudged up the mountain path through the rain that turned to snow and spent the coldest night of my life in my tent shivering my tail off and refueling my soul.

What was enriching and restorative to you before starting grad school? Perhaps listening to live music, spending time with a particular friend or friend group, shooting hoops in the park, trying new recipes, taking a tai chi or pottery or kickboxing class or some other activity that lights you up. Scheduling your version of rejuvenation during grad school will ground you.

Let's talk about exercise. As you know, it's good for your physical and mental health. It has powerful antidepressant and antianxiety properties. Yet, in grad school we easily come to see our bodies as mere transport systems for our precious brains. We neglect them and feel annoyed when our backs hurt after sitting at the computer for hours at a time. For many of us, after a long day of classes, lab work, teaching, meetings, commuting, or other commitments, pushing ourselves to get out for a run or to the gym is just not going to happen.

So let's be realistic. How did you exercise before starting grad school? Going for walks? Going to the gym? Yoga, barre, or other exercise class? If you have access to these resources near your home or school, the path of least resistance is to continue doing the kind of exercise that you did previously on your less busy days. This is likely not the moment to remake yourself as an exerciser extraordinaire. If you are not exercising at all, start by building a half hour each week into your schedule. If you can gradually increase that to two and possibly even three times per week, you are golden! "But I literally don't have time!" you say. I bet you that, if anything, your productivity will increase by adding two or three half-hour chunks of moderate exercise per week. Plus, you'll live longer. So you *will* get more time in the end!

Graduate School Culture

Each grad school and each program within each grad school has its own culture and language. Like all cultures, there are norms of engagement as well as taboos. Even if you attend school in the place where you grew up, and certainly if you've moved from out of state or country, or recently served in the military, you'll likely feel disoriented and uncertain at first. You might wonder things like, "What is an ABD? Should I call my professor 'Rosa,' 'Professor Gomez,' or 'Dr. Gomez'? Should I be formal with my cohort or can I relax and be myself? I've emailed my advisor twice about meeting and haven't heard back. What should I do?" The rules will rarely be spelled out for you. You'll have to do some anthropological observation as well as ask direct questions. Other students, faculty, and administrative staff are good resources.

Surely, some aspects of graduate study will be different from what you imagined. You will have moments when you feel that you don't fit in, either to your program or department, or even your field. You may observe peers or professors who seem delighted to fill every free second devouring the latest journal articles in the field, while in your heart of hearts, you prefer to spend your free time playing video games. You will likely experience aspects of your studies as boring and tedious; you may wonder, "Am I cut out for this?" or "Did I make the right choice?" These are very common concerns among graduate students. If significant doubts persist, find a safe space to process your thoughts and feelings, such as a close friend, family member, or counselor.

A frequent topic of conversation each semester in the confidential student groups I run is doubt about the grad school route. People talk in earnest about what makes them feel ill fit for their current paths, and some think through other possible alternatives. Even those with the intention to stay love to devise colorful and outrageous (for them) escape fantasies. One student proclaimed that he would become a "gym rat porn star," another planned to open a bakery, and a third dreamed of moving to New Zealand to work as a sheep hand. Each of these fantasies convey the wish to escape their over-intellectualized existences for a physical, tactile adventure.

Many grad students (and professors) experience the imposter phenomenon—the feeling that we are not actually capable of doing what we are doing and will soon be discovered as fraudulent. Our backgrounds can contribute to this feeling. If no one in our families attended college, if no one in grad school looks or sounds like our families, if we were told in one or many ways that we are not capable, or even if none of the above are true, we may feel this way. Check out chapter 2, Faking It: Imposter Syndrome in Graduate School.

Build Community

Grad school can make you feel utterly on your own. Compared with your undergraduate training, you will likely spend more time alone. It is often increasingly isolating as the years go by, particularly in doctoral programs. With this knowledge in hand, you may want to prioritize building connections with people when you have the chance. Coursework ends after the first few years. While this will give you more time to do your own work, having meaningful contact with others in academia may take extra effort. If you meet people you like in class, ask them to coffee. If your department has a student lounge, spend an hour or two there each week. It may not be your most productive work time, but you may make connections or learn information that is actually a lot more useful than an hour of reading.

When you have opportunities to connect with students in years ahead of you, take them. For example, if you are paired with a more advanced "buddy," take your buddy up on the lunch invitation. If advanced students present or comment at colloquium about topics that interest you, approach them afterwards to continue the conversation. These students have a wealth of knowledge about which professors to seek out and which to steer clear of, what to expect at qualifying exams, which courses require the least amount of time, which professors should not be on a committee together, and the like. Along a similar vein, there can be benefits from reaching out to students in years below yours. If for no other reason, their questions to you will help you realize how much you have learned and accomplished in a short amount of time. Any of these people could also become project collaborators, your writing group for your thesis or dissertation, and/or friends. That said, keep your antenna up for competitive students who may offer "advice" or try to gain information from you without the best intentions. For more about peer dynamics in grad school, see chapter 6, Navigating Group Dynamics in Graduate School.

Similarly with faculty, get to know them and let them know you. For many of us, this will take more effort. This may be particularly challenging for some international students coming from hierarchical educational systems in which casually chatting with faculty is not the norm. Other marginalized groups that have learned to be wary of and/ or deferential to authority might also understandably find this opportunity quite effortful and intimidating. Yet, avoiding faculty will keep you marginalized in grad school. Getting to know them will give you a sense of whether you want to take their course, whether you want them to be on your committee, whether you could picture asking them for a recommendation letter down the road, and so on. If you are familiar to faculty members, they will be more likely to say yes. If this is particularly challenging for you, then set small achievable goals for yourself.

One way to access professors is to use office hours. You can ask questions related to a course you are taking with the professor or discuss possible research ideas. Many departments have monthly colloquia. Step 1: Go to the colloquium. Step 2: Speak to (at least) one faculty member. Step 3: Repeat. Do what you can to make this as easy as possible for yourself. If, for example, as a member of a racial minority group, approaching a faculty member who is also a member of a racial minority group feels easier, do that. If approaching a faculty member with a friend feels easier, go for it. Keep interactions relatively professional, even if you are discussing informal topics. When alcohol is involved, be careful. If you partake, drink in moderation. You don't want to be THAT student.

While building relationships with faculty, setting healthy boundaries is also important. Given the power differential, professors should not be regularly asking you to do favors for them that are outside of your role. Yet, I have heard of grad students doing everything from picking up dry cleaning to babysitting without pay for faculty. One student I knew sensed that her advisor wanted her companionship. Over time, she began to feel that she needed to accompany her advisor to the movies in order to be able to discuss her dissertation with her. These are obvious examples of boundary crossings. However, there is much gray area. What is within your role as an advisee, supervisee, or research assistant? If you are not sure about something, talk it over with people whose opinions you trust. You may not be able to change the behavior of faculty, but you can choose how you interact and respond. Make careful choices about what you offer, including emotional labor.

Your relationship with your advisor is particularly important. A positive mentor relationship is associated with lower depression and anxiety.[2] Chapter 8, Cultivating and Sustaining Good Mentorship, addresses how to choose and work effectively with your mentor and what to do if problems develop. If you are in the biomedical sciences, also see chapter 12, Biomedical Pathways: Graduate Student Well-Being in the Biomedical Sciences.

Every department has politics. There will be divisions among various subgroups, histories of animosity between professors, competitiveness for resources, and other uncomfortable issues. At first you will be unaware or only vaguely aware of them. Hopefully, your faculty is mature enough to avoid recruiting you into battle. You did not come to graduate school to learn how to cope with thorny interpersonal workplace dynamics. However, you will likely learn a lot about this topic. Try to find a trustworthy peer group with whom to discuss what you sense. Be aware of divisions when you choose your thesis or dissertation committee members. You could easily get caught in the crossfire if you have warring members. If you feel pulled to join a camp during your time as a grad student, do your best to remain diplomatic.

Be respectful and friendly in your interactions with department coordinators and all other support staff. Keep in mind that they often have power over a wide range of logistical aspects of your student life. They may assign resources, such as offices, be responsible for inputting changes in your status into the system, and alerting you (or not) if there are problems. They likely have better access to your professors and advisor than you. Let's say your advisor has gone MIA the very week that the letter of recommendation you requested for your grant application is due; the department coordinator may or may not go the extra mile to help you get their attention. The few minutes you spent asking about their children or the apple you shared when they mentioned they were starving could go a long way.

Maintain Relationships with Family and Friends

You will likely be busier than you were before starting grad school, and therefore will probably have less time to spend with the people you care about. Busy as you are, though, make sure to spend some time with those closest to you. If you have children, see chapter 9, When Thesis Meets Diapers: Journeys of Graduate Student Parents. The time spent together will benefit your relationships and you. You may need to be more planful about this—scheduling date nights or dinner visits, clarifying when you will stop working each evening, even scheduling phone or WhatsApp dates.

Similarly, communicate with your loved ones about what you need, like uninterrupted blocks of work time. This may mean explaining that for a period of several hours during the day, you will not be checking texts. If you live with loved ones who, despite your requests, cannot seem to resist interrupting you while you are working, you might need to find an alternative work space. As midterm and finals weeks approach, let loved ones know what to expect. If they are upset by your lack of availability during certain times, try to listen nondefensively to their complaints (often easier said than done!). Remind them why you are in grad school and that it is temporary. Tell them that you also miss spending time with them. Thank them for trying to understand. When they are supportive (which in some cases will just mean leaving you alone), thank them for supporting you. Perhaps you have a partner or family member with whom you can discuss ideas or who can help with editing. Involving them in the process and expressing appreciation for their interest and input can help them feel included and important.

Most people who have not been to graduate school do not understand what you are doing. They do not understand the particular complex set of challenges, the time commitment, or the reality that a graduate degree will not necessarily immediately earn you an eager employer offering a six-figure salary upon graduation. Yet since nearly everyone has completed some schooling, whether it was middle school, high school, or college, they may *think* they understand. Some loved ones might look down on your decision to attend grad school. They may ask you repeatedly when you will be done. If you are already feeling ambivalent, self-critical, or frustrated about your grad school experiences, these comments will not help. Others might extol what you are doing ("I've been telling all my friends, we're gonna have a doctor in the family!"), which may increase the pressure you feel to succeed.

If you are the first in your family to go to grad school, the experiences that you have can set you apart from your family and friends. Your class status changes educationally and may financially once you graduate. This can be very challenging. One student from Alabama explained that his $20,000 student stipend, barely a living wage in an expensive city, was more than any of his family members had ever earned working full time. His father was not getting the heart surgery he needed because he could not afford it. The student felt callous for spending his time struggling with history texts when his family had "real problems." Another student spoke about her experiences going home for the holidays, where everyone saw her as "the golden one who got away." Her older siblings were both unemployed and living in their mom's small apartment. She believed they couldn't fathom her new existence: pushing herself through crying spells and panic attacks to produce written work and utter a few words in class. She also felt intense guilt for moving away and not helping her mother. Sometimes students become paralyzed during the dissertation phase because graduating would further distance them from the people and culture of their upbringing.

If the above is resonating for you, you may feel out of place both with family and at school. You may feel you cannot speak about school struggles with family and old friends. Similarly, you may believe that your new grad school community would not understand or would judge the issues that are daily reality for your family. This is a lot for you to hold on your own. If this feels alienating or burdensome, finding a space where you can speak about both worlds might help. The students I mentioned above shared what they did in therapy groups—after taking time to build trust with the other members. They found solace in discovering that some of their fellow students had similar experiences. You may want family to know more about what your current life entails but don't know how to even begin the conversation. Decide who it is worthwhile to try to explain your experiences to, and in what level of detail. You can show them relevant sections of this book and other resources to help them understand.

Managing Money

One of the biggest challenges that grad students face is financial. You may have applied for fellowships, taken out loans, tapped into savings, and/or relied on family support. All of this is stressful and affects how much you have to work in addition to school, where and how you can afford to live, and how much you can afford to take time away. In addition to the practicalities of your financial situation, we each have our own complicated relationship with money. Given the importance and complexity of this issue, this book includes two chapters about money in graduate school: chapter 14, Financing a Graduate Degree: The Practicalities, has practical financial planning information for grad students, and chapter 15, Financing a Graduate Degree: The Psychology, addresses the many meanings and associated feelings grad students have related to money.

Dealing with Discrimination

Despite what we might wish about universities being enlightened settings, racism, sexism, antisemitism, homophobia, xenophobia, and all forms of discrimination that abound in the broader world also exist in universities. Students who are Black, Indigenous, and/or people of color (BIPoC) are the targets of stereotypes and/or are ignored.[3] Women are interrupted more frequently than men. People with disabilities are overlooked. Each year at our counseling center, several young, female (often Asian) international graduate students seek counseling because they have had their authority undermined by one or two male undergraduate students who repeatedly question and/or verbally attack them in the classes they teach. Cis female students tell me about faculty members commenting about them or approaching them sexually. One student recently told me about a departmental talk she attended in which the derogatory "n" word, used as an example, was spoken repeatedly and comfortably by the White tenured faculty speaker. Unfortunately, these incidents can (and did) happen even in a liberal, progressive, diverse, urban, social-justice-oriented university setting.

Common reactions to the above experiences include anger, a sense of powerlessness, a sense of pressure to be perfect, anxiety, depression, questioning of abilities, and/or avoidance of the institution. Rather than giving in to the pull to isolate and avoid, try reaching out for support and comradery. Yes, easier said than done! If there are other students in historically marginalized groups in your program, check in with them. If there are minority faculty members, request to meet with them. If you have the opportunity to meet minority students or professors in other programs or institutions, for example at conferences, seek them out. Ask them how they have coped with discrimination in their careers. If they seem receptive, tell them about your experiences. Consider reporting noteworthy events to the diversity officer or Title IX coordinator at your university. Counseling is another potential source of support. Consider what would most help you to regain a sense of mobilization and connection to the reasons that you came to grad school. Chapter 7, Bearing the Baggage of Racial Microaggressions in Graduate School: A Black Woman's Reflections on Ways to Lessen the Load, chapter 5, The Power of Being Different: Navigating Grad School as International Students, chapter 10, "We're Here, We're Queer!" LGBTQ in Graduate School, chapter 11, "To Be Your Best Self": Surviving and Thriving as a Trans Grad Student, and chapter 13, Who Am I? My Multicultural Selves, include more on this topic.

Despite individual and institutional discrimination, the number and percentage of racial minority graduate students increased significantly between 2000 and 2015. Enrollment of Hispanic students increased by 119 percent, enrollment of Black students increased by 99 percent, and enrollment of Asian American/Pacific Islander and Native American/Alaskan Native students also increased more than the 23 percent increase among White students. In fact, currently across the United States, nearly half of the graduate student population are racial minorities. More than half of the grad school population identify as female though, like racial minorities, they continue to be underrepresented in certain prestigious, high-paying fields.[4] Less is known about other minority groups such as LGBTQIA+ groups and students with disabilities

because this information is usually not requested on grad school applications. If you are in a group that is often discriminated against, some
days will be hard. Remind yourself that by being in grad school, you are
courageously living the change that you want to see.

Grad School Is Freakin' Hard

Rates of depression and anxiety are estimated to be six times higher
among graduate students than national averages. Several large studies
of graduate students from a wide range of institutions and departments
conclude that rates of depression are estimated to be 39 to 47 percent.
Students in Arts and Humanities seem to be hit the hardest, with approximately 60 percent of these students having depression.[5,6,7] Across
the literature, the top predictors of graduate student well-being were:
positive advisory relationship, positive outlook on career prospects,
work-life balance, health, supportive relationships in and outside of
graduate school, financial confidence, and academic engagement and
progress.[8,9] While the research cited does not prove that grad school
causes mental illness, the many stressors that students endure along the
way certainly do not help! Within the chapters of *Thriving in Graduate
School*, we address each of the above-listed domains.

How Do You Know If You "Need Professional Help"?

Let's rethink what might sound like a condemning catchphrase. We
can all benefit from a time and space where someone listens carefully
to us, cares about how we are doing, and knows methods to help us
cope. With the collaborative guidance of a professional, we can think
through and plan out how to improve the quality of our lives. But
how do you know if all this is really worth the time and cost to you?
Generally speaking, if your concerns are interfering with your ability
to function and/or quality of your existence, it's a good idea to make
an appointment. If you are regularly lying awake at night worrying,
if you are feeling down much of the time for weeks, if you frequently
avoid certain social settings due to fears of being judged, if you've
blacked out from drinking more than once in the past few months, if
you are regularly distracted by thoughts about your weight, if you are

repeating the same hurtful patterns in romantic relationships . . . and many, many more examples, do yourself the kindness of meeting with a professional. Going through a transition, experiencing a trauma or loss, feeling unsatisfied, or not knowing what you want from life are also good reasons to go.

Managing Preexisting Mental Health Conditions in Graduate School

If you are starting graduate school knowing that you have a mental health condition, a very important task at the beginning of your first year is to set up a treatment team for yourself. Your university counseling center may be able to provide that care or at least provide referrals to good in-network or affordable practitioners. Find out what services they offer. Each September, a handful of wise first-year students approach our student counseling center explaining, "I'm doing okay now, but I've had some hard times in the past and want to be ready if they return in graduate school." These preparatory steps hold these students in good stead. If you hit a rough patch in grad school, you will be so very grateful to already have providers whom you trust for support. Being in ongoing treatment will likely soften and shorten tough periods.

If you take medication, make sure that you have a local prescribing person who is knowledgeable and affordable and with whom you are comfortable. Do not wait until two days before your prescription runs out. It usually takes weeks to schedule an appointment with a psychiatrist, and many don't prescribe at a first meeting.

Sometimes people who have taken medication for years stop taking it when they start grad school imagining that grad school will be a whole new life. Please resist the urge to do this! Many aspects of your life will be changing. The changes, even if they are for the better, will likely increase your stress levels at first. This is not the best time to throw another potential stressor into the mix. Also, the more variables that you change in your life at once, the less you know what is causing what. If you start having panic attacks or mood dips, you will not know if this is medication-related or due to one of your other life changes. Plan out medication decreases together with your provider at duller moments.

If you have been in therapy or even have considered going, find a therapist. Since you will likely attend appointments weekly, make sure that the office is conveniently located and, of course, that you feel comfortable with and respected by the person. You may have to meet with several therapists before you find someone who is a good fit for you. Often students become overwhelmed if they have to find services outside of the student counseling center through their insurance. Indeed, this is what I have to say about figuring out health insurance plans in the United States: &@$%{€"!#+*#$$???!!! (My editor made me take out the profanities. Perhaps she hasn't dealt with insurance companies.) Yet, it is crucial to know. Do take the time to look online or call your insurance company to understand your plan.

When you call your insurance company, take a deep breath, have another mundane task at hand for when you are on hold, have your list of questions and a place to write down answers. Don't hesitate to ask again (and again) if you don't understand what (the hell) the representative is saying. Write down the name of the representative, date, time, and what they told you. Here are some important questions: What is my co-pay per session? What is my deductible (amount I need to pay out-of-pocket before the insurance company starts paying)? Does my deductible reset each calendar year? What is my session limit per year? Where can I find a list of in-network providers? Do I need to preauthorize (call the insurance company to let them know) before my first and/or subsequent visits? Do I have out-of-network benefits (if I want to see a therapist who is not in the network)? If so, what percentage of the fee is reimbursed? Is there a cap?

Consider joining a student support group. These are groups, usually run through the student counseling center, in which students from different programs build bonds with each other, offer support to one another, and share useful information about fellowships, teaching tips, and other good stuff. Some students join preemptively, knowing that there will be turbulence along the way, and others join when they hit the bumps. Lest you worry that being in a group like this indicates that you are a poor student or weak human being, I am delighted to bust that myth for you. During twelve years of running two to three weekly groups at our university counseling center, I've had the pleasure of getting to know some of the most (externally and internally) impressive, successful, and resilient students who graduate from the university. By creating space for their mental health, thinking about what they want and need, and being in an environment where people are open about their vulnerabilities, these students become well equipped to handle the challenges that their tenure-track jobs or other prestigious positions pose down the road.

These recommendations are not easy, particularly if you are moving and/or changing insurance for grad school. For those of us whose moods or anxiety levels are especially sensitive to change, starting grad school may feel like a crisis in and of itself. If so, compassionately remind yourself each day (or hour) that transition is hard and that in a few weeks you will likely settle into a routine. Let the difficulty of each day serve as a reminder to prioritize your self-care and treatment.

Navigating Grad School with a Disability

If you have one or more disabilities, you may have extra navigating to do in grad school to set yourself up to thrive. Of course, this can feel daunting. What will people's attitudes and reactions be? Should you request accommodations (if you have a choice)? What is the culture of the disabilities office in your school? How will your department and advisor react? What will the ongoing process of obtaining accommodations be like? If you have a visible disability, you may be bracing yourself for people's reactions. If you have a disability that is not visible, you may wonder who to tell, if anyone, beyond those who are necessary to gain accommodations. Please have compassion for yourself as you take on these challenges, navigate the awkward or painful moments, and make the difficult requests. I have seen a number of remarkable students with disabilities succeed in grad school by communicating with those around them about what they need and making space to process the feelings that come up through their journeys. Chapter 4, The Struggle Is Real! Accessing Help from Counseling and Disability Services, addresses the process of navigating graduate school with disabilities.

Remember to Enjoy the Grad School Perks

You get to spend your time thinking deeply about topics that (hopefully still) interest you. One student compared her life now to when she worked a temp job: "An hour felt like a freakin' mind-numbing year! I haven't felt that level of boredom in the three years I've been here, and I used to feel it every day." Like this student, hopefully you will regularly feel stimulated. As you immerse yourself in new ideas, perspectives, and ways of thinking, you might discover that your belief system and/or identity evolves in meaningful ways. This process can come with its own challenges, such as feeling more distant from non–grad school friends and family or feeling temporarily disoriented. Yet, the sense of enlightenment, purpose, and vibrancy that usually accompanies the shifts tends to outweigh the growing pains.

You get to spend time with smart people who share similar interests. While this is not a guarantee that you'll like them, it increases the likelihood that you'll have meaningful interactions. Plus, grueling circumstances can build deep bonds. Many people develop lifelong friendships in grad school.

You are awesome for doing this! The world benefits from people who think deeply, skillfully, and creatively about things. Societies are improved by members who can analyze information and situations critically, not just accept them at face value. Even before you started, you may have planned for years, traveled across continents or oceans, worked hard to save money, gathered letters of recommendation, convinced loved ones, and written many drafts of essays. Some of you wrestled with inner and outer voices saying "You can't do it"—perhaps because of your class, race, gender, and/or the plethora of other reasons we hear and tell ourselves that message. And yet, here you are. You're doing it!

Takeaways for Students

- Identify and stay focused on your academic, professional, *and* social grad school goals. Prioritize tasks accordingly. Success in grad school means that you have gotten what you wanted out of grad school.
- Optimize your work periods by choosing times and places to work where you can focus and by setting bite-size, achievable work goals.
- Examine your inner rules and adjust those that are unhelpful in grad school. For example, shift "Anything short of perfection is

failure" to "I'll do the best I can with the time and resources I have."

- Invest time and energy into building relationships with other students, faculty, and administrative staff.
- Protect time each week for restorative activities and connecting with loved ones.
- Communicate with close others about what you're going through, what you need, and how to balance that with what they need.
- In the face of discrimination, allow yourself time to process what happened and connect with helpful others.
- Tune in to your mental health needs. Reach out for support if your functioning or quality of life is suffering.
- Check out other chapters in this book on topics that are relevant to you.
- Remember to enjoy the perks!

Suggestions for Faculty

You are on the front lines. The quality of your connection with your students will impact their success and well-being. You may also be the first to notice if they are struggling. Here are suggestions to set them up for success and to respond if they need mental health support.

- Meet with each of your advisees individually as often as time permits. Clarify what they can expect from you, what you expect from them, and your preferred ways to communicate (email, phone, text, etc.).
  - o Help them articulate their goals for graduate school. Respect that their goals and interests might differ from yours.
  - o Help them figure out what to prioritize in order to pursue their goals.
- When you see students having difficulty with something you struggled with in graduate school (or still struggle with), share your experiences. It can help them have patience with themselves to realize that even those they admire have challenges and persevere.
- Include multicultural materials and perspectives in your classes.

- Do not expect minority students to be spokespeople for their groups. (They may already be feeling overwhelmed and scrutinized and this increases their burden.)
- Do your best to confront racist/sexist/homophobic etc. comments in your classes. This can be challenging but will likely go a long way towards restoring a modicum of safety for students who are feeling targeted.
- Model work-life balance.
- Be outspoken about the benefits of counseling and other mental health services.
- Develop relationships with faculty members whom you trust and set up regular get-togethers to discuss challenges that arise in your teaching and mentoring.

Students Who Are Struggling
- You may recognize that students are struggling based on their academic work (marked decline in quality, comments about despair or death, etc.), their behavior (withdrawn, tearful, highly disorganized, etc.), their appearance (deterioration in hygiene, noteworthy weight changes, etc.), or from reports by concerned peers.
- Try to get a sense of what is wrong. Do not try to be their therapist or diagnose them. Just develop a clear description of what you observe and if appropriate, check in with the student about how they're doing.
- Consult with a mental health professional through campus counseling.
- Discuss your concerns with the department chair, the student's advisor, and/or the behavioral intervention team (or other similar body) when appropriate. Develop a collaborative plan to support the student.
- Have a list of resources on hand that include counseling services, health services, women's centers, and crisis hotlines, in case it is appropriate to offer them to students.
- Set clear boundaries with students who have difficulties with boundaries. For example, if they text you repeatedly about a wide range of issues, you can ask that they only text during business hours and/or on certain topics, such as scheduling.

- Document the behaviors of students of great concern, as well as your attempts to address the problems.
- If a student is being verbally aggressive or threatening in class, follow your school's protocol for handling disruptive students.
- Caring for students in distress can take a significant toll on you! Make sure that you build time into your schedule to replenish yourself—time with close others, exercise, and so on.

Suggestions for Administrators

By building an institutional culture of healthy learning environments, by prioritizing collaboration and mentorship, and by investing in robust student life supports, you dramatically improve chances of success and decrease risk of student deterioration.

- Reward faculty for the quality of their teaching and mentorship. Give awards publicly and tie promotions to excellence in these areas.
- Provide times and spaces for students to connect with faculty, such as brown bag lunch discussions, drop-in hours, and colloquia.
  o Encourage faculty to have friendly, informative web presences on the university website, including their photograph. This will increase their accessibility to students.
- Require departments to have up-to-date handbooks detailing expectations for students and faculty in advisory relationships, requirements for qualifying exams/papers, and what is needed for graduation. One of the most common complaints we hear from students is lack of clarity on what is expected from them and what is reasonable for them to request.
- Provide times and spaces for students to connect with one another, such as comfortable, centrally located student lounges, student support groups, peer mentorship/"buddy" programs, and student-run clubs.
  o Help publicize student-led activities and student government during orientations and on the university website.
- Create a protocol for faculty to follow when a student is of concern. Orient all faculty, including adjuncts, to this protocol.

- Create avenues for faculty and staff with a range of specialties to share information and consult with each other about students of concern. For example, many universities have Behavioral Intervention Teams that meet regularly and include representatives from faculty, security, student affairs, and a consulting mental health professional.
- Create clear policies and procedures to follow in the cases of sexual harassment, sexual assault, and other hate-crime allegations.
- Provide diversity training for faculty. Include literature about specific challenges that minority graduate students may face.
- Encourage faculty to include multicultural perspectives and use minority-inclusive materials in their classes.
- Support offices that support student well-being, such as student counseling centers, health centers, and women's centers. Encourage regular outreach by these offices.
  o At student orientations, in newsletters, in email blasts, and with other forms of communication, tout the benefits of mental health services.

Suggestions for Mental Health Professionals

- Orient the beginning grad student to aspects of grad school that are different from their prior schooling and/or jobs. Help them make sense of their grad school's culture.
- Help the student identify and stay focused on their grad school goals—academic, professional, *and* social. Help them prioritize daily tasks accordingly.
- If students are struggling to complete assignments on time, help them figure out when, where, and how they work best.
- Guide students to reflect on inner rules that get in their way.
- Encourage students to invest time in building connections with faculty and peers. If this is anxiety provoking for students, help them take small achievable steps in this direction. If setting healthy boundaries is difficult for a student, work with them on this.
- For your workaholic students, make sure they take time each week for relaxation and pleasure. This may be easier for them to do if

prescribed by a mental health professional. Help them understand how this can actually increase their productivity.

- Work collaboratively with students to understand how different parts of their identities impact their experiences in graduate school. For example, many students feel that they don't belong. Explore in what contexts they feel like outsiders and what contributes to those feelings.
- Familiarize yourself with the literature about discrimination in grad school. If your client is a minority in their program, allow space to discuss experiences they may have of discrimination. Students will differ in how and how much they talk about this topic with you. Your visible identities will likely impact how comfortable students will feel to do so. Support their attempts to open up with you.
  o After painful experiences of discrimination, help students figure out how to regain a sense of motivation and connection with trustworthy others on campus.
- If possible, run grad student support and process groups. Grad groups can meet certain student needs more effectively than individual counseling and are an efficient use of counselor resources.
- Find creative ways to reach students who might not otherwise seek counseling—through social media, workshops in university departments, having a visible presence at events, and offering academic consultations. If students have positive experiences with you through nonstigmatized avenues, they are more likely to pursue counseling when needed.

The above interventions are suggestions to be implemented selectively based on the individual client and the kind of help they are seeking.

CHAPTER TWO

⌒

Faking It

Impostor Syndrome in Graduate School

Alice Mangan

"Wait, I was *accepted?*" Yvette thought to herself as she reread the letter for a second time. "How is this possible? They *must* have made a mistake."

On the afternoon Yvette received her acceptance letter granting her entry into a prestigious, highly selective doctoral program in philosophy, she was overwhelmed by a sense of shock. This wasn't the only thing that Yvette was feeling. Accompanying her shock was a sense of unworthiness and dread and the persistent thought that there must have been some error made by the admissions office. How could she possibly have been accepted to *this* program? Despite her strong academic record, stellar recommendations, and numerous qualifications, she had applied with the belief that she would *never* be admitted—and somehow this belief itself had actually allowed her to apply! But now that she had been accepted, how would she possibly make it? Surely, she thought, it would only be a matter of time before her secret was revealed to everyone: Yvette was a fraud.

Perhaps Yvette's experience feels familiar to you. If so, you are in good company, joining the ranks of many graduate students who go to extraordinary and exhausting lengths to cover up their perceived deficits, live in fear of being "found out," and are unable to feel the appropriate gratification for the achievements they continue to rack up.

In fact, many people across gender, race, ethnicity, immigration status, sexual orientation, class—people across all dimensions and intersections of identity—have had this kind of pervasive feeling of self-doubt and crippling fear of being exposed as phonies. Even Michelle Obama is not immune! During her recent book tour, speaking to an audience of three hundred students at a school in England, Mrs. Obama shared, "It doesn't go away, that feeling that you shouldn't take me seriously. What do I know? I share that with you because we all have doubts about our abilities, about our power, and what power is."[1] So what is this experience that can plague even a person as accomplished as Michelle Obama?

The Impostor Phenomenon

In the late 1970s, Dr. Pauline Clance and Dr. Suzanne Imes, two psychologists at Georgia State University, identified a troubling trend among their female students and colleagues and set to work to better understand what was happening.[2] After extensive interviews, therapeutic encounters, and educational experiences with a sample of more than 150 high-achieving women, Clance and Imes found notable patterns among these women: widespread feelings of intellectual phoniness, persistent doubts about their own intellects and abilities, and the belief that they had pulled the wool over the eyes of any person who thought otherwise. These women were unable to shake this sense of fraudulence even in spite of impressive academic and professional achievement, high levels of praise and recognition from those in positions of power, and numerous accolades for their work. On the basis of this groundbreaking work, Clance and Imes coined the term "impostor phenomenon" to encapsulate the experiences of this cohort of women.

The impostor phenomenon, commonly referred to as the impostor syndrome, but also called the impostor experience and impostorism, is the psychological experience of believing that one's successes are not the result of actual capability, talent, or proficiency but rather are the result of luck, sheer hard work, or having tricked or fooled others.[3] The impostor syndrome is typified by feelings of inadequacy even when evidence to the contrary is abundantly available and apparent. Those who experience impostor syndrome may be plagued by chronic feelings of self-doubt and intellectual fraudulence, suggestive of difficulty with adequately internalizing an enduring and positive sense of one's own achievements, talents, and abilities. A person with imposter syndrome chalks up her successes to external factors whereas setbacks are further proof of her perceived internal limitations.

Not surprisingly, people who experience the impostor phenomenon may encounter emotional, social, and behavioral symptoms.[4] For example, it is not uncommon for individuals who feel like impostors to face performance anxiety and social anxiety. Students may dread having to present ideas in seminars or give a paper at a conference. Department cocktail parties are forms of torture, and even casual coffee dates to discuss ideas with peers become reasons to sweat. Perfectionism, a tendency toward harsh self-criticism, and self-imposed pressures to excel may plague those who suffer from this experience. Some students may work and rework single words or sentences until achieving what they perceive as (close to) perfect before submitting a course paper. People who feel like impostors may develop depressive symptoms, excessive amounts of worry, and sleep disturbances such as frequent nighttime waking, difficulty falling asleep, or difficulty waking and getting out of bed. Motivation may grind to a halt, giving rise to impressive stints of procrastination for people who struggle with feeling like a fraud.

Lest you begin to think, "I'm doomed! There's no hope for me!" let me provide some reassurance. As a woman who has confronted her fair share of moments of feeling like a fraud, I am here to say: It is possible to shift this experience of self! This chapter will provide you with a deeper understanding of the experience and possible roots of impostor syndrome, while also bolstering your sense of confidence and hope by suggesting specific strategies designed to alleviate your suffering. But first, a little more background.

Impostorism: Not Just White Women!

Clance and Imes' seminal study set the stage for further interrogation of this phenomenon across populations. Their research sample was notably limited to White middle-class to upper-middle-class women. Subsequent research of impostor syndrome has blossomed to consider the impostor phenomenon through the lenses of race, class, and other dimensions of identity.

Clance and Imes initially predicted that women would have significantly higher instances of impostor syndrome due to common sex-role stereotyping of women as less capable than men.[5] Since then, further studies have uncovered the reality that men, too, have their share of struggles with feelings of inadequacy and fears of exposure.[6] Peter, a fourth-year doctoral student in sociology, had made his way to dissertation proposal phase despite being plagued by avoidance throughout his years of coursework. Peter possessed an impressive depth and breadth of knowledge and a capacity for keenly nuanced thinking but struggled to respond to emails, schedule meetings, and finish papers. Rather than corralling these gifts and directing them toward meaningful and productive engagement with his work, Peter instead used them in grandiose verbal displays designed to hide his deep shame, self-doubt, and feelings of fraudulence. Unfortunately, the positive attention Peter received in these moments did little to bolster his confidence or motivate him to more deeply engage; any gratification he experienced was fleeting.

Stymied by his struggle to progress with his proposal, Peter sought help from a therapist at his university's counseling center. In this therapeutic relationship, Peter began to develop an appreciation of the underlying causes for his struggles. He felt supported by his therapist, who helped him learn and implement strategies to confront his tendency to procrastinate while employing mindfulness techniques to ease the suffering caused by his negative thinking.

Students crossing socioeconomic class divides may be susceptible to the impostor syndrome.[7] Janelle was the first in her family to enter and graduate from college, and the first to pursue a graduate degree. During her first year in a doctoral program in anthropology, Janelle struggled to find her confidence among the many talented students in her cohort seemingly groomed for a life in academia. She felt woefully inadequate, disadvantaged, and out of place as she sat in seminars surrounded by the shiny-faced pedigreed Ivy Leaguers in her cohort. She dove into her work, burning the midnight oil well into the night, consuming the canonical works of her discipline, keeping on top of due dates, but never felt confident enough to share her ideas in class.

Born and raised in a working-class family in an economically depressed coal region of Kentucky, Janelle was the pride and joy of her large, tightly knit family. And yet, she recognized how increasingly distant she felt from them. Janelle started to feel as though she was neither here nor there, but rather straddling two worlds: No longer could she identify with all of the markers of her family culture; neither could she fully settle into this elite world of words and ideas. Aware of how un-settled she felt, Janelle began to journal about her experience and found online accounts written by others with similar experiences. Janelle was comforted by this sense of connection and started to feel more able to challenge the manner in which she was limiting herself. These solitary interventions provided impetus for her to make connections to others with similar experiences within the larger university community.

The experience of people of color in graduate school may likewise be constrained by impostorism,[8] most often intertwined with and exac-erbated by minority stress status, a unique set of stressors experienced by minority students and linked to encounters with racism and dis-crimination.[9] A magna cum laude graduate of a prestigious historically Black college, Kevin rode a robust wave of academic achievement to graduate school to pursue a doctorate in linguistics. Among the twelve students in his cohort, Kevin was the only Black student, an experi-ence that, while not wholly unfamiliar, felt quite distant from his four years of undergrad. Whereas his sense of well-being, belonging, and connection during his time in college was consistent and secure, in the context of his graduate school experience, Kevin felt isolated. He frequently questioned whether he belonged in graduate school, despite his achievements. Kevin routinely fielded racial microaggressions; for example, overhearing members of his cohort complaining about not getting fellowships because "they probably gave them to the minority students." As a result, he found himself questioning the motivations of other students or professors as they sought out his ideas or invited him to lunch. He became aware of worrying about whether he was adequately representing not only himself and his family, but the larger Black community. At the same time, Kevin felt concerned that others were judging him according to ages-old and damaging stereotypes of Black men in the United States. Even with his long history of academic and social successes, Kevin's sense of inadequacy grew, and his previ-ously solid self-esteem began to plummet.

After several difficult months, Kevin reached out to friends from un-dergrad who, like him, were pursuing advanced degrees. He shared his experience and felt buoyed as he heard his peers recount similar experi-ences. Motivated by these conversations, Kevin sought out additional sources of connection and support, joining an affinity group on campus for students of color and linking to an organization for minority students that paired students with mentors.

These stories represent just a few of the many stories of impostorism. Students from all walks of life, particularly those students for whom academia is not the most welcoming place, find themselves questioning their abilities, their knowledge, their dreams, and their right to occupy space in the academy.

Exercise: Recounting
Your Own Relationship to Impostor Syndrome

Do any of the vignettes resonate with you? Perhaps as you've read, memories have emerged from moments of feeling like a fraud and worries that others would discover your fraudulence. Have you ever felt, by virtue of your gender, race, class, immigration status, disability status, or other identity characteristics, that you didn't "belong" or had less of a voice? That others wouldn't take you seriously? Do you remember feeling like teachers, professors, or others had made a "mistake" if they complimented you or responded to you as competent? Have there been situations in which you have engaged in a lot of impression management, making sure to cultivate a particular image of yourself for others so as to increase the likelihood they would think well of you?

Take a moment to reflect on these questions. Visualize the details that come to mind: Where were you? Who were you with? What were you doing? How were you feeling and what were you thinking?

Now consider the moments you felt relief from these feelings of fraudulence. Can you identify the factors during these moments that might have led to this relief? A conversation with a friend? A run in the park? Writing in a journal?

Factors in the Development
and Maintenance of the Impostor Syndrome

At this point, you may have some suspicions about the potential roots that give rise to the development of the imposter syndrome. Let's take a closer look at some of the causal and correlating factors that have been identified through the research on the impostor syndrome. As you read, consider your own experience. Do any of these explanations touch upon elements that may contribute to your experience of feelings of inadequacy and self-doubt? When we consciously connect to potential antecedents of an emotional experience, we can erect a kind of containing and organizing mental structure that often provides some relief from distress.

Sociocultural Factors

While no one is necessarily immune from the experience of impostor syndrome, some communities are more vulnerable to the experience of impostorism as a result of sociocultural factors. Legacies of systemic and institutionalized bias, discrimination, and inequality on the basis of race, ethnicity, gender identity and expression, class, sexual orientation, immigration status, language and dialect, and disability have material and psychic consequences.

Among these consequences is the very real risk of *belonging uncertainty*,[10] an insecurity about the quality and sturdiness of one's social connections that leads a person to question their sense of belonging. As a result of social stigmatization, members of minority groups are more likely to experience belonging uncertainty.[11] Belonging uncertainty undermines a felt sense of social connectedness so vital to succeeding in academic endeavors. Studies focused on the experience of African American and Black students have demonstrated that *minority status stress*, described above, contributes to belonging uncertainty, exacerbates feelings of isolation, and gives rise to mood symptoms and anxiety.[12] Indeed, minority status stress can lead to a sense of intellectual fraudulence.[13]

Decades past the second-wave feminist revolution, women continue to battle against enduring and limiting stereotypes and gender-based expectations of behavior. The negative sociocultural scripts about women's intelligence, abilities, and emotionality undermine women's sense of efficacy and belonging and can lead women to question their capabilities—indeed, their very place in the academy. The damaging notions that abound about what it is to be a woman who is assertive, let alone aggressive, may unwittingly cause a female student to question her strivings for success.

Examples from across and within identities abound: Students from working-class and economically poor backgrounds must work against enduring stigmas that link class to intellectual capacity and sophistication. Many immigrant students must confront bias on the basis of language, with accent becoming a lightning rod for not only discrimination, but shame. LGBTQ+ students find themselves fielding microaggressions regularly, contending with heteronormative narratives and outright homophobia. Students with visible and invisible disabilities must do the exceptionally hard work of proving they are capable of complex thinking and work, even when the very term "disability" seems to suggest they are not. These forces, and many, many more, create significant emotional labor for those students who occupy a space on the margins in terms of identities and contribute to higher chances of feeling like a fraud.

Influences from Families of Origin

Each of us is deeply influenced by the families of which we are a part, and every family—arguably—has its gifts and its limitations. In their initial work on impostor syndrome, Clance and Imes theorized that the roots of imposter feelings lie in the families of origin of the women in their studies.[14] Now, lest this section read as an indictment on your family of origin or childhood experience, I welcome you to imagine that alongside the ways in which your family tendencies might have contributed to a vulnerability to imposter syndrome, you also imagine the ways in which your family helped you to get to where you are! That said, understanding the ways in which the norms of your family system might have set the stage for feelings of fraudulence can be helpful.

Children receive tremendous emotional and psychological benefit from having their feelings and wishes affirmed in their primary relationships.[15] Validation of this kind goes a long way in helping a child to develop a stable sense of self. In the chronic absence of this kind of a validating environment, children come to learn that they should hide parts of themselves and instead come to develop false personas or idealized versions of themselves for which they receive validation. Children can start to become dependent on external validation and admiration from others, may be even more sensitive to criticism, and engage defensive strategies to ward off moments of exposure and shame. You may be able to draw a line through the dots here, to imagine the way in which this childhood experience can prime a person for feelings of impostorism in adulthood.

Findings from research on the family backgrounds of people who experienced imposter syndrome revealed a number of generalizable characteristics.[16] Individuals who experience imposter syndrome are more likely to come from families in which a felt sense of support may be lacking. There may be higher levels of conflict and rigidly enforced rules and procedures, and expressions of emotions may be circumscribed. A more recent study found that children who were parentified in their family—that is, they performed emotional or functional roles typically performed by parents and for which these children were developmentally unready—were more likely to struggle with imposter syndrome as adults.[17] When a person grows up in an environment typified by such norms, they may struggle with insecurity, shaky self-esteem, and a weak sense of their own abilities, thus priming the person for imposter feelings.

Individual Traits and Tendencies

A good amount of research has been done to understand the role particular traits and tendencies may play in the development or maintenance of imposter syndrome. As you read this section, consider if any of the descriptions resonate with you. If they do, remember that these are merely a part of the complex, dynamic whole that makes up who you are! And further, keep in mind that identifying certain tendencies or characteristics may be an important starting point in helping you to transform your experience of impostorism.

Those who struggle with impostor syndrome may have a strong tendency toward negative thinking and self-doubt, not dissimilar to the experience of those who struggle with depression.[18] This does not mean that every person who experiences imposter feelings is depressed, nor does this mean that imposter syndrome causes depression. That said, negative thinking and self-doubt, characteristic of depression, can affect productivity and may lead to feelings of impostorism.

Along these lines, people experiencing impostor syndrome may suffer from low self-esteem,[19] weak self-efficacy, and a tendency to undervalue or even devalue themselves.[20] This tendency toward devaluation may be connected to the imposter's attempt to live up to a highly ideal-ized, unrealistic, and self-defeating version of himself.[21]

Research has shown a correlation between trait anxiety and impos-tor syndrome;[22] that is, if you tend to be anxious, you may be more likely to feel like a fraud. Perhaps not surprisingly, introversion has been positively correlated to imposter syndrome,[23] and those who de-scribe themselves as introverts are more likely to describe themselves as shy and anxious.

People who struggle with imposter feelings tend to view intelligence as fixed rather than something that is malleable, growing and changing over time.[24] This belief leads imposters to respond to failures in a less than resilient manner: feeling helpless, withdrawing from learning, en-gaging in self-blame, and feeling anxious or ashamed. In contrast, those who are able to see intellect as malleable are motivated by learning rather than the impression they make on others, and this motivation often supports a more resilient and adaptive response to challenges.[25]

Perhaps not surprisingly, perfectionism is a trait that is common among those who feel like impostors[26] and is often utilized as a method to gain others' approval.[27] Associated to perfectionism is procrastina-tion, which tends to give rise to deep feelings of shame, both tenden-cies for those who struggle with imposter syndrome.[28] You can read more about procrastination, and how to overcome it, in chapter 17 of this book.

Phew! Now that you have deeper understanding of the possible fac-tors that prime us toward feelings of impostorism, let's turn our atten-tion to this important question: How do I stop feeling like an impostor?

So Now What? Strategies
for Addressing Impostor Syndrome

Often those of us who experience imposter syndrome find ourselves suf-fering alone, imagining that this is the price we must pay to be in gradu-ate school. If you are struggling with feelings of impostorism, know that you are far from alone, and that you can feel better!

In this section, I offer a number of proactive steps you can take and strategies you can engage in order to transform this painful experience.

As you read, imagine yourself trying out one or more of these suggestions, and perhaps allow yourself to come up with additional strategies for addressing your experience of impostor syndrome.

Connect to Others

When we are suffering, it is not unusual to feel or become isolated from others. However, isolation only exacerbates our suffering. Perhaps one of the most important things for you to do is to reach out to others in order to build connections, reduce isolation, and start to feel better. There are a number of different ways you might do this.

Affinity Groups

Affinity groups are generally organized around dimensions of identity that are vulnerable to underrepresentation or misrepresentation in dominant spheres. Such groups may be specific to race or ethnicity, immigration status, disability, gender, LGBTQ+ status, or various intersections of identities. Affinity groups can be powerful spaces in which to explore the particular experiences of being a graduate student who is a member of a minority group. These groups have the potential to provide both relief and support, as members find their own experiences represented or validated in the experiences of others. Groups such as these reduce feelings of isolation, may strengthen confidence and self-esteem, and can serve as links to a variety of other resources.

No affinity groups at your university? Create one! Enlist support from your department chair or administrator. Perhaps visit the office for student services or the counseling center at your school. Those who work at colleges and universities generally have a strong investment in helping students *feel* their best so that they can *do* their best.

Mentors

Those who have gone before us on this journey of graduate school can offer authentic and meaningful support as we progress in our own journey. For students who are members of minority groups, finding mentors who share this minority status can offer invaluable emotional and material support. Mentors can serve as resources, sounding boards, and models of what is possible to achieve when we put our minds to it.

Seek Support from a Therapist or Therapy Group

Seeking support from a therapist or therapy group when we are struggling can be invaluable. Psychologists, social workers, and other mental health counselors who work in counseling centers at universities are well-versed in supporting students who are struggling to own their achievements and come out from behind the mask of imposter syndrome. Groups specifically for students struggling with imposter syndrome can be uniquely beneficial. These groups provide multiple voices to counter an individual member's experiences of self-doubt and feelings of fraudulence. Moreover, they serve as powerful reminders that we are not alone in our experience, but among good (and successful) company.

Open Up to Trusted Friends and Family

Sharing your experience of impostor syndrome with family members or friends you trust and on whom you can rely provides relief from the experience of isolation so frequently a part of impostorism. Friends or family may have stories of their own struggles that can provide validation for your experience. Feeling heard and seen by those we love and are loved by relieves our suffering, offering up a kind of warm and cozy psychic blanket with which to wrap ourselves.

Recognize and Learn to Challenge Negative Thinking

A tenet of cognitive behavioral approaches to therapy is that our thoughts, feelings, and behaviors are connected and reciprocally influential. When we feel anxious, we create thoughts to explain that anxiety, and this affects our behavior or response. Those of us who struggle with impostorism tend to create negative rather than adaptive thoughts that correspond to our feeling states. These thoughts reinforce negative ideas we have about ourselves and may lead to less adaptive behaviors. We inadvertently end up getting in our own way!

How can you break this cycle? First, start to observe yourself, identifying the negative thoughts that come to mind when you feel anxious (or sad, or angry). As you start to identify your negative thoughts, you may begin to notice certain patterns or trends across the thoughts you create about yourself and your experience. You may notice that your thoughts actually make you feel worse and reinforce limiting beliefs about yourself.

After some observation of your thought patterns, begin to practice greeting your negative thoughts with suspicion. Imagine holding your thoughts up as objects to be observed. Consider this: You are finishing a paper for an upcoming conference. You find yourself thinking, "This paper is terrible!" "Everyone who hears this paper will see all the holes in my thinking!" "There's no way I'll ever get a job!" You probably can agree that these thoughts will only stoke even higher levels of anxiety and fuel self-doubt.

Next, objectively test the reasonableness of these negative thoughts. You may find that your thoughts are imbalanced and not fully grounded in facts or evidence. Then, try to come up with a thought that is *actually reasonable*. For example, "This paper has strengths and areas that could be further developed." "My performance at this conference isn't going to make or break me on the job market." "Most people will listen and hear the strengths of my argument, and even if they do challenge me, this feedback could be useful to me!" In comparison to the previous negative thoughts, how do you imagine you will feel if you had these alternate thoughts? Chances are, your anxiety would rapidly decrease, you might experience a calm, grounded feeling, and you may even be able to reconnect to your capabilities.

Develop a Mantra
When we are in a moment of self-doubt or fear, we can quickly move to negative thinking, which provides further fuel for difficult emotions. Try to catch yourself in these moments. Recount to yourself a predetermined mantra to provide some grounding and stability. Here are some ideas: "I deserve to be here." "I have many things to offer." "Here I am, right now. Learning." "I don't have to know everything." Let my suggestions spur the creation of your own mantras, ones that you can easily recall, ones that resonate for you and serve as touchstones throughout your week.

Keep a Journal
Journaling may feel like yet another task in your long list of things to do while a graduate student. And yet, taking five to ten minutes each day to document your experience can be enormously grounding. Find yourself a special notebook and pen to use as a journal. For me, it's a medium-size, blank-paged, soft-cover Moleskin notebook and a Pilot

Precise V5 RT pen. I carry these supplies in my backpack and have them at the ready whenever I might need to record or reflect.

A simple way to start is list making. Lists are quick and easy and can actually be enjoyable to create! Here are some prompts for you to start with: What are my successes? What did I accomplish today? What am I good at? What gives me pleasure? What are my goals? What words describe me? Who gave me positive feedback, and what did they share? What am I hoping for?

Move Your Body!

Engaging in physical activity is key in reducing stress, lessening anxiety, and managing depressive symptoms. When we take a long walk, go for a run, hop on our bike, do yoga, or even get our hands in the dirt, we release feel-good endorphins into our system. These endorphins go a long way in alleviating stress and other symptoms that come along for the ride when we feel like a fraud. Exercise helps us gain confidence, can be a social endeavor, and, in general, is a healthy coping mechanism.

Not a person who exercises? Well, start with something you enjoy and can do easily. Commit to engaging in the activity for a certain number of minutes, a certain number of times a week. Start small and make the goal reasonable and achievable. Pair the activity with something else that is pleasurable. Listen to music on your headphones as you go for a run. Talk on the phone with your best friend as you take a walk. Go for coffee after your yoga class. Notice how your body and mind feel after you move. Take note of the positive effects, perhaps even writing that note in that journal you've begun to keep!

Interrogate Your Fraudulence

While this idea may seem counterintuitive, sometimes our negative self-perceptions serve an unconscious function. It can be an illuminating exercise to consider the possibility that feelings of fraudulence serve a purpose. Perhaps feeling like a fake inadvertently lets you off the hook, fuels avoidance, and keeps you from pushing yourself into a position of success? Perhaps you were taught not to brag about yourself, and feeling like a fraud protects you from feelings of self-importance or arrogance that seem even worse? Balance the potential benefits of your impostorism with its drawbacks to determine if it is a worthwhile strategy towards your future goals and values.

Stop Comparing Yourself!

You know what I'm talking about. There she is, the ideal graduate student in your cohort. Each week she seems to somehow do all the readings, always has a brilliant interpretation or comment, and seems to integrate theory effortlessly. Perhaps she is applying for and being awarded grants. Maybe she succeeds in getting an article published after only one revision. She is the easy object of idealization, the one you weigh yourself against, coming up short again and again. But comparisons like this lead you to mistakenly imagine that the only way to succeed is to be another person; the only path forward in your graduate career is the one this other has taken. This simply isn't true. Not only does this idealization of the other stymie your own ability to be present in *your* journey of learning, but it also reduces the complexity of this other person. She, like you, has her own growth areas, her own struggles, and her own self-doubt. Your knowledge, capabilities, talents, growth areas, and learning are your own, and the process you engage to learn is yours too.

Remember, Learning = Disequilibrium!

Of the many things we have gained from the work of the Swiss psychologist Jean Piaget is the concept of equilibrium.[29] Simply put, Piaget theorized that when we encounter something new, we try to make sense of it by drawing on the schemata that we've built from previous encounters with ideas and experiences. But when we can't fit the new ideas or experiences into the schemata available to us, we enter an uncomfortable state of disequilibrium. This disequilibrium, while uncomfortable, is also elemental to learning! We seek to make sense, at least in part to reduce the discomfort that comes from a state of disequilibrium. As Piaget conceptualized, we begin a process of "accommodation" that involves a revision of existing schemata and, at times, the building of new schema. This is learning! Remember, you are *in graduate school to learn*. You aren't expected to know everything yet. Your job is to be in a state of learning: greeting and tolerating disequilibrium, tweaking existing schemata and creating new schema, and—as Piaget imagined—assimilating this new knowledge into the ever-evolving cognitive core that is a part of you.

Take in External Validation
When we struggle with feelings of impostorism, we typically have a hard time believing the positive reinforcement we receive from others about our work, abilities, or potential. It may feel easier to discount a peer's compliments or believe you have once again fooled your professor into thinking you actually know something. Practice taking external validation seriously. Imagine that others actually know what they are talking about, and that what they are witnessing and responding to is a part of you, not something you have tricked them into thinking. Internalize this external validation, maybe even begin to test out believing it.

You Can Do It!

The pressure-cooker microcosm that is academia can easily feed the flames of impostorism, especially for those of us who occupy marginalized identities. As a person whose journey through graduate school included more than enough difficult experiences of impostorism, I know how hard it can be. I also know that it is possible to change your experience by enlisting support and learning to implement adaptive strategies, allowing you to experience graduate school absent the mask of impostorism. My hope is that this chapter built your awareness of the markers of and underlying contributions to imposter syndrome and offered solid strategies for combatting it. Rather than "faking" your way through graduate school, you *can* have an authentic experience and engage in *real* learning while simultaneously accepting your growth areas and internalizing all of your successes!

Takeaways for Students

- Remember: *You are not alone*. Many students sitting right next to you in class are feeling something similar. Many professors in your program faced their own challenges during their time as students.
- Connect to others. Reach out to supportive friends, family members, classmates. Start to open up about your experience.

- Prioritize self-care. Develop and maintain healthy sleep habits, healthy eating and drinking, moving your body.
- Challenge your negative thoughts. Replace these thoughts with more reasonable, balanced, and hopeful ideas that will boost your mood and motivate you to engage.
- Go visit the counseling center at your university. Therapists who work at university counseling centers are well-versed in the complexities faced by students. They are there to help you by providing individual and group counseling, resources, and other kinds of support during times of struggle.

Suggestions for Administrators and Professors

- Cultivate empathy for your students, imagining their experiences and remembering your own from graduate school.
- Keep in mind that many students—even those who may present as confident—are vulnerable to feelings of inadequacy, self-doubt, and fraudulence. Remember that students who are members of marginalized communities or identities may be at higher risk for these feelings.
- Create multiple and varied opportunities for students to come together as a community, to interact with one another and with faculty and administration.
- Support student affinity groups as well as mentorship opportunities.
- Commit to building reliable, consistent, respectful connections and relationships with your advisees.
- If you feel comfortable doing so, share your own experiences with the imposter syndrome in grad school and/or beyond.
- Help students connect to others in the discipline outside of your particular university.
- Actively mentor students as they engage in their scholarship. Be supportive of their research endeavors, pursuit of grants and other funding, and participation in conferences.
- If you feel concerned about a student in your class or program, make an effort to connect in a way that is genuine and respectful of the student's needs for privacy and autonomy.

- Consult with professionals in the counseling center to better understand the causes for and signs of student distress.
- Connect students in need to support services such as the counseling center and offices for accessibility.

Suggestions for Therapists and Counselors

- If you aren't already, become familiar with the impostor phenomenon!
- Offer group treatment for students who may struggle with impostorism. Ensure that the therapists who lead the group are well versed in and able to address the particular experiences of students who feel like imposters.
- Develop and maintain therapy groups for students with disabilities, LGBTQ+ students, immigrant students, and other possibly marginalized groups.
- Utilize cognitive behavioral strategies in individual sessions with students presenting with impostor syndrome to uproot the tendency toward negative thinking and maladaptive behaviors.
- Support students in learning and practicing mindfulness techniques to ease anxiety through individual and group treatment as well as outreach in the community.
- Provide outreach opportunities for students to learn about imposter syndrome.
- Educate faculty and administration about imposter syndrome so that they are better equipped to support all students in their journey through graduate school.
- If appropriate, invest in the relationships you have with faculty and administration to ensure continuity of care for students and to foster durable and healthy alliances between the counseling center and other entities at the university.

~

CHAPTER THREE

So . . . It's Not Just Me?

Coping with Stress and Anxiety in Graduate School

Lauren Wisely

Whether you are contemplating applying to graduate school or are in the frenzied midst of it, "grad school" has probably taken up an inordinate amount of your mental, emotional, and physical energy. Perhaps you're someone who just knew what you wanted to be when you grew up, or you're still trying to figure it out and having doubts about your career path. Grad school is so often a mixed bag of your hopes, dreams, and fears. This chapter will focus on how to deal with the fears part, because once grad school begins, it's the fears that can sometimes take over.

The Long Road

The decision and process to get into graduate school is long and arduous. Years of hard work, academic success, and sacrifice leading to more years of hard work, academic success (fingers crossed), and sacrifice—yay! I haven't met anyone yet who has gone through the process with nothing but determination, optimism, and confidence (regardless if their social media account implies otherwise). Typically, grad school is a stage in life of more or less constant stress, including doubts and exhaustion, in every possible sense of the word. Now that I have made you even more depressed, take heed—it gets better. There are ways to make it more bearable and even tolerable. You're working towards some big goals and that's pretty awesome. Keep in mind the helpful idiom "Nothing worth doing is ever easy!"

There Is More to You Than Being a Grad Student

In the weeks leading up to my first day of grad school, I had nightmares and weird dreams. A recurring theme was that either I signed on for a huge mistake or I would be out of my element in any number of possible ways. I was also scared I would be paying it off for the rest of my life (okay—that part turned out to be true). The first day of orientation came along and there was a helpful/not-so-helpful meeting with older graduate students to give us the scoop on what to expect. This was half pep talk and half scare sh#%*less presentation. The most senior graduate student, who was the most outspoken, described the next few years of our lives something like this: "Kiss your family, your friends, your partner goodbye! You're in grad school now, and there's nothing but grad school for the next five to seven years. It will take over your every waking minute, this is your life!" The beginning of Guns N' Roses's "Welcome to the Jungle" would've been a good opener for this talk. It reminded me of the scene from *Jaws* when the old, life-worn shark fisherman scratched his nails along the blackboard to get everyone's attention. My immediate thought was, "Oh well, I wonder if I can get my tuition deposit back." Yes, I had career aspirations that required an advanced degree, but at what cost? Was it true that I had to make the choice between everything else in life and this? Now, here I am on the other side, and I can tell you unequivocally: No, you don't have to choose between all other parts of your life and grad school. Yes, it's a lot, yes, it's overwhelming at times, but surviving and thriving in grad school requires not losing yourself in the process.

If someone were to ask you "What do you do?" the first response most people give is to name their profession (at least in US culture). Our sense of self is so tied to our professional identities, often at the detriment of so many other aspects of what makes us who we are. Students in graduate and professional programs tend to have a higher tendency to attach a sense of self and self-worth to their career goals. Indeed, in many ways grad school can become a world unto itself, taking over every other aspect of your life. Certainly, being a grad student can and should be a source of pride. After all, excelling at higher education is impressive in itself; but putting all of one's eggs in one basket can be risky. If you eat, sleep, and dream grad school, burnout is much more likely. Even if you're pursing a lifetime goal in your dream profession, you are more than a grad student or a "future" whatever. When your whole ego is wrapped tightly around one aspect of yourself, it makes you vulnerable for increased anxiety and depression. Having other interests and passions allows you to have some distance and therefore perspective on the stresses and challenges inherent in grad school. There will be toxic people who you have to deal with, whether they are professors, advisors, supervisors, or fellow students. There will be unfair or unrealistic expectations placed on you. There will be times you feel overwhelmed or lost. It is easier to get through these challenges if you have other interests outside the world of grad school. The emotional toll of these stressors is diminished when you realize school and professional pursuits are one aspect of you; they do not define you. Relationships outside of the program, other interests or hobbies you are invested in, pets, travel, volunteering, involvement in a community or religious group, creative activities, the options are plentiful . . . don't neglect the other aspects of yourself, and if you have, get back in touch with who you were before grad school, what mattered to you before, or pursue some passion yet undiscovered. These aren't suggestions for the extracurricular activities of your youth, meant to pad a resume and give the appearance of a well-rounded person—they're about being a whole person in spite of the huge time, energy, and financial demands school has placed upon you.

Thoughts Are Not Necessarily Facts

A thoroughly nonscientific survey of most prevalent thoughts during graduate school can be summed up thusly,

"Do I really want to do this?" . . . *"Yay! I got in!"* . . . *"Is this really happening?"* . . . *"Do I really want to do this?"* . . . *"What if everyone is smarter/better than me and they'll see that I really don't belong here?"* . . . *"I have no idea what I'm doing."* . . . *"I CAN do this!"* . . . *"I CAN'T do this!"* . . . *"Holy %$&#! I really can't do this!"* . . . *"Maybe, I can do this?"* . . . *"Do*

I really want to do this?" . . . *"Okay, just get through this week"* . . . and repeat until you graduate.

Not to stereotype, but graduate students tend to ruminate and over-think things. The brain that got you this far academically is probably a best frenemy to you. All the goal-directed behavior, planning, and organizational skills that have aided and abetted this achievement have a darker side. The darker side is the worries, the "what-ifs," and the worst-case scenarios. Striving for success is a wonderful motivator to be sure, but the flip side, fear of failure, may be more salient for you. This fear of failure often manifests as thoughts, some of which were described above. They can usually be distilled into "If___, Then___" assumptions. How you fill in those blanks is personal, but common themes are "If I don't get this done (and perfectly), then everything is over for me" or "If I'm struggling, then I'm not cut out for this" or "If I have one failure or setback, then I will never succeed." It's not that negative thoughts or assumptions can never be accurate, but they are usually overblown. Perfectionism and graduate study have a tendency to go together. You may credit your success thus far with having ex-ceedingly high expectations for yourself. You may, on some level, credit the thoughts that nag you about never being good enough as also being a motivator for your hard work and achievement. Once while watch-ing the winter Olympic Games, I noticed something striking. On the sidelines were coaches who looked stressed, angry, and hostile pushing their athletes ever harder. Yet there were other coaches who looked like a calming force for stressed athletes, who were there with encour-agement and a hug—regardless. Here's the point: Both are competing at the Olympic level. So, while you may believe that being hard on yourself, or internalizing the unreasonable expectations of others, may get you far, it's not the only way. It's sort of like the proverbial angel and devil on your shoulder; we all have that punitive, critical, demand-ing coach and the forgiving, encouraging, supportive one echoing in our minds—the question is where you turn up the volume.

Our thoughts are not ourselves. We tend to experience our internal monologue as ourselves, but thoughts are better understood as a stimu-lus that can just pop up like anything else we experience. When you put your hand in cold water, you don't think "I'm a cold person." You understand that your hand won't be cold when you take it out of the water. You experience yourself as separate from the sensation. Yet the thoughts and emotions we experience can feel like part of us. Learning how to create a little wedge between our thoughts and ourselves is a wonderful little trick. Thoughts are influenced by a multitude of factors. Some are long-standing and hard to change, including our temperament, early environment and relationships, trauma history, and typical mood. Some factors are far more transient, like how much caffeine you recently drank or if you got adequate sleep last night.

Even though thoughts are often not factual, our brain has a funny way of mistaking thoughts for facts. "I'm such an idiot!" is a thought, not a fact, but it triggers a cascade of emotion, and that can potentially turn into maladaptive behaviors. Maladaptive behaviors can include things such as avoiding tasks and procrastination, and they can escalate to shutting down, withdrawing from relationships, or reliance on substances to get by. We can't necessarily change all the factors that contribute to the negative thoughts we have, but it's worthwhile to become aware of what your personal negative thinking patterns are. We all have well-worn grooves in our minds, automatic thoughts that play more or less on a loop. These are different for each person, but recognizing your particular top-five negative thoughts can help you to recognize their influence and learn to turn down their volume over time. Here are some examples of these types of deep-down negative thoughts that fuel negative emotions and behavior: "I'm a failure," "I'm an idiot," "Nobody really likes/loves me," "I'm an embarrassment," "I can't trust anyone," "Everyone is judging me," "I am undeserving," "I'm worthless," or "I'm defective." Take a few minutes and think about the times you are feeling anxious or depressed. Try to figure out which thoughts are fueling those states. Make a list of what yours might be.

Self-awareness is a process whereby you can better understand your particular set of beliefs, thoughts, emotions, and tendencies. It's a skill that can be strengthened like any other, through practice—whether on your own or with the help of a therapist. Self-awareness is different from self-consciousness. Self-awareness is a tool we can use to understand the factors that influence us, while self-consciousness is typically feeling a spotlight on you at all times and second-guessing your every move.

Learning to Become More Mindful

Mindfulness is a great way to exercise your self-awareness muscles. It's a way to take a step back and become an observer of what is going through your mind. Thoughts come and thoughts go, simple as that. It's our reactions to these thoughts that give them power. There are many books on mindfulness, such as *Mindfulness: An Eight-Week Plan for Finding Peace in a Frantic World* by Marc Williams and Danny Penman and *The Mindfulness and Acceptance Workbook for Anxiety* by John Forsyth and Georg Eifert. There are also some great apps, such as Calm, Insight Timer, and Headspace to help get you started. Mindfulness fits well into the graduate student lifestyle because it's relatively easy to learn as a skill and doesn't take a long time to practice. You don't need to become a Jedi master for this to work (though I imagine they'd be *really* good at it). At its core, mindfulness is the act of noticing. With practice you come to see that you are not your thoughts—it's like the difference between watching a train pass by from a grassy hilltop, watching each car go past, versus being a passenger on that train, along for the ride. With practice you can learn to be an observer; watching the thoughts as they go by . . . acknowledging "oh, there's that thought again" . . . and letting it go without having it take hold of you. The problems of overwhelming stress, anxiety, and depression sometimes evolve from wanting to go from being a passive passenger on that train to becoming the conductor, controlling our thoughts, controlling our emotions. People attempt control by telling themselves some version of "STOP IT!!" or through stifling and suppression techniques that aren't really effective in the long term. By learning how to observe these experiences; watching that train pass by, making observations without judgment—we diminish the power of negative thoughts and emotional states. Paradoxically, not trying so hard to control everything leads to a greater ability for control (okay, that does sound a *little* Jedi).

Emotional Gravitron

You have likely heard the term "emotional roller coaster," but roller coasters tend to be pretty fun and over quickly. The Gravitron, on the other hand, is a ride you may be familiar with from amusement parks as a kid—a 1980s version of a demonic spaceship—it spins, really fast, with loud music blaring. Like a lab specimen, you get suctioned to the wall of the ride, stuck to padded vinyl through centrifugal force. It seems never ending and if you're like me, you walk away with a raging headache and severe nausea. Why am I talking about my nemesis childhood ride? Because emotional "roller coaster" sounds too much like easy fun compared to the spinning disorientation that grad school can sometimes feel like. When you're on that ride, all you can do is stick to the gross, sticky (oh God, is it wet??) vinyl wall and wait for it to be over. The point of this little metaphor of the Emotional Gravitron is that sometimes emotions just have to be endured. This is the skill of Acceptance. This, too, is part of mindfulness, understanding the temporary nature of all difficult emotional states and life stressors. We can endure what is difficult when we keep in mind that it won't last forever. Negative emotions pass more quickly by taking deep breaths and doing things to improve your mood, such as self-soothing techniques, to be discussed later.

Building emotional resilience involves a few fundamentals: first, acceptance that negative moods and emotions are unavoidable; pain is inherent to the human condition. I once heard suffering described as "the result of everything we do trying to avoid pain." Seeing emotional pain as a temporary state that will pass (it always does!) helps it to pass quicker. People aren't meant to be happy all the time (or even most of the time). I'm suspicious of anyone who claims enduring joyfulness (if it lasts longer than four hours, I would suggest you consult a doctor). What helps is quasi-embracing the bad, so that the good tastes sweeter. Some mantras that have helped me remember this are simply "this too shall pass" and "it is what it is."

Another essential to emotional resilience is changing what you can to make things better in the long-term. The core skill here is one of balance between the opposing forces of acceptance and change. Some things you need to endure—such as your thesis or dissertation—while with other things you can effect some level of change to make it tolerable, or even, dare I say, good. An example of this from my grad school days was a class with an ineffective teacher (what we had to accept). An advanced statistics professor taught by turning her back to students and endlessly solving complicated equations on the board.

We couldn't follow what she was doing, and she didn't seem to think it required explanation. Needless to say, none of us were really learning statistics, which was the first math class I had taken in a very long time that I actually needed to apply in real life. We were all expected to run statistical analysis as part of our dissertation research, so understanding how to do this was crucial. We couldn't change the class or professor, as it was the only section offered for our small graduate program, but we didn't want to accept failing the class or not learning the material. I'm not sure who to credit for the idea, but as a class we brainstormed ideas for how to deal with this problem and decided to teach one another the material. Every week a couple of students would independently learn the material—through the textbook, websites, or online tutorials—and then present it to the rest of the class. We all took turns as the tutor/professor to our classmates, and by doing so we actually learned advanced statistics. We held our own class right after the actual one in an empty classroom nearby—accept what you can't change and problem-solve solutions for what you can. Also remember that sometimes, as a special treat, it's okay to allow yourself to say F&%$ it! and just abandon some things all together. You don't have to say yes to every opportunity.

Skills for Determining
What to Accept and What to Change

One good exercise that's particularly useful when feeling overwhelmed is to just make a list of the things that are making you feel that way. Just free associate. I recommend a nice big pad and your favorite pen and writing down every single thing adding to your stress. I recommend paper because you are going to want to physically cross stuff off this list—it is much more cathartic than pressing the delete key. When you make this list, it should probably approximate something Santa would have on a scroll before Christmas. If it doesn't, then think harder—there is more stuff stressing you out than you realize. You can include categories such as: relationships, school, workload, finances, physical/mental health, household, the condition of the world, addictive behaviors (checking your computer and phone screens counts!). Likely, you'll have this big, nasty list of real problems, while a few may be exaggerated or imagined (if you are like most of us); include them all. Next, make a list of all the things, real or imagined, that build you up and give you a sense of purpose, peace, and solace. These are your protective factors, and this is where you build up resiliency. Examples of these would include loving and supportive relationships, fun activities and hobbies, long- and short-term goals, an imagined future, basically whatever sparks joy (so to speak).

Don't despair if this list is depressingly short. Often the quality of protective factors can outweigh the quantity of stressors. Following this, you can figure out ways to deal with the items on the stressors list. This is a to-do list of sorts. You can deal with them now, this week, this month, this year, maybe sometime in the far future, or, you may realize, probably never (you get to cross those off the list first). On your list of stressors there will be things you can't change—like a troubling health condition in a loved one. Those are the items you need to work to accept as part of the pain inherent in life and move to seek balance with that list of positives. Once you have a *realistic* (and I can't stress this word enough) timeline for dealing with the stressors, you need to think about the *How*. Sometimes the *How* requires help from others or consultation with an advisor or a therapist. Write the *How* down next to the *What* and the *When*. Since you're a grad student, it may be helpful to imagine this exercise as a table with the list of stressors in the first column, and the next column is the whether you need to accept or change it (even if only a little). If you have to accept something stressful, think of those protective factors that may help—self-care, relationships, things to look forward to. If you can effect some change, think of how you may do so—strategies and problem solving. The last column is for when you'd like to deal with it—bigger problems and tasks should be broken down into smaller bite-size ones.

Self-Care

People talk a lot about the importance of self-care. I see a fair amount of social media posts of happy people drinking with their friends labeled #selfcare, but that's not quite it (though it can be a component!). It is possible to overdo self-care if it's all about what makes you feel good in the moment, tossing aside your long-term goals. As with most things in life—it's all about balance. True self-care involves making choices mindfully and with purpose that improve your emotional state in line with your life goals. These can be nicely indulgent practices such as eating favorite foods, taking a relaxing bath, getting a massage, buying yourself something you've been wanting, or getting tickets to an event you've been looking forward to. It can also involve practices that don't feel great in the moment—better nutrition, increased exercise, leaving a toxic relationship—but have good results in the long term. Self-care is about taking time to prioritize oneself or one's mental health above other things that beg for our time and energy. It is noticing when you need a break or a boost and granting it to yourself without guilt. This book contains a chapter on procrastination, which is related to this idea of balancing the "wants" and the "shoulds" in life.

One aspect of self-care is self-soothing. Self-soothing is anything you do to relax yourself and endure emotional distress. It is best done using your five senses. In my clinical practice I often have people put together a tool kit of things that are soothing and promote relaxation. Here are some examples for your own tool kit:

Sight: things you like to look at: photos of happy memories, slide shows of places you want to travel to and explore, or beautiful scenery. My go-to is "chonky" (pleasantly fat) animals—they are ridiculously adorable! How can you be stressed looking at a superfat kitty, just lying there like an amorphous puddle of soft fluffy chub! I digress.

Smell: any kind of aromatherapy that makes you feel calmer and relaxed.

Hearing: create upbeat playlists to jolt you into a better mood or a sad one to immerse yourself in, cry, feel validated, and come out the other side.

Touch: hot bath or shower, petting an animal (the chonkier the better!), getting a pedicure or massage, sex.

Taste: just everything you can consume preferably with sugar/salt/fat (in moderation of course). One piece of chocolate eaten slowly and mindfully can go a long way.

Try making a self-soothe tool kit of your own.

The Healthy Brain Basics

Your brain may be a vastly complex organic machine, but it has some design flaws. The very essence of who we are is contained in a couple of pounds of squishy gray stuff and (not to get too technical) things can go wonky. Inadequate sleep, hormones, chronic exposure to stress and anxiety, traumatic events, prolonged depression; these things can alter the structure and chemistry that dictate how we feel, think, and view the world and ourselves. Therapy, medication, and healthy habits can help fix or moderate these, just as with all other systems in the body. There is no real distinction between mental health and physical health.

Sleep is one of the easiest things to neglect as a student. Who needs sleep when you have caffeine? You do! More specifically, your brain does. While the mysteries of sleep are not fully understood, what we do know is that it's essential to brain functioning—both cognitive and emotional. Anyone who has been around an overtired toddler can surely attest to the transformative properties of adequate sleep. A good deal of anxiety and depressive symptoms can be tied to sleep deprivation. If you miss sleep do your best to catch up on it, and sleep in when you can. Of course, this is not always easy, particularly for graduate student parents! This is often the first and relatively easiest thing to change to improve functioning.

You already know that you have to eat healthy and exercise regularly for optimal health. Maybe you aren't aware how much it impacts your mind as well. Brains underfunction on snacks alone. Time is precious when you're as busy and pressured as a grad student. Eating healthy and getting exercise takes time—time you really don't have. Yet you don't need an expensive gym membership or a meal plan. Small positive choices accumulate over time. Some techniques to help you eat better can be simple, such as when you cook—cook a lot so that you'll have healthy leftovers you can eat throughout the week. Take stairs instead of elevators and walk or bike when you can. Taking care of your health improves your ability to function on all levels.

Connect to Others

Back in college, nights of watching comically bad movies on late-night cable meant being exposed to relentless commercials for a program that promised to make anyone a successful business entrepreneur. This was clearly a sketchy get-rich-quick scheme—but at two a.m. those ads can become pretty convincing. One of my roommates gave in one night and ordered the program. What came in the mail was a guide that promised to take you down the path to unlimited success. Though I can't remember the name of the scheme, I do remember one piece of advice from the business guru: Friends, family, and relationships in general were classified under the heading "time thieves." Time thieves take you away from what's really important—making money. This was a theme that described how "success" depends on a level of extreme independence and a degree of social isolation, because relationships are distractions from the greater goals (big piles of cash and the luxury items that come with it). In our apartment we jokingly started to refer to each other as "time thieves" whenever we had to get back to studying—our cat was the worst time thief of all. I have heard variations on this theme many times, from many sources—relationships have to take a backseat if you're serious about your career. I would argue the opposite—healthy relationships are what makes the work worth doing. You don't have to make a choice between the two (and no, the get-rich program didn't work, and the business guru eventually went to jail for fraud). However, you may have times when you need to prioritize one over the other.

Having connections to others is a basic human need—critically important to mental health. Whether it's friends, family, or romantic relationships—having others (or even just one other person) who support you, who validate you, who make you feel loved and cared for is probably the most important factor for being able to weather whatever life throws at you. The demands of grad school can be difficult precisely because it often requires moving away from those social supports (whether physically or just in terms of time spent). For many students, grad school can be a time of intense loneliness. Sometimes the sense of "otherness" can be isolating when you feel unrepresented or like you don't fit in with those around you. A sense of belonging can be cultivated, but it often needs to be actively sought out. Many schools have student associations for specific groups such as LGBTQ, racial minority, and international students that can offer a sense of support and belonging. In addition to campus-based groups, there are apps, such as Meetup and Bumble BFF among others, that link people based upon shared interests or activities. While some people are fortunate to have been born into a family or community where support is freely given, many of us have to figure out how to build healthy relationships on our own. Relationships require work to survive and thrive. The work of relationships can easily fall by the wayside when there are papers to write, tests to take, and research to finish. Taking the time to invest in keeping and building important bonds is never time wasted. So, go ahead, ask that classmate of yours whom you seem to click with to meet up for coffee. Yet beware of toxic relationships. If there are people in your life who cause you to feel unworthy, less than, or ashamed, you may need to assess how to set serious boundaries or step away from the relationship.

Connect to Nature, Beauty, and the Awe-Inspiring

Moments of awe and wonder are healing to the soul. When we are young children, the whole wide world inspires joy and wonder. Sadly, we tend to lose that along the way. I'm lucky to live near the ocean and so I stop by the beach often. Here is an observation: Young children on the beach are really experiencing the beach, while adults are doing other stuff. The kids are examining the variety of things you can find in a handful of sand, digging holes, watching the waves burying their feet, catching little critters in a bucket. They are present—experiencing what it is to be at the beach, the vastness of the ocean, the power of the waves, all the forms of life swimming, crawling, flying above them, the heat of the sand, the cool of the water. It's wonderful to behold, and truly there is the occasional adult in it too—not obsessively taking the perfectly framed selfie for Instagram—just taking in the beach. That brings us back to mindfulness; the little kids get it, they are present, they are observing, they are participating in the moment. Nature, in general, is great for this. A walk in a forest can do wonders. A walk through a museum or experiencing a concert or a play can do this too. Beauty can be found on a trip to a gorgeous destination. It can also be found in a potted plant, a poem that speaks to you, a painting that moves you. Allow yourself to open up to the awareness of the incredible in the everyday—similar to young children. Let go of the cynicism and judgment that diminish your inborn sense of awe.

Connect to Something Bigger

A sense of meaning and purpose is vital. You don't need to be out "saving the world," but being involved in something "bigger than yourself" keeps the existential crisis at bay. It doesn't matter what you do—whether it's your career, volunteering, through support and care of loved ones, social justice advocacy, or by creating something beautiful and sharing it with the world. The need to be involved in something greater comes from deep within. There is a longing there that needs to be nourished. Creativity in general is something that can become neglected in favor of career aspirations. Again, children are wellsprings of creativity. Their minds are not constrained—they make, they imagine, they do things without worrying how it will be judged by others. Finding a creative outlet is a terrific stress relief and can take so many forms—the usual modalities of art, music, writing . . . but also things like gardening, cooking, building something, or fighting for a cause you believe in. These are a big part of life's passions, and engaging with your passions is nourishment for the soul; being cut off from them is soul-sapping. What are some things you are passionate about? What activities help you to connect to something bigger?

Keeping Perspective

Understanding that people aren't meant to be happy all the time is vital. Those people who seem perpetually happy and fulfilled on Facebook or Instagram? They aren't—no one is. Comparisons aren't helpful, you never really know what other people are struggling with behind the scenes. If you find yourself making comparisons and holding yourself to absurdly high expectations (I have a hunch most graduate students fall into this category), you aren't doing yourself any favors. Kick the internalized bully to the curb and remind yourself that some of the most important lessons in life come from failure, come from pain. We have a wide range of emotions, some are wonderful and uplifting, some are scary and upsetting, all are necessary and a part of the human experience. If we can tolerate the anxiety, sadness, feelings of inadequacy and insecurity as normal and not some moral failing, they will pass more quickly and will not be amplified. This isn't to say that real bullies or toxic people don't exist. The proportion of students en-dorsing mental health problems has skyrocketed in recent years—from both better understanding, yes, but also due to generational factors that have added more stressors (such as debt, negative impacts of technol-ogy, racism, discrimination, social isolation, and an increasingly hostile cultural climate). There is a growing cultural divide, often with college campuses being a hotbed for exacerbating tensions. We are exposed to reports of mass violence, social injustice, and discrimination with alarming frequency. This isn't a call to stick your head in the sand and accept the unacceptable. If empathy and a sense of justice call on you to take a stand, then certainly don't ignore those rumblings. This is more specifically about the negative perspective that comes if we internalize that toxicity.

One analogy I find helpful in grounding and finding perspective is to imagine waves washing over you. If you have ever entered the ocean, you know that the sheer force of the waves push and pull you to a de-gree that you don't have control over. There is a famous quote, attrib-uted to a bunch of different sources, that states "You cannot stop the waves from coming, but you can learn how to surf." So no, you cannot control everything, but often we find we can gain enough control when needed in order to make it through. It is better to let the tears flow, and go with the flow, than try to hold it all in. It will flow back to joy and happiness if you don't judge yourself harshly for the fear and sadness.

A sense of humor is required to get through it all. It's hard to be de-pressed or anxious and laughing simultaneously (not impossible mind you, but hard). Embrace the weirdness of life as a graduate student and find humor in the absurdity. For Harry Potter fans, this is how Professor Lupin teaches the students to relax when faced with their worst fears—turn them into something laughable. A sense of humor is very individualized, and you are the best curator of whatever it is that makes you smile. Make a playlist of movies, shows, or videos. Go on websites like PhDcomics.com or follow accounts like LEGO Grad Student to commiserate with your fellow unfortunate souls. When you find yourself reading the same paragraph over and over, or staring at a blinking cursor for too long—that's a good signal to give yourself a ten- to thirty-minute break and find something that makes you laugh to reset your brain and your mood.

Help When You Need It

Everyone needs help and support sometimes—this is not weakness. This isn't a failure. This is a truth of the human condition. Truly incredible things have been born out of profoundly deep struggles. Some of those resources will be relying on friends or family, some will be professional help, sometimes it could be taking and staying on a course of medication that helps you. There are advisors, mentors, counselors, and fellow students to help guide you along the way. There are support groups online, there are text and phone help lines. You don't need to figure it all out on your own. What are the components of your support system? Is there anything useful that you could add now that you're in grad school? Grad school is a world unto itself. It takes hard work, intelligence, and perseverance to be sure. In order to get through it more or less unscathed (or at least intact), these life skills need as much of your attention as study skills. You're asking a lot from your brain as a grad student. A little reciprocity goes a long way. Yes, there is a light at the end of the tunnel, but it always helps to make the tunnel a little brighter along the way.

Takeaways for Students

- Eat healthy.
- Get some sleep.
- Keep expectations and negative thoughts in check.
- Be more mindful.
- Reward your hard work with a little indulgence and self-care.
- Be a better friend to yourself and to those in your life who matter to you.
- Stay involved in other interests and passions.
- Create.
- Take the bad with the good.
- Get involved in something meaningful to you.
- Remember that you're not alone.

Suggestions for Faculty and Administration

- Balance expectations with empathy—remember, there is always a compassionate way to address issues.

- Balance the push toward success and mastery with support as needed.
- Be mindful not to perpetuate myths that add stress to grad school, such as "there is only one way to be successful" or "self-sacrifice is required to achieve goals"; avoid back-in-my-day comparisons.
- Flexibility can go a long way to helping students reach their goals. Often reasonable accommodations can be made to best suit an individual student's needs when difficulties arise.
- Respect students as adults; it is easy to fall into an adults/kids dynamic in academia, but recognizing students as professionals-in-training creates a more collaborative environment and increases self-efficacy.
- Always strive for cultural competency and sensitivity and be aware of how power differentials and social disparities are at play.
- Help to build a supportive academic community where students can feel they have a "home base" and a sense of belonging.
- Help to create and support a system of peer-to-peer mentorship for students.
- Know where to refer, without judgment, for mental health resources on and off campus and create an atmosphere where struggle is not stigmatized.

Suggestions for Mental Health Professionals

- Be mindful that grad students often strive to be the "best" therapy clients as well and can minimize issues due to this; always check in with the clearly stated understanding that "it's okay to be struggling."
- Be careful not to pathologize; diagnoses have their place and can help make sense of things, but don't lose sight of the whole person.
- It is easy to overidentify with grad student clients; keep in mind every student is unique and be careful of assumptions due to similarities with your own history.
- Have the courage to support student clients even if it means creating some conflict with faculty, administration, or coaching staff; at times students need advocates in addition to therapists.

- Create a collection of resources that can be shared such as books, articles, videos, apps, and links to other support services and groups.
- Remember the suggestions on self-care and maintaining balance are important for you too.

CHAPTER FOUR

~

The Struggle Is Real!

Accessing Help from
Counseling and Disability Services

Inez Strama

Graduate school is tough. No ifs, ands, or buts about it. If you've read this far, skipped ahead to this chapter, and/or already have personal experience being a grad student, then you know that the struggle is real. If you're a grad student living with a disability—whether it's a learning, speech, mobility/physical disability, visual or hearing impairment, chronic illness, or mental health condition—then you also know that you're navigating that struggle with a unique set of needs and challenges. Often, these challenges are not only about your disability, but also about the stereotypes, microaggressions, and systemic barriers you may face as a result.

About 8 percent of master's students and 7 percent of doctoral students report having a disability.[1] Many students, especially those with hidden disabilities (e.g., learning and/or psychological) are often reluctant to disclose their status.[2] If you don't have a disability, this chapter is still applicable to you. That's because I can guarantee you that at some point in your tenure as a grad student, you or someone you know will seek out help from a mental health professional. How do I know that? Because . . . drumroll please . . . THE. STRUGGLE. IS. REAL. Rinse and repeat. The struggle is real. Rinse and repeat. Just how real? Well, let's revisit some of the statistics laid out in chapter 1.

Perhaps the most sobering stat is that graduate students are more than six times as likely as the general population to experience depression and anxiety.[3] The majority of doctoral students report "more than average" or "tremendous" stress, with the most significant contributors to this stress being academic issues.[4] Lest you master's students think that this doesn't apply to you, rest assured that you report similar difficulties. These include decreased exercise, worse sleep, worse diet, and overall worse mental health since beginning graduate school.[5] Among graduate students who report suffering from depression or anxiety, more than 50 percent also report an unhealthy work-life balance.[6] Here's the good news: The things that predict graduate student well-being are the very things that counseling can help you develop: better work-life balance, improved outlook on career prospects, supportive relationships, and academic engagement and progress.[7]

I have four goals for this chapter. The first is to tell you what you can expect from counseling and disability services. My second goal is to discuss the unique challenges and complexities of disclosing a disability as a grad student. My third goal is to identify some common barriers and obstacles that get in the way of asking for help, bust some myths that contribute to the stigma, and, hopefully, demystify the whole process so that you're more likely to seek out help if you find yourself needing it. Lastly, my fourth goal is to briefly highlight some other student support services that may help you. Taken together, my hope is that by the end of this chapter, you will feel more knowledgeable about and empowered to utilize the services available to you during your tenure as a grad student.

Counseling Services

When visiting a counseling center, what you can generally expect is to be greeted by an administrative assistant or receptionist who will likely ask for your school ID and have you complete some paperwork. This usually consists of an informed consent, a summary of your rights, and the protections and limits of confidentiality. Ensuring confidentiality is not only in adherence with the law but also a part of our ethical code and a mandate of clinical training. What you tell a counselor is generally kept between the two of you, and, by law, your counselor is not allowed to share this with anyone, including professors or other university staff, unless you explicitly request otherwise. The exceptions to this will be explained to you, but they generally have to do with times when there might be a concern about your or someone else's immediate safety. Even in those rare exceptions, only the absolute minimal amount of information necessary is shared.

In addition to this kind of informed consent, you may also be asked to provide some information about yourself, including your demographics and mental health history. You will then meet with a counselor who will ask you some questions to determine how best they can help you, which may mean receiving services at the center or obtaining a referral. The primary goal in the initial meeting(s) is for you to share information about your main concerns and the broader context of your life in order to determine what clinical services would be the best fit for you.

Statistically, international, Asian American, and African American graduate students are all less likely to use counseling services than their domestic and White peers.[8] If you identify as a member of a marginalized group, ask about what services are offered that are culturally affirmative, such as workshops on culture shock, LGBTQIA+ focused support groups, and the availability of counselors of color, either in-house or through referrals. If you are given a referral, you may have some other questions, including cost. See chapter 1 for questions to ask about your insurance. If you don't have insurance, let the counselor know so that they can help you find affordable referrals. Some low-cost mental health centers and providers adjust their fee based on what you are able to pay, also known as a "sliding-scale fee."

Some other questions you could ask a potential new therapist are:[9] "What would a usual session be like?" and "How would you help me address my issues?" If you have some therapy background, you could ask what theoretical orientations inform the therapist's work. Many students wonder if any questions are inappropriate to ask a therapist. You can ask whatever you want, and you will learn a lot from how the therapist chooses to answer. If you ask a personal question that the therapist does not feel comfortable answering, how do they handle the situation? If they maintain an open and connected stance even while maintaining professional boundaries, this is a good sign. Most important is how you feel speaking with them. Do you feel respected? Do you feel that you could open up with them? Do you feel that you could learn something from this person?

Once you're actually working with a therapist, your initial sessions will likely focus on identifying goals. Ideally, this is a collaborative process in which you are an active participant. Your therapist will provide support, listen in a nonjudgmental way, help you clarify your thoughts, feelings, and values, and work with you to generate alternate ways of viewing yourself and your situation. Be as open and honest as possible. You may learn and practice new skills, make meaning of your history and/or identities, and bring unrecognized patterns into awareness, among other possibilities. The exact emphasis will depend on you (your preferences, your background, and your goals) as well as your therapist's perspective and focus.

You will rarely get direct advice about what you should or shouldn't do, since we tend to think you're best served discovering this for yourself. However, you can certainly ask for concrete feedback, guidance, and assistance with problem-solving. Ideally, your therapist will take your whole self into account when working with you: your strengths, resources, relationships, health, attitudes, multiple identities, cultural context, family history, and so on. It is absolutely normal to be nervous, self-conscious, and/or have a variety of other potentially unpleasant feelings at the outset. Please share them with your therapist and be honest if something you're doing together isn't working for you. There will often be emotional ups and downs along the way: Sometimes you might make rapid progress and other times you might feel really stuck. This is all normal.

Disability Services

According to the Americans with Disabilities Act (ADA) of 1990, the ADA Amendments Act of 2008, and Section 504 of the Rehabilitation Act of 1973, as a student with a disability, you're entitled to reasonable accommodations that protect you from discrimination and provide equitable access to your school's academic materials, activities, and programs. International students, this includes you too! While schools are not required to "fundamentally alter" their academic standards, how they interpret the law about what they consider reasonable will vary.[10]

Recently, there has been an increasing shift in higher education towards proactively putting students on equal ground and designing academic environments to be more universal from the outset—that is, by providing multiple and flexible learning options that are more inclusive of different students' needs.[11] In other words, disability is increasingly being viewed from a diversity rather than a medical lens, as an identity that intersects with all the other identities you carry rather than as a deficit and/or deviation from a socially constructed norm.

This means that if you have a disability, your access to equal opportunity for academic success is greater than it's ever been before. Within this cultural context, or perhaps because of it, more and more students with disabilities, but especially those with hidden emotional and psychological disabilities, are attending graduate school (even if they're still reluctant to disclose). Anecdotally, all of the colleagues I spoke with while writing this chapter who work in higher education disability services said the same thing: They're seeing more and more students with anxiety, depression, and ADHD.

Just as with counseling, there will be a similar variation in the level of support offered. Some schools will only have a disability services coordinator, 504/ADA compliance officer/coordinator, or other similarly named point person. Other schools will have this person as well as a fully staffed disability office equipped with a variety of services. Find out what the disability climate is at your school. Call disability services, peruse their website, and/or speak with current students and faculty. Ask them how students with disabilities are generally viewed and treated, how a student with your disability has been accommodated in the past, and whether they have the types of accommodations you need.

In addition, ask how closely they work with other departments on campus (e.g., counseling, health, and security/public safety). You'll also want to know how the intersection of your identities as a student and an employee is treated with regard to your disability. For example, if you will be teaching, will you still get your accommodations for those classes through disability services or will you need to go through Human Resources? Your school might be equipped to support you in the classroom but ill-equipped to support you in your different roles outside of it.

The answers to these kinds of questions will give you a sense of how inclusive an environment you're walking into. If you have a physical/mobility disability, for example, it's not enough for you to know whether all the buildings you'll need to be in are up to code (e.g., including any off-site fellowships, apprenticeships, practicum placements, etc.). You'll also want to know how accessible the spaces within those buildings actually are. Can the library easily accommodate a wheelchair? What about campus-wide events? Are they held in accessible rooms? If you have a hearing or visual impairment, then you'll want to know if institutional announcements are distributed using accessible technology. If you have a learning disability, are there any supports offered beyond accommodations, such as tutoring, academic coaching/mentoring, time-management workshops, a writing center, and so on?

While it is your right to have services, you still have to advocate for yourself by exploring how robust or minimal the services are at your specific school and by self-initiating them when you arrive. If your ability to advocate for yourself is impaired by virtue of your disability, for example, because of a mental health issue or communication disorder, then get help in finding out whether advocacy is part of the services offered. You don't have to advocate for yourself by yourself!

The required documentation in order to demonstrate that you have a qualifying disability needs to be current from a qualified professional who can speak to the nature of your disability and its functional limitations, and it must provide recommendations for accommodations. If you had an IEP and/or 403(b) plan in high school, for example, but didn't receive any services in college, these won't suffice as up-to-date documentation, but they may be a good starting point. Find out how flexible the disability office is in working with you while you obtain the necessary documentation.

When you arrive, what you can generally expect is a meeting with someone from the disability office (or the 504 coordinator) in order to establish what your needs are. If you have a qualifying disability and the requisite documentation to support this, you should bring it with you to that first meeting. If you don't, you can expect a conversation about how to go about getting it and what supports can be provided, if any, in the interim. The person you meet with will review your documentation and may ask you questions about your past accommodations, including their benefits and limitations. Taken together, they will determine what accommodations the school can provide.

You might not get every accommodation you ask for. If you request electronic distance learning, for example, but a fundamental standard of your program is in-person attendance, then the school can deny your request. This exemplifies the importance of researching your program ahead of time and familiarizing yourself with their expectations and requirements and the appeals process. While your school has the right to deny an accommodation request if they deem it unreasonable or find that it fundamentally alters their programming, you have the right to appeal this decision and are entitled to due process while a resolution is worked out, usually through the 504 coordinator.

Once the accommodations are decided and agreed upon, the disability office will draft a letter(s)/email(s) together with you, and you will decide which professors and/or administrators should receive it. If your accommodations differ from course to course, then multiple letters will be sent and only the accommodations relevant to that course will be shared with each professor. The letter(s) specifies what the accommodations are and verifies that there is documentation on file to support them. The specific disability or nature of the disability is not disclosed and only the very bare information necessary for the professor to know is shared. Similar to counseling, your right to confidentiality about your disability is protected by law. The professor(s) is not allowed to disclose this information to anyone else, and if they have questions or concerns, they are expected to speak with the person who sent them the accommodations letter, not to you directly.

As your academic trajectory unfolds, you will revisit what your needs are. New letters will be sent every semester, if you so choose. Some students only need accommodations for one semester (e.g., if their mobility is impaired temporarily after a surgery, accident, or illness), while others will need them every semester; the choice of whether to send letters and to whom is always up to you. The person you meet with in disability services can help you determine this in a collaborative and ongoing fashion.

The type of accommodations you can expect will vary greatly depending on your needs and your specific school, but some examples are: extended or divided time on tests and/or writing assignments, taking tests in distraction-reduced environments, preferential class-room seating, early registration and early availability of syllabi and texts, alternative and electronic formats of exams, audio-recorded lectures, note-takers/scribes, recording pens, ergonomic furniture and computer accessories, reduced course load, modified deadlines, excused absences, personal FM systems/hearing devices, text and screen en-largement and braille keyboards, housing accommodations, and assis-tive technology and software.

Negotiating Disability Disclosure

Know what accommodations exist and come prepared to be supported. At the same time, as of this writing, it is still your responsibility to provide the necessary documentation to enroll in the accommodations available to you. For those of you with visible disabilities, you often won't have a choice about whether to disclose your disability identity in grad school. For those of you with less visible disabilities, you are faced with the difficult decision of whether to disclose and "come out" as having a disability or, if possible, attempt to "pass" as someone with-out a disability. Either way, disability disclosure is fraught with benefits and risks. It is not experienced the same way by everyone and can be largely influenced by what other identities you carry.

Maria[12] is a biracial African American and Latina queer cisgender female. She wrestled with disclosing her depression and learning dis-ability in grad school because of racist and sexist stereotypes she was used to receiving about being both "lazy" and "dramatic." She was understandably wary of her disabilities being viewed from these lenses. As a student of critical theory, she was also cautious about how her experience as a woman of color would be perceived by her professors, most of whom were White males. With a collaborative partnership between myself as her counselor and the disabilities coordinator at her school, we all worked together to identify the courses and professors she felt safe to disclose to and explored the costs and benefits of disclosing versus hiding her disability from others.

In grad school, the decision about whether to disclose your disabil-ity can feel particularly hard because the relationships that you have to build with faculty become much more critical to your overall success than they were in college. Plus, they often involve multiple roles. When I was in grad school, the same faculty member served as 1) my professor when she taught me in multiple courses, 2) my boss when I worked as her teaching assistant, 3) my patron when I worked at the school library, 4) my mentor when she'd have me over for dinner with other members of my cohort, 5) my colleague when we presented at a conference together, 6) my reference when I applied to internships and jobs, and 7) ultimately my dissertation chair. Talk about confusing role transitions! There are politics in each department and no written rules about how to navigate them. If the nature of your disability is such that you have difficulties picking up on social cues or if you have social anxiety, for example, this can be highly distressing. You may worry about whether disclosing will help you navigate this maze or make it worse.

In addition, feedback about your work in grad school tends to be much more direct, personalized, fluid, and ongoing than it was as an undergraduate. If you're getting an MFA, for example, you will be asked repeatedly to defend your artistic choices and sensibilities and critiqued accordingly, making it very easy for the professional feedback to feel personal. If you have a disability, you may already feel scrutinized. Being in grad school feeds right into that and can amplify the sense of being under a microscope. If you're a student in the health professions, disclosing your disability means exposing yourself to the risk of being viewed and treated as a patient rather than a colleague. You may also receive pressure from well-intentioned others in your life, including those in your department, program, or school, to disclose your disability even if you don't want to.

The choice, if you carry an invisible disability, is up to you. That said, it bears repeating that while the struggle is very real, so are your rights. If you're hesitant about disclosing, at least have a conversation about it with someone you trust, such as a wise, discreet friend or a counselor. Identifying whether your concerns are motivated by past experience, something you're picking up on in the environment, and/or other factors will ultimately help you clarify your reluctance, make meaning of it, and determine what, if anything, you want to do about it.

Myths, Misconceptions, Stereotypes, and Stigmas

Now that you have a general sense of counseling and disability services, let's talk more in depth about the things that get in the way of asking for help, beyond a lack of knowledge. Only 30 percent of graduate students report ever having utilized some form of mental health services while in graduate school.[13] This is significantly lower than 50 percent of students reporting having mental health issues (e.g., anxiety and depression).[14] Clearly, there are barriers to asking for help.

General Barriers

Grad students who share a campus with undergrads, for example, can feel as though counseling and disability services are only intended for the undergrads. Not living on campus and working contributes to this sense of disconnection. They either don't realize that they're equally entitled to them or find it awkward to receive services in the same place as the students they are teaching. At the same time, students are often nervous about these services. This can be true regardless of whether you've received help in the past or not. If you have a preexisting condition or disability, it can be tempting to see grad school as a new beginning. Alternatively, if you previously didn't have access to support, had a negative experience, or didn't feel comfortable or safe seeking it out, you may expect that grad school will be more of the same and not even consider that different options might exist for you.

If you're struggling for the first time, asking for help may not only feel like a foreign concept, but it may feel threatening to the self-concept you do have, the one that defines you as the competent, capable, and resourceful grad student that you are. Integrating help-seeking into that definition, without it being tinged with shame or embarrassment, can be tricky. Although not meant to be an exhaustive list, below are some of the most common myths, misconceptions, stereotypes, and stigmas that prevent grad students from accessing help.

"I Shouldn't Need Special Treatment" or "It Means I'm Weak"

Deciding to pursue graduate education, let alone actually applying and getting in, takes a fair amount of hard work, grit, determination, and a history of achievement. Once you arrive and the imposter syndrome sets in (see chapter 2 on this topic), you naturally start to fear being found out as a fraud. Within this context, it makes sense that you would be reluctant to do anything that might signal that you don't have it all figured out. In reality, of course you don't because a) you're human and b) you're specifically in grad school to learn, discover, and figure things out. On top of that, you're contending with insidious messages from society, and maybe even your family and/or culture, that tell you that you're not enough as you are, and that asking for and receiving help is weakness. If you have a disability, you're also contending with the historical reality that disabilities have been—and in some sectors, continue to be—treated as a deficiency or a limitation.

I get it. I totally appreciate how and why an "I can do it on my own" attitude has value and may have even galvanized you to this point. Unfortunately, doing it on your own is not an option in grad school, which is much more of a "contact" sport than college, fundamentally based on dialogue and mutual engagement. You can certainly survive it in a self-contained fashion, but your ability to thrive in it will be limited if you're not also willing to be vulnerable and seek out help when you need it. So, do your best to recognize these toxic messages for what they are and how they may no longer be serving you. In fact, they may even be holding you back.

For Adreanne, a second-year master's student, these messages manifest in the belief that if she only tried a little harder and pushed herself a little further, she could get a hold of the anxiety that she was experiencing as she was preparing to graduate. She was having difficulties sleeping, her mind was constantly racing, and she sometimes found it hard to breathe. She grew up in a rural, White, working-class family, and she was the first in her family to go to college, let alone grad school. Although she had suffered from anxiety for a long time, she was only beginning to appreciate its full impact on her life. She had also never been in any kind of mental health treatment before. She came to see me in the hopes of better understanding what was going on, but she was admittedly reluctant. She thought that it meant that there was something wrong with her and that she simply wasn't strong enough to manage it on her own. While her parents both worked multiple jobs growing up, she helped raise her two siblings and was working herself by the age of twelve, contributing to the household income. She was a star student, paid her way through school, had close, loving, and supportive friendships, and had two job offers on the table after graduation. Her primary concern was choosing the right one.

There was no doubt that this was a strong woman, but for Adreanne, the message she internalized from both her family and rural community was that counseling is only for people who are too weak to handle their own problems. In this context, her coming to counseling was an extraordinary act of courage and a testament to her resourcefulness. We discovered that not only was it very important for her not to be seen as weak, but also that she believed things had to be a struggle in order for them to be worthwhile or valid; they couldn't just be easy. When Adreanne realized this, she reevaluated this belief and began to see the enormous amount of pressure she was putting on herself to make the "right" decision about a job.

As a result, we were able to critically examine and ultimately clarify her values. She realized that she had deep gratitude towards her parents and her community at large for the work ethic that they instilled in her, but that she was also tired, burned out, and needed a break. She had practically been working full-time her whole life. While she was disappointed about letting go of the job opportunity that was seemingly more prestigious, she understood, in a new way, that this did not mean that she was weak. Instead, she viewed it as an act of kindness towards herself, something she realized was a skill to develop further. She also felt freer to choose what beliefs she wanted to hold onto because they served her well, while discarding the ones that didn't. She was still anxious, but the anxiety had started to loosen its grip and she felt more in control.

Fen, on the other hand, was a young cisgender man from China at the beginning of his doctoral program. He had already received his master's degree and had a history of depression. He had been in treatment before and found it helpful, was taking psychiatric medication, and initially came just to continue with counseling. He had never had academic accommodations, which he viewed as an unfair advantage and something that was virtually unheard of in his culture. He already felt "defective" and believed strongly that this was an issue he needed to resolve on his own, certainly not something that he should be getting "special treatment" for.

At the same time, he was sometimes missing his classes in order to make his appointments with his psychiatrist, and he was struggling to concentrate during his exams. The transition to his doctoral program was more difficult than he had anticipated. Over time, he was able to recognize the ways in which he was overemphasizing his own role in his difficulties and underemphasizing the role of the external stressors he was contending with. He also started to appreciate how his ability to contend with those stressors was indeed different from that of his peers who didn't struggle with depression. However, he realized that this didn't mean he was inherently inferior to or less competent than they were. In fact, his depression had taught him a lot about how to be a critical thinker, how to confront difficult and painful feelings, and how to ask for help.

I showed Fen the popular equity versus equality picture of three people attempting to watch a baseball game (Google it!): Under "equality," three people of different heights are all standing on the same size crate, giving them three different views of the game; under "equity," the same three people now have the same view of the game because they re-organized the crates such that the tallest person has no crate, the middle person has one, and the shortest person has two.

This struck a chord and he realized that not only did he need another crate, but that he was entitled to an unobstructed view of the game, which in his case was grad school. He started to see that accommodations would not be an advantage, but rather a way of evening the playing field, giving him the leg up that he needed. He agreed to have at least one conversation with the disabilities coordinator and was surprised to learn that he was eligible for flexibility around his missed attendance for his psychiatry appointments and a distraction-reduced environment to take his exams. He also felt comforted by the idea that these weren't permanent, something that he experienced firsthand when I saw him several semesters later and he wasn't using any accommodations because his depression was in remission.

"I Don't Want to Be a Burden"
Another common myth that gets in the way of asking for help is the idea that you're being a burden by receiving services. In counseling, this tends to play out as a belief that your problems are too small or not

severe enough to warrant attention. In disability services, this tends to play out as the belief that you don't need accommodations, that you can get by without them, and/or that they're "unnecessary." In both, this can also play out as a worry about diverting resources from other students who "really" need them. The reality is that both offices see all kinds of students with all kinds of difficulties. Just because you see them as small, doesn't mean that we do, and we certainly won't dismiss you or your concerns. In addition, whether you utilize the services or not, you're paying for them with your tuition, so you might as well get your money's worth. And, the longer you wait and the more difficult things get for you, the fewer resources and options may be available to you. Trust me, you are not being a burden.

"I'm Not That Kind of Person" or "That's Not for Me"

These are the closely related cousins of "I don't want to be a burden" and often have to do with the misconception that counseling and disability services are only for "certain" people. Just by virtue of you being a grad student, you are that person. While it is absolutely true that counseling is for students with chronic mental illness, other valid reasons for seeking services are adjustment, academic, identity, and/ or relational concerns. For example, more than one-third of graduate students said they would seek help for an academic problem, one-fourth for career-related problems, and more than half for emotional problems.[15]

Some career-related concerns might be changes in funding to your anticipated fellowship or the pressure to publish more articles and attend more conferences. Some academic problems might be struggling to finish your thesis or dissertation, insecurity, or not feeling supported by your adviser. Not being the best and the smartest for the first time can also be quite the culture shock and a blow to your self-esteem. Mental health issues are not necessarily forever. If you're struggling today, that doesn't mean you will be for the rest of your life. Many students struggle at the beginning of grad school but then do just fine after their first year. Others do fine the whole time but struggle when it comes time to write their thesis or dissertation. Embrace that you can be "that" person and get the help before things get too unmanageable. Similarly, be curious about the myth that grad school is a fresh start.

Those of you who subscribe to this myth may stop taking your medication and feel as though the fact that you got into grad school means that you're a whole new you. Sure, you're a grad student now. However, truly consider whether this means that getting the help that you're used to is no longer relevant to you.

Another stigma many students express about not being "that" person has to do with cultural and/or family norms. This includes sharing personal information with an outsider or being frowned upon or considered not "right." Most students who feel this way come to trust that what they share really does remain confidential and usually find great relief in hearing some of their thoughts and feelings put to words out loud for the first time. They start to see how sharing in therapy is different from gossiping, exposing, blaming, or snitching and usually come to value the process.

If you have a disability, while you may not have received accommodations in the past, the increased demands and expectations but decreased structure and guidance of grad school may necessitate them for the first time. You may have learned to "pass" but are finding that difficult to sustain. Or, maybe you're really struggling for the first time under the weight of the increased reading and writing demands and you have an underlying learning disability that's never been diagnosed because you've learned to compensate for and work around it. At least keep disability services in your mind as a potential support. There are also many excellent and not at all burdensome reasons to seek out disability services that don't have to do with chronic illness and/or lifelong disabilities. These include transient, temporary, or well-managed health issues, such as recovery from surgery, an accident, IBS, endometriosis, Chron's or any similar disease that has unpredictable "flare-ups" or episodes, and many, many others.

"I Tried This Before and I Didn't Get Anything Out of It"

Lastly, many students have either had such negative or neutral experiences with help-seeking in the past that they are understandably skeptical about the efficacy of counseling or accommodations. There are things you can do to get the most out of therapy, such as being as authentically yourself as possible, recognizing and respecting your own pace, being aware of censored thoughts and feelings, focusing on what is most important to you, taking risks, giving the therapeutic relation-ship time to develop, and putting in the work outside of your sessions. However, none of these matter if your therapist is not a good match for you. You might need to meet with a few therapists before you find the right one. Goodness of fit is paramount to building a solid therapeutic foundation. I implore you to consider giving it another try with this in mind. The same goes for disability services. You may have had nega-tive experiences receiving accommodations in the past, but remember that accommodations in grad school have the potential to be different, especially if the disability climate at your school is more inclusive than what you experienced in college.

Now that you have the lay of the land of counseling and disability services, I'd like to briefly mention three other auxiliary services that can support your mental health and well-being in grad school: 1) health services, 2) Title IX services, and 3) equity and inclusion services.

Health, Title IX, and Equity and Inclusion Services

Health services is about taking care of your physical health. This in-cludes everything from urgent care and first aid to health maintenance and routine gynecologic care and contraception. For some of you, these services will be offered at an office, medical center, or depart-ment within your school. If your school does not provide these kinds of services internally, it can direct you to local resources that do. If this is the case, Student Affairs, Student Life, or the equivalent of this office on your campus is a good place to start. I encourage you to locate health services sooner rather than later upon your arrival in grad school. At the very least, you'll know where to go and who to contact when you get sick. If there's any experience that compromises your immunity, it's grad school: 44 percent of graduate students report being sick or ill during the semester.[16]

Prioritizing your health will be of paramount importance to your overall success. Among the predictors of graduate student well-being I mentioned earlier, self-reported physical health was number two on the list, followed only by career prospects.[17] Your mind and your body are in constant communication with each other, and the mental exhaustion of having endless deadlines, changing your routines every semester, going from one obligation to the next, barely having time to cook, and losing sleep during exams can seriously run you down physically. At the same time, not feeling well physically can negatively impact your mood, decrease your concentration, and impair your memory, making the completion of your tasks as a grad student virtually impossible.

Another important service to familiarize yourself with is your school's Title IX (pronounced "nine," like the number) office. Title IX is a federal civil rights law that was passed as part of the Education Amendments of 1972. It prohibits discrimination on the basis of sex in any educational institution that receives federal funding, which includes the vast majority of US schools. What this means is that you are legally entitled to learn and work in an environment free from fear of sexual harassment and sexual violence. Specifically, your school is legally required to respond to and remedy any reports of a hostile educational environment based on sexual misconduct. If it doesn't, it risks losing its federal funding. It also means that if you are accused of sexual misconduct as a student, you are entitled to due process and a fair investigation.

Hopefully, you will never have a reason to seek out your school's Title IX office. However, as was crystallized through the #MeToo movement, sexual misconduct is common. Additionally, as a psychologist who's been involved in more than a few Title IX cases over the years, I can tell you that when students have experienced some kind of sexual violation, it has often made a huge difference in their process to know that there was a designated person (usually called the Title IX coordinator) they could report the incident(s) to if they so choose. That last part, *if they so choose*, is important to underscore.

As part of Title IX (and its related federal statute known as the Clery Act), almost all faculty, staff, and administrators are considered mandated reporters. This means that if you disclose an incident of sexual misconduct to them, they are required to share this with the aforementioned Title IX coordinator. Once a formal report has been made, the Title IX coordinator is similarly required to act. What this action looks like will depend on the individual report and the circumstances surrounding it. The point is that it's no longer entirely within your control. The only staff members who are exempt from reporting are counselors, health service providers, and clergy.

If you report to a counselor, they will hopefully inform you of the resources available to you, including your Title IX reporting options, but they will not disclose that information to anyone else. Some students are very clear that they want to file a Title IX report and have benefitted tremendously from doing so. One student, for example, received assistance from the Title IX coordinator in switching their lab section so that they wouldn't have to be in the same class as their accused rapist during the investigation. Another student received a "no-contact" order, prohibiting their accused perpetrator, who wasn't a student, from being on campus grounds. It is equally important to note that some students have chosen to file a Title IX report and regretted it because it wound up doing more harm than good, often because of how re-traumatizing they found it to tell their story to so many people when they hadn't fully processed it themselves. Furthermore, there are students who feel comforted by the idea that the Title IX office exists, but choose not to make a report. This is such an individualized choice and there is no right or wrong answer.

At many schools, the Title IX office is housed within the Office of Institutional Diversity and Equity, the Compliance and Diversity Office, or some other similarly named office. Whatever the name, it's important for you to know that equity and inclusion services exist and that they offer so much more than just the Title IX services described above. As the name implies, equity and inclusion services are intended to support schools in fostering diverse, equitable, and inclusive academic environments that comply with civil and human rights laws and respond to reports of discrimination. Some schools will also have an ombudsperson on campus, who is an official appointed to serve as a neutral and impartial party that clarifies policies and procedures and assists you in resolving any complaints you may have (beyond just those related to incidents of discrimination). The point is that graduate school is fraught with power dynamics. Sometimes, in order to effectively navigate those dynamics, you need a designated safe space or person with whom to talk them through.

In sum, remember that the graduate school struggle is real and that there are tons of resources at your disposal to navigate it, in whatever configuration feels best for you. I hope that if you don't feel inspired, you're at least walking away rethinking some things. Thank you for your time in reading this chapter, and I wish you well on your journey.

Takeaways for Students

- Do a self-assessment: Consider all of your various identities and determine what your needs are in order for you to thrive in graduate school.
- Do an institutional assessment: Identify the resources available to help you, including familiarizing yourself with counseling and disability services, as well as health, Title IX, and equity and inclusion services.
- Know your rights: Be aware of how graduate school is different from college and that the services you're legally entitled to may be different from those that you're used to.
- Be gentle with yourself: Make self-care and balancing your work with the rest of your life a priority, including sleep, diet, exercise, and relationships.
- Ask for help: Identify safe individuals you can talk to sooner rather than later and consider joining a support group. The struggle is real and you don't have to go it alone!

Suggestions for Administrators, Faculty, and Advisors on Counseling Services

- Examine your own beliefs, values, and biases about the stigma and effectiveness of counseling.
- Allow students to describe their difficulties to you if they want and listen carefully. Avoid labels, judgments, generalizations, and/ or dismissive or critical statements. Normalize their concerns and remind them that counseling services are (usually) free, confidential, and nonjudgmental. For example:

> "I know it can be hard to ask for help. I'm really glad you're sharing this with me. Have you thought about looking at the counseling website? I know lots of students who've met with someone there and have really appreciated it."

- Remember that you can help identify students who are in distress and suggest counseling as a resource, but you don't have to be that resource yourself. Some signs that you may have overextended yourself include feeling stressed out or overwhelmed by a student's needs, feeling angry with a student, feeling afraid, having thoughts of rescuing a student, or reliving similar experiences of your own. If you're experiencing any of these, please speak with a trusted colleague and/or make an appointment with a therapist for yourself (through your Employee Assistance Program or personal insurance off campus).
- Familiarize yourself with your school's policies about how to respond if a student expresses concerns about their mental health to you, especially if you're worried about their immediate safety. Consider consulting with a mental health professional at counseling services directly.

Suggestions for Administrators, Faculty, and Advisors on Disability Services

- Receive and provide training and effective campus-wide communication on disability issues across all institutional stakeholders.
- Engage in a self-study to determine how inclusive your institution is towards students with disabilities and consider having the Office of Equity and Inclusion or its equivalent as the lead on such a study.
- Include students with disabilities in disability and diversity initiatives.
- Respect students' decisions around self-disclosure.
- Develop standards to support the process of self-disclosure and create clear mechanisms for receiving accommodations and appealing denials. Consider including less visible or hidden disabilities as examples in your materials.
- Don't "out" your students with disabilities, even if it's in an attempt to be inclusive (e.g., by providing extra support or encouragement to a student with a disability; they don't need anything extra, just equitable and fair access). Regardless of your inten-

tions, it's against the law and has the potential to seriously dam-
age your relationship with those students.

- You're not entitled to know what the disability is when a student in your class has accommodations. If you're not sure how
to handle a disability- or accommodations-related issue with a
student, consult with the 504 coordinator, disabilities office, or
its equivalent on your campus.

- Ensure that not only does every syllabus have an accessibility or
diversity inclusion statement, but also any paperwork students
complete when they register to teach a course, work in a lab, do
an off-campus fellowship, and so on. Signal to all students (not
just those with disabilities) that you value inclusive learning environments and that you're committed to maximizing access in all
of your students' academic and professional settings.

- Make all communications and material accessible, including
campus-wide events, announcements, apprenticeships, and fellowships.

Suggestions for Mental Health Professionals
Working with Graduate Students with Disabilities

- Be mindful of your own biases, attitudes towards, and level of
exposure to people with disabilities.

- Take stock of how accessible your office and clinical paperwork is.
Could someone with a visual impairment complete your informed
consent? Would someone with a mobility issue be able to comfortably maneuver around your waiting room?

- Work collaboratively with students to construct or deepen their
narrative and meaning-making of their disability identity. If they
have a less visible or hidden disability, for example, explore in
what contexts they feel as though they have to "pass" and when
they feel safe enough to "come out." How does this identity intersect with their other identities?

- Language is especially important when working with students
with disabilities as they contend with labels on a regular basis. Listen for how they talk about their disability, what messages they've

internalized about how others have spoken about it, and ask them how they would like you to refer to it. Do they call it a disability, an impairment, a condition, a disorder, a part of themselves, an identity? Do they see themselves as a victim, a spokesperson, an advocate?

- Familiarize yourself with the barriers that exist for students with disabilities.
- Familiarize yourself with strengths-based therapeutic approaches, the incorporation of advocacy into your clinical work, and the relevance of resilience as a skill in working with students with disabilities.
- Determine whether it might be helpful for you to collaborate with the disability services at your client's school. If you're providing documentation on their behalf, be clear about what the guidelines or expectations are so that you don't inadvertently delay accommodations. Be judicious about what accommodations you recommend and review them with your client. Make sure that they're appropriate to your client's individual needs.
- If your client has had their disability for a long time, be sensitive to how this facet of their identity is managing the adjustment to grad school given the new and often unexpected challenges they are facing, especially around role conflicts.
- If your client is reluctant to seek out accommodations, explore their apprehension. Are their concerns realistic? Validate their feelings while providing them with information and psychoeducation about their rights and the process. Help them to identify additional or alternate allies and supports at their institution, as clinically indicated. See if a support group for students with disabilities is an option.
- If your client temporarily injures themselves, gets sick, or is otherwise struggling with their health in grad school, remind them of disability services. They may not make the connection that this new life circumstance qualifies them for help.

PART II

I AM NOT ALONE!

~

CHAPTER FIVE

The Power of Being Different

Navigating Grad School as International Students

Vivi Wei-Chun Hua

My Story

During my first few years in the United States, I lived every day feeling self-conscious. I was acutely aware of how I was different from my peers in school and others around me. I looked different. I dressed differently. I had to pause and catch my breath when speaking English. And I believe I may have often appeared confused and behaved awkwardly. In these and many other ways, I felt I was existing in isolation. Time in the classroom was difficult. I was shocked at how important it was to participate in class in the United States. I was amazed by how easily my American peers raised their hands and how eloquently they expressed their opinions—something that took me a while to get used to and a lot of conscious effort to try to emulate. Class discussions about multiculturalism were something that should have been relevant to me. Yet, I felt irrelevant in the midst of these discussions and wondered how I should identify myself. Asian? Asian American? Immigrant? To me, "international student" was perhaps the term that captured my identity the best. Yet, it was such a new concept for me to have to identify myself with a label and carry this label with me wherever I went.

Time outside of class was perhaps even more uncomfortable. From afar, I watched my peers hanging out in the student lounge, unable to bring myself closer to them. I heard them chatting but didn't understand what they were saying. I didn't know any of the TV shows they were talking about. I didn't understand why they were laughing. I went to the library or went back to my apartment nearby. Ah! I could finally breathe again. Much of my time I spent alone studying and doing schoolwork. Though I often got good grades on exams and reports, to my peers I was perhaps always struggling, always trying to catch up with them. Fortunately, I had a few peers who were interested in getting to know me and talked to me beyond "How ya doin'?" My relationships with them eased the discomfort and anxiety I felt in school and made me feel I, too, could hang out in the student lounge.

My personal life was also challenging. It was my first time away from home and living on my own. I no longer came home to dinner ready on the table. Dirty laundry was not cleaned automatically. Life was no longer just about studying but about juggling to keep my everyday going. When the holiday season came, I looked out of my apartment window and saw my neighbors gathering and celebrating with their family and friends. I wished I could also take a bus or a short flight back home. Phone calls with my family every day became the only way to feel their presence in my immediate life. Stopping by the Chinese take-out restaurant on my way home became my almost daily routine to feel the warmth of a family, home, for a few minutes.

Being an international student meant my stay in the United States relied on my student visa status. Toward the end of my graduate studies, my visa situation became something that could potentially take away all I'd built in the United States. Within a year after graduation, I had to find a job that would sponsor a work visa, which would require me to commit three years of my career. If I couldn't do this, I would have to drop everything and go home! In a field where foreign workers are rare, the job search to me was not just about my qualifications. Equally important was potential employers' policy on hiring foreign workers and whether or not they had the funding to provide visa sponsorships.

People have asked me what it was like to study in the United States. Feeling "unrooted" perhaps best described my experience. Academically, the schools I went to in Taiwan were usually not known to my peers and professionals in the United States. There was not enough reference data for them to judge my competence until I had the opportunity to demonstrate my capabilities in front of them. This made me feel as if all my past efforts and accomplishments in Taiwan had become irrelevant—I had to go back to square one, prove myself all over again, and build my network and relationships from scratch. Culturally, I was constantly observing how people in the United States behaved in various situations, setting aside a big part of myself as I figured out how to fit in. Regardless, it was a humbling experience for me. I began to realize how privileged I was when I was in Taiwan—the privilege of being a member of the majority group and the privilege of benefiting from the resources that my family had worked hard to build over generations. I came to understand why there were groups of people who often claimed that they were treated unfairly. I came to appreciate the hardships of being a minority in a society and the feeling of being invisible and being subject to systemic discrimination and microaggressions.[1]

My cultural and immigrant background became a focus as I made decisions about practicum experiences and job applications. I remember wondering, "Do I look too different?" "Am I good enough?" "Am I an outsider in American society?" "Is my international student status going to jeopardize my chance of getting into a competitive or prestigious training site?" "Is my best chance with sites where my cultural and linguistic background would be considered an asset rather than baggage?" Feeling disabled as a non-English-native speaker and not-so-fully-integrated member of US society, my pride was injured. My confidence hit rock bottom. "How am I going to get any interviews for internship if I continue to feel defeated?" "How am I going to, not just graduate but do well, if I continue to doubt myself?"

I had to make an intentional, drastic mental shift during the summer as I was competing for a US-wide internship. I had to force myself to "just believe in" the outcome I wanted to achieve, despite all of my doubts, fears, and what-ifs. I had to redirect my attention numerous times every day to align my actions towards that belief. Through many years of similar struggles and support from many people, I've accomplished many things that I once thought impossible, including obtaining my permanent resident status using my qualifications rather than through a sponsor. I came to realize that there is a unique place for me as a person in US society and that I have a lot to contribute through my career as a psychologist. There may be many systemic barriers that

I'll never be able to overcome or break, but this can't define my value or deny what I've learned throughout the years as an international student. While my uniqueness may not necessarily be recognized by everyone, there will be some who will be able to see its value.

As an international grad student, I yearned for someone who understood—someone who could openly share with me what it was like for them to go through this process, how they overcame all the struggles. I longed for someone to validate that what I felt was "normal" and made sense. If you can relate to any of my experiences, I want you to know: You are not alone. I know how hard it is to leave your family and friends and study in a foreign country. Depending on your home country, the language, culture, and values in the United States can be very different from what you are familiar with. You may feel that you don't fit in with things or people around you. You may feel like escaping from situations that feel so unnatural and uncomfortable to you. You may start to doubt your competence and wonder whether or not you are smart enough to be pursuing your graduate studies in the United States.

One strategy I used was to seek out peers who came here when they were younger or who had substantial cross-cultural experience. I remember asking them: "How long did it take you to become fluent in English?" "How did you learn to speak up in class?" "How long did it take you to feel comfortable in a new country?" "How did you make friends with the locals?" The more I learned about their experiences, the more assured I felt that I, too, could and would survive in the United States.

My aim through this chapter is to answer many of your questions. I hope this chapter will be a good companion to you as you navigate the landscape of life in the United States as an international grad student. I encourage you to stay hopeful and not be deterred by the challenges on your journey. There are a few things to keep in mind when reading this chapter: 1) Please note that statements about different cultures are made in a general sense and that individual differences and variances exist within each culture. 2) Advice provided in this chapter aims to help you develop new skills based on the skills and strengths you already have. My hope is to help guide your first steps toward success in your life in the United States. There are different perspectives and approaches to managing life circumstances. Some of my suggestions may reflect my worldview and values. Please take what resonates with you and consider the possibility of being "curious" and "experimenting" with suggestions that you are not yet certain will help. 3) I encourage you to take a "developmental approach." This means that you do not see yourself as having "deficits," but rather you just haven't yet developed certain skills. Know that your skill sets will grow with time, repeated practice, and modifications. 4) Pseudonyms are used in this chapter when discussing specific international students in order to protect their confidentiality.

This chapter will focus on:

1. Culture shock about US academic practices and how to overcome it.
2. Key skills to develop for your success in the United States.
3. Some mundane but important things to know about living in the United States.
4. Thinking and planning ahead for your visa situation postgraduation.
5. Recharging your battery and exploring things outside of school.
6. Redefining yourself and developing into the person you desire.

Tips for international grad students are provided at the end of the chapter as a quick reference. Recommendations for educational institutions, graduate programs, faculty members, and mental health professionals are also included as possible ways to provide a supportive environment for international grad students.

Culture Shock[2]: Academic Practices in the United States

The level of difference between the US culture and the culture of the country where you came from plays an important role in determining the amount of adjustment you will have to make. In the United States, there tends to be much focus and value placed upon presentation skills and verbal reasoning skills, whereas in many other cultures students are supposed to work hard, be disciplined, and focus on getting good grades. Beyond test results, in the United States, participation in class and being proactive about one's learning needs are two important ways for professors to understand and assess a student's learning status.

Speak Up, Please!

Generally speaking, international students from certain Asian countries may find it difficult to speak up in class, engage in back-and-forth discussions, or express opinions that are different from professors. This is usually less of an adjustment for students from some Western countries as their academic practices tend to be more similar to those in the United States. If this is an area of challenge for you, how do you overcome the barriers of different classroom expectations? Below are some specific recommendations for you to experiment with.

Prepare at Least One Question to Ask in Each Class

This gives you a chance to preview and/or review class materials, organize your thoughts, identify questions you have, and practice asking questions before the class. The goal of this step is to practice speaking in class and interacting with your professors and peers. For many students, the more practice the easier it gets.

When You Can, Be More Spontaneous

Asking questions in each class will eventually help speaking spontaneously in class feel less daunting. Following the pace of the classroom discussions will also be easier for you with time. When you are ready, you can try to be more spontaneous by being more engaged in the real-time discussions and asking questions that may occur to you. You can also start to express your own thoughts and opinions. Again, this is about gradually expanding your comfort zone by building new skills on top of the ones you've already acquired. Know that there are likely to be setbacks or times when you feel frustrated or embarrassed. Don't let that hold you back from bravely taking more risks. You should know that many American-born students also struggle with sharing and expressing their opinions. Take a small break from this process if you need to recharge your battery. Talk to your friends or family if it helps to discuss the challenges you experience here. Then, try again when you gather enough energy and courage!

Be Proactive!
Another academic practice in the United States that can feel unnatural to some international students is the expectation for students to be responsible for their learning process. While this expectation sounds fair and makes sense to everyone, it may be a new concept for some international students. One way to be proactive about your learning process is to approach your professors when you encounter difficulties with class materials or assignments. For international students from certain cultures, this can be an uncomfortable action that needs to be consciously encouraged and repeatedly reinforced. In some societies, professors are highly regarded and carry an authoritative image, whereby there is more of a distance between professors and students. Most international students I've worked with share the belief that they should try their best to resolve their academic problems on their own and that they should not trouble or bother their professors unless they really have to. In my experience and observation, the academic culture in the United States tends to encourage the opposite. Professors in the United States often enjoy getting to know their students. They encourage students to take initiative when it comes to learning and welcome students to use their office hours. For many international grad students, this is a huge adjustment that takes courage and some practice to feel more comfortable with over time.

Jasmine is a doctoral student who came to see me because she had been struggling to complete her dissertation. Upon exploration, she appeared to feel disillusioned about her advisor because he had not been as helpful to her graduate studies and dissertation progress as she would have liked. As someone who was taught to listen to her teachers and authority figures growing up, Jasmine felt nervous about the idea of approaching her advisor to discuss her concerns. My clinical impression was that she and her advisor may have very different communication styles as she often felt misunderstood or dismissed by him. After a close-up look at their typical interaction in meetings, Jasmine modified the way she approached her advisor. She learned that when she was able to clearly express her needs, her advisor was actually quite responsive and provided the support she was looking for.

You Don't Need to Be Perfect.[3]
Yes, really! When I say this to international grad students, this seems to help them let go of the pressure of needing to be perfect and start experimenting with some of my suggestions. The pressure of needing to be perfect often takes away the space for students to make mistakes that are often part of the learning process. When students feel they can't make mistakes, they are likely to be self-conscious about their performance and worry about how they may come across to their professors and peers. Some of the international students I've worked with feel the need to present their best work and best selves possible in class. They feel when they speak up in class, it should be a well-thought-out comment or at least they should sound smart. If this sounds like you, I encourage you to pay close attention to the questions and comments made by your peers in class. You might find that their comments and questions can vary in quality and that what really matters is to know where you are in your learning process, ask questions to help you understand class materials better, and enjoy the process of exchanging ideas with your peers and professors.

Pause & Think:

- What's been your experience in the US classroom? In what ways are the US academic practices the same as or different from what you are used to?
- What might be some of the US academic practices you would consider adopting? Put them on a list and think about how you would go about acquiring them one by one.

Key Skills to Have under Your Belt

There are many skills required to help you succeed as an international student in the United States, both in terms of your graduate studies and your everyday life. Based on my experience and work with international students, there are a few key skills that, once acquired, are likely to make you feel more at ease and confident. These skills help you express yourself and connect with people. If they are not your areas of strength at this moment, I encourage you to spend time and effort working on them.

English Skills

Your English skills are likely to be good enough to pass required English competency for admission to US graduate schools. However, if you are not a native English speaker or if you did not use English on a regular basis in your home country, there is likely to be a period of time in the United States when you will be challenged to keep up with classroom discussions or conversations with local Americans. No matter where you are with your English skills in the areas of listening, reading, speaking, and writing, I recommend that you continue to work on them, paying additional attention to areas in which you feel relatively limited. For example, some international students may be better with writing and reading English yet need to work on their speaking proficiency.

Do the opposite of what you might feel like doing as you seek to improve your English skills. When we don't feel confident of our English skills, we may avoid opportunities to use them. I suggest that you "do the opposite." Identify and use opportunities to practice English on a regular basis. I know for some of you putting yourself out there and risking the possibility of making mistakes will require courage. It may also require patience and perseverance as communicating in a foreign language can be exhausting, especially during your first couple of years in the United States. I promise, you are improving little by little each time! Some of the tips you may consider to help you do the opposite:

1. Befriend native English speakers and other international students who you have to use English with.
2. Use resources from the student writing center in your school to work on your grammar, vocabulary, and sentence structures.
3. Contact the International Student Office to find out if there are other English resources available to international students so that you can practice English in a supported environment, such as a Language Exchange Program.
4. Use mass media, such as news, TV shows, movies, radio and podcasts, to combine English learning with fun and leisure activities.

Pause & Think:

* How do you assess your English skills in the areas of listening, speaking, reading, and writing? Is there any area that would require significant work? What are some resources you can use to improve your English skills, on and off campus?

Presentation Skills

There are a lot of opportunities for you to make presentations in graduate school. It is a major way for your peers and professors to learn about your thinking, your work, and you. Use each time as an opportunity to practice and learn how to improve your presentation skills. If you haven't had much experience making presentations in the past, or if you don't feel quite confident of your presentation skills, I encourage you to work on them and seek feedback from your professors and peers.

What I often hear from international students is that they feel nervous about making presentations. They worry they will forget what they planned to say when under the spotlight or that they might freeze in front of the class, not knowing what to do. Know that it's quite common for people to feel nervous before and during presentations, even if they are native English speakers. I recommend that you **think about the goal of your presentations**. Oftentimes, people focus on their performance, rather than think about "What do I want the audience to learn or take away from my presentation?" Shifting the focus from yourself to your audience and preparing for the presentation with this mindset, you are more likely to deliver a presentation that will be useful to your audience. Plus, you'll likely feel less anxious. In terms of specific techniques and skills to give a good presentation, there are many aspects to think about, such as how to present the information itself, your voice and the tone you use, your pace, how to engage your audience, potential interaction with the audience, storytelling, and more. I suggest you search for related information through your program or the university teaching and writing centers. You can also search for videos or internet tutorials about presentations that may be helpful to you. Remember, the best approach to managing your anxiety and nervousness about giving presentations is to gain as much "exposure" as possible to the experience you are not yet comfortable with and modify your approach through repeated practice and feedback from others.

Pause & Think:

- What are your typical reactions when you have to make a presentation? Do you tend to shy away from it or do you look forward to the opportunity?
- If you become a great presenter one day, what will you look like? Imagine yourself delivering an engaging presentation. What is your presentation about? What are you wearing? How are you using your hand gestures and physical movements? How do you sound? Do you make eye contact with your audience? Do you interact with them? How does the audience respond to you? Visualize all of these aspects in as much detail as possible, as if you were watching a video about you.
- Use the information you gathered in the step above to help you assess your current presentation skills. What are the things you're already good at? What are the areas you want to work on in order to get closer and closer to the image of yourself in the visualization? Write them down and work on each of them whenever you have the opportunity.

Networking Skills

Relative to many other cultures, the US culture overall values one's ability to socialize and connect with other people. The concept of networking is quite present in many different sectors in US society and is *not* just for business people or for people who are looking for a job. Groups and activities are organized to facilitate the process of connecting people with one another over mutual career or personal interests. A difficult reality many international students face is that by coming to the United States for grad school, they lose the network they've built back home and have to start all over again in America. Fortunately, you can start building your network in the United States as your life here unfolds. Having a balanced network and social support is associated with better cross-cultural adjustment.[4]

Attend meetings on campus or your program's colloquia and keep abreast of local conventions or annual conferences organized by nationwide associations in your field of study. Consider joining professional associations. They are usually interested in attracting students to their membership. Typically, there would be activities or programs designed to encourage student participation, such as matching students with mentors in common areas of academic/professional interests, volunteer opportunities in a conference-planning committee, and opportunities to earn scholarships or awards for your research and work. These can also be great venues for international grad students to connect with scholars and professionals from similar cultural backgrounds. Being connected with someone who has travelled a similar path can be hugely reinforcing and helpful to your career development.

What to do at a networking event? Some of you may feel nervous about walking up to someone you don't know and striking up a conversation with them. As an international student you may wonder whether or not there are protocols to follow in such events. Typically, in the United States there appears to be an implicit expectation for conversation participants to take turns sharing their thoughts or sometimes their experiences on the topic being discussed. An international grad student I worked with, Yuting, often felt nervous about joining networking or social events where she had to talk to strangers. She worried that she wouldn't know what to say to people or if she knew what to say, she might become so nervous that she would freeze on the spot. She worried that people might find her boring and wouldn't be interested in talking to her. Initially, Yuting avoided these events. However, she reached a point where she *needed* to start talking to a bigger pool of people in order to find out about potential internship opportunities. She was soon going to graduate and was under pressure to overcome her worries and fears. During therapy sessions, in addition to processing underlying issues that were holding her back from meeting new people and expanding her network, it was important to prepare her for networking events. We discussed implicit expectations and did role plays on common conversation scenarios in networking. Together, we developed a few sentences she would use to introduce herself. We did role plays to give Yuting an idea of what to expect and how it might feel when she was in the actual interaction. By practicing in advance using different possible scenarios, she felt prepared and more confident in those settings.

Pause & Think:

- What's your immediate reaction to the word "networking"? What's been your experience with networking?
- How would you introduce yourself at a conference or an internship fair? Prepare a few sentences you can use for different occasions.
- In addition to professional events, plenty of activities and meetup groups are organized for social, fun purposes. You should be able to find them on and off campus. What are some events you are interested in exploring?

The Mundane but Important Stuff

Aside from the academic and social aspects, many international students often have to go through a big learning curve when seeking health care or when it comes to protecting their rights in the United States.

Health Care
Obtaining health-care services in the United States can be challenging. There are important things to keep in mind when looking for health-care providers. Typically, providers can be divided into two categories in terms of their participation in insurance plans: in-network and out-of-network.

In-Network Providers
If a provider accepts your insurance plan, they would be an in-network provider for you. Depending on your insurance policy, you may or may not pay a co-pay (a fee that a patient is responsible for) during a visit. In-network providers would usually submit insurance claims for you and be paid by your insurance company for the remaining portion of their contracted service fees. You can search for providers in your network on the website of your insurance company or call your insurance company and speak with a representative about this.

Out-of-Network Providers

If a provider does not accept your insurance plan, they would be an out-of-network provider for you. With out-of-network providers, there would usually be an amount of annual deductible that patients have to pay, in order for the insurance company to start reimbursing patients at a certain percentage. The annual deductible amount and the reimbursement percentage vary from plan to plan. Patients are usually expected to pay the full service fee at each visit, and providers usually provide a bill for patients to submit the claim on their own. That being said, different out-of-network providers may have different practices regarding payments. Some would just collect the coinsurance portion (the percentage of an acknowledged fee that will not be reimbursed by the insurance company) from patients during each visit and may submit claims on behalf of patients.

The health-care system and health insurance plans in the United States are in general very complicated. Americans and seasoned insurance billing specialists often get confused! Pay special attention to certain services that people wouldn't regularly use, such as emergency room visits, use of ambulance, hospitalizations, and specialist services such as physical therapy, acupuncture, and so on. Some of these services may not be covered or may have special requirements before they would be covered by certain insurance plans. Generally, it's safe to err on the side of caution. A general rule: Before using any service, always ask your providers and/or your health insurance company whether or not the service would be covered by your insurance plan as well as the fees you would be responsible for. It's recommended to verify the information from multiple sources. This would minimize the likelihood of receiving "surprise bills" from your providers or your insurance company.

Protecting Your Rights

During your stay in the United States, you are likely to encounter situations where you enter a legal agreement with others. It is critical that you pay close attention to the terms detailing responsibilities and rights of both parties in the legal relationship. Make sure the terms are reasonable and acceptable to you before you sign any agreement. Results of negotiations need to be clearly documented in the agreement to avoid potential confusion.

A common situation that international students often encounter is signing a lease for an apartment. A good practice is to make sure that all of the agreements reached between you and the landlord are in writing to ensure clarity on responsibilities and rights. For example: What is the security deposit amount? When is the rent due every month? Any penalty for late payments? What utilities are included in the rent (e.g., hot water, gas, heat, electricity, etc.)? What are the policies regarding lease renewal, subletting the apartment to a third person, having a pet? Whose responsibility is it to fix or replace certain items in the apartment? What is the landlord's contact information in case of any questions or emergencies?

Learning to be clear about your rights and obligations before entering a legal agreement is an important part of the process of becoming independent, especially if this is your first time away from home.

Think Ahead about Your Plan Postgraduation

Though you may have just started your life in the United States, it's not too early to start thinking about your plan after your graduation. The temporary status of a student visa can often cause uncertainty and anxiety to many international grad students, especially toward the end of their studies. Think ahead if you do plan to stay and eventually settle down in the United States. There are immigration hurdles that you need to be aware of. My advice is for you to consult with immigration attorneys (shout out to CUNY Citizenship Now for free legal advice) and identify ways through which you can maximize your chance to stay. If your potential job market is not in an academic setting or not in a sector where employers regularly sponsor foreign workers, it would likely require extra effort to identify viable channels to obtain a work visa and permanent residency. If you don't want to go through a sponsor and choose a route that requires you to demonstrate your professional impact on a national or international level, I recommend that you start building your credentials as early as possible; an immigration attorney with a track record of successful petitions for applicants in your field may provide helpful insight in this process.

Recharge Your Battery:
Life Outside of School in the United States

Remember to recharge your battery after all of the studying and hard work! Exploring life outside of school is a great way to keep yourself balanced! Making good use of your free time and school breaks will likely enrich your experience in this country. Get up from your desk. Step out of your lab. Join local events that are open to the public, such as music in the park, art exhibitions, or parades for various groups. These are some ways to learn about things your local American fellows care about and to feel part of the greater community outside of school. You may also consider traveling to other parts of the United States to experience changes of the American landscape and variations of American culture and lifestyle. On major holidays or special occasions, your local peers or friends may invite you to dinner or parties. Take advantage of these opportunities! This would be a great way to mix and mingle with Americans and learn how they celebrate important cultural or life events. Finally, there is generally a strong bar culture in the United States where people socialize with one another. Keep an open mind and use your judgment when exploring this option.

Redefine Yourself: Develop into the Person You Desire

While you will go through an adjustment period and encounter many challenges on your journey as an international grad student, what comes with this process are opportunities to grow, expand, and ulti- mately redefine yourself. By challenging yourself and stretching your comfort zone in ways suggested in this chapter and/or many others that you discover, little by little, you will start seeing yourself in a different light, a light that reflects your conscious choices rather than expecta- tions or social forces around you. As you are busy settling into your graduate studies and life in this country, remember to take a moment to connect with yourself every so often and think about what you want to get out of this experience of studying abroad beyond advancement in education and career. Cross-cultural contexts provide ample space for individuals to reflect on themselves, "experiment" with new things, and decide what new traits they want to pick up and what no longer works for them.

Weihan came to me because he was very depressed. He did poorly on his first midterm exams at grad school. He was worried that he would fail the classes and be expelled from school. He questioned whether or not he chose the right field of study for himself as he felt totally lost in class and found it difficult to connect with his peers in the program, though a big portion of them came from the same country as him. Upon exploration, Weihan seemed to have previously gone through a similar situation in a US undergrad program but the issues were overall manageable to him, in large part due to the support of his girlfriend at that time. While he may have moved past the impact of the breakup, he felt isolated and didn't know how to deal with the situation he faced in grad school, academically or socially. Weihan was hesitant to meet with his professors for guidance to prevent his academic situation from getting worse despite my recommendation to do so. Socially, Weihan described himself as someone who "only" felt comfortable with certain types of people and settings and was reluctant to venture out of his comfort zone. While providing empathy to Weihan, we discussed how his hesitance and self-perception could be getting in the way of his adjustment in grad school and in the United States. With encouragement, Weihan took time to "experiment" with new ways to meet his academic and social needs. He started to feel more effective in managing stress and gradually began to see himself as someone who was capable of taking care of himself, someone who was able to connect with a wider range of people, someone who knew how to live his life more fully and vividly. This is my wish for many of you—to take hold of opportunities on your journey as an international grad student to grow, expand, and develop into the person you desire!

Some Final Reminders

To start your life on the right foot, there are many things that are essential for you to set up as soon as you arrive in the United States. Here are some things to consider:

1. Apply for student housing or find your own apartment off campus.
2. Apply for a Social Security Number (SSN). You will be asked for your SSN on many occasions during your stay in the United

States. Speak with your international student advisor about this.

3. Open a bank account and apply for a credit card. It's important to start building your credit history in the United States as soon as possible. Your credit history will likely be checked when applying for housing off campus or getting a loan.

4. Enroll in health insurance. Health-care costs in the United States can be very high if you don't have insurance coverage. Typically, schools will offer health insurance plans for local and international students.

5. Identify ways you can commute to school (if applicable). Familiarize yourself with the local transportation system.

6. Obtain a driver's license in your state though you might not necessarily drive. A driver's license is a form of identification you can easily carry with you compared to your passport.

7. Stay in touch with your international student advisor or the Office for International Students about your visa and travel documents.

8. Join groups for international students and/or ethnic minority students.[5] It's not only a great way to meet new friends but an important venue where you could discuss shared experiences in the United States, obtain validation, and empower one another to effectively manage unjust or nuanced intercultural/interracial situations.

9. Make friends with local Americans in school, in the greater professional community, and in your daily environment.[6]

10. Join a local religious community if you belong to a religion or if you would like to explore this area.

11. Speak with your program office regarding job opportunities on campus. Apply for scholarships, fellowships, assistantships, or grants. They can help subsidize your tuition or living expenses as income options are limited for international students in the United States. They may also help build your professional credentials.

12. Speak with your international student advisor to find out under what circumstances you would need to file taxes. You can also go to the website of Internal Revenue Services (IRS) to look up relevant information.

13. Use school resources, such as the Student Writing Center and the Student Career Center, for your academic and career needs.
14. Know when to seek professional counseling support. The Student Counseling Center can be a tremendous help if you struggle to maintain your regular daily functioning, such as significant changes in your sleep pattern, diet, social withdrawal, loss of interest in things you usually enjoy, trouble staying focused in school, or other mental health symptoms. It's recommended even if you don't experience much of the above but need additional support to cope with school and cross-cultural experiences in the United States.

You should be able to obtain information about most of the above by speaking with your international student advisor, the Office for International Students in your school, or your graduate program. Connecting with other international students is also an important way to get helpful tips for different aspects of living and studying in the United States.

Takeaways for International Graduate Students

- The amount of adjustment you may go through is likely determined by the degree of difference between the US culture and the culture of your country of origin.
- You may experience culture shock about the academic practices in the United States. To acclimate to the American classroom culture, it is important to speak up in class and be proactive about your learning. Prepare at least one question to ask in each class. Be spontaneous and engage in real-time classroom discussions so you gradually feel more comfortable. Remember, you don't need to be perfect! Know where you are in your learning process and proactively approach your professors about your learning needs.
- Work on your English skills, presentation skills, and networking skills. Your ability to express yourself and connect with people will play an important role in your success in the United States.
- Health care in the United States can be very costly. When seeking services, always ask your providers and/or insurance company

whether the services are covered by your insurance plan as well as the fees you would be responsible for.

- Protect your rights when you enter a legal agreement. Make sure all negotiated terms are documented in writing for clarity of responsibilities and rights.
- If you plan to stay and settle down in the United States after you graduate, start thinking about how to minimize immigration hurdles you might encounter as early as possible. Consult with immigration attorneys regarding potential options for you to obtain a work visa and/or permanent residency.
- Explore things outside of school to help recharge your battery and keep a balanced life in the United States. Join local events, travel to other parts of the United States, experience how Americans celebrate important holidays or occasions, and so on.
- On your journey as an international grad student, take advantage of opportunities to grow, expand, and develop into the person you desire to be!

Suggestions for Administrators, Faculty, and Staff

Universities, graduate programs, and faculty members play a vital role in international grad students' success in school and in the United States. Recommendations are listed below.

- Create a page for international students on the school/program website. Provide current information on visa, academic matters, English writing and speaking programs, financial aid, job opportunities, housing, health care, and student organizations. It should be clear to international students as to who they can contact directly if they have further questions.[7]
- Assist international grad students in solving some of their financial concerns. Schools and graduate programs are encouraged to provide scholarships, fellowships, or other financial aid to students to help alleviate some of their educational or living expenses in the United States. Job opportunities on campus would help provide a sense of purpose for international grad students in their adjustment process.

- Assign senior international students in the program/on campus as mentors to facilitate the adjustment process of incoming international students.
- Provide ongoing training and workshops on intercultural/multicultural communication for international grad students, local students, faculty members, and school staff. [8]
- Encourage international students to engage in student organizations of their own and other cultures.
- Create interaction opportunities for international grad students and local students through integrated housing arrangements. [9]
- Provide a safe channel for international grad students to voice and address concerns about intercultural/multicultural practices of the school and graduate program.

Suggestions for Mental Health Professionals

Depending on your clinical training and background, international students and the issues they often encounter may not necessarily be familiar to you. Below are some suggestions that could help you navigate your work with them with confidence.

- During the screening/intake, inquire about the language the student feels most comfortable using. If it's a language you don't speak, refer the student to professionals who communicate fluently in the preferred language and who have experience with the student's presenting issues.
- If the student overall has a good command of English but is not a native speaker, consider matching the speed of your speech to that of the student and speak clearly. Let the student know that they can always stop you if there's anything they don't understand or if they need clarifications.
- Review journal articles or published materials to learn about international students in the United States, their needs and common struggles. Use the information gathered as your knowledge base about this population and don't make assumptions. Know that there will be differences and variations on the individual level.

- Reflect on your personal thoughts and feelings about the student's race, ethnicity, culture of origin, language, and so forth. What are some of the biases you may have about individuals of the same/ similar background? In what ways might the biases affect how you work with the student?
- When appropriate, it's okay to let the student know that you are not familiar with their cultural background, values, or practices. To the extent that it does not cause additional burden to the student, ask questions that would help you understand the student's context, life experiences, and worldview.
- As with other populations, offering clinical interpretations/recommendations in a tentative way will convey a sense of humility, acknowledging that you don't necessarily know everything and that you respect their values and choices.
- Provide information about useful resources that they may not otherwise be aware of.
- Seek consultation or supervision from colleagues who have extensive experience working with international students.

~

CHAPTER SIX

Navigating Group
Dynamics in Graduate School

Kristan Baker

Congratulations! You've made it into graduate school! This is no small feat. Did you know that more than 2.2 million people apply to graduate schools every year?[1] Just 9.3 percent of adults older than age twenty-five have a master's degree, and only about 2 percent have a doctoral degree.[2] Your commitment, focus, and hard work have paid off, and you are now in a position to reach new academic heights, realize life goals, and achieve your professional dreams.

Over the next two to sixish years (depending on your program and degree), you're going to expand your knowledge base and strengthen your skill set. This is what you expect to get out of any graduate program. After all, to earn an MBA, you go to business school to learn finance, profit margins, and statistical analysis; in an MFA program, you'll study great artists, learn art history, and have exhibitions of your work; to earn your doctorate, you will study and master an academic discipline in order to earn a degree necessary for your career. But one of the most important lessons, no matter your field of study, is nonacademic. It's this: *You must learn how to navigate interpersonal and group dynamics.* Mastering this skill is one of the major keys to your success in graduate school and beyond.

Sometimes you interact with people in a way that helps you and other times in a way that undermines your intentions and goals.

Awareness of this fact can help you to be thoughtful and proactive as you engage with others. Getting strong recommendation letters, getting that extra push from a mentor, making the most of a networking opportunity, forming meaningful peer relationships, working well within a team, all help to increase your chance of getting to wherever it is you want to go academically and professionally. This can be a lot to keep track of and manage on top of your academic demands, but the bottom line is that in graduate school, *you have to deal with people*. *The better that you understand how to navigate interpersonal and group dynamics, the better equipped you are to thrive.*

Fortunately, you already have lots of experience. Functioning with others, often in groups, is something that has been a part of your life from practically day one. It starts with your family, continues in preschool, develops further in grades K through 12, and you certainly dealt with group dynamics in college. Now that you are in graduate school, however, you are going to be with new groups of people who are also top students in a setting that will most likely be more focused and more demanding than what you experienced in prior schooling. With that comes a new set of group dynamics to consider and navigate. So, it's a good time to take a look at your interpersonal toolbox and see what you have, and what you might need, to aid you on this journey through graduate school.

Family Dynamics

Meg,[3] a biochemistry doctoral student, was caught off guard on the first day of her second year of graduate school when she walked into her biochemistry lab class and discovered the other five students already present, talking with the professor. Throughout college and during the first year of graduate school, Meg was always the early bird who got to class before anyone else to chat with professors. And this professor was one she really wanted to impress. Meg had felt flattered and relieved when the professor selected her for this specialized lab. She saw it as recognition of her hard work throughout her first year and confirmation of the budding mentor-mentee relationship that was forming between them. But now she felt that familiar pit in her stomach, the one that was often present at dinner time when she was growing up, when she and her siblings vied for their parents' attention. Meg found herself wishing this was an independent study lab just for her. But it wasn't, and she quickly realized she was going to have to figure out how to work well in this group of students in order to make the most of this opportunity.

With graduate school comes groups. And like Meg, you can't avoid them. They come in all different shapes and sizes. In the beginning, your primary group will most likely be with the other members of your entering class. Your program may require that your graduate group take a lot of classes together. Other programs may encourage more independence and flexibility for students to progress through the program via different schedules. Still other programs may require your class to break into smaller or specialized groups by joining labs, specific research projects, or disciplinary tracks. There will be groups in your graduate program where you can choose whether you are a member or not, and other groups where you won't have that choice. The common denominator for any group scenario is *you* and what *you* bring to the table in terms of your wants, needs, characteristics, and goals. Therefore, in approaching your graduate school experience, it may be helpful to consider your first group experiences in life (your family) and how it helped shape how you interact with others.

Family is central to a person's socialization process. With all the function and dysfunction that comes with the territory, the family serves as a person's introduction to interacting with others. It is from this that we learn how our behavior is often connected to how another person behaves, especially if the behavior has a direct or indirect impact on how our survival needs are met. Family teaches us:

- Hierarchical frameworks. Generally, parents or caregivers are at the top of this hierarchy. In some cultures, the oldest sons and daughters also hold unique cultural roles in the family.
- That there are spoken and unspoken group rules. For example, in some cultures it is an unspoken rule to not share family troubles with outsiders (e.g., counselors). To do so risks shaming or alienating the family member.
- That there are different communication styles. Individualistic cultures tend to value independent thought and assertive communication; collectivist cultures tend to value communication styles that minimize conflict among group members.

- How to adapt to systemic changes. Some family systems are more comfortable with adapting to change, while others are more resistant.
- How problems get solved. Some family cultures depend on elders to problem solve (e.g., parents, grandparents, religious leaders) for the entire family.

We learn that each family group can be made up of subgroups, like parent-child and sibling-sibling. We learn that we fall into certain interpersonal patterns, and each person has a functional role in a family that is maintained by the group rules of that family system.

It can be helpful to look to your past to get a clearer vision of your present. Understanding your role in your family unit, how your family unit was structured, and how your family members interacted with each other can help you see similar dynamics and patterns play out in graduate school. And you may find that the family lessons you learned and the family role you developed can continue to play out in other social and professional groups in your life. You can think of it in terms of having a family narrative that provides a guidebook for how you make your way through the world. This can come in handy as graduate programs often resemble a family system with many spoken and unspoken group rules to learn and live by. For example, your professors may function as parental figures, with their own teaching styles and manners of providing support. They may be distant or accessible, demanding or lenient, or a combination of many other styles that can capture a parenting approach. There may be sibling-type dynamics at play with the other students in the graduate program, vying and competing for approval and recognition from the parents/professors as well as the resources provided by the program, such as assistantships, fellowships, publications, internships, and research teams. All of these factors can contribute to how you function in your graduate groups. They can tap into your family system experiences and activate the strategies you developed to survive and manage the myriad interpersonal dynamics at play within a group. This can have benefits as well as drawbacks.

Ben, a sociology doctoral student, for example, found himself stepping into a heated debate between two of his classmates during a class discussion. He didn't know why he felt the need to intervene. Ben was on very friendly terms with both classmates. Most of the time the class was a close-knit group. But now he felt very uncomfortable with the tension that was increasing between the two students. Ben was also aware that the professor seemed to be wary of what was going on in the class. Before he knew exactly what he was doing, Ben started mediating the debate, explaining both sides of his classmates' argument and linking their similarities. He was trying to forge a reconciliation before a rift would exist in the class. Ben's strategy worked. The debate came to an end, the tension subsided with his classmates, and the professor seemed to relax. The professor even praised Ben for his quick thinking and adroit handling of the two-sided discussion. Ben felt thrilled with his success and relieved that the tension was gone. Yet, he also felt emotionally drained and self-conscious that he became the focus of the professor's positive attention, especially since it came at the expense of his friends.

After the class, Ben's classmates took him aside and expressed their frustration with Ben that they couldn't work out the conflict themselves. They noted how Ben "stole the spotlight," and they worried the professor would judge them for needing mediation to resolve a debate. Since that class, Ben was certain his two classmates started behaving more distantly towards him. Ben talked about this situation with his younger sister, and she noted that he often took this very same role in their family. She pointed out the times from their childhood when their divorced parents would argue over the visitation schedule, and Ben, not even a teenager, would help them negotiate in a more peaceful manner. Ben reflected upon this and realized he needed to consider some factors before he intervened as a mediator in a class conflict again. He wondered how much of getting involved was his own need to feel safe and comfortable.

Ben's mediator role may or may not sound familiar to your own family role. It is helpful, however, to examine which role resonates with you. Reflect upon interpersonal patterns (all the good, all the bad, and, yes, all the ugly) that tend to pop up in your life and can be defined as a role you developed through interactions with your family. As a guide, below are some family roles[4] to consider. Read through them to see if you recognize ways you tend to act in groups.

- The Boss: This person likes to take the reins and lead the group into action. The Boss was the "responsible" child who the family could depend on to get things done with little to no prompting. The Boss brings order to the family unit by being directive, goal-oriented, and a delegator. This person is a high achiever who strives for excellence by laying the trail for themselves and others to follow. The Boss has many strengths, but sometimes this person can go too far with wanting to be the only leader and not allow others to be right or have a viable answer. In many cultures, men are socialized to take on the boss role, particularly relative to women. This sometimes leads to domineering and patronizing behavior in academic settings.

- The Caretaker: This person often senses the needs of others before they realize their own needs. The Caretaker is a master of attunement and is an expert at providing support for other members of the family. This person tends to take on the task of problem-solving for the family in an effort to minimize harm and increase happiness in the family unit. Conflict tends to throw Caretakers off as it splits their protection efforts among family members. Caretakers are not as mindful or comfortable focusing on their own needs and may depend on others needing them to feel whole.
- The Peacemaker: The Peacemaker resembles the Caretaker in that this person tends to be very vigilant of how well the family is functioning. The goal of the Peacemaker is to maintain stability and harmony in the family unit. When conflict arises, the Peacemaker quickly activates their negotiating and mediating skills to minimize bad feeling between members. Being on alert to ensure the family is unified can take an emotional toll on the Peacemaker. The Peacemaker's well-being can depend a little too much on how well the other members are functioning.
- The Rebel: This person is a rule-breaker and a contrarian to the family system. The Rebel is a maverick, an independent thinker, a nonconformer. This person tends to resent and resist pressure to conform to the family system. While the Rebel can be a disrupter to the family system, this person plays an important role in the family by pushing the members to consider new rules and systems, being the "devil's advocate," and challenging the family dysfunction and injustice. Rebels can become self-destructive, however, when they disregard the importance of connections and slip more into an anarchist role.

- The Rationalizer: This person often grounds the family function-ing in cool-headed logic and reasoning. The Rationalizer helps to stabilize the family unit by providing a more matter-of-fact, un-emotional approach to problem-solving. While this interpersonal style often allows the Rationalizer to feel and emit calm during family conflict, this person is susceptible to shy away from more emotionally rich and rewarding experiences, which can also be frustrating for the other family members.
- Create your own role label: If none of the roles above hit the mark for how you see yourself, go ahead and create your own label.

Exercise:

When you select the role that best captures you (or you create one that is a better reflection of your role), make a list for each of the fol-lowing categories:

- Professional or academic group (vs. actual family) situations that activate my family role.
- Ways in which playing my family role helps me in these groups.
- Ways in which my family role hinders me in these groups.

Consider these questions as well: Does playing this role energize you and help you to strengthen your motivation and confidence? Or does it require a lot of mental and emotional energy that depletes you and compromises your ability to function in other areas of your academic life? Or both? You may see yourself in multiple roles. If this is the case, examine what circumstances determine which role gets activated and repeat the exercise.

Equipped with this knowledge, you are in a much better position to gauge how strongly your own family narrative directs your thoughts, feelings, and actions within a group. From there, you can better map out and manage group scenarios that work to your advantage or those that put you at a disadvantage.

Group Dynamics

Meg made her way into the lab and sat with the other students. She was the only person from her entering class. The other students were ahead of her in school by one or two years. Meg didn't know them very well. She had seen them around the student common areas, but she didn't have much of an impression of them. Everyone stopped talking when she walked over. Meg felt self-conscious and a little unsure of what do to next. She liked being prepared and having routines; she liked to be the seasoned person in the room who people went to for answers. Now she didn't know what to expect, and that made her nervous. The professor introduced Meg to the other students. She noted that two of them seemed friendly and welcoming. The other three seemed more reserved and skeptical about her coming on board the lab team. Meg was doing her best to read the room. She knew she didn't need to become best friends with everyone, but she needed to figure out how to get accepted into the team enough to get guidance from advanced students when needed and to remain in the good graces of her professor.

We have all been in Meg's shoes. We have been the new kid in the classroom, the new hire at work, the new neighbor on the block, the new person in a friend circle or some other group-based setting. We have also been on the other side when a new person comes into one of our established groups. There's a lot of assessing going on from all the members to figure out how the new social order will, or won't, work. As a group, we are drawn towards establishing and maintaining order, stability, and homeostasis. One of the most popular team-building exercises capitalizes on this need for homeostasis by introducing an unpredictable, destabilizing element into the environment for the group to work through. I am referring to those times in school, work retreats, or a training where everyone counts off by numbers to be sorted into groups to solve a problem or perform a task. As much as you may groan when this activity gets introduced, this strategy provides lots of information about how a group of people form a functioning team. Everyone does some sort of assessment of the situation and figures out their navigation strategies to make it through this exercise. Typically, we all wish to be in groups where we'll be the most comfortable.

Exercise:
Imagine you're doing this type of exercise. What is your assessment of yourself? Are you someone who starts to immediately size up who will be in the same group as you? Are there people in the room you are

praying won't be in your group? Are you hoping certain other people will be in your group?

As the group comes together, people are already seeking out familiarity and anchoring down in their comfort zones. Some are comfortable as leaders and spokespeople. Some are comfortable at being task-oriented and following instructions. Everyone has a role to play in the group. Ideally, each person's role will be complementary to the other group members, and the group will come together quickly to produce positive results. There are many times, however, where there is much more haggling, maneuvering, and posturing that goes on in the group that will affect how well the members work together.

In graduate school, some shape or form of this group exercise happens all the time. This begins with the people entering the program with you. You had no control over who made it into your program. In this group you will have varying degrees in common with your classmates. You might recognize a kindred spirit among some of them, while others may rub you the wrong way. (But don't worry, this will likely change throughout the course of your graduate school experience. Your first-year rivals sometimes become your best friends by year two.) The first year is often about getting to know your classmates, learning how to work with those you like and those you don't. To add to the dynamics, this learning process will take place under the observation of your professors. The first year provides many opportunities to show how well you navigate relationships with your classmates and professors. The benefits of this are many; having a positive reputation with your professors and peers can get you a lot further in your academic journey than if you are not seen as a team player. It also sets the stage for how you integrate into other groups that will come your way. Your reputation will proceed you. The more positive it is, the easier it will be to gain friends, advocates, and allies that will come in handy as you venture into new opportunities or find yourself in rough waters with other students or professors (more to come on this in the next section).

With this in mind, it is a good time to continue your self-journey into who you are in groups, which group dynamics play to your strengths and which will be more challenging. Building on the family role, there are other avenues to explore when figuring all of this out. For example, Meg had a sense of why she was nervous entering that lab.

In addition to realizing she had sibling-types to vie for her professor's attention, she wasn't comfortable being the new person in the group because she felt unprepared and uncertain about what to expect. She also felt the need to please her professor and wanted to be accepted by her fellow lab students. Understanding your interpersonal needs and preferences can serve as a useful guide to navigate group dynamics.

Exercise:
Here are some questions, inspired by the psychologist William Schutz, PhD,[5] to begin the self-exploration process (helpful hint: do not treat this as a judgment exercise, but rather an exercise in self-awareness):

- Do I need to be included in groups or is this something I don't really care about?
- Do I prefer to work with people or would I rather work alone?
- Do I need to be accepted by others or is the acceptance of others not a priority to me?
- Would I like to make friends in a new group or would I rather keep strict boundaries between my personal and professional life?
- Do I need to be the leader of the group and control the group process? Do I prefer to follow someone else's lead and stay out of the spotlight? Or do I need to challenge the leader's authority?
- How comfortable am I with giving up my group role to someone else?
- How do I respond to authority? Do I need to follow the rules? Or do I feel restricted by, or fight against the rules?
- Do I need time to prepare to be in a group or do I prefer to jump headfirst into an unknown situation?
- Do I embrace conflict in a group or is it something I dread?

Not everyone will have definitive answers for these questions, as many of the answers can depend on the situation. For example, your answers will most likely be different during your first year of graduate school when you are new to the program from when you are well established in the program and about to complete your courses. Meg, who likes to be the expert, may be more willing to cede the leadership role in her first year on the lab team, but less willing during her third year.

Your answers can also depend on the other personalities in the group. There may be a lot of strong personalities vying for the leadership roles, or a group where most of the people prefer to avoid leadership. These are just two of the many personality combinations that can happen in a group. Given all of this variability, it is helpful to get a grasp on your own set of needs and preferences that lay the foundation of who you are so that you can recognize when you need to adjust your strategies to attain the best results.

If you want to explore these types of interpersonal questions further, I recommend you check out Dr. Schutz's personality assessment measure, the Fundamental Interpersonal Relations Orientation-Behavior (FIRO-B™).[6] This self-report tool focuses on how your interpersonal needs shape how you approach working with others in a group. You may find completing such an assessment helps to better expand and organize your understanding of yourself in relation to others.

When reflecting on the above questions, you may see qualities that are associated with "extroverts" and "introverts." It may be tempting to oversimplify the categories and determine that extroverts seek out and thrive in groups, while introverts don't. Avoid this temptation! Not only are there many outgoing introverts and shy extroverts in the world, each bring valuable, often complementary, qualities to the group setting. While being talkative, action-oriented, social, and outwardly enthusiastic can work very well in a group setting, so can being more reserved, less impulsive, observant, and contemplative. Before I fall into the oversimplification trap, my main point is to not confine yourself to a certain "sociability" label when considering how well you can function within a group setting. Rather, identify what interpersonal needs and qualities you bring to group dynamics, and then match them to the specific spoken and unspoken rules of a particular group. This will help you expand your strategic options and create opportunities to connect with complementary others.

Standing Out and Fitting In

The first few lab classes went well for Meg. She caught on quickly to the research and felt she was already making a notable contribution to the team. There was one lab mate, Jenny, with whom she was especially close. They bonded over being the only two women in the program. She was grateful to have another female to work with in such a male-dominated field. With the support of Jenny's friendship, Meg felt more relaxed and secure in the group. Together they made a good team within the team. They were often paired together during the mini-team competitions that the professor held to generate more research results. And they often won. Their accomplishments were recognized by the professor and their lab mates. As a result, Meg felt more confident. She spoke up often, answered questions with ease, and made herself readily available to be a team player.

At the end of the semester, Meg was the first first-year lab student to win the coveted "Best Researcher" award, which came with department-wide recognition and a financial award. She was thrilled that her hard work paid off. Her lab mates congratulated her and the professor led the team in a toast to Meg's accomplishment. At the end of the lab session, however, she noticed that Jenny left the room without her. Another lab mate took Meg aside and warned her not to get "a big head," as she was still the "low person on the totem pole." Meg, stunned, left the room feeling confused that she now felt anxious that she won the award.

Meg's experience highlights how graduate school is full of the ups and downs that come with standing out among peers. Having a positive experience in graduate school is often a balance between striving to stand out among your peers while finding ways to fit in. Being visible and standing out for your hard work, skills, and accomplishments has its obvious personal and professional rewards. Knowing how to blend and fit in with your peers also has personal and professional benefits related to social support, developing friendships, social networking, and generating opportunities for professional collaborations. It is very gratifying when the balance is achieved, but there are times when "standing out" clashes with "fitting in," and very real professional and personal challenges emerge. Meg, for example, won a prestigious professional award, but this generated envy among her lab mates, even with her close friend. It can be disheartening to realize that, for all of the camaraderie that develops between students, graduate school, by its nature, promotes and thrives on competition.

Competition for attention, recognition, opportunity, and resources is a crucial part of the graduate school experience. Competition has benefits. It can motivate you to perform well, to attain goals, to push beyond your comfort zones, and to achieve more than you would without it. Competition in graduate school also provides a lot of practice of what to expect in getting hired and working in the "real world"—preparing you to work with others in order to attain your short-term and long-term professional goals.

Even with all the positive aspects of competition, it comes with "strings attached," as it adds a layer of stress to an already stress-inducing environment. Whether you are a person who is very comfortable and confident with competition, someone who finds competition to be fraught with anxiety, or somewhere in between, it is helpful to understand your relationship with competition so that you can anticipate where and when your insecurities and anxieties will surface, and then address them in the most effective way possible.

Exercise:
Here are some questions to ask yourself:

- Are you someone who craves or avoids competition?
- Growing up, did you have to compete with other family members for resources, attention, or other needs?
- Was competition fostered or squashed in your family?
- How was competition emphasized or minimized in your previous school experiences?
- What types of outlets were available for you to express competitiveness (e.g., being on sports teams, debate teams)?
- When did competition help or hinder you in meeting goals?
- How do you feel competing against friends?
- How does your culture shape your thoughts, feelings, and behaviors about competition?
- Has your gender and/or race impacted how you approach competition?

While pondering these questions, identify and link your responses with coping strategies you have used during competitive situations. For example, think of a time you were required to compete against another student. Did you take up the challenge with gusto and ease? Or did it require a lot of self-talk and/or prompting from your teacher to get you to engage in the competition? Take stock of the coping strategies you used. For instance, did you give yourself a pep talk? Did you do some breathing exercises? Did you imagine your opponent in a funny suit? Reflecting on how you handled competition in the past will help you identify your strengths and areas where you could use some assistance in developing your confidence and skill in the competition arena.

Part of what makes competition tricky is you are also coping with people being competitive with you. The exhilaration of success in a competition is often accompanied by the dread of envy. What would you do if you were Meg? How would you approach a friend who you beat in a competition? How would you embrace your success while coping with the envious reaction of others? How would you react if you were Meg's friend? Or if one of your peers received something you coveted? A part of navigating the choppy waters of competition is being mindful of all the different sides of the win-lose scenario. Consider the benefits of being a gracious winner and loser. This might mean treating your friends as you would like to be treated if you experienced a win or a loss. Allow yourself to take pride in your accomplishments and avoid letting others bring you down. Be mindful when you are feeling envious and create some self-check points. Channel those undermining, self-defeating feelings towards a more productive use. What could my envy be telling me? How might I address that more productively in my life and career? There will be other opportunities that will present themselves. The key is to keep yourself in the game. Remain visible to your professors and peers in a positive way and you will be in a prime position to get the most out of your graduate school experience.

Discrimination based on race, sex, sexual orientation, gender identity, disability, religion, or pregnancy is a toxic form of the standing-out and fitting-in dilemma. Discrimination is against the law, and there are institutional, federal, and state protections against such behaviors, such as Title IX, which prohibits discrimination on the basis of the sex of a person. Unfortunately, these protections do not guarantee that discrimination, overt and covert, won't occur in graduate school. Roger, a Caribbean American male, was in his first year of his MBA program when he was reviewing internship sites he wanted to apply to for the following year's practicum. When Roger and his classmates were comparing notes about the internship application process, some of his Caucasian classmates made comments about "the benefits of affirmative action." This angered Roger and he was thankful when one of his other classmates called them out for their remarks. The classmates mumbled some apologies and said they were "joking." Roger didn't really buy their apologies but shrugged it off as he didn't want to give them the satisfaction of getting under his skin. What hit him harder, however, was when the professor, a Caucasian female, came over to the group to review their choices. When Roger showed his preference list, the professor quickly crossed out three internship sites, explaining that Roger didn't fit the sites' "intern profile." When asked to explain what she meant, the professor stated that those sites didn't "kowtow to the race card." Angered by this interaction, Roger consulted his family, friends, and a professor he trusted.

After many discussions, Roger decided to speak with the university's Ombudsman Office to get further guidance about his options from an independent source. The ombudsman officer helped direct Roger to his school's chief diversity officer. A complaint was filed, which ultimately concluded with an informal resolution, where the professor apologized and agreed to further diversity training. If it didn't get resolved informally, another option for Roger could have been to consult a lawyer. All Roger wanted was to make sure he had as fair a shot as his fellow students at furthering his professional goals. The stress of filing the complaint took a toll on Roger, as did navigating his awkward relationship with the professor afterward. Yet, he knew he would have felt worse had he not acted. It takes a lot of courage, tenacity, guidance, and support to navigate through discrimination in graduate school. Each person must make their own decision about whether and how to act in response to being the target of discrimination. Often it can feel like there is no good option. Whether or not one takes direct institutional or legal action, it is important to recognize that these experiences can be painful, overwhelming, and exhausting. Allowing oneself space to process the situation and getting support from others who understand and care can be helpful for healing.

Managing Challenging Group Dynamics

After leaving the lab room, Meg went looking for Jenny (the close friend and lab mate who left the room without Meg after she won an award). Meg wanted to make sure everything was fine between them. Fortunately, Meg didn't have to go far. Jenny was coming to look for her. Jenny apologized for walking out of the lab without her, but admitted she needed a few minutes to work through her disappointment in not getting the coveted award. Meg said she appreciated Jenny, noting she learned a lot from working together. Meg let Jenny know she planned on telling this to their lab professor. She also asked Jenny for advice regarding their lab mate who warned Meg to "stay in her place." Meg and Jenny explored Meg's options. Meg developed a plan where she would first talk with the lab mate about the comment. And if that didn't work, she would talk with the professor. Meg was nervous about the plan, but she was determined not to feel self-conscious about being a strong member of the research team. Jenny said she would support Meg through this process.

While these hard parts of group dynamics can feel daunting, they will be fertile ground for lots of personal and professional growth. And it is navigating through the challenges of group dynamics where you will learn valuable lessons of trust, collaboration, negotiation, and how to handle the thrills of victory and agonies of defeat. As Meg and Jenny illustrate, conflicts can be worked out, and for the majority of the time, people will come out stronger by working through the challenges.

Cliques

There will be times in your graduate program where you will feel like you are back in high school. Subgroups and coalitions form within groups, and sometimes these subgroups turn into cliques. Most of us (if not all) have experienced what it is like being on the outside or the inside of a clique. What makes a clique different from a regular tight-knit group of friends is its exclusive nature and a reputation for alienating others who aren't members of the clique. Sarah, a fourth-year student in a clinical psychology PsyD program, was impacted by a clique in her class cohort. For the first two years in her program, three of her eight classmates formed a clique, and they were not nice to Sarah. These three classmates would talk about her in voices loud enough to hear; about her hair, her appearance, her voice. She had no clue why she was the target of ridicule by this clique. Sarah tried to ignore them and relied on other students in the program for more positive interactions.

Starting in the third year, Sarah spent less time in classes with the clique due to choosing different specialties. By chance, Sarah ended up in the same externship with one of the clique members. She was surprised that this person ended up being really nice to Sarah and apologized for being mean to her. They even became close friends. (Still to this day!) Not all situations like this turn out so well, but there are strategies to managing cliques. First and foremost, remind yourself that you are *not* in high school anymore. It can be painful and trigger old insecurities to be on the outside of a clique, but there are also many benefits to not being in a clique. You have more freedom to be who you truly are on your terms, and you don't have to abide by the clique's rules about who you can and can't be friends with. It may be tempting to form or join a clique to avoid being a target of one, but just think about the amount of emotional and mental energy it takes to maintain your clique membership. There are too many rules in a clique, so it is beneficial to steer your energies towards social connections that are much more flexible and inviting. Also, professors tend not to be fond of high school behavior, so cliques don't necessarily give you an advantage in getting recognized for your skills and achievements.

"Good" Group versus "Bad" Group

I have heard many current and former graduate students say that their faculty and administrators labeled the graduate class groups in the program. It is very gratifying to be in the class group labeled as the "smart" group, the "overachiever" group, or the "best" group. You may find yourself, however, in the "difficult" group, the "challenging" group," or the "not-very-well-liked" group. It just so happens that I was in a class group that was labeled "difficult." We were a small group of women who were not falling into step with the politics of the program. While we were hardworking achievers, we also had the reputation of "having a lot of balls (ironically enough)" in challenging our professors. As I saw this reputation forming, it struck me as funny since I am a people-pleaser by nature (I have a sneaky suspicion that I was the most people-pleasing person of the bunch). We bonded as a group and took pride in our reputation as being strong-willed. It was irritating at times to have to defend ourselves and clarify to others that we were more complex than our "difficult" reputation allowed. But we were fortunate that it did not hinder us from making strong, productive, individual connections with our professors and from being selected for assistantships and special teams.

Our class happened to follow a class that was very popular with the faculty. They were very much the "good group" in our program. While it could have been easy for the two classes to dislike each other based on our reputations, we actually got along as a whole. We avoided the pitfalls of being pitted against each other. We acknowledged our different reputations and often teased each other about our respective labels. Our class was fortunate to have such a supportive class ahead of us. When this doesn't happen, the "good" group versus "bad" group can be much more of a tricky minefield to navigate; there is more risk for conflict and high drama that can take you off course. If this is the case, or your class's reputation is hurting your academic opportunities, then be proactive about nipping the reputation in the bud. If possible, try to avoid getting into conflicts with other class groups. Keep focused on your academic goals and continue to seek out and foster positive relationships with your fellow students and faculty members. Also, reframe the situation by asking yourself, "Why do the faculty have to label classes this way?" Perhaps this has more to do with faculty personalities and may reflect some dysfunction in their relationships with each other. For example, the faculty in my program were split on how they viewed my class: Some saw us as independent thinkers while others saw us as difficult. This split seemed to mirror the divide between the faculties' theoretical orientation (cognitive behavioral vs. psychodynamic), which may have indicated problems between the faculty members that were then projected onto my class.

Students versus Faculty
We all hope and expect going into graduate school to find mentors, advocates, and allies in our faculty members. Unfortunately, this is not always the case. Rifts between classes and faculty happen. Rifts can stem from personality differences and teaching styles. Sometimes a vicious cycle develops where the professor is convinced the class group doesn't like them, which leads the professor to dislike the class, which leads to the class really not liking them. These types of conflicts are often managed in the classroom and don't extend beyond the end of the course. It is important to keep a bigger-picture perspective on what

your goals are and who will help you achieve those goals. Be aware if a "groupthink" situation is developing. In its simplified form, that's where the group members start to get caught up in a dynamic where agreeing with each other is paramount rather than making the right decision. Dissenting opinions are not allowed in this group dynamic. An indicator that groupthink is happening is if no one is allowed to be the "devil's advocate." Keep this on your radar and address it as best you can. Being mired in groupthink can lead to having "blind spots" for making smart, productive choices about your academic relationships and professional courses of action.

Other rifts, however, can stem from more serious ethical concerns of conduct. Jon and Leslie were two first-year students who joined a research team in their anthropology doctoral program. There were two other students from the class ahead of them that were a part of the team. During the course of research, Jon witnessed the professor become very angry with one of the research participants. The professor started yelling at the participant. Upset, Jon brought this to the attention of his fellow teammates. After much discussion, they decided to have a meeting with the professor to discuss what happened with the participant. The professor was very dismissive of the team's questions and concerns. The student group met with one another afterwards. Jon and Leslie stated that they would leave the team in protest. The other two students stated that they were staying on the team. After consulting with some other students and faculty members, Jon filed a complaint against his professor, which triggered an investigation. Ultimately, the investigation resulted in the professor losing his research grant, and the two students who had remained on the team lost their assistantships. While Jon felt confident that he did the right thing, he was worried that the students who were impacted would resent him, and that the other faculty members and students would look at him as a "troublemaker." In the end, Jon's relationship with the two students became strained but he gained a mentor in a professor who admired his willingness to act on his ethical beliefs. It is unfortunate when this type of group dynamic happens. Going through something like this can be stressful. It is during these times where relying on an established support system (hopefully a mix of family, friends, and trusted professors) will be essential in helping navigate these types of stormy waters.

Conclusion

A lot of group dynamics that take place in graduate school were introduced in this chapter. It is important to make the ups and downs of working with your fellow students and faculty members worth your while. Take advantage of your time in graduate school to practice, hone, strengthen, and revise your interpersonal skills. You will have many fun, fulfilling, and frustrating experiences to work from as you navigate your way through graduate school. Self-exploration is a good navigation tool from which to build a framework—a compass, if you will. You may be surprised how much "knowing thyself" can translate into you being better equipped to be the captain of your ship, to better reap the rewards and tackle the challenges of your graduate school journey. You got this!

Takeaways for Graduate Students

Below are some basic management strategies for your consideration when confronted with a group dynamic that is interfering with your ability to progress in your goals.

- First, assess the situation to see if it rises to the occasion of warranting direct action. There may be times where avoiding or ignoring the conflict (like in the clique example above) and/or redirecting your energies may be the better solution.
- If the situation warrants direct action on your part, address the issue sooner rather than later. Confronting an issue can be nerve-racking, but it will be a lot easier managing it on the front end.
- First try to work it out with the person(s) directly. Doing this can keep the drama to a minimum, and there is a good chance that both of you will gain a better understanding of each other.
- If it is apparent that it is neither feasible nor smart to go to the person first, or you tried this strategy and it didn't work out, seek out support and guidance from a faculty member with whom you have a positive relationship. This person can help you identify your options and strategies and can also point you to possible administration policies in your program that can help resolve the situation.

- Other people to consider if you feel like you are not getting the guidance or results you are seeking: the department chairperson or executive officer; the school's ombudsman; a person in your program who is identified as a student advocate; student affairs; the student counseling center.
- While being a strong self-advocate, also be respectful, fair, and solution-focused. Be open and willing to discuss your part in a situation.
- Seek guidance and support as needed from your support system. Ask them to be a "devil's advocate" to your stance so that you can better assess your position and the position of others.
- Remind yourself that working through conflict can help you to be a stronger, more confident student and person.

Suggestions for Administrative Staff

- Be aware and mindful of how group dynamics can impact a student's experience in your program.
- Be cognizant of how broader systemic dynamics—such as larger university politics—can impact departmental, cohort, and lab dynamics.
- Provide written materials about the rewards and challenges of group dynamics during the orientation process. This chapter is a good first step!
- Be aware of how faculty members promote, encourage, and address competition and cooperation with their students.
- Have trainings/workshops for faculty regarding forming productive group dynamics and addressing toxic group dynamics.
- Have a student mentor program that includes a focus on group dynamics and how to manage challenging group dynamics.
- Have a protocol for student-student and student-faculty conflict resolution.
- Reinforce and promote policies and procedures that address and protect against discrimination (both overt and covert). Provide a safe environment and have a clear protocol for students if there is a concern about discrimination.

- Have an ombudsman system within the program, on top of the institution's ombudsman office.
- Have mental health resources available for students.

Suggestions for Faculty Members

- Be mindful of how you promote, encourage, and address competition and collaboration in your classroom.
- Be a positive role model of collaboration and working through professional conflicts.
- Be proactive about addressing toxic group dynamics.
- Do not tolerate discrimination. Know the discrimination protocols. Promote a safe environment for a student to voice a concern about discrimination.

Suggestions for Mental Health Professionals

- Ask your clients about the group dynamics in their graduate program, and how they are positively and/or negatively impacted by them.
- Support your clients' self-exploration process regarding how they function within a group and how this is played out in the graduate school setting.
- Help your clients identify and strengthen productive coping strategies for managing challenging group dynamics.
- Support, guide, and act on behalf of your client if they are being discriminated against.

CHAPTER SEVEN

Bearing the Baggage of Racial Microaggressions in Graduate School

A Black Woman's Reflections on Ways to Lessen the Load

Adjoa Osei

I saw the monkey. I saw the banana. A research tool utilized in a study with African children as participants. My body heard the professor's joke of how the exercise was culturally relevant and stiffened like a board. My mind pretended it did not and went blank. I looked at two of my Black classmates. Their eyes told me that a memory was forming that I could not ignore. Who was going to interrupt this professor's presentation and point out the insensitivity of his joke? Is it supposed to be me? I cringed at the thought of me, an early career, Black female doctoral student directly challenging a White male professor about a potentially racist statement. I scanned the room and saw the non-responsive, intently listening faces of my fellow peers and professors. Was it only the Black students in the room that recognized the harmful implications of what he said, specifically a statement that could be interpreted as dehumanizing toward people of African descent?

This time, I am going to be completely emotionally honest. I reason with myself. I completed my dissertation. I finished my internship. I am a licensed clinical psychologist. I am employed in a supportive psychology department. I have a private practice. You have made it this far. I say aloud, telling your story will not take those accomplishments away from you or significantly endanger your current livelihood. The doubt slowly creeps into my mind about whether this chapter will be helpful

137

for anyone. Are my experiences valid? Hopefully, whoever reads this and can relate feels validated and understood. Hopefully, whoever reads this and cannot relate can take a couple of deep breaths to let the words on these pages settle before dismissing my narrative. And some of you may find yourselves switching between these two perspectives with each sentence.

With each word I type, I find myself searching for ways to reduce the anxiety. Engaging in magical thinking that there is some specific action I can do to prevent something bad from happening. While I have frequently shared my experiences on being a Black doctoral student in formal and informal settings, I always feel that same sense of hesitancy at the back of my throat, trying to filter my words or mute my voice. The question revolves in my head. If I say too much, how will this harm me? In graduate school, the bad things always seemed clear, anything that would put me on the dreaded path of not being able to graduate, and I am sure many students can relate to this fear. It always seemed like there was something hanging over my head like a slightly bent umbrella that easily could snap with a gust of wind or too many raindrops if I said or did the wrong thing. A passing grade. A supervisory relationship. A potential mentor. An end-of-year evaluation. A recommendation letter. An externship acceptance. A dissertation defense. In this case, the dread persists even while I am not sure what badness I am attempting to avoid as I write this chapter.

My hope with this chapter is to revisit racial microaggressions that I experienced while pursuing a doctoral degree in clinical psychology and to examine the challenges that I had in addressing them at the time. Racial microaggressions are everyday behaviors like slights, insults, and invalidations that offend people of color by generally well-intentioned White people. In addition, White people may not be aware that they have exhibited racially demeaning speech or behaviors toward people of color.[1] By sharing these distinct moments, my goal is to develop a counternarrative that illuminates the challenges that students of color face in pursuit of higher education specifically with regards to race-related encounters and to reassure these students about the validity of their experiences. Counternarratives are a tool to challenge dominant narratives centered in racial privilege and to make visible the stories of marginalized communities that are often silenced.[2] For example, the

"Am I Going Crazy?!" narrative was based on qualitative interviews of Black and Latinx doctoral students. The narrative revealed that graduate students of color often encountered experiences of racism, censored themselves in response to racialized moments, questioned self-efficacy, debated whether it was worth it to pursue a doctoral degree, adapted their behavior to adopt norms of their discipline, felt stifled in scholarly pursuits, and relied on supportive relationships with peers.[3] Reading this study as a graduate student was an empowering moment for me because it made visible what I was going through and my concerns felt armored with legitimacy from a published study. It also reflected that the conscious and unconscious racism graduate students of color often encountered in their academic programs were worth exploring and examining in research.

In addition to using my examples to create a validating and affirming environment within this chapter, I want to look at these racial microaggressions with a fresh new pair of prescription lenses and think about how I would handle them now, given my professional growth and deepened knowledge about racial microaggressions and strategies for addressing them. As I self-reflect in the spaces of these pages, I will also encourage you to take time to identify and process your own racial microaggressions with relevant questions and exercises. Along with revisiting and processing, I will be reviewing helpful strategies and assertive ways to address racial microaggressions in higher education. Hopefully, you will be able to find some that you are already using as well as broaden your repertoire of skills.

The Monkey That Followed Me

The monkey and the banana along with the phrase "so we made it culturally relevant" are forever stained in my brain and are a definitive moment for me that perfectly captures my graduate school experience and dilemmas around navigating race-related experiences. One afternoon, early on in my doctoral program, students and faculty from my department gathered for a colloquium. One of our core faculty members was presenting research he conducted on children in a rural African village. He was showing research tools that were used during the study, which included a puzzle of a monkey with a banana. When he initially posted the image, I did not notice any discomfort. It was when he described the purpose of the exercise that the research participants were asked to do and made the offhand comment, "so we made it culturally relevant," accompanied by a smile, that I noticed the waves of shock traveling through my body. As I mentioned earlier, it was when I made eye contact with other Black students and saw those knowing looks of hurt that the impact of the racial microaggression started to register in my mind. There is a history of caricature dehumanizing Africans and people of African descent by portraying or referring to them as animalistic and savage. His joke reinforced this stereotype by suggesting that his research tool was relatable and culturally sensitive to African children and their environment, essentially suggesting that African children were like monkeys in search of bananas.

I cannot speak to the awareness of the professor and the meaning behind his joke, but I can describe the impact it had on me. Along with feelings of anger and sadness, I questioned how and if I wanted to respond to this in a public space. It seemed like a huge risk in the moment to openly challenge and criticize a professor who I did not know very well, especially in front of my cohort and other faculty. If I displayed emotional honesty and spoke with passion, I risked making people feel uncomfortable or being dismissed as the stereotype of an angry Black woman. I was also concerned about the power dynamics of our relationship and the possibility of any conscious or unconscious retaliation. I decided to stay silent as my emotions went from a simmer to a boil. Racial stereotypes about African countries and people of African descent swirled around in my head, and I was disappointed that no one in a position of power, specifically a faculty member, pointed out the insensitivity of his joke.

After the colloquium, I met several times informally with fellow Black students in my cohort and we processed the experience together. My concerns felt validated when I saw that they experienced similar emotions and had debated what would be an appropriate response. While I was reluctant to say anything about the incident, my classmate decided after our talk that she would speak to the program director. Unfortunately, our program director told her to disregard the racial microaggression due to concerns that this professor might target her. I realize now that my informal meetings with other Black graduate students served as a "counterspace." "Counterspaces" are safe academic and social spaces in which students of color can challenge stereotypes and racial microaggressions. They can occur in formal and informal settings, such as peer groups and student organizations.[4] Throughout my academic career, I developed several "counterspaces" in which I could authentically talk about my challenges with race-related experiences and get valuable feedback, such as mentor and peer relationships, therapy, and the New York chapter of the Association of Black Psychologists.

In looking back, the most important thing I have learned from that moment is taking the time to process my thoughts and feelings in a safe space after encountering racist actions. I often initially feel shock and then shame if I do not address the offensive speech or behavior at the time. I realize now that there is nothing shameful about taking the time to process my experience with people that I trust. "Counterspaces" allow me to identify and reflect on my thoughts and feelings, take time to care for myself, and receive feedback on potential interventions. After the colloquium, I would still have met with my fellow Black students and utilized the "counterspace" to validate my concerns and challenge the racial microaggression. I also still would not have spoken to the professor due to several reasons: 1) it was early on in my academic program and I was concerned about making a negative impression, 2) I did not have a relationship with this professor and was concerned about the power dynamic, and 3) there was a possibility of retaliation.

In regard to additional interventions, I would have benefitted from supporting my classmate by speaking to the program director as well. Going on record with my complaints could have further illuminated the harmful impact of the racial microaggression and reflected that this was not only my classmate's concern. I also believe this would have been a form of "beasting," which focuses on how Black undergraduate students present a counternarrative that is self and culturally affirming. Rather than focusing on the person who offended, Black students openly challenged racist encounters by centering their own value and that of Black communities with highlighting intellectual merit, promoting Black diversity, and highlighting Black history, culture, and perspectives.[5] Whether we met with the program director as a group or individually, the conversation would shift from exploring the professor's intent or trying to placate my classmate's objection to actually acknowledging the importance of our perspectives as graduate students of color. With our lived experiences and knowledge, we could demonstrate that there needed to be an ongoing dialogue about racial microaggressions in the program rather than sweeping these moments under the rug. Even if things did not significantly change right after a conversation with the program director, a seed would be planted and that seed could be watered over and over again as more racial microaggressions unfortunately occurred in our program.

Exercise #1

Now with the below exercise, I want to create a "counterspace" within the pages of this chapter and give you time to process a racial microaggression. Think about a time in which a White person said something that was racially insensitive or offensive to you. Focus less on the person's intention and whether that person was consciously or unconsciously aware of what was offensive and more on your experience of the microaggression and what was upsetting to you. Grab a pen and paper or electronic device to write on and take some time to jot down your thoughts and feelings to the below questions. There are no right or wrong answers. This is about reflecting on your experience, not coming up with an appropriate response or intervention.

1. What were your immediate thoughts, feelings, and bodily sensations after the racial microaggression occurred? If you cannot remember what you were thinking or feeling at the time, what comes up for you now as you imagine the experience?
2. Describe your relationship with this person. Close? Distant? Any power differentials?
3. How did you respond verbally or nonverbally at the time? Was there anything you wanted to say or do at the time that you were hesitant to say or do? What contributed to the hesitancy?
4. Think about people or places in which you would feel safe enough to discuss this racial microaggression. What validating things would you need to see or hear at the time? If you cannot think of a person or place, imagine me sitting across from you,

intently listening to your experience. What things would you want me to say or do?

The Sting of Words of Encouragement

Internship. Even saying the word still gives me anxiety. In order to graduate from the clinical psychology doctoral program, we had to apply for and complete a full-time, yearlong internship. It was a competitive, grueling, multistep process that included writing essays, obtaining recommendation letters, submitting applications, interviewing, and a match process that involved ranking internship sites and being ranked by sites. My cohort was noncompetitive and willingly shared information with each other, which helped ease the burden. We were all balls of anxiety bouncing off of each other and pushing each other forward with support.

Even with all the genuine support and guidance, I still felt nervous and discouraged that I only had four interviews and was concerned about my chances of matching for an internship. At some point during the application process, I had a meeting with a prior supervisor who I worked with early on in my clinical training and who had provided me with a recommendation letter for internship. I do not recall the purpose of our meeting, but I remember sharing my anxiety about upcoming interviews and the overall internship process. She looked at me with a mix of kindness and pity and said something like, "You will be fine. They are always looking for minority candidates." In that moment, all the things that my supervisor wrote in my recommendation letter that she believed made me a strong candidate for an internship were reduced to me being a diversity hire. There is nothing wrong with internship programs actively working to diversify their programs and recruit graduate students of color. However, the comment suggested that I did not need to be anxious or worry about having actual qualifications for the position because my dark skin color would grant me an automatic pass. Her intent appeared to be to reassure me, and yet I was conflicted about my feelings and how best to respond to her. This is one of those racial microaggressions that I remember burying underneath a frozen, awkward smile, and I do not think that afterwards I even mentioned the experience to anyone.

I include this as an example because it is reflective of many interpersonal racial microaggressions that I experienced in graduate school. They walked the blurred line of offensiveness while triggering thoughts and feelings related to prior microaggressions and race-related experiences. With this example, I was taken back to four years of high school in which I was one of the only Black students in honors English classes. Each semester, I was on the verge of failing out with grades that danced between a B- and a C and yet, I would somehow make it into the class the next year. I remember feeling incompetent at the time and wondering if I belonged in the class or if they needed to meet a quota of having a Black face in the room. Was my former supervisor truly seeing all of me or was I the Black face in the room to her?

A freeze response masked by an awkward laugh or smile is my typical response to interpersonal microaggressions, and then I devote countless mental energy later questioning whether I was allowed to be offended by it. As I revisit this racial microaggression, it becomes clearer to me that this is a moment in which I would feel more comfortable now speaking the truth of my experience and utilizing a microintervention. I worked closely with this supervisor for a year, we had a good working relationship, she had written me a strong letter of recommendation, and I did not fear any retaliation due to no longer being her supervisee. Microinterventions serve two functions of enhancing psychological well-being and sense of control and provide a range of responses that directly challenge or mitigate the effects of microaggressions. They are everyday words or actions that provide validation, affirmation of one's value and identities, support and encouragement, and reassurance that the target of the microaggression is not alone.[6] What I primarily needed in that conversation with my supervisor was validation of my thoughts and feelings around being offended and encouragement that I had the right to challenge and to educate her on the impact of her words.

Microinterventions can be divided into four strategic goals of 1) making the "invisible" visible, 2) disarming the microaggression, 3) educating the offender about the metacommunications they send, and 4) seeking external support when needed.[7] With making the "invisible" visible, the focus is on bringing the hidden meaning behind the comment or action into the perpetrator's awareness by using tactics like making the metacommunication explicit, challenging the stereotype, and asking for clarification.[8] For example, I could have humorously said to my supervisor, "Don't get me wrong, I love being Black, but I also know from your recommendation letter that I have more to offer an internship than my racial background" or I could have asked for clarification, "Did you realize that your comment suggests that I would only be appreciated for my diversity versus all of the qualities that make me a strong candidate?" The strategic goal of disarming the microaggression is to interrupt the comments or actions through highlighting the harmful impact, confronting what was said or done, or showing disagreement verbally and nonverbally.[9] In that moment, some statements I would make now are "I have to be honest in that I disagree with what you said" or "I do not view what you said in the same way, because it hurts to think that is the only reason you believe I would match for an internship." Educating the offender centers on facilitating a dialogue with the perpetrator of the microaggression by identifying what was offensive, relating it to their beliefs and values, and having them consider the viewpoint of marginalized members.[10] This is probably the strategy that I would have utilized, because I think my supervisor could have benefitted from recognizing the difference between the intent and impact of her words. I imagine myself saying, "I know that we both can tell that I am anxious and you want to reassure me, but your comment makes me feel like a token. It suggests that the only reason you think I am a competitive candidate is because of a program's need for racially diverse applicants." Lastly in situations in which targets of racial microaggressions believe it may not be safe or effective to directly address the situation, they can seek external support from supportive people, community services, therapy, and those with authoritative power in the institution.[11] As I mentioned earlier, it was important for me to have safe spaces in which I could validate and challenge my experiences with racism.

Microinterventions are often situation specific; how we use them could depend on a number of factors like our mood, energy level, nature of the relationship, power differentials, the culture of the academic program, and whether we think the person will be receptive to our feedback. However, it can be helpful to know for yourself which interventions come to you naturally and which ones are more challenging to use in situations. For example, as I was writing my potential responses in the prior paragraph, I found that I could think of several responses to educate the offender, but I stumbled with thinking of ways to disarm the microaggression. It is harder for me to directly confront microaggressions by disarming them because of my fear of being invalidated and appearing aggressive.

Exercise #2

This exercise will focus on practicing microinterventions.

Take a look at the microaggression that you reflected on earlier and practice using each microintervention in that situation. Try not to worry about whether the intervention would be effective or not and focus more on how it feels for you to use the microintervention. Which ones do you recognize as interventions that you might have used? Which ones do you find to be challenging? Which ones do you find to be easier to use?

When You're Playing the Game and Want Your Friends to Win Too

At some point, I learned the rules of the game and settled into the reality of my graduate program. There was not a specific moment that changed my perspective, but with time it became clearer that this was not going to be the academic home in which I would feel a full sense of comfort and safety. As graduate students of color, it can often feel like we are being held to a different standard. I recognized that I did not have the luxury of some of my White peers to ask for an extension on a deadline, to take an incomplete in a class, or to skip a colloquium. The aforementioned are real examples from my program and does not fully describe what I was experiencing when I witnessed them. It was more of a mix of jealousy, sadness, and resignation. I came to terms with the fact that my light switch needed to be on, and I could not be caught slipping in any situation.

Even so, I was proud of the progress I made, grateful for the genuine connections I formed with some professors and supervisors, and appreciative of the supportive relationships with my cohort. That last point I cannot emphasize enough—my cohort definitely made graduate school more manageable. We could lean on each other for assistance with assignments, find relief in never-ending jokes, share snacks when a stomach grumbled, and turn up when we actually had free time. So when the dissertation beast reared its ugly head, I naturally leaned into my support network at school to figure out ways to calm and lead the beast. In particular, I was participating regularly in anxiety-fueled communications with two close friends. We all shared the same core faculty member on our dissertation committees. He was a committee member on mine and the dissertation chair for my two friends. The dissertation chair is responsible for helping a doctoral candidate navigate the dissertation process, and the chair provides valuable feedback before other committee members are allowed to review your proposal.

It was the beginning of the fall semester and we were under a strict deadline to propose our dissertation to our committee so that we would be allowed to apply for internship. If your dissertation chair did not feel that you were ready to propose your idea, this meant that you would not be able to apply for internship and would be spending an additional year in the program. Needless to say, it was a recipe for stress, anxiety, and intense pressure, and none of us wanted to mess up the meal. I cannot recall if it was before or after I successfully proposed my dissertation idea, and I do not remember whether it was initially a text or phone call, but the pain in my friend's voice is what shapes the memory. She learned about a month before we could submit internship applications that she would not be allowed to propose her dissertation. Flashbacks of the summer came to my mind and feelings of anger and guilt arose about the ways in which she had been mistreated by her dissertation chair.

Throughout the process, evidenced in frequent conversations about dissertation progress with my two friends (one a Black woman and the other a White man), I noticed that they were being treated very differently by their dissertation chair, a White man. My White friend was in regular contact with his dissertation chair even while I believe the professor was on vacation. While the dissertation chair could be tough in his feedback, he still seemed to be actively involved and guiding my friend toward being able to meet the deadline. However, with my Black friend, he seemed to be constantly creating obstacles, harsher with his criticism, and passive toward providing clear direction. A month before the fall semester with the crucial deadline, he told her that they could not be in contact at all while he was traveling. This means that when the semester started, she was under unnecessary pressure and time constraints to get his approval.

When my friend would vent her frustrations about her dissertation chair, I struggled with how best to support her. I felt helpless and was unsure of how much to be solution-focused and how much to validate her concerns by highlighting the way in which I felt she was being treated differently by her dissertation chair. If I shared specific information, would it be validating or would it be demoralizing? Also, I did not know if I should be providing more concrete assistance, such as problem-solving around ways to advocate for herself or offering to provide feedback on her dissertation proposal. There was also the part of me that was focused on my own dissertation proposal and scared to ruffle any feathers since we shared the same committee member.

I include this example because as graduate students of color, we are impacted not only by racial microaggressions that directly affect us but also by the ways in which our fellow peers are negatively treated within the program. Again, I cannot speak to this professor's intent, but his actions suggest that he was engaging in demeaning ways toward his Black supervisee. And he was holding his White supervisee to a different standard. For example, with his White supervisee, he would provide constructive, direct feedback and with his Black supervisee, along with providing feedback, he would make disparaging comments about her writing and stated that he would be burdened with having to write her dissertation for her. In addition, he provided his Black supervisee with a vague, additional assignment that took time away from working on her dissertation proposal. In these moments, you are not always going to know what to do, and it is okay if you cannot think of an appropriate intervention. As a bystander, the intervention may not be as direct or powerful as you want. Sometimes, the intervention is about holding space so that your fellow classmate can tell you what they need or want and checking in with yourself to see if you have the resources to support them. Luckily, we are still friends and I had the opportunity recently to ask her what she needed from me at the time. As I was writing this chapter and reflecting, I kept feeling guilty and thinking that I did not do enough concrete actions to help my friend. My friend told me that she struggled with embarrassment and what she needed most from me was to be believed. How would things have felt differently if I had directly asked what she needed rather than making assumptions at the time? I believed in her and knew that she was more than capable, and maybe the experience would have been less isolating if I had been able to communicate that directly to her.

Exercise #3

With this exercise, I want you to think about your supportive network within your graduate program and to gain a better sense of what you might be needing from your peers.

1. How would you describe your relationship with peers? Supportive or not supportive? Close or distant?
2. If there are students of color in your program, how is your relationship similar or different in comparison to other students?
3. With regard to support, what do you think you are needing or wanting from your peers and how comfortable do you feel asking for it?
4. Is there a fellow classmate who you are concerned about and what would it be like to check in with them?

Concluding Thoughts

We made it. This chapter is for us by us. As I text my friend to ask some follow-up questions regarding her experience in graduate school and I feel that fear arise again questioning the benefit of publicly sharing our challenges, I am reminded that we and other fellow students of color graduated despite the obstacles that were unfairly placed on our courses. As a Black psychology doctoral student, at times I questioned whether my identities were fully seen and considered in my graduate program and whether I could speak openly and safely about the racial microaggressions I experienced at the time. While racial microaggressions are unfortunately still too frequent occurrences, I now feel more capable and empowered to address them when I choose to, and I also feel in a position of power to help other graduate students of color navigate their courses. Through multiple roles, it is rewarding to be able to assist graduate students by being an interviewer, supervisor, mentor, and dissertation committee member and facilitating didactics and workshops. Graduate school is challenging at a professional and personal level, and as students of color, we face additional barriers centered around race-related experiences. When facing racial microaggressions, we can find ourselves struggling to sort out our thoughts and emotions as well as developing an appropriate response or intervention. I hope with this chapter you feel less alone and better equipped to address these challenges in the future. This chapter is for you and me. This chapter is for us by us.

Takeaways for Graduate Students (of Color)

- Take time to remind yourself that regardless of the path that led you into graduate school, you belong in the academic room and your experiences are valid.
- Find safe "counterspaces" in which you feel seen and validated and can openly talk about any academic challenges and racial microaggressions.
- "Counterspaces" can be things like supportive peer and faculty relationships, diversity organizations, mentors, and therapists.
- If possible, form connections with other graduate students of color, whether inside or outside of your academic program, and schedule time to regularly check in with each other regarding needs and progress.
- There is no right or wrong way to respond to a racial microaggression. It is okay to not respond and focus on yourself. It is also fine to take your time to process your thoughts and feelings and get feedback before developing a response or microintervention.
- When developing an intervention, take into account power differentials and negative consequences of responding to the offender.
- Think about any potential harm toward yourself and your academic career and which consequences you can live with if you decide to implement an intervention.

Suggestions for Faculty and Administrators

- It is important to recognize that diversity and retention efforts should not focus only on recruiting diverse students.

- The cultural environment of academic programs should be examined for any potential formal and informal barriers to graduate students of color.
- It is recommended that academic departments have their own diversity and inclusion committees that can consist of faculty, alumni, current graduate students, and consultants.
- A diversity and inclusion committee could perform several functions, such as reviewing academic content, organizing workshops and didactics, and serving as a mediating space for faculty and graduate students to address race-related experiences and concerns.
- It is important to note that faculty is going to differ regarding levels of self-awareness and commitment around addressing diversity issues.
- Administrators should ensure that mandatory trainings that focus on topics such as power and privilege, intersectionality, conscious and unconscious racism, and racial microaggressions are being conducted for all staff.
- Faculty and administrators should familiarize themselves with microinterventions and self-reflect on moments in which they have been offenders, allies, or targets of racial microaggressions.
- When graduate students of color address racial microaggressions, faculty and administrators should be receptive and validating toward students' experiences.
- Faculty and administrators should encourage a collaborative approach when addressing racial microaggressions and discuss appropriate interventions and next steps.

Suggestions for Mental Health Professionals

- In working with students of color, it is important to familiarize yourself with current research that addresses issues around diversity, recruitment, and retention in graduate programs.
- Therapy can serve as a "counterspace," and mental health professionals should make an effort to focus on validation as well as on how to respond or implement change.
- Mental health professionals should have potential resources that can connect students with supportive environments outside of their academic programs.

- It is important to understand the complexity of racial microaggressions and to be aware of research around microinterventions.
- Mental health professionals should take time to self-reflect on moments in which they have been offenders, allies, or targets of racial microaggressions.

∼

CHAPTER EIGHT

Cultivating and Maintaining Good Mentorship

Martin D. Ruck, Juliana Karras-Jean Gilles,
and Isabelle M. Elisha

Good mentorship in graduate school is integral to student success and well-being.[1] Getting the mentorship you need will take work. There are some important things to keep in mind as you consider how to and how not to choose an advisor. Since some strategies work better than others, we will give advice for how to: work effectively with your advisor, address problems when they arise, and get your mentorship needs met inside *and* outside of the advisory relationship. Knowing how to tackle different situations that may come up with an advisor can help you head off problems even before they start, so throughout the chapter we use practical examples and end with an exercise to help you identify your goals and mentorship needs.

Procuring the "Perfect" Mentorship

There is no "perfect" mentor. Mentors are humans with complex lives, insecurities, and competing demands on their time, energy, and resources. Depending on how long they have been in academia, you may be their fifth or forty-fifth student. You may also be their only student or one among many advisees. Regardless of how experienced your mentor is, as with any relationship, it is unlikely that all of your needs will be met. However, a quality relationship with your mentor(s) can ensure your successful progression through graduate school. In cultivating a productive relationship with your mentor, an intersectional lens[2] is useful for considering how your ethnicity, gender, and/or other social identities interconnect to shape your lived experiences, including your relationship with your mentor. For example, someone who shares your ethnic/racial identity may have some similar experiences; however, your interactions with the same people or systems may differ due to other factors such as gender identity, socioeconomic background, or religious affiliation.[3] Our unique lived experiences will inform how we orient our way through graduate school. Understanding this can help you figure out what you need for your advisory relationship(s) to succeed. Throughout this chapter, we will employ an intersectional approach to discuss illustrative examples of different mentor-mentee interactions that may arise.

Goodness of Fit

Although you will likely be paired with an advisor whose research interests align with yours, this does not guarantee a good fit. Similarly, if a mentor shares your social identities (e.g., ethnic/racial, gender), it does not guarantee that they will provide the support you need. Knowing that support can come from mentors who do not share your social identities can be helpful.[4]

Central to the mentor-mentee relationship is how your advisor provides feedback on your work.[5] Graduate training is not about only receiving praise. Your mentor should push you beyond your current abilities, ideally by encouraging you to expand your skills, while supporting your progress along the way. However, tension may arise if you do not feel supported in reaching your goals. The mapping activity at the end of this chapter will help you discern what type of feedback you find helpful and what is potentially problematic. Feedback from advisors that feels excessively harsh to one of your fellow students may not have the same impact on you. Part of navigating the advisory relationship is understanding that your own perception plays a major role in it. How you interpret your mentor's tone and your reaction to it is largely subjective and depends on the interactions between your own and your advisor's personalities, your prior training, and the norms of your program. For that reason, it is important that you try to gain an understanding of your mentor's style early in the relationship.

To determine your advisor's style, consider asking them about their graduate training, how their mentors provided them with feedback, and what their idea of "good" mentorship is. For example, each of the coauthors of this chapter at some point had to work through feeling overwhelmed or upset by feedback from a mentor. Knowing that your mentor came from a tradition of in-depth critique with limited praise can prevent you from being discouraged by receiving a paper full of red-tracked changes and comments. Although it can feel off-putting—especially if your undergraduate writing was highly praised—this may reflect your advisor trying to get you to write like a more seasoned scholar rather than a student. Near the end of the chapter, we provide a reflective activity which will allow you to proactively handle those stressors that may impede your progress.

Pretenure/Posttenure Mentor Trade-offs

Academic careers have a developmental path, and where your mentor is on this path can shape your experience. Graduate programs may provide faculty with student achievement milestones, but your mentor's own career-stage-based needs or expectations will shape what they require from their students. Tenure-track (TT) professors move through three "levels," starting with assistant, then associate, and full professor. The greatest challenge TT faculty face is moving from assistant to associate, as this typically aligns with earning "tenure." Understanding your mentor's professional journey can help you understand the unique pressures they face, and thus better navigate your relationship with them.

Junior faculty who are striving toward tenure typically invest extensive time and energy into their research program while seeking to establish themselves within the institution and learning to navigate institutional politics. Under the "publish or perish" ideology that dominates academia, during tenure reviews teaching and mentoring are not awarded equal weight compared to publishing.[6] As a result, junior faculty are likely to be focused on establishing productive research programs; for some this means giving graduate students significant responsibilities and opportunities. But, as they work toward tenure, there may be fewer authorship opportunities and more "thank you for your contribution" notes. Junior faculty mentors may have the expectation (or requirement) to be first author on any publication with student(s). Alternatively, working with junior faculty may give you more opportunities to take an active role in the full life cycle of research or a hands-on role in grant-writing, as these faculty are more likely to be engaged extensively with these activities and therefore may benefit from graduate student assistance.

Conversely, tenured or more senior faculty often have more established research programs and professional networks. Since pressures for publication become less intense as faculty become more senior,[7] there may be more opportunities for you to coauthor publications as lead author, with them playing a supporting role. But it is also possible that their productivity is more limited. This depends on the faculty member, their research, and their field—all of which vary widely. Relatedly, as faculty become more senior, they often see less benefit from participating in activities such as academic conferences—as a result they may have limited interest in student-level opportunities for professional development. If a faculty member has been in academia for fifteen-plus years, they may be less cognizant of changes in what makes graduate students competitive on the job market—which can limit their ability to most effectively support your transition out of graduate school. However, senior faculty may be particularly skilled in successfully navigating the politics of your program. They may have insights about their colleagues' working styles that junior faculty do not have or are unwilling to share. For example, senior faculty may be better able to direct you toward good members of your mentorship network and steer you away from faculty who may not be ideal for you. In addition, senior faculty often wield more social capital and are thus better positioned to advocate on your behalf.

Ultimately, working with more junior or more senior faculty both have their pros and cons. To figure out who may be the better fit for you to work with, take note not only of where they are in their professional journey, but also consider how they approach their work. Ask yourself if they have a *collaborator* or *competitor* orientation? Do they have mainly solo publications? Or a team of collaborators? In what order are their graduate students positioned on publications? Do they have publications with multiple students or just one? As personal rivalry and discontent can tear at the fabric of a mentorship relation-ship, it's important to gauge your advisor's working style regardless of their level. As in the example below, Randy learned the hard way that concretizing expectations is key to sustaining a positive working rela-tionship with your mentor.

> At the end of Randy's first year as a student in a master's program, his faculty mentor who is working toward tenure invites him to help prepare a manuscript for publication. Randy is asked to write up sections in the literature review, on which he receives positive feedback and is asked to further expand them. Versions of Randy's sections are included in the final manuscript. Later on, the faculty mentor also asks Randy to help with the analysis, complete the reference check, prepare tables and figures, do a final read through of the whole document, and upload the submission in the journal's manuscript portal. Throughout, Randy went above and beyond what was asked of him. While uploading the final files, Randy discovers that the faculty mentor did not consider his con-tributions to merit authorship. Rather, Randy's name is among students listed in the acknowledgments.
>
> Randy felt frustrated and confused that his involvement did not merit authorship. He learned that this faculty mentor's criteria for authorship differed from other faculty mentors his peers worked with. Ultimately, this experience led to a rift between Randy and his mentor, pushing Randy to pursue a working relationship with another faculty member he believed was more likely to include him as an author on publications to which he contributed.

This experience taught Randy that assumptions regarding author-ship can never be made. Instead, before contributing to papers, he learned to explicitly ask what "counts" for authorship.

Boundaries

It can be difficult to find the right balance between your personal needs and the practical ones that come with being a graduate student. Ideally, your mentor-mentee relationship provides room for both a sense of col-legiality and comradery—but whether you need more warmth or more guidance depends on what style helps you progress. When considering the ideal social dynamics with your mentor, however, you ultimately need a potential collaborator who can help launch you professionally rather than a confidant. This dynamic is due in part to the unique nature of the mentor-mentee relationship, wherein there lies an inherent power imbalance.

Mentor-mentee relationships vary based on numerous factors. Junior faculty are often younger, having more recently completed graduate school. Closeness in age and experience may create a temptation to develop close friendships with graduate students that do not necessarily take into account the power imbalance. This may lead to unexpected issues that strain the relationship, particularly if the distinction between professional and personal becomes blurred. Here, it is important to remember that, ultimately, your advisor's primary role is to be your academic and professional mentor, not your buddy. Moreover, the graduate training model requires your mentor to act as the main gatekeeper of your progression through graduate school. Your mentor is preparing you to transition from being a student to a colleague. As a result, over time you should gain or be entrusted with more autonomy as your responsibilities change. Your mentor will, however, always retain some form of "seniority" over you. In choosing a mentor, take note of faculty who overly infantilize their graduate students, as their power should instead be leveraged toward elevating their students. Mentors display this by valuing intellectual equity and fostering a growth-oriented mentor-mentee relationship that evolves positively over time.

Avoid viewing your advisor as static; rather, just as you are growing and developing, so are they. It is helpful to maintain your intersectional lens and to focus on being growth-oriented in your expectations of yourself and your advisor. As relationships take time, you may not be privy to the intersecting identities or day-to-day life of your mentor(s). Your mentor may encounter pressing personal issues that you are not aware of but are impacted by. Although the boundaries of an appropriate mentor relationship are fuzzy, communicating your needs while respecting theirs is instrumental in developing a positive relationship with your mentor.

Self-Advocacy

As in any long-term relationship, during your graduate journey conflicts with your mentors will arise. The very nature of the student-mentor relationship as one where you are a subordinate *and* a colleague-in-training may make tensions inevitable. A challenge in resolving these conflicts may be learning how and when to advocate for yourself. Self-advocacy is key to developing a sense of agency that advances your progress. A sense of agency refers to the ability to consider options, form meanings, and engage in activities that reflect your own individual wishes and goals.[8] Between program requirements and your mentors' guidelines, too often a sense of agency may be absent from your graduate journey.

One tool for cultivating agency is to become aware of the standards by which student progress is measured in your department and discipline. Prioritize experiences that allow you to meet that standard, and remember that being visible, present, and communicative is as important as setting clear boundaries. When navigating your graduate school progression, be aware that your mentor(s) may have their own idea of a schedule for you that may not be compatible with your ideal. To communicate your best-case scenario schedule and goals with your mentor, the mapping activity will help you identify your needs and goals. But, be aware that they may not be respected, thus it can be to your advantage to have your own more realistic schedule and goals that you do not share. If a problem arises, your first line of defense is the university's or department's graduate student handbook, so become familiar with the rules for student progress.

The standard measure for student progress tends to be whether you are reaching milestones that are necessary to get a degree. With the goal of graduating in mind, try to be thoughtful in picking and choosing your activities. Although it may look great on your curriculum vitae (CV) to be on multiple academic service committees, they can drain your time. Learn to be protective of your time and ensure that you have a clear sense of what's expected of you before agreeing to get involved in any academic endeavor. Prior to committing to an activity, identify what the outcome or "compensation" for your participation will be. This is especially important for students from underrepresented groups who are more likely to be asked to participate in endeavors that would make them a representative for their ethnic/social group, as illustrated by Kenya's story.

Kenya is a doctoral candidate in a field where research and publishing are the standard measures for progress. She is one of just two African

American students in her PhD program. Kenya has noticed that she is asked to serve on committees and attend departmental social events more often than graduate students from other ethnic groups. While no one has explicitly stated that they want her participation because of her ethnicity, she suspects that might be the case. Kenya is happy to be an engaged, active, and visible member of the program, but she realizes that the time she spends on committee work might be better spent on her research. Recently one of her dissertation committee members, Professor Jones, expressed concern that she was not making progress on her dissertation. He also asked Kenya to be a student representative on the program's admissions committee. Kenya is already on two other committees, has a part-time job, and is on a panel for first-generation college students. She does not want to join another committee as she fears that the time spent in meetings and reviewing applications will take away from her writing. Still, she does not want to offend Professor Jones.

While it may be personally meaningful to participate in academic service, sometimes the best activity is self-advocacy. Remaining focused on the goal of getting your degree and not overextending yourself is key to meeting your goals. As a student, your power is somewhat limited, but after completing your degree, you will be in a stronger position to advocate for others and avoid some of the tokenism that can happen in academic spaces that are not diverse.

Navigating Tensions

Tensions between faculty and students are usually unspoken but important to be aware of. For students whose social identities have been historically underrepresented in higher education, maintaining a sense of agency can be particularly challenging if conflicts arise. Faculty are humans who hold underlying assumptions regarding students' skills or interests and in some cases, prejudice. Faculty misunderstanding how cultural factors shape students' graduate journey is not uncommon.[9] As all humans hold implicit biases, this cuts across disciplines, with even the most well-intentioned faculty making problematic assumptions.

If you encounter stereotyping, discomfort, or even outright discrimination, there is no guaranteed strategy that will yield the result you desire. Discussing the issue with a school counselor or someone you trust who is familiar with graduate school can help you process the experience. Some students may feel comfortable addressing these issues directly with their advisor. In other instances, the faculty member's insensitivity may preclude this from being a viable option. Looking up university policies and resources is important, as universities typically provide students with access to an ombudsperson or departmental student faculty advocate who can help address and resolve conflicts. Sometimes the ultimate form of self-advocacy students must employ in graduate school, however, is deciding to change advisors, as outlined below.

During the first year of her doctoral program, Gloria was paired with a senior faculty mentor whose research was reasonably aligned with her interests. Through advising meetings, Gloria realized quickly that she and her advisor had very different working styles. Whenever Gloria asked for clarification about her advisor's feedback, the advisor became defensive and stopped Gloria from diverging from the advisor's perspective. During one particularly uncomfortable meeting, Gloria's advisor responded to her questions by saying: "I thought Asian women were supposed to be submissive. You sure aren't." Seeing Gloria's distressed facial expression, the advisor assured her that the comment was a joke, not an attempt to offend. Gloria was very upset by the comment but feared that reporting it would further delay her progress. She reasoned that her advisor was simply awkward and told herself to be patient. Gloria was determined to make the best of a difficult situation, but anytime she tried to voice needs that conflicted with her advisor's plans for her, the advisor shut her out. Attempts to address her concerns with her advisor led to the advisor "ghosting" Gloria. With no resolution by the beginning of her second year, she initiated a conversation with her advisor about her timeline and goals. The same issues resurfaced, with her advisor being noncommittal and unresponsive to Gloria's desire to complete exam requirements in a timely fashion to keep on track with her cohort. Gloria consulted with upper-level students, who helped her identify another faculty member whose work aligned with her interests and was willing to take on new advisees. Before communicating the shift to her original advisor, Gloria secured the support of the graduate student faculty advocate and a commitment from her new advisor.

It was in Gloria's best interest to make this switch well before she moved toward qualifying exams or the dissertation proposal stage. As students advance, it is often more difficult to change advisors, but it is still possible. In Gloria's situation, her progress was thwarted by a dysfunctional relationship. Faculty advisors know that student progress often depends on their responsivity. By ignoring her messages, Gloria's advisor made a conscious decision to delay her progress. In addition, the offensive stereotype the advisor used to deflect Gloria's questions reflects the type of microaggressions often experienced by students of color.[10] Microaggressions in the form of comments or actions that make derogatory inferences about one's ethnic group are draining and disarming. They force the recipient to diverge from their course of action and lead them onto a time-consuming track where they question and reassess interactions. In Gloria's case, the experience temporarily stopped her from advocating for herself. Even if the use of the stereotype was unintentional, students should be aware that tolerating an advisor's "awkwardness" or outright bigotry may seem to be the safest course of action, but it is likely not a winning strategy as this behavior may continue if left unaddressed. This is why it is important to cultivate a network for mentorship and support that extends beyond a single advisor. More experienced students, faculty, and administrators can aid graduate students in processing adverse experiences and deciding how to proceed. This is particularly important for students from ethnic/ racial minority groups who may have difficulty finding faculty who understand the challenges they face. For students from all backgrounds, finding academic mentors who are available and willing to listen to them is essential.[11]

Curating a Mentorship Network

Expectations, requirements, and mentorship standards vary by program and discipline. Making it through graduate school depends on figuring out your program's written and unwritten rules as well as your mentor's preferences. Some programs require you to assemble a graduate committee while in others you may work with only one or two faculty members. Triangulating multiple faculty's perspectives can be valuable in navigating the informal rules that guide your program. However, an important caveat is that some advisors are possessive of their students and may not respond well to your developing relationships with other faculty. In addition, there may be tensions between faculty members of which you are unaware. In order to build a strong mentorship support network, be sure to get a sense of your advisor's attitude toward your working with other faculty. Some advisors may explicitly state that they do not want you to collaborate with faculty member X, but it may be more likely to be implicit and subtle. For this reason, it is a good idea to talk to other graduate students about their experiences with faculty.

Another strategy for developing a network of mentors is to take courses with faculty whose work interests you. This is a common strategy for developing relationships with faculty beyond your primary advisor. As you get to know more faculty, you can curate a network of mentors by maximizing relationships with faculty who can provide you with support that builds on the groundwork you have done with your primary mentor. To begin this process, explore your program's faculty webpage to gain familiarity with faculty members' areas of expertise. Then, identify courses taught by faculty whose work interests you. These two steps will be important parts of mapping a strategic approach to getting the mentorship you need. Keep in mind that your "best" academic mentor may not be a faculty member.[12,13] Rather, you should remain open to reaching out to postdoc or supportive upper-level graduate students. Their progression through graduate school is more recent than that of faculty, which may enable them to provide you with unique insights for successfully navigating the particular climate of your program.

Relatedly, a successful mentorship network is about more than academic progress.[14] It also acts as a community of support that can nurture your interconnected identities.[15] All students benefit from such support, but it is especially significant for students from underrepresented backgrounds who may be alienated through even casual interactions. We see this in Sam's story.

> Sam is hardworking and has an enviable CV for a master's student. Sam identifies as nonbinary and prefers to use the pronouns "they," "their," and "them." However, as the only nonbinary person in the program, Sam struggles with the fact that some faculty and fellow students are unsure how to use the correct gender-neutral pronouns and frequently misgender Sam. Sam has had to figure out when to correct colleagues

and faculty. For example, after an awkward exchange with a professor who questioned Sam's preferred pronouns, Sam needed advice. The absence of nonbinary faculty at the institution meant having to search more broadly for mentorship. Through an online search, Sam found a social media group for gender-nonconforming academics. Although none of the group members are from Sam's academic discipline, Sam has had some very positive and empowering mentorship experiences through the group. Because of a shared gender identity, the group is supportive and understanding in ways that well-meaning departmental colleagues cannot be. Sam finds membership in the group to be nurturing and cannot imagine making it through grad school without the group's support.

For students like Sam who identify with the LGBTQ+ community but are not actively engaged in LGBTQ+ research, it may be challenging to meet academics who share that aspect of their identity. But, by finding a way to link with other nonbinary faculty and students via social media–based support networks, Sam could feel more connected and empowered. Research examining stressors among graduate students indicates that feelings of isolation can disrupt your progress.[16] Using social media and identity-based associations to enhance your network of support can help you develop a better sense of balance.[17] Conversing and exchanging resources with people who experience oppressions that are similar to the ones you face can help you gain perspective. There is value in engaging with people who either share aspects of your experience or are committed allies, even when their areas of academic focus do not align with yours.[18]

Leveraging Your Network

When you leave graduate school, the hope is that you have developed an array of skills that will position you to succeed in your postgraduate pursuits. As such, you should prioritize getting involved with research and opportunities to develop the skills you will need to succeed. Some benefits of a diverse mentorship network include not only the insights yielded by their distinct personal backgrounds, but also their years of experience and expertise. Working exclusively with a single advisor runs the risk of limiting access to opportunities that could be instrumental in your professional development, as illustrated by Maria's experience below.

Maria is a doctoral candidate at a prestigious institution who works with Professor Sanchez, a highly respected researcher. She has been first author on several articles published in the top journals in her field. She is currently on the job market seeking a tenure-track position. Her preference is to end up at an R1 (universities with the highest research activity) institution, but she is applying to a wide variety of institutions. Based on her qualifications, Maria expected to be able to pick and choose from a number of offers. Much to her surprise, despite having successful interviews at major institutions, she's only been offered positions at smaller colleges. To better understand why, Professor Sanchez reached out to colleagues who were on search committees for an explanation. He was told that while Maria is viewed as brilliant, her work appears indistinguishable from his. A colleague at one institution went as far as to suggest that they would rather not hire his clone.

Maria's work was seen as indistinguishable from her well-established faculty advisor's scholarship. Some hiring committees might have asked Maria how her work differed from that of Professor Sanchez, but usually the job candidate bears responsibility for communicating this. Clearly describing how your program of research differs from your advisor's work showcases the uniqueness of your own work, thus preventing direct comparison with your advisor's work. In addition, some might contend that Professor Sanchez's role as a mentor does not extend beyond providing Maria with opportunities in areas he is familiar with. Thus, it is your responsibility as a student to find opportunities beyond those offered by your advisor to help you develop your individual identity as a scholar. One major benefit of going outside of your immediate advisory network is the possibility of acquiring new skills, as illustrated by Veronica's experience.

While mapping the analytical strategy for her dissertation proposal, Veronica found a complex methodology that perfectly aligned with her research aims. But, when she presented this idea to her advisor and dissertation committee chair, her advisor was concerned that Veronica had not previously used this approach or software before. The chair also did not have any familiarity with the approach and could not therefore provide guidance. Veronica recognized that her chair's concerns were valid; however, she was confident in her ability to figure it out. The meeting ended with the chair urging Veronica to consider another approach, so she took it upon herself to reach out to another faculty member in her program who had used this exact methodology and asked whether they could provide analytical support. The faculty member enthusiastically agreed to provide support. Fortunately, this faculty member also had a good relationship with Veronica's chair, so Veronica's chair agreed and worked with Veronica to formalize the plan; the additional faculty member became a member of Veronica's committee and provided invaluable methodological support. As a result of this experience, Veronica developed lasting mentorship relationships with both her chair and the committee member. She has continued to successfully collaborate with them since completing her degree.

Veronica was not only able to develop new analytical expertise, but also to advocate for herself with the support of a new member of her mentorship network. While she may or may not reuse this analytic approach, it adds an element to her work that is distinct from her mentor.

Teaching

Research experience is essential, but when you go on the job market, having skills and experiences beyond research can make you more versatile. Take advantage of opportunities to teach, act as a teaching assistant (TA), or guest lecture, as teaching requires you to be comfortable with public speaking, to organize your thoughts, and to learn to explain your topic to an audience that does not share your expertise. All three of those skills are applicable to other activities. Opportunities for teaching will vary by institution. For example, some graduate programs have a teaching requirement while others do not. There are also institutions where students who teach a course outside of their assigned funding package are not paid, but receive academic credit instead. Gather a sense of what is possible through conversations with faculty and other graduate students.

Teaching opportunities also allow you to document your professional development. For example, student evaluations provide evidence of your performance as an educator. If you are the sole instructor for a course, be sure to request a formal teaching observation from a faculty member and have the feedback included as a letter for your file. If you are acting as a TA, ask the instructor if you can lecture a class and request a formal observation of your teaching. Consider also asking the instructor whether questions can be added to the student evaluation about your work as a TA so that you can get student-level evaluation of your TA role. When you go on the job market, these observations and evaluations can be included in your teaching portfolio. If your primary advisor has not observed your teaching, you should consider discussing your teaching evaluations with them so they can speak to this aspect of your professional development in any letters of recommendations they may be asked to provide for you.

Mapping Your Mentorship Needs

Good graduate mentorship requires mentors who are available, supportive, and invested in your development as an emerging scholar. But the quality of your training depends on you being proactive in identifying your needs and communicating them in a timely, professional manner with your mentor. Time is one of the most precious resources in graduate school—thereby it is in your best interest to think about and/or map out some of your professional and personal goals early on. The mapping activity provided below will help you identify *where* and *how* your primary mentor can support you and what goals may require you to build a mentorship network.

In addition to identifying and communicating your goals, it is important that you stay on your mentor's radar. As faculty are likely working with students who are each at different stages in their progression, use your "planning" meetings to ensure that your advisor is aware of those deadlines that will allow you to make timely progression through your graduate program. Keep in mind that comprehensive examinations often require formal paperwork and there may be annual deadlines and required signatures from your advisor and other key faculty, such as the department chair. The student handbook for your program should outline these details; however, it is a good idea to talk with students who have recently completed these milestones to make yourself aware of any "unwritten" guidelines. Ultimately, it is up to you to stay informed and communicate your goals so that your advisor can support you as needed.

Reflective Mapping Activity
Find a quiet space to reflect for thirty minutes. On a blank paper in landscape orientation, draw two adjacent circles that overlap slightly. Write *Personal* in the left-hand circle and *Professional* in the right-hand

circle. Then, fill both out by responding to the following questions: (1) What motivates me and brings me satisfaction? (2) What are my greatest strengths and skills? (3) What are some areas in my life where I would like to grow? (4) Why do I want to grow in these areas? (5) What do I need to help me grow in these areas? and (6) How will I know that I've grown in these areas?

On a second page, map how to meet your goals by working backwards using your *Personal/Professional* circles as guides. Rotate your paper to a landscape orientation, making space for six columns by drawing lines from the top to the bottom. Working from left to right, title each section as follows with their corresponding guiding question: (1) Goals—*What are my personal and professional aims?* (2) Knowledge/ Skills to Develop—*What do I need to meet my goals?* (3) Resources and Support Needed—*What do I need to develop these capacities?* (4) Action Items—*How will I acquire those resources?* (5) Indicators of Success— *How will I measure my progress?* (6) Goal Completion Dates—*By when do I hope to achieve my goal(s)?*

Expanding the brainstorming you completed in your *Personal/ Professional* circles, complete each of the six sections by starting from your Goal(s) column and working from left to right toward your Goal Completion Dates. Use the guiding questions to respond to each section, starting with one or multiple goals. Once each section is filled, draw connector lines between sections, and consider whether any goals require duplicate resources or whether you need to revise any goals or completion dates after considering the extent of what will be required to achieve those goals within the original time frame. *Personal* goal areas may include health and wellness (e.g., regular exercise, weekly digital detoxes, self-care routines), familial or relational needs (e.g., advancing your relationship with a significant other), and financial goals (e.g., paying off student loans). While *Professional* goals include the obvious goal of completing your degree, it may be more helpful to break down the elements of your timing and programmatic requirements that you need to complete to get there. Additional *Professional* goals may include publications, teaching experience, networking, conference submissions, and so on.

Think of this as a living organizational tool, to revisit and update regularly. As it is normal for your interests and goals to evolve as you progress through graduate school, we recommend revisiting this map each semester and revising it if you need to. Prior to meeting(s) with your mentor, use it to help identify your priority *Professional* goals to discuss with them to keep you on track. Make it part of your routine to create agenda items to discuss with your mentor, document decisions made in that meeting, and recap those decisions via email or some written documentation you share with your mentor to ensure you're on the same page and have a clear sense of direction. If possible, schedule a subsequent meeting with your mentor to ensure you have a tangible date by which to check in and goals to be completed by then. Depending on the relationship with your mentor, it may be appropriate to discuss some of your *Personal* goals; however, as time is one of your most precious resources in graduate school, ask yourself what is the best way for you to use that meeting time with your mentor to maximize that relationship.

Takeaways for Students

- Use a tool like the mapping activity to help articulate your goals and plan your route to achieve them.
- Remember a successful mentorship experience depends on communicating with your advisor, remaining aware of your program's requirements, and revising your plans as needed.
- Successful progress in graduate school requires you to be consistent and active, approach mentor relationships as ongoing works in progress, recognize where and how you can cultivate the supports you need to be successful, and advocate for yourself to meet your goals.
- If your advisor relationship becomes maladaptive, discriminatory, or even outright abusive (e.g., emotionally), advocate for yourself by being flexible and open to working with other faculty or changing advisors, seeking additional supports (e.g., academic allies, thesis committee, psychological counseling), or filing a complaint with the program and/or institution.

Suggestions for Faculty and Administrators

- Be open, empathic, and validating of how hard it is for students to bring up issues with their advisors due to the power differential.

- Educate yourself on the multiple intersecting identities and roles beyond that of grad student that can complicate students' academic and professional progress.
- Your experience is valuable and graduate students benefit from your sharing it. The sharing humanizes you and can help graduate students feel less isolated.
- Think about how the job market has changed over time. What do graduate students need to know? Are there additional resources or workshops your institution should be providing? How can you be supportive as students transition into postgraduate life?
- Ask yourself regularly: How do inequality, power, and privilege shape your own and graduate students' perceptions, opportunities, and experiences?

Suggestions for Mental Health Professionals

- Become more knowledgeable about challenges students may face with their mentors, advisors, and principal investigators (PIs). Reading this chapter is a great first step!
- Be open, empathic, and validating of how hard it is for students to address issues with their advisors due to the power differential.
- Do not assume that all advisor issues originate from the student. Consider the possible contributions of the advisor, the program, and the institution.
- Educate yourself on the multiple intersecting identities and roles beyond that of grad student that can complicate students' academic and professional progress.
- Offer thesis and dissertation groups with space for advisor issues to be discussed.
- Offer yearly workshops on working more effectively with advisors, mentors, and PIs.
- Offer academic consultations, which may be less stigmatizing for students to request and attend than individual counseling.
- Ask yourself regularly: How do inequality, power, and privilege shape your own and graduate students' perceptions, opportunities, and experiences?

PART III

~

WHO AM I,
AND WHY AM I HERE?

~

CHAPTER NINE

When Thesis Meets Diapers

Journeys of Graduate Student Parents

Nicole Benedicto Elden

So, you decided to be a graduate student and a parent at the same time! Well, I'm glad you're here because we have a lot to discuss. Did you know that approximately 5 to 10 percent[1,2] of grad students are parents or become parents while they are in grad school? You're certainly not alone even if you sometimes feel like no one can understand. That's right, there are other grad parents out there who are mind-numbingly sleep deprived, juggling worries about school, advisors, jobs, thesis, kids, spouses, parents, asking themselves *What the hell am I doing*, and ruminating daily about the joys of dropping out. The good news is that if you truly want a graduate degree, if you are willing to seek help and be flexible, then your degree is achievable. In fact, many grad parents who attained their degrees this way have told me that it is worthwhile.

As a surviving grad parent, I still cherish the memory of hearing my name called as I was hooded (a convocation ceremony for the doctoral degree) and my daughter's sweet, explosive voice in the audience saying "That's my mamma!" I remember clutching that degree in my hand, sobbing and thinking *I REALLY DESERVE THIS!* This sentiment was not coming from a place of arrogance but from memories of the many, many sacrifices, personally and professionally, that I had to make to be on that stage obtaining that piece of paper. Aside from giving birth to my daughter, that was the proudest moment of my entire life!

Of course, I cannot share with you the glory of the destination without also sharing the meandering paths, the detours, and all the agonizing (sometimes bruising) bumps along the way. After all, there is another truth to being a parent in grad school. It can be painfully hard! Perhaps I can exemplify this best by sharing with you another day in my life as a grad parent.

I look wistfully out the coffee shop window to the beauty of Prospect Park. I wonder if I will ever get to enjoy that park with my toddler without the specter of my dissertation haunting me! Before long, uncontrollable tears are rolling down my cheeks. I wipe my tears away as the waitress brings me coffee and looks at me sympathetically. I can tell she is curious why I cry every time I'm there. but I'm too embarrassed of my tears and feel unworthy of her sympathy.

Memories of earlier that morning continue to assail and overwhelm me. It is 10:00 a.m. and I am saying goodbye to my three-year-old to work on a dissertation I have come to despise. Her little hands are clasped tightly around my neck and tears are streaming down her face and landing on my cheek.

"No Mamma, don't go. Stay with me!!"

I unclasp her hands, look into her incredibly sad brown eyes, kiss her tears, and explain once again the reason I am leaving her. The same reason I've given her every Saturday morning for the past two years.

"Mamma has to finish her work but as soon as it is 4:00 p.m. Mamma will be back and we will spend the rest of the afternoon doing whatever you want . . . I promise . . . so start thinking about what you would like to do . . . anything you want."

I say this with confidence and enthusiasm for her sake, but the facade fades away as soon as I walk out the door. I start to feel a pounding in my head, and I realize I have been holding my breath and pushing down a lump in my throat. My familiar and constant companions emerge— sadness, worry, doubt, guilt, shame, and rage. What kind of mother am I to leave my child that way? Should I just quit and focus on parenting and my job . . . but what about all my efforts, six years of my life . . . not to mention all that money?! I am also the first in my family to pursue a doctorate. What kind of role model would I be to my daughter, to other Filipino American grad students, and to myself if I quit? Why am I not done with my dissertation yet? Why can't I get the help I need to finish this? Nothing I do these days seems to be good enough.

I share this very private and painful experience with you because I have heard versions of it recounted over and over for the past twenty years from high-achieving grad parents overwhelmingly challenged to complete their master's or doctoral degrees. The specific work and thesis they are trying to complete may differ. The number and age of the children they are fretting over may change. They may be dealing with different family issues, academic and work conflicts, and identity issues. However, the sadness, joy, worry, doubt, pride, shame, excitement, rage, and, above all, *guilt* remains consistent.

I have four main goals for this chapter: 1) To help you develop self-reflection and self-compassion for the many grad parent tasks, roles, and expectations that you are juggling; 2) To convey the message that you are not alone through examples of the lived experiences of real-life grad parents, past and present, who share with you their myriad internal, interpersonal, and sociocultural experiences and conflicts; 3) To incorporate practical and pragmatic tools and strategies to help you hone and maintain your mental well-being; 4) To help you better navigate your interpersonal and social relationships. Furthermore, if your loved ones, friends, professors, advisors, administrators, and counselors wish to better support you, you can recommend that they read this book so they can develop empathy and understanding for all that you are grappling with. They may even gain strategies on how to help you through your journey.

Please remember that each grad parent is unique and striving to balance different tasks, roles, and expectations. As a result, some narratives and experiences articulated in this chapter will resonate with you while others may not. Similarly, there is no one strategy or tool that fits every person's needs. I hope that you will embrace flexibility and challenge rather than complacency and rigidity. Try a strategy out. If it works, great! If it doesn't, try to modify it to fit your specific situation. If it does not work for you at all, move on to other strategies. Along the way, you may just learn some valuable insights about yourself, your child, and your academic and life journey.

So Many Tasks, So Little Time

It is often worthwhile to take a macro evaluation of all the tasks you are juggling. Many grad parents are in a continuous fog of sleep deprivation, constant scheduling, and activity, and they are afraid to slow down. When I ask students to make a list of all they are balancing, they look at me as if I'm trying to get in the way of their forward motion. I am not, but I am asking you to slow down! What can emerge is a more realistic view of what you are managing, how you have been functioning, and hopefully a forward motion that is more thoughtful and considerate of what you truly want in life.

Exercise:

- Grab a journal and please list all the tasks you are currently balancing (*Not a Joke*)!
- What emotions surfaced as you wrote your list?

There is no right or wrong response, but your feelings can communicate a lot about your emotional well-being. While doing this and other exercises, you might experience some discomfort with an awakening realization of all you have been doing. Perhaps you'll become very emotional as you gain significant insight and self-compassion. It is also possible that you will feel completely overwhelmed and flooded with emotion and be unable to continue reading this chapter. Whatever emotions come up for you, pay attention! Just like your thoughts, your emotions may be communicating their unmet needs to you and screaming for you to listen. Furthermore, if your emotions are overwhelming, there is no shame in seeking out help from family, friends, and supportive professionals, such as religious leaders and/or mental health counselors. The shame would be in not seeking help and continuing to suffer.

Those Forgotten Hours
Strewn along the road of parenthood and graduate school are memorabilia you cherish and hold dear along with those you suppress with every fiber of your being. The former includes bedtime cuddles and kisses, your successful proposal defense, and finally reconnecting with your partner over the weekend. The latter includes diapers of various sizes and smells, textbooks you have come to hate, and your partner's depressive episode (or was that yours?). We can also muse together about all the seemingly *forgotten hours* that can comprise your parenting and thesis time. Forgot-

ten hours are all the hours you cannot think of when someone asks, "What did you do today?" Taking the time to reflect on these forgotten hours will help you realize just how much you actually do day to day!

As a parent, forgotten hours include thirty-minute burping sessions, elaborate bedtime rituals and stroller rocks, watching every move they make while in the playground, and all those difficult talks you had to have with your depressed teen and the school principal. It also includes never-ending nanny, day care, and school interviews and those screaming fights with your partner about radically different theories of parenting. Basically, forgotten hours are all the invisible activities that likely take up hours and hours of your week!

Exercise:

- Grab that journal again! Take a moment to list, acknowledge, and respect some of your parenting forgotten hours.

Unfortunately, you also have to contend with many grad student forgotten hours that are often unremembered and uncounted. This includes all the stacks of research articles you have to read just to determine that they do not belong in your paper/thesis or the incomplete paper on racial identity that you just can't write because it triggers your own racial identity conflicts. What about the data analysis that requires eight hours to transcribe just one of your interviews? Even more disheartening are those numerous emails you carefully and meticulously crafted to entice your advisor to *please, please* meet with you. Forgotten hours are frustrating because they take up so much space in your life, yet they are so easily minimized and forgotten.

Exercise:

- Take a moment to list, acknowledge, and respect some of your grad student forgotten hours.

Role Conflicts

The tasks and responsibilities inherent in the role of grad student and parent can be immense and difficult, but when they occur simultaneously they can be downright overwhelming. I still remember comforting a fellow grad parent who sobbed resentful, bitter tears as she had to cancel her dissertation defense due to her child becoming sick with the flu. She then wept self-reproaching tears for feeling this way as she cradled her vulnerable, sick child. Understanding the difficulty of managing conflicting roles is particularly important because being a grad student and a parent are rarely the only two roles one juggles. Most grad parents navigate additional roles as international students, teachers, workers, partners, caregivers to their own parents/in-laws, social activists, and friends.

Exercise:

- Take a moment to list and acknowledge all the roles you are balancing.

Interrole conflict aptly describes how expectations from one role can conflict with expectations from another role, leading to limited and overtaxed time and energy resources.[3] This is particularly applicable to grad parents. Being an overachieving lot, your typical response to interrole conflict is to increase your self-expectations and outputs in order to achieve the demands of all the competing roles. Although resilient and admirable when expectations are realistic, this can be heartbreaking when it becomes unmanageable. Nicholas Beutell and Jeffrey Greenhaus[4] offered a more effective way to cope with interrole conflict. They advise individuals to employ the help of others to set newer, more realistic structural expectations (e.g., change deadlines, defense and graduation dates; leave of absence) and also to change or moderate one's attitudes and perceptions of role expectations (e.g., reevaluating always being the best; giving up some control of academic, child, and home responsibilities). Later in this chapter, you will hear from various grad parents who have creatively and successfully utilized some of these very strategies!

Reflect on all that you are doing and offer yourself some self-compassion. Grad students, in general, are not very good at self-compassion. They are often driven to succeed by internal and external pressures that value productivity and external reinforcement. *More, harder, faster* is often the mantra rather than *enough, slow down,* and *good job.* Let's look at the relevance of self-compassion and the reasons why it can be so hard for grad parents to attain.

Self-Compassion

Having self-compassion is so important because without it, you become blind to the ways in which you are doing your best and perhaps even thriving despite it all. When your focus is solely on what you did not do (or what you did wrong), then you are not utilizing objective reality. Instead, you are minimizing the positives and maximizing the negatives in your life and work. Perhaps this way of thinking was manageable before you became a grad parent, but now the consequences may be detrimental and undermining. Self-compassion entails working from the reality of your particular situation and setting goals realistically so that they are healthier and more achievable. It's true, self-compassion not only requires taking stock of your life and developing empathy but may also entail changing goals, disappointing others, and reevaluating your idea of being the best at everything, every time.

It is important to point out that certain societal parenting myths can sometimes be complicit in your difficulty acquiring self-compassion. For example, many women grew up with the myth of the "superwoman," defined as a mother who parents, has a career, and manages the household with little complaint.[5] This is a picture of a grad parent that is often unattainable, because even those who thrive in their grad parent roles still experience many moments of feeling overwhelmed, guilty, and helpless. Likewise, many fathers, particularly those who share equal caregiving responsibilities with their partners (either by choice or by necessity), frequently experience intense stress[6,7] but fear being criticized and labeled if they share the adjustment difficulties they encounter in their new roles. This myth minimizes and neglects the difficulties that many contemporary fathers experience and sometimes labels and pathologizes adjustment issues as misogyny or entitlement. As a result, fathers can often feel isolated in their despair, lack the outlets to process their experience, and become locked in a cycle of defensive anger, confusion, and self-blame. Both these myths are further perpetuated by the lack of contemporary parenting models available for emulation.

Additionally, grad parents who are international students, those who belong to certain racial and ethnic groups, and those who are members of the LGBTQIA+ community often encounter unique and damaging myths about their parenting. There may be discrimination or stereotyping of a certain group's parenting skills (e.g., as unhealthy or irresponsible) or a devaluing of a certain group's parenting style (e.g., Western-style parenting valued over Eastern). This can lead to extra pressure and hypervigilance in their parenting along with difficulties in seeking help and developing or maintaining self-compassion. For example, a grad parent who identifies as gender nonconforming, and uses the pronouns they/them/theirs, shared with me recently their struggle to prove that they are good and loving parents to their child (by the way, they are!). "We have people around us who believe we should not be parents at all. People look at us with suspicion and sometimes alarm . . . so every insecure thought or mistake we make with our child feels so pressured and dangerous!" These myths are not only internal notions that an individual grad parent contends with but are notions infused into the very fabric of our society. Therefore, they are often hurtful and damaging beliefs that people convey overtly or covertly.

Finally, there are academic myths[8] that prize knowledge, ability, productivity, and sacrifice above all else. These myths can deter a grad parent's attainment of self-compassion. Furthermore, they may reinforce the tendency to remain silent and isolated when difficulties arise.

When you lack self-compassion you also become more vulnerable to the negative judgments of others, particularly those who have not walked in your shoes. So many grad parents have complained to me about not being understood by those around them that I feel compelled to address this issue explicitly. Let me confirm and validate your experiences. Those who have not had to navigate all these roles at once *Do Not Understand*. Your nonparent classmates and professors do not understand. Your partner who never went to graduate school does not understand. Your mother who raised four kids but was a stay-at-home mom does not understand. Your friends and family who negatively judge your difficulty including them in your hectic schedule do not understand. They may be caring and mean well and they may even offer you some sound advice, but, rest assured, they do not understand or see all that you are doing. Unfortunately, criticisms and judgments from others can lead to extreme stress, impede you from taking stock of how much you have achieved, and distract you from taking advantage of the growth and learning that is such a vital part of this journey. As such, having an internal reserve of self-compassion becomes even more crucial.

The Good, the Bad, and the Baby

The "Good" refers to the benefits of being a grad parent. Sadly, these benefits are often shrouded by the challenges and, therefore, seldom acknowledged or even discussed. Many grad parents tell me they only become aware of these benefits after completing their degrees. This is a shame because awareness may shift one's perspective, help modulate emotions, and improve overall mental health. Research has shown that improved mental health leads to greater capacities in parenting[9] and in the role of grad student.[10] The "Bad" refers to the many challenges of being a grad parent. We already identified some of these earlier, but we will continue to explore them through vignettes from real-life grad parents. Ironically, these challenges can sometimes be the gateway to personal and professional growth. Finally, the "Baby" refers to . . . well, the babies. There is the child (or children) that has irrevocably changed the course of your life. Then there is your thesis or dissertation—your baby born after many years of painful critiques and insecure musings.

In the next section, you will have the opportunity to get to know some courageous grad parents who grappled with the Good, the Bad and their Babies! They struggled, attained self-compassion, and reevaluated and reprioritized the tasks and goals in their life. In the process, they discovered invaluable insights about themselves, their relationships, and even their sociocultural environment. I hope that as you read their narratives it will embody some of your own feelings, thoughts, and experiences. That being said, each narrative is based on a composite of many different students that I have known professionally and personally. They may sound like you, but rest assured, they are not you! I have also incorporated many helpful strategies and tools in the narratives that, I hope, will be a useful complement to the resources you already have as you evolve into the successful and healthy grad parent you were meant to be!

Student Perks

A benefit of being a grad parent is having summer/winter vacations and holidays off with your kids. Of course, when I say "vacation" I am well aware that you may actually be working at a job and be simply on an academic vacation. Even if you are fortunate enough not to need a job, you will likely be working on papers, your thesis, or your dissertation during your vacation. At least, you will have some control of how to manage these tasks around your family time without the added stress of an academic calendar. Kevin, a parent and master's student in sociology, describes his summers off as his "ideal parenting time." For him, summer is a time when he feels most able to be the parent he yearns to be. He and his partner, Paulo, diligently outlined a summer plan that worked best for their family. Kevin shared how having a schedule that allowed him to parent their six-year-old daughter during the day, unencumbered by weekly assignments and deadlines, allowed him to give her the focus and attention they both needed to bond and connect. Three nights a week and for four hours on Saturdays, he would go to the local library to work on his thesis while Paulo took care of their daughter. Sunday was their family time together.

This measured and structured summer timetable allowed Kevin to "feel good as a parent, like I could be the nurturing, loving, focused parent to her that I struggled to be during the academic year and that I never experienced in my own childhood." It motivated him to make the most of his work time and it also helped him reconnect with Paulo, "since during the academic year we hardly had time together. Our schedule week to week was just mayhem!" As is evident in this example, collaborative schedules often require actively engaging and negotiating for help and time with your partner or loved one. Another important aspect of having the summer off for Kevin and Paulo was the reprieve from the financial burden of full-time child care, which often left them "child-care broke" during the academic year. Fortunately for Kevin, Paulo made enough money that he did not have to work. Many grad students do not have this privilege (see the chapter on finances and graduate school).

Another benefit of being a grad parent is that you can, within reason, extend your grad school tenure past the typical two years to complete a master's and five years to complete a doctorate. All this would require is a loosening of your rigidly held graduation schedule, the approval of your program, and the financial means to pay for the additional years. For example, it is possible to defer starting your program altogether, to go from a full-time student to a part-time student, or to take a leave of absence. If you are a typical overachieving grad student, I can already picture that scowl on your face. I know, I know, you want to complete your degree within your original planned timetable! I didn't say that it would be a comfortable option, only that this option is possible because you are a student rather than an employee. Furthermore, if you have found yourself taking on too much during a semester and are unable to complete all your assignments, you have the option of asking for an extension or taking an incomplete so you can finish the work at a later date. This may seem incomprehensible to you now, but it has saved a great many grad parents from having an emotional breakdown and/or simply dropping out.

Institutional Benefits
Although universities still have a very, very long way to go in truly supporting grad parents, some positive changes have been taking place in the past decade. For one, the majority of universities now have parental leave options, which enable parents to take time off without losing certain benefits. This is particularly important for students who fear losing their scholarship, grants, and insurance due to a parental leave. Furthermore, more universities are offering this to fathers, mothers, and LGBTQIA+ parents, which greatly addresses the changing landscape of the modern American family, where diverse family compositions are more common and increased egalitarianism is often necessary.[11]

Another potential institutional support that may be offered are in-house child-care centers and/or summer camps. The City University of New York's Graduate Center, where I work, offers grad students the opportunity to enroll their children in a low-fee, on-site day care program through the Child Care Center. So many of the financially strapped and guilt-ridden parents I spoke to expressed relief and gratitude for this cost-effective service, and they cherished the opportunity to check in on their children during the day. Unfortunately, the wait-list at the center is so extensive that I often encourage new parents to sign up their children right after birth (or before)! There is even a pumping room for nursing parents, greatly reducing the possibility of inadvertently flashing their advisors, professors, and colleagues alike. Yes, it happens!

Additionally, check with the student counseling centers for parenting support. For example, our student counseling service partnered with the Child Care Center to offer parenting workshops, parenting support groups, and walk-in services. We also offer our students couples treatment, because parents who experience each other as supports generally do better balancing all their responsibilities. So, it is important that you speak with university administrators and check out institutional programs about services that may help you through this wonderful but exhausting journey.

Evolving into a "Good Enough Grad Parent"

The most common complaint I hear from grad parents is their difficulty balancing the many roles they occupy. Along with this complaint is the constant refrain: "Nothing I do is ever good enough!" When they are with their children, they feel guilty and cannot concentrate because of all the academic demands that interfere with being present. However, when they are working on their academics, they cannot fully concentrate because they feel guilty that they are not with their children. This constant feeling of not being "good enough" in their roles seems to be a recurring anthem of grad parenting and is captured evocatively by the example below.

Ashley was a second-year doctoral candidate in computer science. She always did well enough in grad school despite her waxing and waning bouts of anxiety and depression. Her program was rigorous, primarily populated by male professors, and subscribed to the expectation that to be a "good grad student" one had to be available anytime, for all assignments and events, no matter how unreasonable the notice. Unfortunately, this is quite a common expectation in many grad programs. Her program was also not family friendly and lacked role models of academic parents to emulate. Ashley was actively discouraged from starting a family by professors, administrators, and her cohort. The most common drawback they would cite was missing out on networking, publishing, and job opportunities. However, Ashley and her husband were in their late thirties, and they did not want to miss the opportunity to start a family. This is a very common predicament befalling many grad families.[12]

Once she had her child, Ashley had difficulty maintaining her "good grad student" role and also felt marginalized by those in her program. Her advisor was particularly unsupportive of her decrease in productivity and withdrew much of his attention from her. Because she felt anxious and guilty, she agreed to more unrealistic demands and deadlines from him, which, inevitably, she could not complete. Unfortunately, this paralleled her childhood experience of unsuccessfully trying to gain the attention and love of her neglectful, alcoholic father. Ashley lacked compassion for herself and judged herself to be "just lazy and not smart enough to get it together!" This was also a frequent, painful criticism she heard growing up.

Additionally, Ashley's child suffered from colic and for the first two years hardly ever slept through the night, leaving her overwhelmingly sleep-deprived. When her child started to exhibit behavioral problems, she found herself vacillating between being overly indulgent and passive or reacting to him with anger and impatience. Predictably, his behavioral issues worsened. Ashley believed that she was not a "good student" or a "good mother" and suffered from intense feelings of guilt, shame, despair, and self-blame. She described herself as "just so, so depressed. I was like a hamster stuck on a wheel that never stopped turning . . . I was confused and lost and didn't know how to get off!" Regrettably, she decided the answer was a suicide attempt. Fortunately, she was unsuccessful.

Ashley's suicide attempt was a wake-up call that something had to change. She joined a grad parent support group where she learned that she was not alone in her experiences. In group, members were encouraged to actively reevaluate their definitions of being a good grad parent. In the process, she realized that her expectations were wholly idealistic, unrealistic, and unhealthy but also not uncommon. She felt validated upon learning that other mothers were also socialized to believe that they needed to sacrifice themselves completely for their children and suffered greatly as a result. She was also able to become aware of the unsupportive, unhealthy, and discriminatory environment of her program. Slowly, she developed a sense of perspective and a burgeoning self-compassion for her plight. It became clear that she would need to moderate her role expectations to find a compromise that would lead to a healthier and more manageable life.

The group also discussed the concept of being a "good enough parent."[13] Ashley determined that, for her, this meant accepting that she could not be a stay-at-home mother, who was always there for her child, but she could develop strategies to be more present and attentive during the times she was with her child. This also meant seeking help from a family therapist who helped her see how her inability to empathize and nurture herself made it difficult for her to empathize, nurture, and set boundaries with her child. For example, when she was feeling guilty, she found it difficult to discipline and guide him and would often compensate for her absence by being overly permissive. However, when she was overwhelmed and feeling unnurtured, she would react angrily and punitively towards him. She also realized how her abusive childhood did not teach her how to balance nurturing and disciplining her child.

Eventually, Ashley learned how to respond to her child by focusing on his feelings and his needs rather than on trying to alleviate her own anger, guilt, and insecurities. "It helps for me to ask myself, why is he acting this way? Does he just need comfort or a hug right now? Does he need me to help him figure out why he's upset, maybe with an explanation? Does he need discipline and boundaries?" Additionally, it gave her comfort to learn that there was no one right way to raise a child and that children, in general, can be extremely resilient as long as they feel loved, have a predictable routine, and have parents who are generally stable and reliable. Rather than striving to be her idealized "good parent," she strove to be the more realistic "good enough parent."

Exercise:

- Grab that journal again! List some ways you are a "good enough parent."

Ashley extended the concept of good enough parenting to being a "good enough grad student." This entailed compromising on her goals and setting healthier boundaries with others. For example, she sought accommodations from the office of disabilities to extend her deadlines, took a leave of absence to finish her incompletes, and delayed her graduation date. Additionally, she spoke to the student affairs director and the university ombudsman (an intermediary between students and university personnel) about her experience. This led to the institution emphasizing to programs their parental nondiscrimination policy and their willingness to enforce it. Ashley also deeply examined her anxieties about disappointing authority figures so she could set appropriate boundaries with her advisor.

Exercise:

- List some ways you are a "good enough grad student."

The Grad Parent Triad
When grad school and parenting issues start to become intertwined with traumatic childhood experiences, it can often lead to intense emotion dysregulation. In fact, I have found this phenomenon to be quite common and pervasive and have termed it *The Grad Parent Triad*. To envision this triad, take out a piece of paper and draw a triangle. Label the top corner of the triangle *Childhood Experiences*, the bottom left corner of the triangle *Graduate School Issues*, and the bottom right of the triangle *Parenting Issues*. Between these labels are bidirectional arrows indicating how issues in one realm can influence issues in the other two realms.

Ashley's *Grad Parent Triad* involved her relationship with her abusive father (childhood experiences) and its subsequent impact on her experiences with her advisor (graduate school issues) and her child (parenting issues). For example, she realized she had started to see her advisor as a father figure and sought from him the love, attention, and validation she never received at home. "I had to realize that he is not my father and I don't need him to love or agree with me, I just need him to help me graduate!" By becoming aware of this in therapy, she was able to reset her expectations of him in order to move forward academically. Likewise, Ashley realized that she had great fears about becoming an abusive parent like her father. Therefore, negative thoughts and feelings that emerged while parenting felt very threatening and overwhelming for her. It also led her to react from her own anxieties rather than respond to her child's needs. By meeting other grad parents, she was able to normalize her thoughts and feelings while separating them from her actual behavior. "Now when I am overwhelmed, I take time out for myself . . . I remind myself that I am a good enough mother . . . I run, or lock myself in the bathroom and listen to a relaxation audio. That way I can be calmer and can concentrate more on what my child may actually need in the moment!"

Exercise:

• Take this moment to reflect on the childhood experiences that have been triggered for you since becoming a grad parent.

Reevaluating Your Intersecting Identities

Most grad parents had to reevaluate the tasks required by all their roles and identities to determine what they are willing to sacrifice. Research has shown that the hours spent on household and child-care responsibilities increase according to the number of children in the home of a grad student.[14] As a result, the more children one has the more often questions such as "Do I really want this degree" and "What is really important in my life" take on an urgent quality. In the narrative below, a successful grad parent is forced to explore and reevaluate her multiple identities in order to determine if she wants to continue on her grad school journey.

Latesha was a third-year African American doctoral candidate in political science. She was an extremely successful and well-regarded activist before she started grad school and was a star in her program. She was known for never saying no to opportunities and for her leadership qualities. Her mother raised her on her own, worked two jobs, and drilled into her the importance of success and fighting for social justice. As a result, Latesha was very in touch with her own resilience and strength and felt she could accomplish it all.

Once Latesha had a child she had difficulty balancing the demands of both roles. She often had to choose to prioritize one over the other. This meant "not being good enough" at either role, disappointing others, and often feeling out of control. She also realized the importance of her racial identity and how anxious she was about being viewed as "a stereotype . . . a token . . . or not qualified to be in academia!" In fact, racist and misogynistic notions were conveyed to her through eye rolls and paternalistic/maternalistic comments when she had to miss meetings and classes, drop out of conferences, or say no to opportunities because of her parenting responsibilities. Furthermore, changes in her availability led to being left out of the loop of academic and networking opportunities. This experience of feeling "marginalized in academia" due to parenthood is documented in the literature.[15] By the time she was pregnant with her second child, she was in therapy, tearfully conflicted, and contemplating quitting her program.

Latesha started to untangle the myriad roles (e.g., parent; people of color [POC] role model; partner; social justice activist; grad student; daughter) and identity conflicts that led to her emotional crisis. She realized how much it meant to her to represent POCs within and outside of her program, yet how burdensome it was to "try to dispel every negative stereotype . . . like every move I made had that as an ulterior motive and I felt I was representing everyone in my community!" She also became aware of what being a parent truly meant to her. She idealized her working mom and had always thought she had wanted to be just like her. "Everyone admired her for raising us on her own while working two jobs." However, she grappled with disturbing feelings of guilt, sadness, irritation, and anger every time her toddler would cry or protest when she left her. Long-buried memories of her own sadness, anger, and loneliness being a latchkey kid (a child who would come home to an empty house because their parents had to work) reemerged, interrupting her concentration and sleep. Latesha realized that inter-role conflicts triggered her early experience being parented by a loving but overworked, sometimes unavailable mother. This reexperiencing of one's own childhood and infancy through the process of becoming a parent is a common and well-known psychological phenomenon.[16]

In therapy, Latesha honed her capacity to be attuned to her own value system and to follow her own internal compass. She deeply evaluated how much time away from her child would allow her to feel like a "good enough parent" and how her identity as a parent complemented or conflicted with her other identities. Eventually, Latesha became aware that "I am in grad school because my mom wanted me to have this degree and I was on automatic pilot trying to please her, as usual, but, is this really what I want? I have to make sure the time I sacrifice away from my child and family is actually worth it for me!" She decided to take a leave of absence to give herself time with her children but also to reflect on these questions. In my experience, grad students who take the time needed to deliberate and determine how best to move forward in their lives often have an easier time with their eventual decision. This is in contrast to students who make decisions hastily, driven by insecurity, anxiety, or a negative setback or event.

Latesha eventually decided to leave with her master's degree. Years later, she sent me an email update about her family and her new position in a not-for-profit advocacy group. She told me that she did not regret leaving grad school because she didn't quit impulsively. "I came to realize that I didn't need a doctorate to have the job and life that I really wanted!" She also consults and teaches on race and advocacy issues and is a role model to grad parents in her former doctoral program. This overachiever models that it is actually possible to decide to leave grad school and not feel like a failure!

Setting Appropriate Boundaries

For those who decide to stay in grad school, a common new perspective involves how to engage and interact with those around them and how their academic goals evolve with time. Many shared how they no longer get involved in the dramas of graduate school, are more willing to set boundaries with others, and refrain from "sweating the small stuff." This progression often entailed a harsh setback (e.g., losing a grant, an incomplete, negative feedback), the realization that things cannot go on as usual, and then a change in perspective and behavior.

I can share with you my own experience of this phenomenon. When I was applying for an internship in psychology, I was surrounded by nonparent grad students who anxiously applied to many internship sites. I admit that their stress, mingled with my own, was contagious, and I struggled unsuccessfully and unhealthily to keep up with them. I became overwhelmed, irritable, and physically sick. Inevitably, I felt like I just could not be my best in any realm—as a parent, student, teacher, or partner.

It took time for me to gain the awareness that my expectations for myself were unrealistic and that I had to protect my well-being by setting boundaries. This entailed exiting when anxious talk of internships began and only sharing my plans with those who were understanding of my special circumstances. I often commiserated with a fellow grad parent who, like me, had to minimize the number of sites she applied to due to time, cost, travel, and parenting constraints. We often played the game "what's the worst that could happen" and helped each other see that no outcome was ever a dead end. My fellow grad parent and I were consciously aware that, to be the best we could be in all our roles, we had to be more flexible and forgiving in all our roles. This was a momentous shift. Eventually, we became able to secretly rejoice in this newfound perspective and become in awe of how such a little bundle of infant had the capacity to teach us such an important life lesson.

An alternate perspective is the increased focus, motivation, and boundaries that some grad parents develop to prioritize and complete their degrees. Some shared how their procrastination tendencies were moderated by parenting "because graduating took on an extra importance . . . I could no longer mess around." Kevin, from the earlier example, had never been a procrastinator but was an extreme over-achiever and social justice warrior. When his child became ill and he was unable to complete a paper, he appropriately asked for an extension. The professor responded gruffly to his request and made a snide comment about needing a wife to take care of his children. Kevin felt intensely disrespected and appalled by the homophobic comment. Unfortunately, this tenured professor's homophobia and misogyny were well known. In the past, Kevin would not have hesitated in "taking this fight 100 percent on my shoulder!" However, since becoming a parent it has not been as simple for him. He was defending and graduating that semester and "if I take this on, I know that the next few months will be overwhelming. I will be irritable and grumpy at home, not the parent I want to be. Honestly, I need to defend, get the hell out of here, and start making money for my family!" However, the option of completely ignoring the situation was abhorrent to him.

After much introspection, Kevin decided to meet with other students who had similar encounters with this professor. They, as a group, approached administrators. Rather than taking it on "100 percent," he had to set a boundary. He shared the burden with others and even declined the leadership role. "In this situation, I had to prioritize finishing my degree, being a good parent, and my mental well-being above all else . . . but I also did not ignore the homophobia."

Sociocultural Clashes

Sometimes sociocultural differences are in the forefront of a grad parent's conflicts, as in the case of Claire, who was from the Philippines, and Jon, her African American husband. When working with international students and interracial couples, issues of acculturation, immigration, discrimination, and gender roles are sometimes at the forefront of difficulties.[17] Claire just started a master's program in women's studies while Jon was a pharmacist. The main complaint they brought to couples treatment was their constant fights at home about disciplining their child and the division of household chores. However, embedded in their seemingly minor disagreements, which often escalated into full-scale screaming matches, were deeper conflicts revolving around their cultural, gender, and racial differences triggered by becoming grad parents.

It was apparent that Jon and Claire were tired, depressed, and overwhelmed. They had difficulty seeing each other as a source of understanding and support. Jon was very angry that Claire "was never around . . . she's either in school or doing something for school," and he saw her difficulty declining requests from her program as "irresponsible." He also disagreed vehemently with some of her parenting beliefs, particularly when it came to her "permissive" ideas about eating, sleeping, and activities. "He [their son] is almost four years old and still sleeps with us. She lets him eat whatever he wants and do whatever he wants, she doesn't know how to discipline!" Claire was, likewise, furious at Jon's expectation that she maintain the household and cooking despite her rigorous schedule. "He acts like I am a stay-at-home mom, like it's the 1950s or something . . . but I am in a really hard program and he just doesn't understand how much I have to do. All he does is yell and give orders. He is so selfish!" It took great effort for them to de-escalate, so that they would be able to listen to each other and finally unmask the more vulnerable emotions hidden behind their anger and contempt.

Jon grew up in New York City in a close-knit Baptist family with a very strong patriarch and an equally strong matriarch. His father was a pastor and his mother stayed home and took care of him and his siblings. Although he was considered "the liberal one" in his family of origin, having his own child unearthed uncomfortable, gendered viewpoints. He realized that he greatly resented all the time his wife spent in her program, working on her thesis and/or being at home "but not really at home (at home but working)." However, he also felt guilty for feeling this way "because I believe in gender equality and I always thought that I wanted a wife who worked . . . I just didn't realize all that meant once we had a child!" It was very upsetting for him to realize that he was conflicted about this issue.

Meanwhile, Claire came from a traditional family and grew up in the Philippines. Although both her parents worked, extended family members lived with them (her grandparents, aunts, uncles, and cousins), and they had help around the house. "Everyone took care of the kids, you didn't have to ask!" Claire dearly missed her family and culture and this was greatly exacerbated once she had a child. Instead of having a village to support her and help her with parenting, she felt alone and overwhelmed. She struggled to balance her maternal, marital, and academic roles. She also felt judged by Jon and her in-laws for her non-Western parenting style and found herself "always defending my upbringing." Academically, she had difficulty saying "no" to the constant demands of her advisor. She connected this to her Filipino cultural value of *pakikisama*, which meant getting along, especially with authority figures, and sacrificing one's own needs for others.

Claire felt guilty for not being "good enough" in all her roles and raged at Jon for his constant criticism of her parenting and the household. This was often perpetuated by feminist discussions and readings in her classes that made her worry "that deep down inside he is a misogynist. He just wants me to stay home and take care of him and our son. I am trying to do my best!" Graduate school often triggers intersectional identity awareness and reevaluations and this often impacts relationships with significant others. Jon eventually owned his conflicts but also pointed out all the ways he collaborated at home in parenting and with her academic needs that contradicted her statement that "you don't ever support me!"

Another major issue that came out of their therapy revolved around race and colorism (when an ethnic group values lighter skin tone over darker ones). Jon became incensed every time Claire commented negatively about their son's curly hair and dark complexion and related this to racist and colorist comments he had received from her Filipino family. It became apparent that some of these comments were incredibly hurtful and that they troubled him greatly. This issue also brought back many racist incidents from his childhood and triggered a need in him to "prepare my son to deal with it, like my parents prepared me. There needs to be rules and it needs to be clear . . . it's life or death!" He realized that these messages were conveyed to him primarily by his mother and when Claire "spoiled" their son, he saw this as an indication that she is "not doing her duty in parenting a biracial child."

Claire was able to acknowledge the racist and colorist beliefs of her culture and how hurtful they were to him and to their child. She shared her own internal struggle and conflicts growing up morena (a darker-skinned Filipina). However, she admitted that it was hard for her to fully comprehend his worry. She also argued that some of her parenting decisions were actually based on Filipino cultural values "that you refuse to understand either. You just think the American way is the best way!"

Claire and Jon bravely tackled these complex issues in counseling and were able to garner greater understanding of each other's experience and perspective. This helped in moderating the intensity of their arguments. They marveled at the many times that they would misinterpret and misunderstand each other and became more cognizant of each other's efforts during the week. A major shift occurred when they were able to realize how much they missed being with each other and seeing each other as a support. This enabled them to employ strategies such as scheduling time each week to negotiate responsibilities and chores and setting up a weekly date where they were not allowed to discuss their child at all. Instead, they focused on learning and sharing more about their early childhood experiences and their cultural values. They sought to connect and understand what they learned to their relationship, their academic and career conflicts, and finally to their different parenting styles. They also discovered how these issues led to their lack of boundaries and to their difficulty with assertion with their advisor and boss, respectively. Claire was particularly grateful to identify this *Grad Parent Triad* as it made her feel "less confused and more hopeful." Currently, Claire and Jon are working towards greater intimacy. However, they continue to grapple with their differing worldviews and experiences and sometimes still struggle to partner and parent effectively together. There are no easy fixes when such complex issues emerge.

This is an example of how practical and pragmatic issues of parenting while in graduate school could be further complicated by socio-racial-cultural norms, expectations, and conflicts. The majority of the issues identified here—marital, parenting, and academic cultural adjustment, isolation from home and family, feelings of inadequacy while balancing multiple roles, discrimination, gender role conflicts—have recently been cited as some of the major issues impacting international student families.[18] Because these issues tend to be quite complex and layered, intervening as early as possible can be helpful, and employing the help of objective parties such as religious or mental health counselors is recommended.

Exercise:

- List how sociocultural issues impact you as a grad parent.

Seeking Help

I hope that reading this chapter has helped you become more aware of the benefits and challenges of being a grad parent. I also hope that I have convinced you to invite moments of self-reflection and self-compassion into your daily life! If you remember one thing from this chapter, I hope it will be the importance of seeking help and support from those around you. I am well aware that grad parents, in general, are an independent, self-sufficient lot. You are used to figuring things out on your own and may have difficulty letting go of control. I know that you are highly concerned about being labeled "a bad parent" or "a problem student" and you can feel intense shame when you feel helpless and confused. As a result, you may have great difficulty advocating for your needs. However, being a grad parent requires a lot of help from others. *You Cannot Do It Alone!* This lesson is best learned quickly for you to succeed with your mental health intact.

How do you reconcile your need for help from others given the fact that so many may not truly and fully understand your challenges? This is an important question with no easy answer. After all, each person in your life is unique with different capacities to communicate, understand, empathize, and support. In one scenario, you may decide to share with others, explicitly, your everyday stressors in order to ask them for help and support. Be sure to complete the exercises in this chapter so you can convey accurately what you have been managing and what you need from them. In another scenario, you may decide to simply accept that they will never fully understand (either because they are unwilling or unable) what you are going through. They may not have the capacity to give you the support you need. Subsequently, you may decide to cease from defending and explaining your unique situation and set up boundaries instead. Most likely, you will find a compromise or alternative option somewhere in between these two scenarios. The exercise below offers some useful questions to ask yourself before seeking help.

Exercise:

- What type of support do I want from this person? If it goes well, what would they say or do that would lead to me feeling supported?
- What is the likelihood that they are willing and capable of understanding and giving me what I want? For example, how have they responded in the past?
- What would make it more likely that they will hear me and respond to me in a helpful and supportive manner?
- Am I in the right emotional state to enter into this interaction? When is the right time and place?
- Is it just healthier for me to set boundaries with this person and address this at a later time?
- Who, in my life, is more likely to give me the support I need right now?

As future professors, administrators, advisors, mentors, supervisors, and counselors, you will have more opportunity, influence, and power in helping to create a more family-friendly grad school environment. Being aware of your journey and having self-compassion will allow you to give compassion to future grad parents in order to counter the destructive hazing mentality (e.g., I suffered therefore you should also suffer) that is sometimes pervasive in higher education. So, I hope that you will join me in this endeavor, and that together, we can make grad school accessible to everyone, especially grad parents!

Takeaways for Grad Parents

- Slow down! Take stock of all the roles and tasks you are balancing in life.
- Develop self-compassion. If you don't know how, seek help.
- Remember the benefits and not just the challenges of being a grad parent.
- Remember that challenges can also be opportunities for personal and professional growth.
- Consider moderating your self-expectations and academic/life schedule to address the reality of your current situation.
- Create a structured weekly/monthly/yearly schedule but be flexible and know that changes will occur, sometimes unexpectedly and inconveniently. Then revise!
- Strive to be a "good enough grad parent" rather than always being the best.
- Determine if a Grad Parent Triad is complicit in your difficulties. If so, consider seeking help to understand the impact in your current life and relationships.
- Set boundaries with unsupportive others.
- Ask for and accept help from your institution and from supportive others in your life.
- *Breathe!*

Suggestions for Administrators, Faculty, and Advisors

- Seek out ways to understand and be more supportive of grad parents. Reading this book is a good first step.
- Increase your awareness of your grad parents' role conflicts, including racial, sexual, gender, and sociocultural roles that are often unspoken but impactful.
- Develop awareness of the ways your program or institution may be discriminating against grad parents.

- Advocate to increase family-friendly and inclusive messages in your program and institution. Connect grad parents with current grad parents and grad parent alums.
- Check in more often with your grad parents to counter their sense of isolation and alienation. They will appreciate the time and effort you take to show you care.
- Just listen, don't judge.
- Validate the emotions that come from balancing so many tasks and roles at one time.
- Explicitly express your support and willingness to help.
- Take on a collaborative stance by working together to set realistic goals.
- Reinforce, reinforce, and reinforce the accomplishments of grad parents!
- Be flexible with academic deadlines and defense or graduation dates.
- Understand that grad parents often do not have time in a day to do all they have to do. They will likely miss many academic and social events and meetings. Consider videotaping events or live streaming them.
- Model work-life balance.
- Be aware of available grad parent supports already in place, such as institution and program support (e.g., child-care services, nursing rooms, leave and accommodation options, financial aid) and psychological and emotional supports (e.g., university counseling services).

Suggestions for Mental Health Providers

- Educate yourself on the specific needs and experiences of grad parents. Reading this book is a good first step.
- Empathize and validate their experiences.
- Identify how they are thriving not just how they are being challenged.
- Consider the spectrum of difficulties—from intrapsychic, to interpersonal, to sociocultural.

- Address practical concerns such as unrealistic time and task expectations that may require problem solving and alternative-seeking interventions.
- Address distortions in thoughts and behaviors that may lead to emotion dysregulation.
- Connect their experiences to early childhood experiences. Identify the Grad Parent Triad.
- Help them identify and strive to be their definition of a good enough grad parent.
- Address issues related to role and identity conflicts.
- Offer couples counseling (student counseling centers).
- Offer workshops and groups specific to grad parent needs (student counseling centers).
- Advocate for grad parents within the university, in the community, and with their loved ones (student counseling centers).

CHAPTER TEN

~

"We're Here, We're Queer!"
LGBTQ in Graduate School
Kristen A. Renn

For students minoritized by sexual and gender identities—lesbian, gay, bisexual, transgender, queer (LGBTQ)—graduate school can be a time of empowerment or disempowerment, embracing and expressing identities or staying in/going back into the closet. For many LGBTQ grad students, it's a mix of all of these experiences and feelings. Students arrive at grad school anywhere from their early twenties to late in life, and because sexual and gender identities develop across the lifespan[1] it is possible that *any* grad student could undergo identity shifts before and during school. And because graduate students often choose their programs based on disciplinary strength and academic opportunities rather than, for example, geographic and cultural location, it is possible that someone who was living openly and comfortably as LGBTQ prior to graduate school will need to expend energy to be and feel safe in the grad school context.

A constant in the lives of LGBTQ people is the need to decide over and over whether a context is safe and if so, whether or not to come out or let others know about their sexual and/or gender identity. The term "cis-heteronormative" is a mouthful, but it is useful to describe the assumption that everyone is and ought to be cisgender (that is, their sex assigned at birth—usually male or female—matches their felt gender identity within the binary categories man or woman) and heterosexual. Living in a cis-heteronormative society requires LGBTQ people to constantly have to self-identify, or come out, as other than cisgender and/or other than heterosexual.[2] For LGBTQ graduate students, deciding whether or not to come out begins before application and runs through the job search into careers.

Imagine Briana (pronouns she, her, hers) was president of the LGBTQ student organization at her undergraduate institution, and she is going directly into a graduate program at a flagship public research university in another state, one known for its conservative politics. Briana identifies as an African American lesbian. During her grad school search, she learned that the program she is entering is one of the top-ranked in her field. She combed the university's website for evidence of LGBTQ student organizations and found the LGBT Student Alliance. Yet, she also discovered that nondiscrimination policies that protected LGBTQ people from employment discrimination and harassment were not included on the website. On her application she decided not to include her LGBTQ activism and leadership, fearing it might negatively affect her chances of admission. After she was admitted she visited campus for a recruiting day, during which she stayed closeted while trying to gauge how her program and the university supported students of color and LGBTQ students. She learned from other Black students that campus housing was likely a better option than trying to find a rental off campus, where landlords were cautious about renting to students of color and rowdy undergraduate parties sometimes resulted in harassment of women and people of color. But on-campus graduate housing was only available in shared apartments, and Briana was wary about moving in with a stranger without knowing how they would react to visits from Briana's girlfriend.

Briana found another African American woman in her academic college to be her apartment mate and moved to town to begin her graduate program. Still out to no one in her new setting, she overhead a number of casually homophobic comments from undergrads in the course for which she was a teaching assistant, and the professor instructing the course said nothing. Briana came to trust her advisor and told the advisor about these interactions, taking the risk to identify herself as lesbian. Her advisor was supportive and offered to work on strategies for addressing classroom microaggressions. Briana then decided to come out to other faculty and students in her program, including her apartment mate, who took the news in stride. Briana felt supported and safe. But when she wrote a paper on African American LGBTQ youth, a professor in her program suggested she avoid "hot-button issues" that would make it hard to publish the paper and mark her as a "potential trouble-maker" to future search committees. Unsure whether the professor was responding to her race, her sexual orientation, or both, Briana began to worry about the impact of her identity on her future career.

Along the path from the grad school search to postgrad school careers, LGBTQ students like Briana face innumerable moments of decision about identifying their sexuality and/or gender to others. They scan each setting for signs of safety or threat, seeking allies and supportive faculty and peers.[3] The time and energy spent in this environmental assessment comes out of the same reservoir used for academic and psychosocial transition to and success in graduate school.[4] LGBTQ students deal with the prevailing cis-heteronormativity in all aspects of their graduate experience. There are ways that institutions can reduce this toll, such as increasing the visibility of LGBTQ people through campus organizations or an LGBT campus center, and pro-LGBTQ policies such as nondiscrimination and all-gender washrooms and housing. And the stories of students like Briana are not simply ones of stress and constant calibration; LGBTQ students report ways that their identities become points of connection to others, sources of intellectual creativity, and powerful positive forces in their lives inside and outside the academy. For LGBTQ students coming to graduate school from backgrounds that included bullying, harassment, or fear of negative reactions from family, this new academic chapter may be the first time when they can come out and celebrate their identities. There is no universal story of LGBTQ students in graduate school, but there are some common elements across many LGBTQ students' experiences.

Intersections of LGBTQ Identities with the Roles of Graduate Students

Graduate students fill many roles, and LGBTQ identities can intersect in ways that support or challenge their ability to thrive. First, graduate students are adult learners in classes, laboratories, fieldwork, and other curricular settings. Minoritized sexual orientations and gender identities have been shown to provide "hooks" or opportunities to connect with curriculum for students in a number of disciplines.[5] As in Briana's story, connecting a course assignment to one's identity can provide meaning and personalize the learning experience. Although it may be harder in some academic areas than others to make this connection, even learning statistics can be an opportunity to engage in LGBTQ-related material.[6] Although bench science labs may not provide intellectual connections to LGBTQ identities, social science labs and fieldwork could be places where identities create a bridge to learning new material and concepts. Briana's story also illustrates some downsides to exploring LGBTQ topics in research; the reception she received from one professor (avoid "hot-button issues" if you want to get a job) could be based in racism and homophobia, or it could simply be one person's attempt to offer practical advice for a competitive job market. Whether or not the field would react negatively to Briana's paper, at least one professor in her program is warning her away from identity-related academic work.

Graduate students fill roles other than learner, and typically one role is graduate employee, such as a teaching assistant (TA) or a research assistant (RA). As a TA, Briana was exposed to homophobic micro-aggressions in the class section she taught, and although her advisor was supportive the professor in charge of the course did nothing about the classroom climate. As TAs, LGBTQ graduate students may find themselves in supportive, neutral, or hostile teaching environments. They may choose to self-identify (come out) as LGBTQ or may choose for a variety of reasons not to do so in this setting. The choice is individual and based on personal assessment of risks and benefits, safety and threat. Importantly, developmental theories support this kind of situational identity expression as healthy rather than dysfunctional;[7] although some LGBTQ people may experience stress or feel inauthentic if they are not out across all settings, there is likely no long-term harm that comes from thoughtful individual decisions, such as Briana's, to selectively disclose some aspects of one's identities. Of course, there may be settings in which a graduate TA can be "out and proud," including in courses that engage with gender, sexual orientation, and/or gender identities. But the choice always belongs to the TA.

As research assistants, graduate students may find themselves in settings where LGBTQ identities are celebrated, ignored, or denigrated. The microclimate of research work, whether one-on-one with a research supervisor, in a lab, or in some other constellation of faculty, postdoc, grad, and undergrad researchers, varies and can substantially influence outcomes for an LGBTQ graduate student. In a field where there is great emphasis on whose lab one is part of, getting along with the principal investigator (PI) and others on the team may be seen as paramount, and any introduction of identities or worldviews that do not conform to the assumed majority are considered unwelcome distractions. The interlocking dependencies of funding for grad school, socialization for future career, learning through research, and in the case of international students, visa status, create a power dynamic that can be hard to address if the PI runs a lab in which LGBTQ identities are unwelcome. If that PI controls one's employment, funding, academic program, and student visa, then conformity—at least while in those settings—may be a reasonable course of action. There are LGBTQ PIs across academic fields, including STEM fields where the subject matter may not lean toward identities of any kind, and there are PIs of every sexual orientation and gender identity who create research contexts in which team members of any identity can thrive. As with TAs, LGBTQ RAs have the right and responsibility to gauge risks and benefits, to challenge hostile environments, and to choose when, where, and how to come out to others.

Graduate students have lives outside of classes, teaching, and research. Because sexual orientation and gender identities evolve across the lifespan, and situational identification is a healthy strategy for thriving, a graduate student may be coming to know themselves as LGBTQ or may be telling family, friends, and others for the first time. LGBTQ grad students who are also parents may be interacting with children's schools. LGBTQ students who have lived in the same community for years may be, for the first time, talking with members of their faith community, civic organizations, recreational sports teams, or other everyday acquaintances about sexual orientation and gender identity. Some will tell their parents for the first time. Some will experience a breakup or enter a longed-for relationship; either could be a time when having people to talk to about their identities might be important. In short, LGBTQ grad students have the same kinds of roles outside school that everyone else has, though they may have varying levels of safety and support in sharing their identities in the same ways.

Transgender Graduate Students

Seeking connections on campus, Briana joined the LGBTQ grad student caucus sponsored through the campus LGBT resource center. She found it a good place to be with other people who were experiencing similar questions about academic life, TA and RA responsibilities, and navigating relationships with PIs, mentors, and advisors. Although the group was predominantly White, she found a few other queer and trans people of color (QTPOC, usually pronounced *cutie-pock*) with whom to share the trials and tribulations of life in a college town in a conservative region. One of her new friends, Carter (pronouns he, him, his), identified as an Asian American transman. Carter was studying botany, with plans to pursue a postdoc and then a tenure-track faculty position.

Carter described his trajectory from a biology major at a small, left-leaning liberal arts college to the university. He had presented himself as a cisgender tomboyish lesbian when he arrived at college then encountered transgender and nonbinary students through LGBTQ student activism. These students, together with popular culture, social media, and academic reading about trans people, helped Carter realize that he identified as a transman. Aware of the costly and burdensome process of undergoing gender transition—and not certain he wanted to—Carter completed college knowing he was trans but continuing to identify publicly as a butch lesbian. Coming to graduate school provided some financial autonomy, and, in spite of its location in a conservative state, the university provided grad student health insurance that covered gender-related medical services. Indeed, the city in which the university was located was a regional center for trans-friendly health care. By the time Briana met him, Carter was well into the process of medical transition and taking the necessary steps to change his legal gender before he completed his PhD the next semester.

Carter talked with Briana about the challenges of dealing with providers at the university health services, who were not as open-minded as those at the university-affiliated hospital's gender clinic.

Carter talked about avoiding single-gender restrooms in the building he teaches in, as he'd been harassed there his first year on campus. He described the reaction of his advisor, who was also his PI, to the news of his gender transition; Carter's advisor was generally supportive though admitted he didn't know much about transgender issues. He thought it might "look funny" to have different names (pre- and post-transition) on Carter's curriculum vitae and offered to talk to colleagues, anonymously, on his behalf to get advice. Carter worried about applying for positions that would require transcripts that would have different names on them, not wanting to be outed during the initial stage of the applicant screening process. And Carter's second recommendation writer—a very famous scholar in the field—was reluctant to use the name "Carter" and pronouns he, him, and his in letters, sticking to her stated conviction that to do so before a legal name and gender change would be dishonest; Carter suspected the resistance was rooted in transphobia but felt strongly that this professor's letter would be a "make-or-break" factor in Carter's dossier. To be a botanist coming out of this university without this professor's imprimatur would signal that he was not a strong candidate.

In chapter 11, Genny Beemyn and Abbie E. Goldberg write about the experiences of transgender graduate students. I introduce Carter here to make connections across categories of sexual orientation and gender identity in the experiences of graduate students because although they are different constructs and students have distinct needs, LGB and T identities are often combined in campus programs and services and in the literature on minoritized students. Transgender and nonbinary graduate students have specific experiences and needs that are distinct from those of lesbian, gay, and bisexual students.

Colleges and universities operate with a number of administrative apparatuses that rely on fixed categories of names and sex/gender taken from the student's initial application for admission. An increasing number of institutions are incorporating processes for indicating a "preferred name" on class rosters; this practice is seen as one that can benefit trans students, students who have always used a nickname, or international students who would rather offer an English name than constantly have their name mispronounced.[8] Common software platforms that campuses use for student information systems (e.g.,

Banner, PeopleSoft) allow for customization such that students can indicate preferred name and the pronouns they use. Typically, these are fields that can be changed at any time at the student's request. These platforms generate class lists and can be configured to include pronouns as well as names for instructor use, in learning management systems (LMS), and so forth. Critical documents like transcripts and diplomas may still be issued with the student's legal (at time of application) name, but best practices include the opportunity for any student with proper paperwork to formally change their legal name (first, last, or both) in university records. Unfortunately, as many authors have pointed out, legal name change is costly and beyond the means of many graduate students.[9]

Graduate student health care varies widely, with insurance coverage for gender-related services ranging from very good to very meager or nonexistent. Even when health insurance covers gender-related psychological and medical care, there may be no local providers who can or will provide it. Carter found the on-campus student health center transphobic but the university-affiliated hospital's gender clinic to be an excellent resource; a transgender grad student friend of Carter's at another university in a small town two hours away had to make the drive weekly to access trans-inclusive health care.

Much has been written about the everyday basics of trans-inclusive public facilities on campus: bathrooms, locker rooms, and housing.[10] It should go without saying that any person—undergraduate, grad student, faculty, staff—of any gender needs access to safe places to live, change their clothes, and use a restroom. The provision of gender-inclusive (sometimes called gender-neutral) facilities is not yet a given, however, and when students like Carter have to spend energy to devise workarounds rather than use convenient options for fear of harassment, their overall well-being as a graduate student may suffer.[11]

Strategies and Resources for LGBTQ Graduate Students

LGBTQ graduate students can find support on campus, in their disciplines, and outside academe. Not every LGBTQ grad student will need the same resources, and not every campus will offer the same kinds of opportunities for support. Still, there are usually options. It is important to remember that there is no one way to be LGBTQ in grad school, no one way to be LGBTQ as an academic, no right or wrong time to come out or to stay in the closet. Healthy, satisfying LGBTQ identity can include fluidity over time and situational disclosure and expression of sexual orientation and gender identities.

Campus resources might include those in one's academic department and college, such as an academic advisor, PI, and/or teaching supervisor. LGBTQ faculty in one's program or college, even if outside one's discipline, may be able to provide mentoring or advice on navigating academic life. Other graduate students in or outside the department may be good resources for understanding LGBTQ contexts in the college or wider university. Many public research universities support LGBT resource centers, some of which offer groups or services for graduate students. Graduate student employees (graduate assistants) at LGBT resource centers may be able to offer advice on adjusting to the university, graduate student life, and/or the community. Although many graduate students are funded through their academic departments, working as a graduate assistant at an LGBT resource center, or the women's or gender center, is another option for financing graduate education.[12]

A number of disciplinary societies offer programming and services for graduate students, for academics minoritized along a number of dimensions (e.g., race, gender, sexual orientation), or both. For example, the American Educational Research Association (AERA) has a Special Interest Group on Queer Studies; the American Historical Association has the Committee on Lesbian, Bisexual, Gay, and Transgender History; the American Physical Society formed an Ad Hoc Committee on LGBT+ Issues (C-LGBT) in 2014. There are also some LGBTQ organizations in the wider disciplinary ecosystem: oSTEM (out in STEM) educates about and advocates for LGBTQ people in STEM fields. Graduate students may find the disciplinary or cross-disciplinary groups good places to network, find mentors, and locate peers for collaborations and colleagueship. Many of these groups have active social media presences on Twitter and Facebook, providing low-risk ways to explore what they have to offer and extending their reach to locations where being an out LGBTQ person might be more challenging.

Finally, although graduate students of any identities can sometimes fall down the rabbit hole into their studies, teaching, and research, it is also possible to find support outside academe. The members of the local gay men's gospel choir may not understand what it's like to write qualifying exams, and the lesbian potluck crowd may not know how to deconstruct literary theories, but they can be valuable guides to local culture. LGBTQ and LGBTQ-inclusive sports teams, performing arts groups, yoga and meditation classes, and faith communities provide settings where LGBTQ graduate students may be able to get away from worries about being out and from academic pressures. They are places to learn about the best local coffee shop, queer-owned businesses, which doctors to avoid and which to seek out, and how nonacademic LGBTQ people live their lives. LGBTQ grad students who are parents may find these off-campus groups valuable as they seek day care and schools that will be inclusive of LGBTQ families. There are lots of reasons to explore LGBTQ resources, organizations, and people in the local community off campus.

Conclusion

Graduate school can be a time of great discovery, personal and intellectual. It can also be a time of great stress. For LGBTQ graduate students it may be some combination. Understanding oneself and the support available in one's department, on campus, and in the community is an important start. Faculty, administrators, and others who support the success of LGBTQ graduate students can activate the resources to which they have access—and can advocate for additional programs, policies, services, and facilities as needed. LGBTQ graduate students represent one facet of the future of higher education, and their success today will contribute to all of our success moving forward.

Takeaways for Students

- There is no one way to be LGBTQ in graduate school. It is important to live your own identities and their intersections in ways that feel safe and productive for you. Identities are situational; what was right for you in undergrad or the workforce may not feel right in various settings in grad school. Situational identification is healthy and adaptive.

- It's okay to seek help in figuring out your sexual orientation and gender identities. Professional assistance, such as through campus- or community-based counselors, is one option, and there are a number of other resources available in different ways, depending on your institution and the people there: peers in your department or university, an LGBT campus resource center, and advisors, supervisors, and mentors from before or during grad school.
- LGBTQ identities can be a powerful connection to learning opportunities through research, coursework, or campus engagement. Exploring your own identity or networking with other LGBTQ people in your field provides a fresh perspective on your academic life and the academy.
- You should understand the ways that institutional, local, state, and federal policies and laws protect you from discrimination and know how to report incidents you believe are bias-related. Protection for people minoritized by sexual orientation and/or gender identities varies. It may be different at your graduate institution from the protection offered at your undergraduate school or in the workplace. Look online at your institution for nondiscrimination policies and reporting for bias-related incidents; at some campuses the Title IX office or LGBT resource center office are resources. If there is an ombuds office (sometimes called ombudsman) this is a good place to start; a graduate employees union may also be a good resource, as might a graduate-specific or campus-wide diversity, equity, and inclusion office.

Suggestions for Faculty and Administrators

- Conduct an audit of all campus policies and procedures, from graduate student recruitment through postdegree placement, to look for instances where LGBTQ students might experience negative climate or discrimination or where the institution could improve on programs and services already offered. For example, audit all forms that graduate students complete from application through graduation to see where sex/gender are presented only as binary options and where legal name, as opposed to preferred name, is required. Enlist LGBTQ graduate students in this process, but do not leave them responsible for addressing weaknesses or for advocating for change.

- Require graduate programs to conduct a similar audit. Because so much of graduate education—from recruiting to placing students postdegree—is the responsibility of individual departments and conducted by individual faculty, it can be hard to ensure that all processes and policies are inclusive of students with minoritized sexual orientation and gender identities. Going through audits with one or two departments and providing templates to other units might facilitate the process where there is resistance, inertia, or competing priorities.
- Work with facilities and building management to identify where gender-inclusive restrooms, locker rooms, and housing accommodations will be. If there is not a gender-inclusive option in proximity to every single-gender pairing, create a campus map that clearly indicates where the inclusive facilities are located. Design gender-inclusion into all new buildings and renovations.
- Carefully examine graduate student health insurance options and ensure that they include coverage for gender-related health care and treatment. Determine that gender-related health-care providers are available and covered by graduate student health insurance. If these providers are not local, give all students information about how they can access them.
- Conduct a campus climate assessment that identifies positive and negative experiences for LGBTQ graduate students. There are a number of well-used climate assessments, including new approaches that incorporate heat maps and visual data.[13]
- Disaggregate data so that concerns of LGBTQ graduate students can be identified. Provide opportunities for students to report their experiences as learners, as TA instructors, as graduate assistant (GA) researchers, on the campus, and in the community. Account for the multiple roles of grad students and for multiple identities (e.g., QTPOC).
- Explore how to collect data on students' sexual orientation and gender identity so that these data can be used for tracking progress and identifying opportunities to improve graduate education for LGBTQ students. Knowing, for example, that LGBTQ students

are making their way through X doctoral program but dropping out at disproportionate rates from Y master's program could provide useful context for identifying how best to support student success.

- Develop a network of graduate students, faculty, and staff who are willing to serve as mentors and guides to LGBTQ graduate students. These mentors need not be LGBTQ-identified themselves, and it would be ideal if they came from a range of identities to provide the most diverse network possible for LGBTQ grad students.

Suggestions for Mental Health Professionals

- Understand that sexual orientation and gender identities are evolving and situationally expressed. There is not a single "healthy" LGBTQ identity-development end point.
- LGBTQ graduate students are situated in the university as students and (often) as employees. They may come to grad school directly from undergraduate education or well into their adult lives. Their needs in individual or group counseling settings may reflect these differences in roles and life stages. For example, it may not be appropriate for graduate students to be in group counseling settings with undergraduates whom they teach, or they may be exploring gender identity as adults with spouses and children of their own.

~

CHAPTER ELEVEN

"To Be Your Best Self"

Surviving and Thriving
as a Trans Grad Student

Genny Beemyn and Abbie E. Goldberg

"Grad school presses buttons you did not even know were there," related Loren, a nonbinary PhD student in the social sciences, in an interview with us. His statement applies to many grad students, but it especially encapsulates the external and internal difficulties often faced by trans and gender-nonconforming grad students. This chapter examines the greater challenges that trans grad students may encounter in finding a supportive institution and local community; working with advisors, mentors, and other faculty; developing allies; preparing for a career; and looking for a job. Our findings and recommendations are drawn from quantitative and qualitative research we conducted with current and recent trans grad students from across the United States, including data from more than forty interviews.

Finding an Institution that "Fits"

All individuals who are applying to grad school should carefully research the institutions they are considering, looking at both the program in which they want to study and the larger university. For trans grad students, this examination is especially important because departments and colleges can vary significantly in their level of trans-inclusiveness, and a program that is among the best academically may not be at all trans-supportive. "There's no program [worth it] if you aren't going to be able to finish it" because it is unaccommodating to you as a trans person, stated Sam,[1] an agender PhD student in the social sciences at a large research university.

Common advice among the trans grad students we interviewed was the need for trans prospective students to, in the words of Benjamin, a trans masculine master's student in education, "gather as much information as you possibly can" about the climate for trans people in the department and at the institution in general. Some information may be available on the school's website, especially if it has an LGBTQ+ center, but more likely you will have to reach out to faculty, staff, and other students. Benjamin suggested that trans prospective students "ask the hard questions at the beginning" about an institution's efforts to create a trans-inclusive environment in order to avoid choosing a program and university that will be unsupportive. Even if you do not intend to be out as trans, having a space where trans people are not disparaged is going to be important, and you can avoid having to out yourself in the process of obtaining information by communicating with school officials over the phone (such as speaking with the office manager of the department to which you are considering applying) or through the institution's social media or internet platforms.

Some of the questions you might want to have answered include[2]:

- Does the institution have a nondiscrimination policy that is inclusive of gender identity?
- Are hormones and gender-affirming surgeries covered under the grad student health insurance policy?
- If the campus has a counseling center, are its therapists knowledgeable and experienced working with trans students? If there is not a campus counseling center or if it is not trans-inclusive, are there local trans-supportive mental health services?
- Does the institution enable students to use a chosen name on course rosters, ID cards, and diplomas?
- To what extent does the campus have gender-inclusive restrooms? Are they present in the building(s) in which you would take classes, work, and have an office?

- Does the institution offer LGBTQ+ educational training sessions? If so, does the department you are considering participate in these trainings?
- Is there an LGBTQ+ or trans-specific grad student organization? If so, how active is the group and how well-supported is it by the institution?
- Is there a campus organization for grad students in your field? If so, is it trans-inclusive?
- Does the institution recognize gender diversity in its written materials, public pronouncements, programming, campus groups, and so on, or does it seem heavily rooted in a gender binary?
- Are there out trans faculty members in the department you are considering or at least at the institution?
- If you are considering a department in the humanities or social sciences, does it have faculty members who are conducting research in gender and sexuality studies?
- Can the department or at least the institution connect you with current trans students and recent trans alumni?

Even if the department or university is unable to connect you with trans students, faculty, or alumni, you can reach out yourself to get a better sense of the climate for trans students and for students in general and the extent to which diversity and inclusion are part of a department's values. Some of the questions you might ask of trans and nontrans grad students and graduates include:

- In general, how comfortable are faculty members with trans students? Have there been out trans students in the department previously?
- To what extent do faculty members ask, rather than assume, students' pronouns?
- To what extent is the language used by faculty and administrative staff within the department inclusive of trans people, instead of perpetuating a gender binary?
- Are the experiences of trans people incorporated into the curricula to the extent possible?

Working with Advisors, Mentors, and Other Faculty

Even if you are readily seen as cisgender by others and decide not to be out as trans to the faculty in your intended grad program, you will still want to have an advisor who is not hostile toward trans people to avoid feeling uncomfortable. After all, you will be working closely with this person for the next two to seven years, and for this reason, many of our interviewees suggested that grad students choose their advisor carefully. Gabriel, a trans male PhD student in the health sciences, recommended that prospective grad students meet with different faculty members at the colleges they are considering to be sure that their advisor will have at least a basic knowledge of trans people and be supportive of their needs. In his own grad program, Gabriel did not have such an advisor and felt that he was disadvantaged as a result. Another interviewee, Jake, a PhD student in teacher education at a public research university, likewise regretted not having had an advisor who could serve as a mentor to him as a trans person and help him navigate being a trans educator.

In addition to interviewing faculty members to find the person with whom you can best work, Joseph, a trans male PhD student in biology, suggested approaching students to learn about potential advisors and to get more than one perspective, because different students will often have very different thoughts about the effectiveness of a given professor as a mentor. He also encouraged trans prospective grad students to speak with alums, because they will be more likely to be forthcoming than current students, given that they are no longer working under faculty members at the institution and do not have to worry as much about potential retribution if they speak ill of an advisor. "If a mentor is really bad, most students will be too afraid to talk about it, or worse, they might think it's normal," he stated.

If you will be out or seen as trans in grad school, finding an advisor and other faculty members who will be trans-supportive is even more critical. All grad students want to have an advisor who will help them navigate grad school and position them for a successful career. But as Avery, a genderqueer PhD student in higher education, pointed out, trans grad students can especially benefit from having a faculty member who will help "get stuff out of the way" and "be their ultimate cheerleader," because they will face greater obstacles in college and on the job market. Avery was able to find such an advisor, which is a big part of why they chose to get their PhD at the public research university they now attend.

If you are willing to be out as trans in grad school, one way that you can get a sense of whether you will be accepted by faculty within the departments to which you apply is by disclosing that you are trans within your application materials and in interactions with potential advisors. This was the strategy used by Victor, a trans male PhD student in English. He included his pronouns on his resume, grad school application materials, and in his email signature as a way to help screen out programs and faculty members who were not trans-inclusive. A department that would reject him because he is trans is not one that he would have wanted to be a part of anyway, and he ultimately entered a program that is "hugely supportive" of him as a trans person.

Another interviewee, Kasidy, a genderqueer PhD student in history, likewise encouraged trans people to be out during the grad school application process. Although doing so "can be scary," they say that it is beneficial to know upfront if you will face discrimination. Kasidy had been open about being trans when they applied, which enabled them to find a program that not only embraced them as a gender-nonconforming person but also encouraged their interest in conducting research in trans history.

Depending on your area of study and the college you decide to attend, you may be assigned an advisor who is less than supportive or even antagonistic toward trans people. Research finds that many faculty members repeatedly misgender trans grad students, especially nonbinary individuals, in classes and meetings by using their dead (i.e., birth) name, the wrong pronouns, or an inappropriate form of address like "Mr." or "Ms."[3] In some cases, if the faculty member is simply ignorant about trans people and terminology, you may be able to educate them, if you are willing to risk an uncomfortable or possibly confrontational situation. One of the students who decided to take that chance was Jeffrey, a PhD student in bioengineering at a large public university. In response to a professor making an offhand negative remark about trans people, he met with the faculty member to express his concerns about her comment and felt that their conversation went well. The professor was Jeffrey's principal investigator, so "it was hard for [him] to reveal that [he's] trans for fear of what will happen to [their] professional relationship or what she may say to other faculty and students in [their] department." A trans grad student who is not taking classes with or being advised by a professor, and thus does not have to worry as much about the faculty member holding power over their grades or career, would likely find it easier to challenge the professor's anti-trans statements or instances of being misgendered.

At the same time, some students choose not to confront faculty members who misgender them because they tire of constantly having to remind professors of their appropriate pronouns or feel that correcting them is more inconvenient and awkward than enduring misgendering. Casey, a genderfluid master's student at a private university, was among the students who reacted this way. They stated:

> [When the program director or someone else] misgenders me, I just roll my eyes, just because—like, I feel like sometimes I'm uncomfortable about correcting people [and] I feel like it takes so much of a toll when you're consistently correcting people. A lot of the times I just let it happen, because I would rather talk about what we're talking about than spend time . . . correcting you and . . . having to educate someone on that. Because I think it takes away from . . . what we're talking about, which is probably more important.

In some instances, a faculty member may continue to misgender a trans student, even after they have been corrected, because they do not believe that trans identities, particularly nonbinary identities, are legitimate or real, or because the student does not fit their assumptions about the appearance of a trans people. A student in this latter situation is Ariel, a genderqueer femme PhD student in education at a public university. They often struggle to be seen as nonbinary and referred to by "they/them" pronouns in their department because faculty members see them as "too feminine" to be genderqueer.

A few of the trans grad students we interviewed had especially horrific experiences with advisors and other faculty members. For example, Joseph was sexually harassed by the professor for whom he conducted research, who threatened to impede his progress in grad school and sabotage his career if he did not respond to his advances. Joseph "felt trapped" and "like [he] had no outlet." He explained:

> The people I spoke to seemed to not really believe me or didn't know what to do. Mostly, I just kept it to myself. The stress was like a pressure cooker, and at some point I just broke. I ended up having a really severe nervous breakdown, unable to leave the bathroom in my apartment for over a month. [I] spent a week in a mental hospital.

Joseph endured three and a half years of harassment from the professor—only to lose his research position because the faculty member stated, in Joseph's words, "that he was 'uncomfortable mentoring me.' I thought that was really ironic . . . him not being comfortable with me."

Making his situation worse, Joseph could not find another professor who would take him on when he was so close to the end of his PhD work. In desperation, he reached out to a leading biologist who is trans and who had served as a mentor. The biologist called a faculty member in Joseph's department and convinced the professor to be his advisor. Joseph had to start a new PhD thesis in an entirely different subfield, but he was relieved to be able to finish in his program and extremely grateful to the biologist. "I have *never* felt so supported in my whole life," he stated.

Developing Allies and Supportive Communities

Joseph's experiences serve as a cautionary tale about the particularly vulnerable position that trans grad students can find themselves in and the potential for—and effects of—a lack of institutional accountability. But his story also demonstrates the importance of finding support among trans and nontrans professional colleagues. While the assistance that Joseph received to save his graduate career was an extreme case, many of our interviewees discussed how knowing other trans academics was critical to their scholarly success and mental health, especially if their department or college was not very trans-affirming. Lacking mentors in his program, Gabriel turned to the LGBTQ+ network within his field's professional association for support and was able to receive advice and help from colleagues who were further along in their careers. He also benefitted from belonging to and communicating with other members of a Facebook group for trans grad students. Kasidy is part of the same Facebook group, and Gabriel and Kasidy have found it useful in addressing concerns like how best to come out to the students you teach and how to confront a student who repeatedly misgenders you without alienating them. Like many interviewees, Kasidy suggested that incoming trans students look to build a supportive trans community around them because grad school is "so individual and isolating."

The people we spoke to also indicated that having cis allies was critical to being able to navigate their grad programs, particularly in relieving the burden of having to educate others about trans people and always being the one to respond to instances of misgendering. Casey, for example, indicated how much they appreciated cis students speaking up when a faculty or staff member used the wrong pronouns for them so that they did not have to do so themselves and feel that they were alone in confronting trans erasure. Trans allies could also be helpful in addressing institutional barriers. Evan, a trans male master's student, related this experience:

> [There are] three single-user showers [on campus]. . . . Three times now
> . . . I've gone to use them, because I go to the gym before work, and
> they've been locked. [It's] a big embarrassing scene to get them open,
> and what's the point of having them if they're locked? So I called [co-
> worker on campus] and I was like, "Hey, I don't really want to make
> these phone calls because I'm kind of tired of it, can you deal with this?"
> And they like, totally were there to like, make a phone call.

"Be Picky in Terms of Location": Considering Local Communities

While you will undoubtedly do in-depth research on departments and colleges in your grad school search process, you should also carefully consider the local community, as, unless you live in grad student or family housing, you will spend more time off campus than on it. If you are considering a grad school that is not very trans-affirming or has few resources for trans students, moving to an area that will be supportive may help offset the limitations of the campus. At the same time, the most trans-inclusive department or university may seem a lot less welcoming if you will not feel safe in the area.

The importance of a safe and comfortable local community was stressed by many interviewees, especially those who presented as gender nonconforming or who were readily seen by others as trans. Kasidy, for example, explained that when they were looking at grad schools, they asked themselves questions like, "Could I live and walk on the street looking the way I do and it not be a problem?" and "Can I spend six or seven years in this town?" Kasidy not only found a department and college that were trans-inclusive, but also a local community in which their gender expression was not an issue. Similarly, Terry, a transmasculine PhD student in economics who provided the quote above about being picky, was glad that they were choosy, because their college and the city in which it is located have been extremely supportive of them.

In contrast, Chase, a nonbinary psychology PhD student, decided to attend a college in a rural community that she knew was not very queer- and trans-friendly, because she believed that the value of the program offset the challenges of being in a less-than-tolerant area. Chase gets "looks" from people in the town and has to be careful not to touch her wife in public, for fear of a verbal or physical confrontation. But she has survived in such an environment because she has built a community of friends who help sustain her, and she recommended that for grad students in a similar situation, "surround yourself with people who support you and have your back."

In considering the communities in which your prospective colleges are located, some of the questions you might want answered include:

- What is the general political climate of the area? Would someone who is known as trans feel relatively safe living there?
- Are there LGBTQ-supportive local businesses, health-care providers, and places of worship?
- How visible are local LGBTQ+ and trans communities?
- Are there local LGBTQ+ and trans-specific social, cultural, and political organizations and events? To what extent are these groups and activities inclusive of younger trans people and trans people with multiple minoritized identities, such as trans students of color and trans students with disabilities?
- How difficult will it be to find trans and trans-supportive friends and partners in the area?

- How available is trans-affirming medical care locally, such as trans-supportive endocrinologists and surgeons?
- How available is trans-affirming mental health care locally, including gender therapists?

Prioritizing Mental Health Care

Many grad students experience a tremendous amount of stress, in large part because of their heavy course loads, but also often related to other work and family responsibilities, finances, uncertainty about the future, and, possibly, a lack of support and community. For trans grad students, the pressures can be even more intense, given the constant struggle to manage their gender identity in departmental and college environments that may be less than accepting and the potential for extreme isolation, as there are likely few, if any, other trans grad students in their program.[4] Thus while all grad students may have a need for mental health services, such as therapy and support groups, and can benefit from taking steps to promote their physical well-being (e.g., exercise, meditation, getting enough sleep), trans grad students may have a greater need for self-care than their cis peers. As Jules, a genderqueer PhD student in the humanities, stated, "being a grad student is difficult regardless," so do not make it harder on yourself.

Many interviewees stressed the importance of trans grad students prioritizing their mental and physical health and doing so as soon as they enter grad school, before any issues arise. Jeffrey, for example, suggested that incoming grad students be proactive and immediately locate "all support systems you can find." Even if you do not need them now, he said, you may need them later, and you do not want to be scrambling to get help when you are experiencing a crisis. Chris, a nonbinary PhD student in education, agreed. They felt overwhelmed during their first year of grad school and wished that they had taken the time to look into mental health care options and to find a trans-supportive physician at the outset.

Counseling may be particularly valuable for trans students who are coming out or newly out, adjusting to a new geographical area or position (in this case, transitioning to grad school), considering or starting hormones, or contemplating or wanting to have trans-affirming surgeries. If you seek therapy, some of the questions you should ask include:

- To what extent does the therapist have experience working with trans students with a gender identity similar to yourself (i.e., trans woman, trans man, a nonbinary individual)?
- Will the therapist expect you to teach them or are they familiar with the general experiences of trans people?
- Will the therapist be able to separate the effects of anti-trans oppression from other mental health issues, or will they see every issue as related to being trans?
- Does the therapist recognize that there is not one way to be trans and not one way to transition?
- Will the therapist respect the name and pronouns you use for yourself?
- Will the therapist write letters of support if you want to start hormones or have gender-affirming surgeries?

Prioritizing Other Forms of Self-Care

Along with knowing about and making use of mental and physical health care services, interviewees recommended that incoming trans grad students take care of themselves and their mental health by forming friendships with LGBTQ+ people outside of grad school so that they can get away from work or develop a better perspective on it. Some interviewees, like Kasidy, benefited from having nonacademic friends, as they did not have to talk about grad school with them and could escape the stressors of their program for a while. Other narrators, like Aiden, a trans PhD student in anthropology, relied on nonacademic friends to be able to discuss issues that they were having in school without having to worry about what they said getting back to people on campus. Aiden referred to the support they received outside of grad school as "lifesaving."

Some interviewees discussed pursuing nonacademic interests as a form of self-care. Joseph urged trans grad students to "find hobbies and activities that you love to do, that get you out of your head. Mine was rock climbing. You can't not concentrate on the rocks, because if you do, you'll fall. So it was very effective at getting me to not think about anything else." Haley, an agender master's student in an interdisciplinary studies program, mentioned that, to get away from school, "I like to work with my hands. I do crafts and stuff and I like to bake. I like to watch wholesome TV and then some less wholesome TV."

Most of the interviewees were out as trans to some degree in their departments, and some saw coming out or being out as contributing to their mental well-being, because they did not have to try to hide a central part of their identity or be concerned about who knew. Loren, for example, came out last year, after he had completed most of his degree program, and found that doing so relieved a lot of the anxiety he was feeling at the time. "It was a big relief not having to worry about that aspect," he stated. Moreover, Loren discovered that the process of coming out was a lot less stressful than he had expected, as no one made a big deal of his nonbinary identity and, as he is writing his dissertation, he does not interact with a lot of other students anyway. He recommended that grad students come out, if they can, before or during college "because grad school is stressful enough." A number of other narrators, including Jeffrey, concurred with this advice. While Jeffrey acknowledged that it can be difficult at times to decide between being open about who you are and being closeted, avoiding possible harassment and discrimination, he believes that it is important to have support in your department. It helps to be out to those you think you can trust, he stated, so "don't be afraid to take the leap."

In addition to being out to at least some other students and faculty, interviewees considered advocacy for themselves or for trans people in general to be critical to sustaining themselves in grad school. Through their activism, they frequently felt a sense of personal empowerment and a sense of community with other trans people, as well as a sense of relief and self-satisfaction if their aims were achieved. One of the narrators who successfully lobbied for themselves was Chris, who had been told that their legal name had to be on a particular campus record. Chris did not think that this was true, so they refused to take "no" for an answer, and ultimately they were vindicated when another university official allowed them to use their chosen name on the record. From their experiences, Chris recommended that trans grad students "don't be afraid to stand up for yourself and be your own advocate."

Taking Time Off or Leaving Your Program

For a variety of reasons, including finances, changes in career path or interests, mental health, lack of support, transition-related demands, and stress related to anti-trans discrimination, trans grad students may leave or take time off from school and/or switch institutions.[5] Some trans grad students face greater financial pressures than their cis peers because of the additional expenses of transition-related medical care, which can be compounded if they receive little or no emotional and financial support from their families of origin because of their gender identity. Trans grad students may thus have to spend more time working while going to school and may not be able to turn to their families if they experience anti-trans discrimination or harassment in their department or at the larger institution. These and other stresses may "pile up" and lead trans students to feel that they need to take time off or leave grad school.

If you find yourself in similar circumstances, you should ask yourself what you can do to improve your situation (and your mental health), including:

- Would time off to focus on your mental health, transition-related medical care, and/or financial stability enable you to return to grad school and better focus on your studies?
- Do you have mentors, friends, or family members who might be able to offer you more support to help you stay in school?
- If you are not seeing a therapist, would doing so help you better handle the stressors you are experiencing to stay in school? What other self-care steps might you take to address the stressors?
- Are there individuals to whom you can turn to help you consider the pros and cons of taking time off, and perhaps help you strategize how you might improve your situation?

Preparing for a Career

It is important for you to be thinking about your career path as a trans person. How trans-aware and trans-inclusive is your area of study? Are there visible trans people in your field? Being out as trans in the humanities or social sciences, for example, may be quite different from being out in medicine, law, or engineering. However, you can find out trans professionals in any field, as many professional associations have LGBTQ+ caucuses or sections, such as the GLBT Round Table of the American Library Association, the Gay and Transgender Chemists and Allies Subdivision of the American Chemical Society, and the American Astronomical Society Committee for Sexual-Orientation and Gender Minorities in Astronomy.[6] In fields where the professional associations do not have formally recognized LGBTQ+ affiliates, there are often informal networks, such as LGBT+ Physicists and Spectra: The Association for LGBT Mathematicians.[7] There are also a number of Facebook groups for LGBTQ+ and trans PhD students and academics more generally, which several of our interviewees described as important sites for career support. Casey, for example, stated:

> [A trans scholar] put out a thing on social media . . . "I'll look over any cover letter, resume, for any trans or gender nonconforming . . . especially, like if you're also a person of color." So he went through and looked at my cover letter and gave me a lot of feedback, which I feel like I've never gotten before. So I just feel like, within the community, I can reach out to people if I'm not sure what to do or I need support with something.

Ideally, your advisor or mentor should connect you with others in your field, including other trans scholars and practitioners, if you want them to do so. But even if they help you meet colleagues, you will want to develop relationships on your own that extend beyond your advisor, program, and university. Having been sexually harassed by his advisor, Joseph especially emphasized the need for grad students to reach out to other academics in their field: "Network, do good work for other people outside of the lab, and try to collaborate or find other mentors. Try to distribute the power away from one person as much as possible."

Looking for Jobs

Whether or not you decide to be out as trans in the job search process, you will need to think carefully about how you "package yourself" as an applicant.[8] For example, if you have written or presented on LGBTQ+ or trans topics, do you cite this work on your resume or curriculum vitae? What name is on your transcript(s), and if it is not the name you go by, do you want to legally change it to have the appropriate name on your records? What name and pronouns are you known by to the writers of your letters of reference, and do you need to come out to them (or make an effort to remind them) so that they use the appropriate ones?

In considering the pros and cons of being out as trans on the job market, you may be afraid of the consequences of doing so (e.g., will it limit who invites you to interviews or who hires you?) but also afraid of the consequences of not doing so (e.g., will you find yourself at an institution or in a workplace that is unsupportive of trans people and be miserable there?). For Casey, the most important factor in deciding whether to be open about being trans when applying for a particular university position is their perception of the climate for trans people in the area:

> [Whether I'm out] depends on location of the school, and how safe and comfortable I feel. And because I'm doing a national search, and I don't even know if I'll have a support system wherever I'm going—then I'm much more cautious to share.

Another interviewee, Robin, a masculine of center, genderqueer PhD student in medicine, has chosen not to be out in applying for jobs because there are so few positions available in their particular field. They stated:

> I'm a little bit . . . wary to, publicly . . . be out, kind of, or just draw attention to myself as trans [online or on social media] because I'm worried about—you know, there's like two jobs in the country, and if . . . the person hiring is influenced by this in any way, and Facebook stalks me or whatever, then that's my one job goodbye.

In addition to being concerned about their visibility online as a trans person, Robin worried about what might happen if they were invited to an interview and certain "inconsistencies" were made apparent: "Like, say that they expect one thing, because they see female on the application form, for my gender. And then they meet me and they're like, 'Oh, this person wasn't quite what I was expecting.' . . . I'm not sure what to do about it." Such a scenario had the potential to be uncomfortable, if not humiliating.

The possibility of potential employers discovering their gender iden-tity online was also raised by Brook, a genderqueer PhD student in the sciences at a public university. They had identified themselves as trans in a media interview, which they worried would affect their job search: "It's a little terrifying now with finding a job—because my name is not super common so . . . it's the question like, are they Googling me, is this coming up, like, where can I apply for jobs now?" These concerns demonstrate the importance of being careful about what you say and what might be said about you online, especially if you have a highly identifiable name or are in a relatively small field in which there are few out trans people.

Conclusion

There is no right way to be trans in applying to or attending grad school or in looking for a job afterward, just as there is no right way to be trans in general. No matter what decisions you make about your field of study, the school you attend, and the extent to which you are out, you should do what feels most appropriate for you. What really matters, as Benjamin emphasized, is that "you need to be your best self."

Takeaways for Trans Graduate Students

- Research the trans-related policies of colleges and their climate for trans students when applying to grad schools, including talk-ing to trans students at the institutions, if possible.
- Research the climate for trans people in your chosen department at each of the colleges you are considering (such as whether they have out trans faculty and students and whether they ask for and respect students' pronouns).
- Also research the climate for trans people in each local com-munity and state, as you will want to feel safe and comfortable beyond the campus.
- Once you have started grad school, reach out to other grad stu-dents, especially other trans grad students, at your own and other local colleges to develop a community of supportive people.

- Make taking care of yourself mentally and physically a priority from the beginning of grad school.
- Develop friends and hobbies that are unrelated to school so that you do not have to always live in the academic world.
- Know trans-supportive mental and physical health resources on and off campus before you might need them.
- Find an advisor who has at least a basic knowledge of the experiences of trans people and who will be a strong advocate for you in grad school and on the job market.
- Do not be afraid to stand up for yourself and be your own advocate.
- Find mentors and allies in your field through the LGBTQ+ groups within professional organizations.
- Be out about being trans to the extent that you feel you can because it will lessen the stress you might otherwise experience.

Recommendations for Faculty and Staff Members Who Work with Trans Grad Students

We end this chapter by providing recommendations for all faculty and staff members, and specifically for faculty, mental health professionals, and administrators, to create a more supportive campus environment for trans grad students.

Suggestions for All Faculty and Staff Members

- Learn about the experiences of trans people, particularly the experiences of trans grad students, and the issues they face in higher education.
- Ask, rather than assume, the pronouns of students.
- Do not use gendered language for a student or a group of students—such as he/she, Mr./Ms., sir/ma'am, and "ladies and gentlemen"—without knowing how they identify their gender.
- If you misgender a student, sincerely apologize as soon as you realize your mistake, and learn from your mistake, so that you do not repeat it.

- If you hear someone else misgender a student, be sure to correct them, preferably immediately after they have done so.
- Ask the trans students with whom you work how you can best support them, recognizing that different students have different needs.
- Never disclose the trans identity of a student without their explicit permission.

Suggestions Specifically for Faculty Members

- In the small-size classes you teach, have the students introduce themselves, including sharing their pronouns if they want. In larger classes, avoid calling on or referring to students in gendered ways. Instead, use the students' names or nongendered forms of address (e.g., "as you were saying . . .").
- Where possible, include material by and about trans people in the courses you teach.
- Do not expect the trans students in your classes to speak for all trans people or to speak about their experiences at all.

Suggestions Specifically for Administrators

- Immediately make the changes that trans students suggest to create a more trans-inclusive campus.[9]
- Seek out and listen to the voices of trans students and involve them in the process of developing trans-supportive policies and practices.
- Require all faculty and staff members to attend a training session on the experiences of trans people and the institution's expectations for valuing and respecting trans students.
- Make sure that the staff members who address compliance with Title IX recognize that courts have ruled that gender identity and expression are covered under the law and that repeatedly and consciously misgendering a trans person or denying them access to a restroom that reflects their gender identity are forms of harassment.

- Take part in the Campus Pride Index (www.campusprideindex .org) to gauge and improve the level of LGBTQ+ inclusiveness of your campus and to indicate the institution's trans policies to prospective students.

Suggestions Specifically for Mental Health Professionals

- Recognize that there is not one way to be trans, including not one way to transition.
- Affirm nonbinary trans identities as valid and authentic.
- Consider creating a support or therapy group for trans grad students, as they have different needs than trans undergrads and will not feel comfortable in a group with students whom they may teach.
- Know about campus and local trans resources, including area support groups and the most accessible options for obtaining hormones and gender-affirming surgeries.
- Advocate for your institution to cover long-term therapy, hormones, and gender-affirming surgeries under graduate student health insurance if it does not already do so.

‿

CHAPTER TWELVE

Biomedical Pathways

Graduate Student Well-Being in the Biomedical Sciences

Jess Zonana

Pursuing a graduate degree in the biomedical sciences sets you on a path with great potential reward and many unique challenges. Working for ten years as a psychiatrist for graduate students in biomedical research, I have seen many graduate students navigate their academic and personal pathways. I have had the opportunity to follow students in their twenties, thirties, and forties as they become sophisticated scientists entering new phases of life and identity. My perspective in this chapter is based on my role as a psychiatrist and therapist, not a graduate school administrator, academic mentor, or principal investigator (PI).

This chapter will discuss factors affecting personal well-being as you progress toward a PhD in your biomedical graduate program. Frameworks for thinking about these factors and examples are shared, along with guidance on how to consider your own work habits, personality, and vulnerabilities while pursuing your career goals. This is your own metabolic pathway (*sorry!*). Like most biologic systems, starting a biomedical graduate program disrupts your personal homeostasis. Figuring out what aspects of your life to hold steady and what aspects would benefit you to change is part of growing. Sometimes these changes and challenges can come at a cost to your mental health,[1] and at other times they can upregulate positive developmental pathways.

Biomedical Pathways

Biomedical research is an incredibly alluring career path. No matter what you do on a given day, your work contributes to the understanding, prevention, treatment, and even cure of disease, with the ultimate goal of reducing human suffering. When looking for meaningful career paths, biomedical research is at the top of the list for many students with an interest in science. The big picture can be really important in sustaining you through the day-to-day challenges of any program or job.

Some students enter graduate scientific studies with the goal of becoming a researcher. Others may choose it to continue a course of study in a subject they have enjoyed and/or done well in, to increase education and career opportunities more broadly, or even as a practical route away from another life situation. Not everyone knows if and how they want to apply their degree to work and career later.

Your transition to a biomedical graduate program is unique and personal. You may be directly entering graduate school from undergraduate studies, you may have spent some time working in a lab after college, you may have started a graduate program elsewhere and are transitioning to a new school or program, or you may have worked in a totally different capacity in the world and are now returning to school. Endless circumstances can precede the start of grad school. Some graduate students feel their background puts them at an advantage, others can feel disadvantaged entering their program.

A Sense of Belonging

So now you have a new identity: *graduate student, scientist, researcher.* This is an impressive accomplishment. Satisfaction in this achievement can be complicated by several factors. Any new phase of life requires you to integrate or manage a new aspect of identity. Sometimes it's an added bonus to the other parts of yourself and sometimes it comes with a sense of loss of belonging to a group now in your past. Sometimes your student role must now supersede another important role you have inhabited. This graduate student identity is now added to all your other intersecting identities, giving it unique meaning for you. Cherishing your uniqueness is important—it is also crucial to find some ways to identify with your graduate student identity, even if it is just one small aspect of who you are. Finding a way to embrace your student identity can prevent a sense of isolation.

One way to manage this is to stay connected to your graduate school class or cohort, even if you are not close friends with your classmates. You do share a common identity with all your grad school colleagues, whether you feel like you belong or not. "Imposter syndrome" refers to the feelings or beliefs that success or accomplishment has been undeserved, that one is actually not as competent as they appear and somehow fraudulent. (For more on imposter syndrome, please see chapter 2 in this book.) Imposter syndrome, or associated psychological conflicts, can present a barrier to making and maintaining connections with your classmates and mentors. Connecting with multiple people or groups, even when experiencing imposter syndrome, is protective for managing stressors and crises as you proceed through graduate school. Strategies for this include exploring student activities and clubs, joining student committees and government and peer-mentoring programs, accessing resources such as the university counseling center and offices of student life and/or diversity, living on or near campus, and attending informal social events.

Alex, a twenty-four-year-old graduate student who identifies as a gay, cisgendered, Latino man, is in his second year in the pharmacology department of a large university. He has struggled to focus on his studies over the past six months, feeling obligated to go home most weekends to help during a time of family crisis. His younger sister recently revealed past abuse by their former stepfather, and their mother is having difficulty with this news in addition to losing her job last month.

Alex is the first person in his family to go to college, and now graduate school. He feels separate from his classmates, believing he "missed the window" for making friends by going home so frequently. He also thinks he doesn't know as much as other students, having attended a local university while "everyone else went to Yale." His sister and mother have no idea what he is studying and rarely ask him anything specific about school or science. Alex is assigned to present at journal club next week. He is starting to feel like he doesn't really care anymore about doing well at school. He hasn't chosen the article yet nor started to prepare.

This example highlights how hard it can be to balance the competing demands of family and school, yet also how important it is to start to make connections early within the graduate school community—with peers, faculty, deans, or therapists. Reaching out for help during a crisis is tough if you haven't built some preliminary supports. It can also feel more difficult when you feel your background or culture is different from the majority of your classmates. While recognizing this, it's never too late to start reaching out.

> Alex decides to contact student mental health, and in the course of short-term therapy, realizes that he wants to re-engage with school since this has always been his source of strength and achievement. He starts to let his family work through some of their difficulties without him and sets up study hours for himself where he turns off his phone to better concentrate. He also pushes himself to attend some student events, even though he feels out of place. He felt underprepared for his journal club and is not sure how it went, but he decided to meet with the professor to get help rather than withdraw further.

Invisibility is not your friend, even if it has been a coping strategy in your past. Seeking and connecting with peers and mentors is vital to managing the bumps and obstacles that occur through graduate school. Stay in touch with teachers you like even if through email or a quick hello. Faculty have capacity to take notice of you, but sometimes they need to know that you want them to.

Shy, Reserved, or Socially Anxious?
Benchwork often attracts students who are shy, reserved, or socially anxious. Scientific research does not require constant human interaction, and the metrics for success are not primarily based on social aptitude. Experiments that require repetition and precision attract smart people who might prefer spending stretches of time alone. Solitary pursuits can be quite rewarding. However, these traits can get in the way of navigating academia. Sometimes traits that are an asset in one situation create challenges in other situations. Graduate school can be the first time where flying under the radar may have a negative impact on you. Pushing yourself to reach out *before* things get tough allows you to have more cushion and support during the hard times. Letting at least a few people get to know you, allowing them to care about you, even guide or advise you, creates a foundation not just for survival, but success.

How do you know if your shyness or anxiety is inhibiting your success? An anxiety disorder develops when anxious feelings or behaviors interfere with functioning, do not pass after a specific situation, or worsen over time. A mental health professional can help diagnose a disorder. The good news about problematic anxiety is that it's treatable. Whether you are a "worrier," or someone who withdraws in social situations, or gets panic attacks, or is afraid to show your work until it is perfect, a therapist can help you function better and live more comfortably.

Shyness can also be a personality trait that doesn't need formal treatment. As with all personality traits, it is helpful to identify ways it affects you so that you have more control over its impact. Shyness as a trait can sometimes hold you back from presenting or performing confidently. Basic strategies for overcoming shyness or social inhibitions include asking questions in and after class, attending office hours, attending mentoring events, being a teaching assistant, and practicing public speaking.

Finding Your Lab

Securing placement in a lab is one of the concrete milestones of graduate school. It can bring great relief, motivation, and excitement. However, the process can also be challenging. You may get endless and conflicting advice. Most students understand the importance of being invested in the science and/or methods of a particular lab. Too often overlooked are the internal and interpersonal factors that matter in lab placement. Lab environment and culture, management styles of a principal investigator, size and stability of a lab, personalities of the PI and dominant players all have a huge impact on a student's experience, growth, and success in graduate school. How to weigh these factors is very individual and depends on you.

Guidance on navigating success from an academic and scientific perspective should be sought through mentors, established researchers, and resources in and outside of your graduate programs.[2] Advisors can guide you on strategy regarding scientific inquiry, building research skills, and building a career path. They will also tell you to find out about the principal investigator and the lab—how much and where they publish, how quickly they graduate students, and what the students do after they graduate. Do this research—this is information you need to make an informed decision. The importance of mentorship and that relationship is well-known and reinforced by experts.[3,4] You will rotate through several labs so you can experience a range of lab structures, environments, activities, PIs, and lines of scientific inquiry. Pay attention to the types of work environments and PIs that positively motivate you in your work and life.

It is the rare graduate student who knows exactly what they want and adeptly fosters a relationship with the PI they are courting, landing a spot easily in that lab. Some people have the certainty and interpersonal skills to do this, or the external connections to help with this, but most do not. That's okay. And it's not necessarily predictive of success. Finding a lab can provoke some soul searching if it does not come easily. This can be beneficial, even if it is painful.

Hopefully you are interested in joining a few labs. If there is truly only one lab you want, then weighing PI factors becomes less relevant. Pause and make sure you understand why this can be your only lab, and consider increasing your flexibility. If you do have a few labs where the subject matter is interesting, the consideration of PI factors has more weight in how you choose, and it also gives you a chance to include personal well-being in your lab choice.

Nature Biotechnology reported wildly high prevalence rates of anxiety and depression (41 percent and 39 percent, respectively) in graduate students.[5] Students with less anxiety and depression endorsed more positive statements about their PI/advisor than anxious and depressed graduate students. Only 35 percent of students with high anxiety and 32 percent of students with depression agreed that their PI/advisor provided ample support, and only 37 percent and 35 percent agreed that their PI/advisor was an asset to their career. Regardless of what larger conclusions one draws from this study, it underscores the importance of the student-advisor relationship for the graduate student.

Loss of Milestones

Tests and exam grades can lead to demoralization for students who tend to compare themselves negatively to classmates. Lab work can offer a break from this cycle. Yet exams and classes also provide familiar milestones, a sense of progress, and a sense of belonging to a group who are all doing and working on the same material. These supports can be lost when transitioning to lab.

While classes and tests can provide an opportunity to bond with your cohort, they can also provoke insecurity. Students enter with a wide range of experience and expertise, which can foster competition. It is also easy to feel behind if you are shifting academic focus from your undergraduate work to a new specific topic. Seek out supplemental resources if you feel you might actually be behind, such as tutoring, teaching assistant (TA) sessions, or attending office hours. Letting the professor know you are interested and engaged is paramount.

Lab work, unlike coursework, is not necessarily designed for the student experience. Students are exposed to a very broad range of circumstances, lab environments, expectations, and support. This requires them to be adaptive to their environment and have some awareness and acceptance that competing agendas exist. In addition to overseeing graduate students, principal investigators are also pursuing grants, overseeing postdoctoral students, overseeing all aspects of their research lab, and looking to publish, along with many other academic demands.

Once classes become the less-dominant structure for your work and time, you need to develop a range of milestones that are appropriate to your thesis work. You will also need to learn to value and trust these milestones even if they are less obvious than an "A" on a test or a published paper.

June is a MD-PhD who has secured placement in a neurobiology lab for her thesis. She adores her PI, who is warm and available. June has always felt she has had to work harder than others to pass tests and learn new material. She also chronically worries she will be perceived as not working hard enough. A few months into her research, June shares with her roommate that she has been asking her PI for reassurance at the end of every weekly meeting. Her PI was initially accommodating but now has begun to show impatience with her. Her roommate encourages her to seek reassurance at home and not at work. However, she soon also finds it frustrating that June needs such repetitive and frequent validation from her.

She encourages June to find a therapist through student mental health to help manage her anxiety. Working with her therapist, June comes to understand that she has lost her usual means of reassurance and managing achievement expectations. No longer having grades to validate her progress, she is now urgently looking for other people to provide this. June accepts that this is not working, so she starts to explore other ways of measuring her progress, while practicing skills to feel validated.

This situation also underscores the importance of having different people to reach out to for different things. If the support you are getting is not working, or is jeopardizing relationships in other ways, make sure you are going to the right people for the right things. Seeing a therapist can ease pressure and preserve other relationships when you are struggling.

The Family Paradigm
Applying a family model to labs and graduate school can be useful in navigating your experience. If you had traumatic experiences in your family life growing up or did not have a traditional family, you can still apply this model. It is not meant to reflect actual experience, but to provide a way of thinking about relationships and interactions in your lab situation. This framework is best explored with some flexibility. A PI can serve as a parent figure, your lab colleagues as siblings, and your classmates can inhabit several roles—siblings, cousins, friends. You may also bristle at this family concept if you cherish your independence and take satisfaction in "adulting." But life, no matter what phase, offers endless opportunity for a *good* or *good-enough* parent to make a difference. The ways that this model may be relevant to your actual lived experience is that everyone brings an imprint of prior relationships when creating new ones. We will come back to this, but introducing it here is important as you weigh the PI factors in lab selection.

Settling on a thesis lab usually involves compromise in domains that matter to you, whether it's the exact area of scientific inquiry, the methods you will be asked to employ, the level of prestige of the PI, the work environment, or other factors. It helps to sort out what you think is important before trying to make the decision. To make it even more difficult, you must also manage enormous uncertainty even if you feel confident in your priorities—people may not be as friendly as they seem at first, colleagues may not tell you about their negative experiences, and PIs may believe they are available and accessible even if they're not.

Prioritizing these domains helps you make your compromises. It may end up feeling worth it to choose a PI who people indicate may be "moody" (implying harsh or explosive?) or another who is withdrawn and travels all the time, if the research itself fulfills a dream, or if you feel you can succeed in most environments. But don't use your lab choice to prove this to yourself. Having the ability to tolerate certain personality types may not mean you will thrive under these conditions. In fact, it may trigger negative patterns for you in the long run. Survival is extremely important, but survival as your primary goal sets you up for a struggle. Reflect on who your other "parents" have been in the past—actual parents/guardians and other teachers, coaches, or mentors. Consider these questions: What were they like? Which traits helped me? Which harmed me? Which relationships led to conflict and why? How do I respond to authority? Under what conditions have I blossomed the most? Do I need the same things now as I did then?

Anita has the choice of two different labs for her thesis work. Both labs offer a chance to explore her interest in gut immunology and bacteria. One of the PIs, Dr. A, is more junior and known to be a likeable and fair micromanager. The other, Dr. B, is more famous and described as temperamental. Dr. B's lab has a much wider range of projects going while Dr. A's science is more narrowly focused. Anita is leaning toward Dr. B because she is less sure of what she wants to do, but her friends are urging her to join Dr. A's lab, noting that Dr. B sounds a lot like her undergraduate supervisor, whom she ended up resenting. Ultimately, Anita decides that she needs to prioritize her environment and the process of the next several years, not just the outcome. She joins Dr. A's lab after identifying a positive mentoring relationship as important for this phase of her career.

Trouble Finding a Lab
Sometimes trouble finding a lab is just bad luck. A PI has changed institutions between the time you interviewed and arrived. You might have a great rapport with a lab, or PI, or both, but the funding isn't there. These external factors can have a real impact on options and opportunity, but these are also crucial times to reflect on yourself, your needs, and adaptability.

Sometimes difficulty finding a lab can reflect your own ambivalence about being in graduate school. You may need to reset your criteria or search for barriers. Internal barriers can be tough to acknowledge. Am I avoiding a lab because I think I'm not good enough? Am I rejecting a lab because I am being too arrogant? Am I frustrated about something else and stalling in this decision? A therapist can help with this if you are finding it hard to do on your own.

> Rivka is on her fifth lab rotation after her first four labs were not a good match. At her school, the expectation is to rotate through three labs and then settle on a thesis lab. One lab had offered her a spot, but she felt the work would be tedious with a focus outside of her primary interest. The two labs she had hoped to join already had accepted students from her year; students who seemed arrogant and pushy. She is feeling rejected while also believing the labs available have no real chance of a major "breakthrough." After talking this out with a therapist, she verbalized her wish to make a major scientific discovery during her thesis work. She realized that while she may want to hold on to this goal, it had become an obstacle as a guiding factor for choosing a lab and was getting in the way of starting any work at all.

Lab placement can feel like it permanently alters the course of your life and career. Sure, this can be true, but this lens can be overwhelming or even paralyzing when choosing a lab. For some students, it is more manageable to approach choosing a lab as a practical step in building experience and knowledge for a career in science. Talk over your needs and goals with several people to understand the opportunities available as a result of work in a specific lab. Are the methods more important than the specific scientific questions for you? Do you need preliminary training to go into the field you want to pursue as a postdoc? Will this lab offer a specific skill set or broader experience and which do you want or need?

Collect Several Mentors (Parents)

This is easier said than done—that's why everyone keeps saying it. One mentor can rarely provide the level and range of support a graduate student needs. And different parents are better at different things. The PI-student relationship is complicated and variable, sometimes encumbered by conflict of interest and differing needs of advisor from advisee. There is a lot at stake for everyone, and the work is intense.

Faculty don't always advise well outside their "lane," and everyone carries the bias of their own experience. So even when you are talking to other faculty members or advisors, keep in mind that no advice is absolute. Your job is to integrate and absorb what people are offering onto a new situation—you—so not everything needs to be applied concretely.

Friends and classmates are usually helpful but not adequate for professional and career support. Senior graduate students can offer guidance based on their own experience, which can be useful. But be mindful that this "advice" can also be tainted with aggression, resentment, or competition, sometimes more about them than you. This can be harder to recognize when you are feeling uncertain or vulnerable.

Life In and Out of the Lab

Qualifying Exams

The qualifying exam is a major milestone for biomedical graduate students. In some programs, the exam might be based on lab work you are already doing, in others, the exam specifically requires you to develop an independent proposal, and in still others, the exam is based on applying what you have learned in class to new articles or hypothetical situations. The months leading up to this exam are often a stressful time. It helps to plan for this whether or not you expect it to be difficult. Time management can be especially challenging, particularly if your PI is not attuned or sympathetic to this demand on your time outside of their lab. Before you decide your PI doesn't care, make sure they know this exam is coming up. It may be your responsibility to tell them. Also think about how and when to bring it up, as this can have an impact. Just because this may be an uncomfortable conversation does not mean you should delay. Asking for reduced hours in the lab during the week(s) leading up to the exam is a reasonable request, but framing the request as a demand may not be well received.

Your qualifying exam may also be the first time you have to present in front of a faculty panel. This can exacerbate anxiety or self-esteem issues during this time. As with any time of acute stress, avoid making other major life choices during the exam period if you can. Can you decide on a breakup later? Can you wait to move to that apartment, dorm room, or other housing? If you are starting to think the PhD is not for you, can you complete the qualifying exam and then decide? These decisions can start to feel more urgent when other stressors escalate, like qualifying exams.

Competition and Aggression in the Lab

Competition is important to recognize in any work environment. Nearly all people have a competitive drive, whether acknowledged or unacknowledged. As with most human traits, this can produce both positive and negative consequences. Some people are more aggressive in how they manage this drive, while others may withdraw when confronted with direct competition. Many fall somewhere in between.

Drawing on the family model, competition within a lab can be viewed akin to sibling rivalry. Whether you are a graduate student, postdoc, or senior researcher, in some ways you are all competing for your PI's attention, praise, and professional support. As a more junior graduate student, it can take time to get a sense of lab dynamics and how others manage this competitive drive. In more collegial lab environments, researchers are more able to appreciate and benefit from each other's different skills and success, and overt aggression or undermining behaviors are limited.

In other environments, either consciously or unconsciously, a PI may allow several researchers to set a more aggressive tone, allowing for subtle or even blatant aggressive styles. Sometimes this can result from the PI modeling a similar manner, but it often results from PIs who may be conflict avoidant, untrained in people management, or reluctant to embrace this role. When a lab allows a few personalities to dominate, the culture can favor aggressive over harmonious competition.

Aisha, a third-year graduate student in biophysics, is asked by her PI to present her work at an important conference. She is very pleased because she had heard he usually selects more senior students to present. She is also relieved that her PI feels her work is going well enough to be presented. He has always been pleasant but tough to read. She worries he thinks she isn't working hard or being sloppy, despite knowing otherwise.

Aisha has made a lot of friends throughout school, but the senior students in her lab have been interpersonally hot and cold. After the news of the conference, she begins to feel more uncomfortable in the lab. Julia, a senior graduate student, seems to be talking to her less and deliberately going to lunch without her. She feels like she might be making it up but can't put it aside. Aisha presents at lab meeting for practice, and her PI needles the group by saying "At least we have Aisha to get us some real results—the rest of you take notes!" Afterwards, Julia says, "Well, I guess you know how to become the teacher's pet!" Aisha feels angry at Julia and at her PI for publicly praising her. But . . . she also feels validated by his praise. All these frustrated, thrilled, and guilty feelings morph into anxiety for Aisha, and she starts to feel more apprehensive going to lab, sometimes avoiding people and downplaying her knowledge.

Figuring out how to thrive in your lab environment is a key adaptation of graduate school. This does not mean you have to love being there all the time and become best friends with other students or researchers in the lab. It does mean you have to find ways to thrive as best you can in that environment. Aisha may figure out that withdrawing is not in her best interest, or that other people aren't taking the same stance as Julia, and hopefully she will find ways to manage rather than just wait for her to graduate, which is a popular but painful approach.

If you are feeling uncomfortable in your work environment, seek help for how to manage this. Sometimes your discomfort, if based primarily in anxiety or self-esteem issues, is something you need to manage with help from people outside the lab, or with a therapist if it could potentially have an impact on your functioning or performance. If your discomfort is rooted in the misbehavior of others, you may need to find a way to discuss it with your PI. Don't assume they are observing and ignoring a situation—they truly might not have the attention or the skills to pick up on problematic dynamics.

Lab cultures can also get much more hostile than this. If you are feeling harassed or chronically disrespected in your work environment, you should let someone know. Ideally, you should start with your PI if they are not a direct participant in the problem. You should also seek guidance from your program, a mentor, or an advisor on how to approach this if your PI is not able to help sufficiently. It is difficult as a student to figure out how to best navigate lab or departmental politics. Reaching out for help can feel like going over a PI's head, which students are understandably hesitant to do. It is more likely to create tension if you have not tried to discuss it with your PI first. If you are not sure who to go to, resources like an office of student affairs help students navigate and resolve tough situations. Remember those other faculty members you were assigned? Or the ones you were advised to collect over the past few years? This is when you might benefit from talking to them.

Depression, Anxiety, and Not Showing Up

Jesse is a nonbinary, biracial twenty-four-year-old student in molecular biology who was initially pleased to have landed a spot in their first-choice lab. They had one episode of depression in college but have been feeling pretty good since starting graduate school. They are paired with a postdoc who is finishing up a project using techniques the PI wants Jesse to learn. The postdoc is erratic with Jesse, sometimes impatient and dismissive, other times overly familiar and talkative. The postdoc, who is White, tries to enlist Jesse in talking about race and politics at work, asking questions that seem more provocative than curious. Jesse starts to dread going to lab. This continues and Jesse becomes regretful about joining this lab. They are having trouble sleeping and skipping days without notifying anyone at the lab. The postdoc reports to the PI that Jesse is not putting in any time on the project and not showing up. The PI emails Jesse asking for them to meet.

Not showing up or not responding is damaging to you, even if it provides short-term relief. Whether you are feeling aggressed, victimized, demoralized, or depressed, not showing up rarely helps you and rarely communicates accurately what you are experiencing. If you are starting to dread and avoid going to class or work, this is the time to seek out help inside or outside the lab or report what is happening.

Jared is a shy, anxious fifth-year doctoral student in a computational biology lab whose PI asked him to lead a collaboration with a wet lab who had generated new data sets. Jared had developed several new statistical models, one already published, and he is about to start writing his thesis. The PI is eager to find applications for his methods and pushes him to work on this project simultaneously. The collaborators are aggressive in their time demands, peppering him with emails about how soon they can get results. Jared finds them resistant to feedback on how to apply his model and what it can (and can't) do. Jared is feeling bullied, is angry at his PI for putting him on this project, and starts to not respond to any emails sent from the collaborators. Jared gets an email from his PI asking to meet after receiving complaints from the collaborators.

There are many scenarios that lead students to withdraw or not show up. Sometimes students get depressed and literally cannot make it to lab. Other times, anxiety, anger, or resentment get in the way. If possible, students benefit from seeking help with situations or feelings before they start to affect functioning. This may mean finding a therapist for support if the sources of the conflicts aren't easily addressed.

Finishing

Biomedical graduate students often show a bimodal trend in seeking therapy—preceding the qualifying exam and then again nearing the last year of thesis work. Life stressors accumulate as a graduate student begins to accumulate enough data that puts finishing in the line of sight. "Burnout" becomes a common term applied in the last years of a PhD. The prospect of graduating also means you need a plan for after graduate school and face another major life transition. This may be welcomed, but it still acts as a "stressor" psychologically. The last two years can be a time when the relationship between student and PI can become intensified, conflicted, or acrimonious.

Delay is also common in the final year or years of a PhD. Sometimes experiments just aren't working, and these results are needed to finish your scientific story and graduate. This can lead to feelings of burnout, frustration with your PI or program, or issues of self-esteem related to your value as a scientist. Charging through the finish line can also be difficult if you don't know what you want to do next. One student spent an additional year and a half dragging out experiments, avoiding going to lab, and bickering with his PI despite stating that his number one goal was to "get out of here." Many factors infused this situation, but one major factor was his uncertainty and fear of leaving academia, despite all his feelings of resentment.

Storming Out

The process of finishing a thesis can exacerbate any tensions or negative relationships within a lab. For students eager to leave, additional experiments or assistance on other projects can be frustrating. Students can experience these requests as sadistic, punitive, or retaliatory, all of which can sometimes be true. One student's relationship with her PI crashed and burned in the last year of graduate school as the PI asked her to continue to work on a postdoc's primary project, with the student feeling exploited for her skills. The PI expressed astonishment at the student's reluctance to meet the lab expectation for cross contributions. This relationship, once functional and productive, ended in an adversarial goodbye.

Hostage Crisis

Lina is a thirty-one-year-old international student and has received significant praise for her work. She presented at conferences and has several labs expressing interest in her for postdoctoral work. At her last committee meeting, the faculty were congratulatory, suggested several top journals to submit her work, and approved the plan to submit her thesis. Until this year, Lina had experienced her relationship with her PI as symbiotic, but now she has become both anxious and frustrated about her situation. She feels her PI is not letting her leave, as he continues to require new experiments before submitting her paper to any journal. These requests seemed understandable at first, given the journals they were considering, but now it has been a year. She believes she is now forced to choose to leave without her first-author paper or to stay indefinitely, with the hope he will eventually let her submit.

Hostage situations unfortunately occur and rarely resolve in favor of the student if other program leadership is not involved. Students must advocate for themselves with help outside of the lab, and these politics are tough to manage from the student position. If the PI is a powerful figure at the school, which they often are, it becomes all the more important for the school to have avenues for mediation. Schools can be structured differently, but the program director or an office of academic affairs or student affairs or similar are important resources in these situations.

Setting out criteria, expectations, and a timeline for graduation with your PI is extremely important. You may need to review this as your projects progress or change. Complicating situations can always occur, and taking extra time may be necessary and advantageous for you. PIs will have competing demands in addition to nurturing your career. Experiments may not work out as hoped, so students must allow for some flexibility in their personal timelines to accommodate external pressures. Seek help from your program director or dean's office if a situation becomes essentially coercive or clearly detrimental to your future plans.

Academics or Industry or Out

What do you do with a PhD or master's degree? Somehow you have to figure this out as you are busy doing your work and managing your personal life. The most available advice and influence comes from nearby academics and mentors who all chose to pursue academic careers. Not surprisingly, this advice can be biased in favor of academia. Preserving academic research is important to the creative pursuit of knowledge; scientists are aware of mounting obstacles toward this end and lobbying for change.[6] People also tend to reinforce their own decision making, and seeing mentees pursue similar career paths is validating. Many students feel inhibited in asking for guidance around nonacademic career issues with fear of damaging relationships with mentors. Students report stigma associated with interest in working in industry rather than academics.[7]

Do your best to explore these other options freely if this might be a rewarding path for you. Know that you are not alone when considering "nontraditional" careers. In one study, 70 percent of biomedical graduate students surveyed were "strongly considering" at least one career path not directly involving scientific research, resulting in recommendations to integrate more career development programs into basic science graduate programs.[8]

Takeaways for Students

- Your time as a graduate student can yield immense personal and professional growth if you prepare for obstacles and embrace your version of a graduate student identity.
- Acknowledging your own needs, traits, and vulnerabilities enables you to adapt and prepare for the personalities, politics, and opportunities that surround scientific research.

- Milestones within the lab and research environment may be different from past academic experiences.
- Learning to reach out for support increases your chances for success and prevents crises.
- Avoiding competition may not be possible, but recognizing it in yourself and others can help you manage it.

Suggestions for Faculty and Administrators

- Consider explicit and separate structures for academic mentoring, academic advising, career coaching and psychosocial supports.
- Develop additional outreach and support programs for underrepresented minorities and international graduate students to help address unique challenges and counteract disadvantages these students may face.
- Create and support networking programs for faculty-student contact outside of the classroom and lab.
- Provide and require training for faculty members in project management, personnel management, and conflict resolution.
- Provide resources for graduate students interested in career paths outside of academia.

Suggestions for Mental Health Professionals

- Promote and support accessible mental health services for graduate students.
- Consider psychoeducation programs at your institution to encourage intervention before crises occur.
- Inquire about lab relationships and fulfillment of academic requirements.
- Explore whether students are communicating adequately with their mentors and supervisors.

CHAPTER THIRTEEN

~

Who Am I?

My Multicultural Selves

Michelle Chu-Camba

Each of us holds a unique set of identities and cultural backgrounds that impact our reasons for coming to grad school, our experiences in grad school, and the choices that we make in grad school. Embarking on the graduate school journey can undeniably be a rigorous and overwhelming experience. Not only are you expected to manage academic responsibilities, but additional challenges faced by graduate students may also include relocation (to a different state or country), leaving supports such as family, friends, and significant others, forming new relationships, coping with financial burden, and navigating the long stressful years of commitment involved in attaining a graduate degree. The intersectionality of your identities may add another unique layer of stress as you adjust to your new educational and social environments. Ethnicity, race, gender, culture, religion, sexual orientation, and age are some examples of intersectional identities that can influence your graduate school experience.

Juan, for instance, a Latinx student, the oldest of five children raised in a single-parent, lower socioeconomic status household, held the responsibility of contributing financially to his family. His collectivistic values instilled a sense of familial obligation that, at times, conflicted with his academic pursuits. Juan's male gender, birth rank, socioeconomic background, cultural values, and family dynamics compelled him to work several part-time jobs to ensure that his family was financially cared for while he pursued his academic goals. This often diminished the amount of time he could dedicate to his academic work. It also negatively impacted his engagement with classmates and professors, his ability to network with other professionals, and his pursuit of research opportunities.

Students' identities play a significant role in their overall psychological and emotional functioning. Each of us have *visible* identities, such as the color of our skin, as well as *invisible* identities, such as our sexual orientation. Individuals who perceive their multicultural identities as compatible with each other and with their environment are more likely to report increased well-being.[1] However, tensions between identities or between one or more identities and the environment may lead to feelings of confusion, stress, and alienation. Nonetheless, one's unique identities can also serve as a source of strength by providing valuable support during strenuous life circumstances. For instance, religion and spirituality can sometimes create a sense of community and belonging, generate opportunities for social connectedness with others, and reduce feelings of isolation and loneliness.[2] This, in turn, may protect against depression and anxiety and reduce or moderate substance abuse and other self-destructive tendencies.

A primary goal of this chapter is to explore the experiences of multiculturally diverse graduate students. This chapter will address challenges encountered by students as they navigate their multicultural identities in their academic settings. Identifying these experiences can encourage readers to reflect on their own journeys and how these challenges may have contributed to their personal and academic development. The unique stories shared are intended to help readers consider the multiple intersections of their own identities and are not representative or generalizable to an entire group or subgroup. Suggestions will be offered for how graduate students can cope with and thrive throughout the stressors of graduate school. Finally, this chapter will end with recommendations for how peers, faculty, and mental health professionals can support graduate students based on existing research as well as my clinical experience.

What Is Multiculturalism?

In this chapter, the term "multiculturalism" embodies all unique aspects of an individual. To illustrate the various visible and invisible identities that one may possess, I often use Edward T. Hall's metaphor of a "cultural iceberg"[3] in my clinical work. Imagine a large iceberg sitting in the deep ocean water. Only a small portion of the iceberg's mass can be seen extending above the surface. This visible piece, according to Hall, represents a person's visible identities. These include their physical features, race, gender, spoken language(s), accent, age, and even clothing. These are aspects of us that are difficult to conceal and are easily accessible to those whom we encounter. What many people do not see, however, is the portion of the iceberg hidden beneath the water's surface. As a result, the vast majority of our identities lay hidden beneath the surface, invisible to others. These identities could include level of education, citizenship, sexual orientation, gender identity, political affiliation, family dynamics, past and/or current trauma, and personal worldviews.

Exercise 1: Reflect on Your Identities
I encourage you to pause from reading this chapter and reflect on your own identities—the visible and invisible ones. Can you identify your visible identities? What about the identities that are invisible and often go unnoticed by others? Which identities do you value the most? Do the identities you value change based on the context you are in? Which identities feel the most central to who you are? Which ones feel more peripheral? What has contributed to how you experience your current identities?

There are no right or wrong answers. Reflecting on our identities is sometimes difficult, so if you are finding this exercise challenging, that's a normal reaction! You can always return to the activity at a later time. Furthermore, keep in mind that our personal identities are not static. They evolve as we go through life and encounter different situational and social environments and circumstances.

As students become exposed to a range of communities during their time in graduate school, they may question and/or need to negotiate multiple aspects of their identities. This may have an impact on their social, emotional, and physical wellness. When I was in grad school, I often wrestled with feelings of guilt resulting from my relocation and physical distance from my aging parents. My Chinese American identity places an emphasis on the value of "filial piety," the Confucianism virtue of respecting and caring for one's parents and elderly family members. While caring for aging parents is a general concern for adult children everywhere, my parents being non-native English speakers left me with certain responsibilities (e.g., serving as translator at their medical appointments) that became more difficult to carry out as the academic and clinical workload in grad school intensified. As confusing as it was, I eventually learned to navigate the intense internal conflict presented by my intersecting identities, and I also learned to manage the various responsibilities and expectations tied to my distinct roles. For instance, continuing my filial responsibilities to the best of my ability despite my physical distance was a value that I honored. As a result, making a commitment to visit my parents one weekend per month to help with family responsibilities compartmentalized my roles as a daughter and graduate student. In fact, setting aside a designated weekend to be with my family motivated me to be more productive during the weeks prior. Given the nature of grad school, however, it is beneficial to maintain a flexible mindset recognizing that, at times, it may be unrealistic to fulfill certain responsibilities and roles. Fortunately, my supportive parents, friends, and professors helped me understand the impact of my various identities on my graduate school experience.

In my work as a psychologist in a university counseling center, I've found that interpersonal and intrapersonal challenges associated with students' multicultural identities regularly found their way into our sessions. Although the narratives shared by graduate students are unique, there were several recurring themes that tended to overlap with each of their experiences. This chapter will address two such themes: 1) sense of belonging and 2) language.

Sense of Belonging

Many graduate students have painful stories of feeling alienated and isolated within their environments, whether it be their graduate program, cohort, social groups, and/or communities. How students perceive their personal integration within their environments can impact their feeling of relatedness or connection to others as well as their overall sense of being accepted and valued. There is substantial research that illustrates the positive impact of one's sense of belonging and social connectedness on physical and mental health. Students who reported higher levels of belonging in their educational environment have overall better psychological outcomes than students who demonstrated a lower sense of belonging.[4] People who feel more connected to others have higher resilience and lower levels of anxiety and depression.[5] Being part of a group can help people feel valued while also eliciting feelings of solidarity. The feeling of being valued and appreciated in relationships can have a positive impact on health and improve one's ability to cope with intensely painful emotions. As a result, the additional benefits of social connectedness include decreased mortality risk and increased sense of meaning and purpose in life.[6] Having a sense of belonging has also been linked to positive educational achievements including student's intrinsic motivation, retention, and completion rates.[7]

Sofia, an international student in her thirties, talked about the challenges of holding dual identities—being born and raised in Europe and studying in the United States. In her mid-twenties, she moved to the United States for her educational pursuits. Despite already living in New York for almost a decade, Sofia's European upbringing made her feel as though she still did not have a right to speak about the sociopolitical climate in the United States. "I'm not American . . . do I even have the right to say anything about the Black Lives Matter movement or what's happening in the White House?" However, when asked about her comfort level expressing her thoughts about the current political climate in her native country, Sofia expressed a similar level of sadness and alienation. "When I visited home last year, I found it hard to comment on politics with my family and friends. I mean, I didn't even vote. I couldn't vote because I was here." Sofia also shared her disappointment at the persistent gender-role stereotypes within her patriarchal family that made it even more difficult for her to participate in political discussions with her father and two older brothers, "they're proud of me for being in grad school and they think I'm smart . . . but maybe to a certain degree, they don't take my ideas and political stance seriously. It's like they don't think I know what I'm talking about because I'm not a man."

Sofia's painful disclosure highlighted her "rootless" feelings and the conflicts she experienced in her environments. Her lack of early history in the United States and her absence from her native country contributed to her feelings of uncertainty regarding her role and promoted her sense of being a "temporary guest" in both spaces. Sofia found it challenging to share her voice and ideas about political topics that she cared about. This struggle led to feelings of being devalued and dismissed. Consequently, Sofia found herself often experiencing low mood, weepiness, and a reluctance to participate in courses that required her to engage in sociopolitical debates.

Over the course of our treatment, much of our work focused on validating Sofia's emotional distress and helping her recognize that her voice *matters*. Her early upbringing in a male-dominated family and society promoted a rigid dichotomy of gender roles and expectations. Men were viewed as logical, strong, unemotional, and the primary breadwinner, whereas women were seen as soft-spoken, emotional, weak, and the primary caretakers of the home and children. Sofia's mother and father upheld these gendered roles in their family, which instilled the belief that Sofia was less important than her male counterparts. This, combined with her dual identities, strengthened her view of "not belonging." In our work together, Sofia explored her multicultural identities. She learned to honor both of her cultures (European and American) and integrate these life experiences to form a more rounded sense of self. Our sessions also provided her with the opportunity to better understand her feelings around gender roles and expectations. I encouraged her to gently challenge her own beliefs about herself, which gradually led to her increased confidence in seeking and establishing space for herself. With time, Sofia no longer viewed herself as "rootless," but rather as a resilient woman exploring opportunities to grow.

Exercise 2: Exploring Your Relational Resources and Needs

Using a sheet of paper, draw a circle in the middle of the page and write your name in this circle. Now, draw four more circles outside of and encircling this central image, like planets orbiting around the sun. Draw a line between each circle (planet) and the middle circle (sun). In the outer four circles, write down any individuals and/or groups to whom you are meaningfully connected. Examples may include family, relatives, friends, roommates, academic advisors, religious and spiritual communities, and athletic groups. Feel free to add extra circles if needed. In contrast, if you're noticing a struggle to fill in the outside circles, that's okay! The purpose of this activity is to help identify your social network.

When you have completed the exercise, here are some questions to consider: Do the individual(s) or group(s) identified in the circles live near or far from you? How often do you connect with each other? Which of these individual(s) or group(s) do you tend to seek emotional support from? What about physical support? Do you feel socially satisfied with your current connections? If so, what about these relationships feel nurturing and supportive? If not, what are some aspects that you think may be missing from these connections? At the end of this chapter, I will be sharing some suggestions to help expand your social connections.

Language

Language is central to our sense of belonging and meaningful social connectedness. It plays an influential role in how we communicate and how we engage with others. Language is not merely an instrument for expressing our thoughts, feelings, attitudes, and values, but it is also an expression of our social identities. Language can be expressed verbally and nonverbally and is an important part of how people view themselves in relation to their environments.

Amy, a forty-three-year-old married mother of two teenage sons, originally from Macau, shared her challenging journey as an international student whose first language was not English. Amy recalled having a socially and professionally fulfilling life when living in Asia. However, since relocating to the United States, Amy noticed changes in her mood and self-confidence. She discussed her daily weepiness due to social isolation and the frequent fear of being negatively evaluated by others for her accented English and slow speech: "I know my English is not good. I take a long time to say something. People will smile and nod, but they don't have patience. They don't ask me questions . . . they don't try to get to know me . . . they don't want to be my friend. They think I'm stupid."

For graduate students, language can impact how they are perceived and understood by their peers, colleagues, and professors. Amy experienced harsh self-criticism when she believed she was unable to convey her thoughts, feelings, and needs clearly and concisely. My ability to communicate with Amy in her native language helped establish a sense of kinship between us. She found it "liberating" to converse in Chinese without having to doubt her vocabulary and grammar. During sessions, Amy's lack of confidence conversing in English was normalized and identified as a common challenge encountered by many international students. This acknowledgment seemed to soften her self-criticism and feelings of shame and embarrassment. We discussed the role of language to one's identity and cultural heritage and the value of maintaining it. Over the course of our time together, Amy began to feel less self-conscious speaking in her secondary language and opted to engage in the remaining sessions using English. She viewed the therapy environment as providing a safe opportunity to challenge some of her existing beliefs and self-criticism. At the end of her treatment, Amy looked forward to expanding her social connections by becoming involved in the New York City Chinese communities, as well as events hosted by her graduate program.

Graduate students, over the course of my work in university counseling centers, have shared their struggles navigating aspects of their identities. These students described situations in which their identities were judged negatively due to age, the color of their skin, how they dressed, whether they were abled-bodied, and how they communicated. As a result, many of them believed it was necessary to minimize certain aspects of themselves in order to conform to their academic fields' professional norms. This often came up in how students used language.

Will, a twenty-six-year-old, White, self-identified male, queer, first-year engineering graduate student, discussed the pressure to conceal being in a same-sex relationship to avoid any possible scrutiny from his academic and professional peers and superiors, "I don't know them well enough to feel safe being my authentic self. Who I am attracted to and who I am dating should not impact their professional perception of me . . . but it still does . . . it's still a risk!" Will was also a first-generation college student who frequently experienced feelings of uncertainty about his career trajectory and self-doubt about his capabilities to succeed. He discussed the pressure to adopt a deeper voice to present as more masculine and to use sophisticated vocabulary when interacting with classmates and professors to appear more intelligent. When Will initially sought counseling, he struggled with low mood, anxiety, guilt, and fear of his true identities being discovered. When asked what it was like for him to alter his speech and behavior around others, Will responded with a sigh, "It's exhausting. I'm constantly wearing this mask . . . I feel good in the moment when I think I sound smart or make a good impression, but then there is the guilt of hiding parts of me."

Another student, Monica, a thirty-one-year-old married, Black, female graduate student in her second year of a master's in journalism program, also shared her struggle around language. Monica discussed the constant shift between her use of "Black English" and "White English." "If I spoke and acted the way I do with my family and friends, my classmates and professors would see me as unprofessional . . . maybe threatening . . . the typical 'angry Black woman.' I need to sound White if I want to be seen as intelligent and competent." Monica explained that altering her speech and mannerisms allowed her to be culturally compatible with her academic and professional environments and to appear less threatening as a person of color. "I hate not being real, but if I need to put on this mask to climb this ladder, then I will keep this fake smile and keep this mask on until I get to the top."

Will and Monica both described the process of "code-switching," the modifying of speech and behavioral patterns to align with their surrounding context. Although code-switching can be an advantageous skill, protecting students from unwanted biases against them, such strategy can unfortunately be taxing on one's well-being. Emotional burnout and reduced authentic self-expression are some of the adverse consequences highlighted by these students.

During individual therapy sessions with Will and Monica, they were encouraged to explore the meaning of language and how it related to their various identities. We discussed the function of code-switching (e.g., survival) and the advantages that came with it (e.g., fitting in), along with its negative impact on their overall health (e.g., feeling in-authentic; anxiety about conforming). They considered ways to more flexibly code-switch to increase the academic and professional benefits it offered while also finding ways to be more authentically themselves so as to reduce their psychological distress.

Will recognized the value of not only maintaining his strong sup-port systems from home but also creating a trusted circle in his new environment. Although he initially was hesitant to connect with other classmates, Will gradually became open to the idea of accepting invita-tions to academic gatherings and used the opportunities to get to know his peers. During this time, Will came out to two classmates, whom he felt safe with after establishing friendships with them. "I don't need to tell *everyone* my business. I am who I am and I love who I love . . . and as long as there are people in my life, even if it's just a handful, who accept my authentic self, then that's all that matters." Subsequently, Will's mood improved as he more flexibly used code-switching.

Will also discussed his identity as a first-generation college student and how that impacted his school experience. He shared feelings of loneliness being the only person in his family to have this educational opportunity, and, despite his parents being supportive, he had found it challenging to confide his graduate school struggles to them, "They just don't get it." We explored who could understand and be supportive to him in this way. Will eventually found comfort and understanding in his mentorship relationship with his academic advisor.

Monica, on the other hand, continued to struggle with the use of language, which impacted her sense of belonging. When we were able to explore what was underneath her mask, painful stories of discrimina-tion and oppression were revealed. Monica shared past and present sto-ries of being taunted for her skin color and hair texture. These injurious incidents were perpetrated by both peers and family members, as her skin was darker than most of her relatives. The shortage of faculty of color in her graduate school also contributed to her internalized belief that as a person of color she embodied numerous inherent character flaws. This taught Monica to hide aspects of herself to avoid being a target to those in power. Changing her use of language was a constant reminder of her need for safety and the world being an unsafe place. The insight Monica gained from our sessions helped her recognize the origin of her pain and the value of ongoing therapy to facilitate continued exploration of these areas. Though the notion of further exploring these difficult topics was anxiety-provoking for Monica, I deeply admired how her courage and desire for self-growth carried her forward in her healing journey. Eventually, she joined a support group and was relieved to realize that she was not alone in her experience. This also led her to determine how and with whom in her program she could start to practice being more authentically herself.

Coping Strategies

If any of the themes above resonated with you, then it is important for you to know that you are not alone! Some of your graduate student colleagues are experiencing similar challenges. In this section, I share with you some coping strategies that may be useful.

Seek out Social Support

There is much value in social support and connections in surviving graduate school. Maintaining and creating new relationships can help alleviate and prevent feelings of nonbelonging. For example, places of worship can be a primary source of support. One of my former clients viewed it meaningful to continue her spiritual and religious journey after relocating to New York City. She attended a weekly mosque service in her new community and was able to build meaningful relationships with other attendees. In her words: "I belonged somewhere."

Finding a space in your university that elicits feelings of acceptance and value can be beneficial to your mental and physical health. Consider exploring resources offered by your university such as program events, graduate student groups, and organizations that represent a wide array of cultural, social, and academic interests that are meaningful to you. Are there groups or organizations dedicated to the LGBTQIA+ community? Perhaps a graduate group for racially or ethnically diverse students? Or even a group for graduate student parents?

Participating in team sports is another way to seek out social connections. If this is an area of interest for you, consider searching out intramural activities in your university athletic center or the local community.

Explore Your New Community

Whether you are an in-state, out-of-state, or international student entering graduate school, it can be an intimidating transition as you acclimate to the newness of your surroundings. Therefore, it may be helpful for you to explore your new academic community before starting your program. This opportunity could be used to discover activities and events that exist in the neighborhood. If this is not feasible for you, that's okay! You can use the academic year to explore! While graduate school life is important, one must not neglect other equally important areas of life such as physical health, spiritual wellness, and leisure activities. Talking to your program or university about how to get information about the community can be one of the first places to start! Online research is another.

Nurture Your Existing Social Connections

In addition to building new relationships, it is also helpful to stay connected to loved ones from home. Scheduling weekly calls, video chat, email, text, or, my favorite—mailing a handwritten letter—are some suggestions to maintain your connection and involvement with your loved ones. However, be flexible as your ability to connect with loved ones may vacillate during the academic year. Graduate school can be a lot of work and can take up much of your time!

Connect with Faculty and Mentors

In addition to receiving support from family, friends, and peers, a quality mentoring relationship with faculty can play a significant role in your sense of belonging and your level of satisfaction with your graduate school experience. Students who develop supportive professional relationships in academia demonstrate higher levels of academic performance and achievement, intellectual development, commitment to their chosen field, and retention in their program.[8]

Approaching faculty can be intimidating at first but do not feel pressured to speed the process. Instead, allow for a more gradual and subtle development of the mentoring relationship. If you are looking to connect with a specific faculty, consider using their office hours as an opportunity to not only review class assignments and exams, but also to get to know them on a professional level. Asking them about their research or for advice on a project is a good way to break the ice!

Consider Counseling

I would also like to mention the value of your college and university counseling centers. As you know by now, graduate students encounter a range of stressors that can make it difficult to utilize the coping strategies that they usually rely on. Counseling can provide space for students to work on distressing areas academically and personally. Subsequently, this may lead to greater self-awareness, self-acceptance, improved self-esteem and coping skills, and a greater ability to express and manage emotions. In the cases of Sofia, Will, and Monica, counseling provided them with the opportunity to explore and better understand their intersecting identities and how their identities impact upon their experiences. Each of these individuals flourished in their own ways and ended treatment with a new understanding of themselves.

Of course, not every student feels comfortable requesting counseling services at their academic institution. If this is the case for you, consider contacting the counseling center for referral assistance instead. They may be able to help connect you with a therapist in your community.

Exercise 3

Read the following questions and take a moment to reflect on your needs. You may use a sheet of paper to jot down your thoughts and ideas: What would I like to learn about my new community (e.g., graduate school, residential community)? What kinds of social support and/or connections do I need and/or want in order to thrive in graduate school? What kinds of services at the counseling center are available to me? Which can I benefit from? What other resources can I consider?

Support Your Peers

If you know someone who may be experiencing some of the issues discussed in this chapter, know that you have the possibility of making a difference in their life. How? By simply asking them, "How have you been feeling?" Expressing genuine curiosity and care about their graduate school experiences can go a long way. Demonstrating empathy and listening without judgment can foster a sense of comfort and safety. It can also be validating for them to hear you share your own challenging graduate school experiences. Of course, this is not an occasion to compare stressors, but more an opportunity to normalize their struggles and to communicate that they are not alone. An added benefit of helping others is that it can help you feel good too!

Takeaways for Graduate Students

- Increase your awareness about your visible and invisible identities and their role in your overall psychological and emotional functioning.
- Your personal identities are not static. They evolve as you go through life and encounter different situations, environments, and circumstances.
- Exposure to various communities during your time in grad school may lead you to question and negotiate multiple aspects of your cultural self.
- You may feel a sense of isolation in grad school. Social connectedness is important because it can have a positive impact on your health, ability to cope, sense of meaning, life purpose, and educational achievements.
- Be aware of how language is an expression of your social identities and plays an essential role in how you communicate and engage with others.
- You may engage in various coping strategies such as "code-switching" but become aware of how this may sometimes lead to emotional burnout and reduce your capacity to express yourself authentically.
- You are not alone! Some of your graduate student peers are also experiencing similar challenges.
- Coping strategies include seeking out social support, exploring resources and events in your new community, keeping in touch with family and friends, connecting with faculty and mentors, seeking counseling services, and supporting your peers.

Recommendations for Faculty, Staff, and Administration

- Cultivate a sense of inclusion within academic programs by creating community-oriented peer networks for students. For example, design a "buddy" or "mentor" system connecting advanced students with incoming students.

- Share access to information about resources and networking opportunities through user-friendly websites, university tabling events, and classroom bulletin boards.
- Create opportunities for grad students to connect with each other as well as with faculty and staff. Devoting time and financial resources to designing a thoughtful orientation program can be an encouraging first step for students to begin building community.

Recommendations for Mental Health Professionals

- Provide space for students to explore their intersecting identities and how they impact the students' environments.
- If you are comfortable sharing your own identities, students may really appreciate hearing disclosures from their therapists. Of course, only do so if you deem it clinically relevant.
- Offer a range of group services each semester to provide additional support to students. Be creative! These groups may focus on often neglected topics such as multicultural challenges, life transitions, and navigating marginalized identities.

PART IV

HOW DO I
GET THROUGH IT ALL?

CHAPTER FOURTEEN

~

Financing a Graduate Degree

The Practicalities

Phyllis Schulz

You've made the decision: You are going to graduate school. You're caught up in the excitement of researching your dream programs when it hits you: Graduate school costs serious money. And not just once, but for the duration of your program. How are you ever going to attend school full-time and be able to afford a place to live? Five years of ramen noodles doesn't sound very appealing, after all, you are an adult now. Is it really worth it?

Sound familiar? That's how I felt when I was accepted into a graduate program right out of undergrad. Ultimately, it is what led to my working in financial aid and made me want to help future students. More on that later.

Figuring out how to finance a graduate degree can be confusing and stressful. Is there financial aid for graduate students? How do I apply? Where do I even start? Do I need to supply parental or spousal income information? Can I work and attend graduate school? Even if I find a way to pay for grad school, how do I afford living and housing expenses? This chapter will answer these questions and serve as a guide on what to expect throughout the graduate school life cycle. It will include tips on what to consider when applying to graduate school and how to manage finances on a budget. Resources and information about obtaining grant, fellowship, and other assistance will be included. With the proper tools, students can face financing their education with con-fidence.

Financial Aid

The good news is that there is financial aid available to graduate stu-dents. You won't have to pay those tuition bills out of pocket. You may even be able to secure funding to cover your basic living expenses. The bad news is that understanding the various forms of funding can seem to require a degree in rocket science. Let's break down the various types of financial assistance.

Institutional Aid

Simply put, this is money from your school. Institutional aid can come in various forms: scholarships, fellowships, assistantships, and even loans. The type and amount of institutional aid offered by each school will vary, as schools have varying budgets and priorities.

Scholarships are also known as tuition discounting, because they reduce the amount of tuition a student will have to pay. They can be need-based, which means the school will request that you complete an application to determine if you have the financial need they are looking to support. Other scholarships will be merit-based, meaning that they will be based on your academic record or some other metric. Scholarships are most common for master's, medical, and law degrees but are generally limited.

Fellowships are most frequently associated with doctoral programs. Fellowships are generally considered to be a monetary award to help a student with their academic pursuits. They can cover tuition costs and may include an assistantship or stipend for living expenses. Fellowships offered vary dramatically, even between academic programs at the same school. If you want more information on the fellowships available, you should consult with the academic program you are applying to. They may refer you to another office that has the expertise to answer your questions, but they can let you know what to ask.

I would also recommend speaking to current students—they can tell you about the lived experience, not just the mechanics of the fel-lowship. Since fellowships vary widely, it is important to ask about the timing of payments. If you have rent or a mortgage payment due, your landlord or bank isn't going to be too happy if you don't know when you will be able to pay them. Other questions I would ask current students are: Do you feel that you can live comfortably with your fellowship support or do you need to supplement your income? What do you wish you knew about your financial support before you accepted the offer?

Assistantships are paid positions that typically require that a student provide a service—teaching or research are most common. They may also include a tuition component or access to health insurance. Like fellowships, the terms of assistantship can vary across institutions, but they are usually standardized by the school.

Some institutions may offer institutional loans. The term "loan" usually means that the money needs to be repaid, sometimes with interest. You should read any fine print before accepting an institutional loan. Make sure you are aware of interest rates, repayment terms, and any other fees. In many cases, institutional loans have more favorable terms than market or federal loans. You just want to make sure you know what you are getting into. If you don't repay a loan under the required terms, it can hurt your credit. General life advice: Try not to hurt your credit. It is important. Especially if you ever want to buy a car or a home or apply for certain jobs.

Unfortunately, there is no universal handbook available to compare what kind of aid you can receive across schools. You will have to do research on the programs you are interested in to determine what kind of institutional aid is available. While some school websites will have detailed information available, many will not. You may have to contact the financial aid office or the academic program itself to see what opportunities are available. Questions to ask include:

- What type of institutional aid is available? Is it renewable (in other words, am I guaranteed the same package next year if I want it)?

Some schools will offer generous aid packages for the first year to lure students in, but funding is not guaranteed for the future. As most graduate programs require a longer time commitment, it is important to understand the long-term picture.

- How do I apply for institutional aid?

Some schools will require an application—financial, a personal statement, and so on—while others will base their institutional aid offers on your application for admission.

- When should I apply for institutional aid?

If there is one thing I hope you take away from this chapter, it is that *deadlines matter!* Most schools are working with limited resources and want to help as many students as possible. What is the easiest way to eliminate students from consideration? If they do not meet the deadline to apply. Make sure you know application deadlines and you meet them. It may be the difference between receiving financial assistance to attend your dream school or having to attend a less desired program just because it is the one you can afford.

- If I were to receive institutional aid, are there requirements tied to it?

Most financial aid programs, whether institutional or federal, will have enrollment requirements. You want to know what they are, so that you do not inadvertently lose your funding. Some fellowships and assistantships may require a service component, such as teaching a certain number of hours or performing as a research assistant. Make sure you can meet the service requirement before you accept the fellowship or assistantship offer. All financial aid programs require that a student make satisfactory academic progress. Find out how your school measures this, so you know where you stand.

- What percentage of students receive institutional aid? Does it vary by academic program?

The last question will give you an idea of what to expect. If everyone receives funding, you know you will be funded. If only 25 percent of students receive institutional aid and funding is part of what will drive your decision, you may want to look at other, more generous, programs.

Federal Aid

If you had financial aid as an undergraduate student, some of this terminology may be familiar. Federal aid simply means that the funds are supplied by the federal government. Students are typically eligible for federal aid if they are enrolled in a degree-granting program and are US citizens or permanent residents who are not in default on a prior federal loan. Students must continue to make satisfactory academic progress, as defined by the school they are attending, to continue receiving federal financial aid. If you are a male, you must be registered with Selective Service. Students must be enrolled at least half-time to qualify for graduate federal aid. You should consult with your school to see how they define half-time status as it can vary. Easy to follow, right?

The first step to apply for federal aid is to file the Free Application for Federal Student Aid (FAFSA). It can be filed online at fafsa.ed.gov. It becomes available every October for the following academic year. For example, the FAFSA for the 2023–2024 academic year will be available in October 2022. The FAFSA will ask questions about your educational plans and current financial situation. It will also ask for "prior-prior year" tax information for you and your spouse (where applicable). If you are married on the date you initially file your FAFSA, you are required to include spousal financial information, even if you were not married during the "prior-prior year." Graduate students are not required, however, to submit parental financial information, even if your parents still claim you on their taxes. *Important note*: While you do not need to submit parental information on the FAFSA for federal aid consideration, schools can request that you provide parental information for institutional aid consideration. This is most common at medical and law schools.

Back to "prior-prior year": For the 2023–2024 FAFSA, you will have to supply information on your 2021 taxes. You will have the option to have the IRS import your tax information into your FAFSA. *Take advantage of this option*. It will make your life easier. You will also be asked to indicate the Federal School Code of any school you would like the information sent to. If you do not send the FAFSA information to a school, they cannot offer you federal aid. Most schools have this code available on their websites.

Once you submit the FAFSA, it will be reviewed by the federal processor. They review the application to determine general student eligibility as outlined above. If they can't determine if a student is in fact eligible, they will flag the application and request that the schools follow up. For example, if they cannot verify that the citizenship status you indicated on the FAFSA was correct, they will ask the school to collect the necessary proof. If they think that something about your income doesn't look right, they will flag you for verification, a process that requires schools to verify the financial information you provided. After their review, the federal processor will send the applicant a Student Aid Report (SAR). Students should review the SAR for accuracy and to see if any flags have been placed on their account. The flags will have to be resolved before any federal aid can be disbursed. The school will contact you about next steps.

The SAR will also provide you with an Estimated Family Contribution (EFC). This is the amount the government believes you can contribute towards your education. Based on my experience, very few individuals agree with the government's assessment. So even if the number seems inflated, know that everyone thinks that. If you have faced a significant change to your finances since the tax year reported on the FAFSA, it is worth bringing to the attention of your financial aid office. Depending on the circumstances, they may be able to take your current circumstances into account.

The EFC is used to determine your financial need. Your financial need is calculated by your cost of attendance minus your EFC. Cost of attendance is made up of the cost of your tuition, fees, estimated cost of books, and the school's best estimate of expected living expenses. Some schools will ask you to provide detailed information on your living expenses, while other schools will use their own estimates. *Insider tip:* If you have personal expenses that you need to cover in order to attend school, but your initial loan offer isn't enough to cover the expense, contact the financial aid office. We do have some flexibility to increase your cost of attendance based on your actual expenses. Specific examples of expenses we can consider include: child care while you are in school, transportation costs to and from school, computer purchases, and the like. When in doubt, ask.

Please keep in mind that financial aid can be used to cover basic educational and living expenses. It cannot be used to cover lavish lifestyle choices. I live and work in New York City. Would I love to live in a penthouse overlooking Central Park? Of course. Why don't I? Because I can't afford it and there are plenty of other affordable options. A student should not expect their financial aid to cover such choices.

Important note: The following information is accurate at this time based on legislation passed in 2012. Federal regulations can change and often do. Right now, a number of changes to federal aid programs are being debated in Congress. If you have questions about federal aid policies, you should contact your financial aid office. They will have the most up-to-date information available to you.

Your financial need determines how much need-based aid you can receive. Unfortunately, federal need-based aid is limited at the graduate level. Some schools may have need-based Federal Work Study programs. This means you would find a job on campus and earn a salary that can be used for living expenses. Other schools *may* offer the TEACH grant, which is available to students in programs designed to prepare them to be highly qualified teachers in a federally defined "high need" field. *Note*: If you are offered a TEACH grant, be sure to read the terms carefully. If you do not meet the necessary terms, your TEACH grant can become a loan! Be sure you understand what is required. Many teachers didn't realize that they needed to submit an annual certification to prove that they were meeting the service requirement. To their dismay, they only found out about the requirement after they missed the deadline and their grant had already been converted to a loan.

If you receive need-based aid, it will reduce your financial need. *Note*: Institutional scholarships and fellowships will be considered need-based, even if they were offered based on merit. This means if your cost of attendance was $30,000 and your EFC was $12,000, your financial need will be $18,000. If you received a merit-based scholarship for $20,000, you would not be eligible for any need-based federal aid, since you have no remaining financial need.

The most common form of federal aid available to graduate students is the Direct Loan program. Through this program, you borrow money directly from the Department of Education with the understanding that you will repay the loan through your assigned loan servicer once you leave school. The direct loans are not need-based, so regardless of whether your income is $10,000 or $1,000,000, you will be eligible to borrow.

The amount you can borrow is determined in part by your school-determined cost of attendance minus any other aid you are receiving. A loan eligibility example: Cost of attendance for fall and spring semesters—$30,000 minus $25,000 fellowship and $2,000 scholarship equals $3,000 loan eligibility. Every semester, we hear from students, like Katie, who think this is unfair. Katie was told by her advisor that her $2,000 scholarship was supposed to be used to attend a conference, so she didn't think it should be counted as part of her financial aid. While we sympathize with Katie's situation, the federal regulations are pretty explicit. If a student receives funds for their education that are not considered wages or a reimbursement, it counts as part of their financial aid award. My office also reached out to Katie's advisor to make sure he referred students to our office to find out how such awards can impact their other financial aid.

There are two types of Direct Loans available to graduate students: The Direct Unsubsidized Loan and the Graduate PLUS Loan. Both loans are unsubsidized, meaning that interest will accrue from the day the loan is disbursed to the school until the day the loan is paid off. The loans have fixed interest rates for the life of the loan. The interest rates are determined in June each year and apply to any loan disbursed after July 1. This means that if you borrow a loan in your first year of graduate school it can have a different interest rate than a loan you borrow in your second year. While you are in school, the interest is simple interest. This means that you are only accruing interest on the principal balance. Once you are less than half-time for a period of six consecutive months, you will enter repayment. At that time, any unpaid interest will be capitalized or added into the principal. You will then have a new principal balance that will start accruing interest. *Important note*: There is no penalty for repaying your loan early. If you can make payments towards your loan while you are in school, it will not harm you.

Under current legislation, the Unsubsidized Loan has a 1 percent lower interest rate than the Graduate PLUS Loan. Students can borrow up to $20,500 in a Direct Unsubsidized Loan in a given academic year (*Note*: Students in certain health professional programs may be eligible to borrow more). That said, in the example above, the student would be limited to borrowing $3,000 based on the other eligibility rules. Over their lifetime, graduate students cannot have more than $138,500 in outstanding Direct Subsidized (currently offered to undergraduates only) and Unsubsidized Loan principal debt (*Note*: Again, certain health professional programs may be able to borrow more).

We generally recommend that a student exhaust their Unsubsidized Direct Loan eligibility before borrowing a Graduate PLUS Loan. Why? The Graduate PLUS Loan has a higher interest rate and requires a credit check. Not the kind of credit check you undergo when applying for a car or a mortgage. It is considered a credit-ready credit check. This means that they will not look at things like debt-to-income ratios (because what graduate student would qualify?). Instead they are looking to verify that you do not have an adverse credit history. Graduate PLUS Loans do not have an annual or lifetime cap. Its eligibility is limited by the cost of attendance minus other aid.

Once the loan is disbursed, it will be assigned to a federal loan servicer. Your loan servicer is the agency to whom you will repay your federal loan. It is important that you keep your contact information updated with them. You do not want to miss important information! Most servicers now have paperless options, so as long as you supply a valid email, you should receive most important information. Some information still has to be mailed, so be sure to update your mailing address as well.

As long as you enroll at least half-time, you will not be required to make payments on your loans. Currently, the government does offer a number of different repayment options and even a loan forgiveness program for those working in public service. There is a lot of pending legislation to simplify both programs, so I am not going to go into great detail here. If you have questions about either, contact your financial aid office.

Private Loans

Full disclosure: I hate private loans. Why? Well, first of all, they are completely unregulated. Lenders can pretty much offer whatever terms they choose. This means that their loans have lots of caveats and fine print. From my experience, most borrowers don't bother looking too closely. Most private loans have variable interest rates, so while the interest rate when you apply might be more favorable than the federal loans, it could become much higher over the life of the loan. Repayment terms are often less flexible. The federal loans, meanwhile, offer certain protections for periods of unemployment or returning to school. Private loans often do not. If you have a payment due, it's due regardless of whatever else may be happening in your life. In some cases, they even require payments while the borrower is still in school.

My advice: Only borrow using a private loan if you have absolutely no other option. For example, international students are not eligible for federal aid. With a US cosigner, they are eligible to borrow a private loan. If that is what allows them to continue their education, they should proceed with it.

I've Applied for Financial Aid. Now What?

There is no harm in contacting a school to verify if they received your application and to find out when you can expect a response. In fact, I would recommend it. It will give you peace of mind. Furthermore, deadlines matter! One way to miss a deadline is if your materials are never received. Unfortunately, system and human errors happen all too regularly. Protect your own interests. Schools often also have very different response times. Two schools may have the same financial aid application deadline, but their expected response date could vary by months. The process can be stressful enough. Arm yourself with appropriate expectations.

Once you get your financial aid offer, review it and make sure you fully understand it. If not, ask questions! Do not make assumptions. There is nothing more heartbreaking to me than students who show up for orientation assuming that they understood their funding only to find out that they were wrong. Ask about taxes and health insurance in advance. This is particularly crucial for students from foreign countries who may not understand the US tax or health-care systems.

In some cases, you may be able to negotiate for a better financial aid package. While I do not guarantee it will work, it never hurts to ask! In fact, some schools do keep additional funding aside to help recruit applicants who are hesitating to attend due to finances. They rely on you to self-identify and to inform them of your concerns.

Can I Work While I Am a Student?

As with most financial aid questions, the answer is that it depends. Some programs will discourage pursuing outside work due to the strenuous nature of their program's curriculum. Other programs, such as MBA programs, will encourage working. In most cases, it is a matter of personal preference and your ultimate goals.

I worked full-time while pursuing both my Master's in Public Administration (MPA) and my Doctorate in Higher and Post-Secondary Education. My MPA was easy to pursue while working: Classes were offered in the evening, and the program had no preference about being full-time or part-time. The benefit was that working at my school allowed me to earn a full-time income and have my tuition paid on my behalf. There were a few downsides. My tuition benefit was considered income and taxed rather heavily. I had to take a loan to supplement my income. I also didn't have the time to take part in some of the more exciting externships or projects that involved travel. While that would have been fun, practical me did not think it was necessary.

Working through my doctorate was also not discouraged, especially because I was working in higher education. My boss was flexible if I had to leave early for a class. The tax on my tuition benefit became less of an issue once I completed my coursework. *Insider tip*: Once you finish your coursework and are working on your dissertation, most schools do not charge you the same tuition they would charge someone pursuing coursework. They charge a much lower rate.

Now, this is also where career goals come into play: I was not interested in being a future academic. I like being an administrator, and I am ambitious. It is easier to rise through academic administration when you have a terminal degree. Other students in my cohort were seeking tenure-track positions. For them, working full-time during school would be disadvantageous. Instead, they focused their free hours on building up a curriculum vitae that included various teaching and research responsibilities. Unfortunately, for those who have children while in grad school, balancing both school and family life may leave minimal time for outside work.

What Happens to My Loans from a Prior Degree?

If you have federal loans from a prior degree, you can defer them once you return to school as at least a half-time student. Deferment means that you can stop making payments, provided you meet certain eligibility standards—in this case, being a half-time student. During periods of deferment, subsidized loans do not accrue interest. Unsubsidized loans do accrue interest, but payment is not required. *Insider tip*: If you can pay the interest, it may benefit you financially in the long run. While you are in deferment, interest is accumulating, but it is not being added into the principal. Once you enter repayment status, any unpaid interest will be capitalized or added into the principal balance. If you can pay off the interest before entering repayment, you will not start accruing interest on interest.

Once you are enrolled half-time, your school will update a centralized database, the National Student Loan Clearinghouse (Clearinghouse), with your enrollment status each semester. Most loan servicers will check the Clearinghouse and automatically place your loans into deferment. For those returning to school after a break, please allow four to six weeks for servicer processing, meaning you may need to make a subsequent loan payment after initial enrollment. Please note: There are a handful of smaller loan servicers who still require a paper loan deferment form. Check with your loan servicer to see what their preference is.

Have a private loan from a prior degree? You may or may not be able to defer it. It all depends on what was written in the promissory note that you initially signed. Remember, these loans are unregulated, so the lender can choose not to allow for deferment.

Takeaways for Students

- Deadlines matter!
- Ask questions—do not make assumptions. There is, honestly, no such thing as a silly question. Chances are we have heard it before—and if not, perhaps we should have!
- Understand your funding. While well-meaning friends and advisors may offer friendly advice, your financial aid staff are the experts. Financial aid rules are always changing and often specific to individual situations. Don't assume what was true for a friend will be true for you.
- Befriend your financial aid staff. We generally only see students when there is a problem, but we would love to see you otherwise. Feel free to check in periodically and make sure you are up to date on financial aid issues that matter.
- Bring any hardships to the attention of your financial aid staff. Sometimes we will have solutions. Other times, you will bring a new issue to our attention. We had a number of students, to our surprise, come forward with issues of food insecurity. After further student surveys, we were able to approach a donor about creating an emergency fund for students in similar situations. We are here to help wherever we can.

Suggestions for Administrators and Faculty

- It is sometimes difficult to remember what it was like to be a student living on limited means. Have empathy for your grad students. Listen and validate as they share their financial concerns with you. If you can, share with them your own financial challenges while you were in graduate school.
- Times have changed. The cost of tuition now outpaces inflation. Most students will have to work and/or take out loans in order to complete their education. They don't always have family financial support available to help make their educational dreams a reality. Be flexible with your expectations of today's students as these additional stressors may ultimately mean a longer time to degree completion.

- Please refer any financial aid questions or concerns to your school's financial aid staff. That is what we are here for. We are the office most up to date on the latest financial aid issues and requirements.
- If you notice troubling financial trends, such as food insecurity among students, please do not hesitate to bring them to our attention.

Suggestions for Mental Health Practitioners

- Thank you for what you do. Graduate school is a stressful time for nearly all students, and the support you provide is invaluable.
- Increase your awareness and understanding of the practical financial stressors that grad students often face. I hope this chapter provides some insight.
- Encourage students to befriend the financial aid staff and to check in with them whenever questions or stresses arise.
- If you work in a university counseling center, befriend your financial aid staff yourself! If you notice troubling trends around finances, such as multiple students with food insecurity, you can bring them to the attention of financial aid staff who may be able to take action.
- If you work in a university counseling center, collaborate with and offer information sessions to the financial aid office. In turn, financial aid staff would also be able to refer at-risk students to a resource they trust.

~

CHAPTER FIFTEEN

Financing a Graduate Degree

The Psychology

Stephanie Newman

Jack slides into the therapy chair in my office. "So you know I need a reduced fee, right?" He is a PhD candidate in a humanities discipline, and this is our first appointment. Though we are barely out of the gate, the issue of money is already on the table. After listening for several minutes as Jack details the difficulties of living on loans, supplemented by only a small stipend, I attempt a gentle rejoinder: "It's difficult when funds are tight."

He shakes his head. "That's an understatement. All of my friends are working full-time and earning a decent living. One of my buddies just proposed to his girlfriend. She also works, and with two incomes, they can buy a one-bedroom apartment in a nice part of town. Last week a bunch of my friends went in on basketball season tickets. They go out to restaurants and clubs. And all of them—everyone but me—can afford a gym membership. I feel like such a loser."

Jack is a composite of several clients whose tight finances strain relationships and threaten quality of life. And while money is a topic that is of concern to everyone, it is of particular importance to a subset of graduate students living in poverty, weary from the weight of scraping by, and bearing huge amounts of educational debt. While their friends earn enough to afford homes and cars and to make contributions to retirement funds, end goals like these can feel impossible for grad students navigating daily life in expensive cities.

Too many students know what it's like to skimp to get by, even on food. One client, for example, described to me eating a hot pretzel with mustard while riding the subway to class, savoring every tiny bite because it's all she'd have for dinner that night. Her next fellowship paycheck was three days away. Taking on mountains of debt to pay for tuition, housing, and meals, living a deprived existence, like Jack, while siblings and friends use disposable income to have fun (even as they build their careers and start families) is a very common grad student experience. Some graduate students fear they are falling further and further behind, never to catch up. Others, whose families live in poverty, question their choice to postpone a decent income for years—unable to help their families—in order to pursue graduate education. Any which way, financial strain can be demoralizing with effects on mood, personal outlook, and academic performance.

For those who experience shame, humiliation, or intense self-blame connected with their tight finances, hopefully knowing how widespread this reality is helps it to feel less personal. Know that there are steps that you can take to limit the negative effects of financial strain on mental health; you will find a list of ideas later in this chapter.

The Struggle Is Real

Some cold, hard facts about the financial situation of graduate students in the millennial cohort: According to CNBC,[1] their income has remained flat as the costs of housing and tuition have increased. Thanks to inflation, while the median wealth of middle-income Americans has held for years, according to the Federal Reserve's latest Survey of Consumer Finances,[2] prices for housing and college tuition have risen tremendously. It's no surprise that 62 percent of those in the graduate student cohort report living paycheck to paycheck,[3] while 36 percent of college students don't have enough to eat and report food insecurity.[4] With statistics like these, it's not hard to understand the frustration of one PhD candidate who describes earning $11,700, noting her stipends are not nearly enough to live on. Deeply in debt, she is unsure whether she'll ever be able to pay off her educational loans. While prior genera-tions of postcollege students could dig their way out of debt and reap the rewards of advanced study more easily, the picture is different for today's graduate students.

Many graduate students today live in poverty, barely managing to subsist, which has mental health implications. In a recent large-scale study, career uncertainty was highly correlated with depression and anxiety. The study found that PhD students suffer from depression, anxiety, and suicidal ideation at "astonishingly" high rates.[5] Graduate students who find themselves struggling should not hesitate to ask for mental health support—there are often very low cost or even free op-tions. But how can therapy help anyway?

Money and Psychotherapy

When clients share that they feel drained by the battle to subsist on very limited means, therapists will often connect current emotions (in-cluding those rooted in current realities) to past struggles. Those past hardships can imbue the current experiences of struggle with particular meanings and feelings. The pain of the past can heighten our suffering in the present without us even realizing! In our increasingly expensive and materially focused world,[6] many psychodynamic psychotherapists also use money to explore underlying feelings.[7] Money discussions in therapy allow therapists to help individuals identify specific patterns of behavior and frame characteristic ways of relating. This self-knowledge affords clients more choices. For example, a graduate student who looks inward can approach a difficult situation proactively and minimize emotional pain instead of falling into old patterns and becoming mired in sadness, anger, or envy.

After considering the current climate and lack of upward mobility that poses a very real problem for so many, the question becomes: What can members of the graduate student cohort do to manage daily stresses and cope with their very real fears that their harsh economic realities will persist long into the future? What follows is a set of suggestions for master's and PhD candidates and others similarly situated who feel distraught as they struggle to get by on meager means.

Ways to Be Proactive

Do Not Suffer in Silence

Mental health concerns should be given priority, which means grad students who feel despondent or overwhelmed about finances and/ or other matters should seek counseling. Student counseling centers usually work on a short-term basis. They have lists of clinicians and centers that offer open-ended treatment and accept reduced fees. Likewise, psychoanalytic institutes that offer training for clinicians wanting to learn how to do intensive treatment often offer reduced fees to grad students who agree to attend counseling sessions two or more days per week. The American Psychological Association (APA) and American Psychoanalytic Association (ApsAa) have lists of referral sources, some offering sliding-scale options.

Talk Yourself Out of It

We can't always control our feelings—fear, dread, anxiety, or envy can come on fast and quickly overwhelm us—but we can understand ourselves better and manage overwhelming emotions by applying concrete strategies at even the toughest moments. Thinking it through, getting perspective (e.g., "Hard work generally pays off"; "I might not have money for a fancy meal, but I have friends, family, a course of study I like; I bring value and contribute") can bolster feelings of esteem and gratitude while helping us combat envy and dissatisfaction. By working to change thoughts we can often elevate mood.

If the spiraling mood persists, change the channel—literally. Stop whatever you are doing and give yourself a break. Instead of finishing the difficult Cicero translation or continuing to memorize formulas for an upcoming exam, step away from the laptop. Clear your head and try again a little later. Knowing when to hit pause is an important form of self-care.

Find Fun That You Can Afford

Cities do offer all kinds of entertainment for residents—from free chess games to walks on interesting streets, to readings, concerts in the park, and other events that are offered at no cost. Some institutions, such as New York City's Metropolitan Museum of Art, offer complimentary viewing times. Your university campus likely also has free or low-cost live music, theater, dance, and so on.

Engage with Friends
Instead of going to restaurants, ask friends to cook at home—it was good enough for Bridgette Jones and her crew! If out is better than staying in, cities offer tea and coffee houses where friends can catch up over caffeine instead of a full meal. Friends will understand if you are on a limited budget—they might be too!

Remember That Life Is Not Static, and Set Reasonable Goals
Five years down the road will look different from now, and so will ten and twenty. Chances are you won't be living as a grad student for the rest of your life. Incomes increase, and if you find a partner, having two salaries instead of one in the same home may also change the financial picture.

If you can, look into debt-forgiveness options. Participating in programs offered by the military or seeking jobs postgraduation that offer forgiveness in exchange for working in rural or underserved communities can allow participants to address their debt in a more timely and manageable manner.

Turn the Tables
Instead of getting mired in envy (and it's understandable to have the urge to proclaim: "It's not fair—everyone else has more"; "I work hard, why can't I keep up?"), it's more helpful to focus on gratitude. Saying, "I *get* to" [swim at the university pool], instead of I *have* to [grade a hundred papers] can change perspective if practiced over time. We are not advocating repressing your feelings but moderating them.

Seek Support in Dark Moments
If you do feel distraught over money pressures or other concerns that become overwhelming and bring thoughts of suicide, go to the nearest ER, go to the university counseling center, or call the suicide prevention hotline (1-800-273-8255). It's crucial to reach out and resist the impulse to hold in helplessness and hopelessness that sometimes accompany feeling sad, angry, envious, and overwhelmed. There's never any shame in seeking help. If it can be discussed, it can be addressed.

What about Jack?

For those who are still curious about how therapy works, we return to the composite portrait of Jack. He and I agree to a fee he can afford, an amount per session totaling even less than a typical insurance co-pay. This reduction allows him to come multiple times a week so we can get at the fear and sadness that pervades his daily life. During our work, we discuss a number of concerns, including: his frustration about having no money in an expensive city, his humiliation at trying to date on a low budget (inviting women to a coffee shop when peers go to clubs with bottle service), his envy of his friends who are moving on. Always below the surface is a fear that he has years of poverty ahead.

In session Jack frequently vents about being a "have not" and insists that I am "okay" with his low fee because I charge others "through the nose" and make a "killing" on them. Even though these ideas come from him and can be seen as an expression of negative feelings, perhaps anger at needing help or frustration about feeling stuck, he insists his experience is positive; he has only gratitude towards me.

Our work moves forward with Jack describing the daily pressures of life at his university, including difficulties forming relationships in "such a large, unfriendly" city. Though I know his financial struggles and loneliness are very real, I attempt to talk about money in a more abstract way, believing that doing so will allow us to learn more about his internal life. I listen and empathize in session. When the time is right, I will encourage Jack to attempt deeper exploration.

About five months into the therapy, Jack presents me a wrapped gift, which I set down on my footstool. Telling him I appreciated his kindness, I invite him to say what comes to mind. "You probably think this is some cheap bottle of wine and view me as a loser. And this is what I assume goes on with my friends. I imagine them sitting and laughing at me. It's humiliating."

After making this point, Jack becomes tearful and begins discussing his envy of friends with nice apartments, cars, and parking spots beneath their "luxury buildings." He speaks angrily about his wish for more money and his feelings that he "deserves a break." I suggest that with life becoming so difficult, he feels the urge to spew. I offer that while I don't mind listening, I think it would be helpful to view his "rants" about money as a communication from him to me. He disagrees with my characterization of the session and accuses me of "not getting it." He threatens to leave therapy.

Seeing Jack's pain and wanting to help him understand the connection between his past and current situations and the emotions underlying them, I apologize for misspeaking and using the word "rant." I ask him not to go, but to "live through something with me." There is a charge in the air. Moments later Jack begins to weep as he recalls a time when he was young and "everyone in town looked [him] up and down" because his family didn't have the money to buy him a nice suit and good shoes for a religious service he attended.

In the weeks and months after that session, he becomes curious about the meaning of money, past and present, in his life and acknowledges that his "money rants" keep me at a distance. As he feels more comfortable opening up, he confides about the wish to break out of poverty, start a small business, and build a source of disposable income. Soon after, Jack begins work on an independent venture and notices that his friends are impressed with his progress. As he "changes the game" and earns some money outside of his teaching assistant job and campus stipend, he feels his confidence grow and his envy diminish. From this point forward, Jack feels more able to tolerate the squalor of his grad student housing and long road to graduation. By broadening his perspective and rechanneling his anger and envy into a source of income, he develops a sense of his own agency and becomes less reactive to his immediate environment.

Over the years, I have seen a number of clients like Jack, students in various graduate disciplines who spend years completing their degrees, working hard in their studies, yet struggling all the while to make ends meet. While there are no guarantees of success, and though individual psychologies differ, the process of "living through something"—with me or another therapist—may bring relief and allow clients to feel more hopeful about the future.

Takeaways for Students

- Poverty in grad school is very common: You are not alone!
- The daily experience of living in poverty and/or under huge debt can be exhausting and demoralizing, with effects on mood, personal outlook, and academic performance.

- Understanding the meanings of money to you, and your associations with your current strains, can help reduce your suffering.
- Recognizing your past patterns of behaving and relating can also help you recognize the choices that you have now.
- Find and set aside time for fun that you can afford.
- Spend time with people with whom you feel good.
- Remember the big picture. You are making an investment in grad school now. Down the road, you will likely have more income, and a degree.
- When in distress, seek counseling. There are likely options that you can afford.

Suggestions for Faculty, Staff, and Administrators

- Understand that financial strains can impact students' mental health and academic functioning.
- Recognize that some students may need to work one or more jobs while in school. This may interfere with their ability to be present for nonmandatory department activities and roles.
- When possible, offer financial packages that help students afford the cost of living in your university's location.
- Understand that the economic climate currently is likely more challenging for students than when you went to school.

Suggestions for Mental Health Professionals

- As many of us did not get training in talking about money in graduate school, ask yourself whether this might be a growth area for you.
- Make sure that you understand your own life experiences, feelings, and meanings associated with money.
- Understand that financial strain is very common for grad students. If your grad student clients have not brought up their financial situations and you think talking about finances might be helpful to them, listen for apt moments to ask.
- When appropriate, work on multiple levels with your grad student clients' financial situations: Help students think through and plan

concretely how to make the most of the resources they have—if they would like help with this. Empathize with their difficult realities. Explore with your clients their underlying meanings and feelings associated with their current financial situations.

~

CHAPTER SIXTEEN

Getting the Writing Done

Completing Your
Paper, Thesis, or Dissertation

Karen E. Starr

Writing is such an integral part of graduate school life that one might assume that most graduate students have no difficulty with the writing process. Indeed, chances are if you made it to graduate school, you already have some idea of how to write an academic paper. Yet, many graduate students find themselves overwhelmed by the sheer amount of writing they have to do and unsure about their ability to do it at the graduate level. Even when you are finished with your coursework, if your terminal degree is a master's, you will most likely be required to write a master's thesis. If you are in a doctoral program, you will be required to write a doctoral dissertation that makes an original contribution to your field of study. If this is your first experience in graduate school, neither of these tasks will be familiar to you, and it's not surprising if you are somewhat intimidated by the prospect. But be assured, you are not alone!

For many graduate students, writing a master's thesis or doctoral dissertation can feel like an especially daunting proposition, given the extended scope of the project and the mandate to be original. This scale of project requires the application of a consistent, steady writing discipline across a span of one or more years. It can also be quite a lonely undertaking, as you will no longer have the regular contact with cohort members that classes provided. Of course, it will also not be the only thing you will be doing during that time, so figuring out how to balance the writing process with the rest of your life, including work responsibilities, family, friends, and having fun, is absolutely essential to graduate school success.

This chapter will offer practical strategies for engaging with your writing process in a way that will feel more satisfying and pleasurable and make you more productive. It will cover choosing your topic, organizing your time, becoming unstuck in your writing, overcoming perfectionism, dealing with procrastination, and finishing your incompletes. Because most of the difficulties graduate students have with the writing process arise during the new and unfamiliar experience of developing the master's thesis or doctoral dissertation, this chapter will offer guidance specifically for students facing the challenge of working on these longer projects, including tips for formulating an original idea, communicating that idea effectively, working with your advisor, and moving forward in a process that is more of a marathon than a sprint.

Especially, though not exclusively, with regard to theses and dissertations, the prospect of writing can sometimes feel less like an exciting opportunity to express your ideas and communicate them to others and more like a heavy burden you have to carry with you 24/7. Although writing always entails some discipline, it does not—in fact, should not—have to feel like you're carrying a twenty-five-pound pack on your back as you live your daily life. How you approach the undertaking can make a huge difference in your sense of satisfaction and self-efficacy, as well as in your actual ability to get the writing done.

Choosing a Topic

Make It Interesting

Whether you are writing a paper for a seminar class or thinking about a topic for your doctoral dissertation, the first step on the road to becoming more engaged with your writing process is to make it interesting— that is, interesting to you! Even if the class for which you have to write a paper was dry or boring, or not in your particular area of interest, try to choose a topic for your paper that will engage you creatively. While there are certainly limits to how creative you can be—your paper does have to adhere to the criteria established by the professor for the assignment—what is important is that, as much as is possible, you find a way to engage your own interests and curiosity. A writing project is an excellent opportunity to learn more about a subject you don't know much about but would like to, or to go deeper into an idea you're curious about but have touched on only briefly in class. Being interested in what you're writing about will make the process of writing itself so much more interesting.

If you will be writing a master's thesis or doctoral dissertation, the imperative to make it interesting applies exponentially. In those cases, I would go as far as to say, be passionate! If you're writing a dissertation, being passionate about your topic will help keep you motivated and sustain your interest through the long haul. Especially when it comes to doctoral dissertations, it is not unusual for there to be an element of "me-search" involved in the research; in other words, the area of study is in some way personally meaningful to the researcher.

When you're in the process of choosing your topic, it's a very good sign if you find yourself getting excited about the prospect of exploring your subject. If you're not sure how you feel about potential topics you're considering, try bouncing your ideas off someone else. This person does not have to be someone in academia; it can be a friend or relative. Notice how you feel while you're talking to them. If you're feeling bored, it's probably not the right topic for you. If you find yourself becoming enthusiastic, you are likely on the right track.

One caveat: While it can be highly motivating to be passionate about your topic, be careful not to choose a subject that is too emotionally close to your own life and that might blindside you by making you feel psychologically overwhelmed. For example, if you have experienced sexual trauma yourself, immersing yourself in the study of sexual trauma for the extended period of time required to work on your dissertation might leave you feeling emotionally flooded and, ultimately, stuck in your writing.

Because dissertation research often involves an element of "me-search," issues of identity may unexpectedly come to the fore, sometimes in ways that feel energizing, but at other times, in ways that can feel paralyzing. Becoming aware of these issues and taking them into account is an important first step in resolving them.

Kesha, an African American doctoral student in anthropology, came to me for a consultation because she felt unable to write. Although she had made significant progress and had received positive feedback from her advisor on the chapter drafts she had sent him, Kesha had been avoiding working on her project for more than a year. Embarrassed and ashamed, Kesha was initially at a loss to explain why she felt unable to return to it.

I encouraged her to tell me in detail about her dissertation topic. Kesha explained that she was studying the social and religious affiliations of the community in which she lived. Her data included interviews with community leaders and with friends and acquaintances with whom she herself socialized. As we talked about her project, it gradually became clear that Kesha felt conflicted about her identity as a researcher/scholar within the context of the community in which she herself was a member. She was concerned that some people in her community might not like her research findings or might be hurt or insulted by what she had to say. To her astonishment, Kesha realized that her difficulty was not with the writing per se, but with her anxiety about fully embracing her identity as a researcher and scholar, because if she did so, it might make some people in her community unhappy. For Kesha, bringing her unconscious conflict into the realm of her awareness and putting it into words was enough to free her from feeling trapped by it.

Be Strategic

If you are still doing your coursework but will eventually be writing a thesis or dissertation, try to choose individual paper topics that are related to your main area of interest and that might be relevant to your larger project later on. If you're strategic about choosing your paper topics, by the time you're ready to embark on the research for your dissertation, you will have already familiarized yourself with the literature and will be in a much better position to discern what subspecialty appeals to you and where you might make your own original contribution. That said, if you have no idea what your thesis or dissertation topic will be, it is not necessary for you to figure that out before you start your paper.

Narrow It Down

This imperative applies especially to master's theses and doctoral dissertations. It's important to remember that your goal in writing the thesis or dissertation is not to write a magnum opus, but to successfully complete the requirements of your graduate program. Even if you are planning a career in academia after graduation, you should not view your dissertation as the grand summary of your life's work. In fact, just the opposite is true. The dissertation is only the beginning of your career as a scholar. You do not have to cover everything there is to know about your subject. You just have to choose one aspect of your field of study and see if you might have something new to add. After graduation, you'll have the rest of your academic career ahead of you. If there's something more you're interested in related to your topic, you can pursue it then. Your immediate goal is to finish graduate school.

Narrow your focus so that the project feels manageable to you. The litmus test of whether your topic is narrow enough is whether you can give what has become known as the two-minute "elevator speech." If you're in an elevator with someone and they ask you what your dissertation is about, you should be able to tell them in a sentence or two. Being able to express your ideas fluently and succinctly will also come in handy when you're speaking with faculty or fellow students, as well as in social situations. If you're at a cocktail party and someone asks, "What are you writing about?" you don't want to launch into a long lecture or to fumble around awkwardly trying to make your thoughts coherent. Aside from the negative social consequences, it can feel demoralizing to repeatedly feel like you don't have a good handle on what you're doing. Even while you're in the midst of working on your dissertation, being able to formulate your project in one or two sentences will have the added benefit of reminding you what your focus should be while you're in the process of researching and writing. When you find yourself going down the research rabbit hole, your two-sentence summary can be a useful way to bring yourself back into focus.

Work with Your Advisor
Too often, graduate students are intimidated about the idea of asking their advisor for help in developing their topic. Yet, in fact, the role of advisor is actually to advise. Having a conversation with someone you trust who is knowledgeable in the field can help you get a better sense of where you might make your own contribution. Setting up regular meetings with your advisor can help keep you on track, whether you

are still deciding on your topic, are in the research phase, or have already started writing. If you have chosen a celebrity in your field who is good at being famous but not so good at mentoring, or if your advisor is chronically unavailable for other reasons, then you have more of a challenge. You have a couple of options. You might want to consider switching advisors (yes, people do this!) or speaking to someone else on your committee who is more available, friendlier, or generally more helpful.

Build on Existing Scholarship

You've chosen your topic, begun your research, and then, to your horror, you discover that someone else has just published an article or book in exactly your area of interest. This is not cause for despair! So many graduate students report having this experience that it seems almost inevitable. (When I was choosing a topic for my dissertation, it happened to me, too.) It actually means that you're on the right track—that the topic you've chosen is interesting academically. You can use this newly published article or book to shore up your argument for why your area of investigation matters. Remember, all academic work builds on existing scholarship—that's why literature reviews, citations, and references are so much a part of academic writing. Your task when writing a thesis or dissertation is not to create a whole new body of literature out of thin air, but to build on others' scholarship—whether you are using their work to support your argument or you are developing your argument as a counterpoint to theirs. Your goal is just to add something new to the existing literature—a new perspective, a new integration, a different take—or to examine in depth just one heretofore unexamined unique slice of a very large scholarly pie.

Creating a Writing Schedule

The most common misconception among graduate students embarking upon writing the dissertation is that they should be writing eight to ten hours a day, five to seven days a week. Not only is this an unrealistic goal, it's a surefire way to feel overwhelmed, overworked, and chronically guilty. Very few people, including professional writers, can sustain that kind of full-time physical, emotional, and cognitive endurance.

Moreover, most graduate students are juggling multiple relationships and responsibilities along with graduate school. You may have a spouse or partner, children, an ailing parent to care for, and/or one or more jobs. It is much more realistic, and you are far more likely to make progress in your writing, if you create a writing schedule that takes your everyday life, including time for rest and relaxation, into account.

Carve Out a "Sacred Space" for Writing

Set aside regular times in your schedule that are reserved exclusively for writing and nothing else. This time is not for checking email, reading social media, doing your online shopping, or returning phone calls. You are free to do all of those things at any other time during your day, but not during this designated writing time. Of course, if you need to read or look something up to support your writing, that's fine. But writing should be your main focus during this time.

For this exercise, I recommend using a visual calendar where you can see an entire week at a time and you have ample room for writing in your activities for each day of the week. I like to use an appointment book that shows a week at a time, with each day divided into hours and each hour into fifteen-minute time slots, but you can do this on your phone or even draw a simple calendar on a sheet of paper. The first step is to write in all of your scheduled appointments and responsibilities for the week. Take the rituals of your everyday life into account and try to be as realistic as possible. For example, if you're a parent and you have to take your children to school and pick them up every day, make sure you mark that on your calendar. Schedule in time for meals; don't use your sacred writing time for eating lunch.

Next, think about what is the shortest amount of time in which you can write productively. It's typically quite difficult to pick up right where you left off last time and just sit down at your computer and write, so make sure you give yourself enough time to get back into your writing. Let's say you chose two hours as the minimum amount of time you need to be productive. Look at your week and see where you can realistically carve out one or more two-hour time slots in your schedule. Write those in and then commit to spending that time during the week only on writing. These blocks of time comprise your sacred space for writing.

The advantage of planning your time this way is that outside of the times you set aside as a sacred space for writing, you are free to do whatever else you have to do! As long as you're consistent in sitting down to write during the times you've allocated, you don't have to carry the burden of guilt of "I should be writing" with you during the rest of the day. You will be amazed at how good this feels.

If you are having trouble getting started and the thought of scheduling a two-hour block of time to write makes you want to crawl under the covers, try to carve out writing time for just thirty minutes every day. Once you work for thirty minutes, you may find that another thirty minutes wouldn't be so bad. This technique actually works! For most people, getting started is the hardest part. It's much easier to keep going once you are already doing. Getting in the habit of working on a longer-term project such as a thesis or dissertation every day, even for a short period of time, can make you feel more productive.

Daily contact with your writing project keeps it on your mind and enables ideas to percolate all day. If possible, leave the papers and books you need to work on the section you're writing easily accessible to you. This will make it easier for you to get back to what you were doing after some time away.

Make It Easy
Try to make your writing process as pleasant as possible for you. Think about where and when you work best. Where is the most pleasant place for you to write? At what time of day? If you feel freshest in the morning and enjoy writing at home while you have your coffee, perhaps you can get up a little earlier before the rest of your household wakes up and have some quiet time to write. If you're more of a night owl, plan your writing time for the end of the day. If you prefer to be among people, go to the library or to a cafe to write. If it's a nice day and you could use a change of scenery, take your laptop and go to the park or sit outside in your backyard.

Battling Perfectionism and the Imposter Syndrome

When you're a graduate student, it is pretty typical to be concerned about sounding smart. You may, at some point, find yourself asking,

"Am I really a scholar or am I actually a fraud?" If so, you are not alone! One of the most common reasons graduate students become stuck in their writing is because they are writing for an imagined audience of harsh and critical readers who have taken up residence in their minds. This fantasized internal panel of judges is comprised of scholars who know everything there is to know about your topic and are ready to pounce on any factual error or missed citation. They are cuttingly sarcastic about awkwardly worded sentences or insufficiently explained abstruse ideas. If you are feeling paralyzed and unable to write or find yourself writing, deleting, and rewriting the same paragraph over and over again, you are most likely engaged in a struggle with perfectionism or the imposter syndrome. Fortunately, there are some very useful techniques you can draw upon to make writing less of a battle with the academic ideal and more of a down-to-earth, ordinary, pleasurable experience.

Read Other People's Dissertations
I highly recommend this. If you need to write a dissertation but are feeling intimidated and anxious, it can be extremely helpful to spend some time reading other people's dissertations. Many departments keep their graduates' dissertations in the departmental library. You will be surprised to discover that most of these dissertations are not the great master works you imagine them to be. In fact, the reality is that many of them will be mediocre at best. The feeling, "I can do better than that!" is not only true but also can be extremely motivating.

Be Willing to Make a Mess
Instead of trying to be perfect and ending up not writing anything, allow yourself to be messy! In other words, if you find yourself feeling stuck, give yourself five or ten minutes to "free write." Free writing means writing without worrying about whether what you're writing makes perfect sense, flows correctly, or is worded in an articulate manner. Just get your thoughts on paper or on your computer and keep going. It can be extremely productive to separate out writing from editing. If you allow yourself to be messy, you will find that it's much easier to move forward. You can always go back and edit. Most good writing is actually good editing.

Write as if You're Teaching Someone

Many graduate students make the mistake of thinking that the most important goal to keep in mind when writing is to sound smart. This is not true! In fact, your most important goal when writing is to be clear. If you find yourself worried about sounding smart, you are most likely writing for that imagined audience of harsh and critical readers who know everything there is to know about what you're writing about. This can be paralyzing. Instead—and this is an extremely useful technique—imagine that you're teaching someone who knows very little about your topic. Picture yourself teaching a class of undergraduate or high school students. Explain what you know in a clear and simple manner so that the person reading your paper or dissertation can understand what you're saying and follow along with your argument. A good thing to keep in mind is that readers get anxious when they can't follow your logic or don't understand what you're saying. Your goal is to make your reader less anxious by spelling out your argument step by step and by writing in clear language. It's fine to use academic jargon here and there if it is pertinent to your topic and helps explain what you're trying to communicate, but the overuse of esoteric terms for the sole purpose of sounding smart is very annoying to the reader.

Don't Be Afraid to Work in the Wrong Order

Give yourself permission to do what feels easiest first. If you find yourself procrastinating because the next chapter in your dissertation feels too daunting, start working on a different chapter that feels more manageable. It doesn't matter if you're writing chapter 3 before you write chapter 2. What matters is that you're writing. Working on what feels easiest first helps to keep you moving forward and helps to build your confidence that you can actually do this.

Write Notes to Yourself

If you've got a great idea that you're developing and you know where you want to go next but don't have time to continue writing, write "Next, I want to introduce x, y, and z and explain how they're related. They all have the same features of 1 and 2, and that explains my theory of A." When you come back tomorrow, you will already know what to say next. All that will be left is to say it.

Alternatively, if you know what you want to write about but are stuck on how to say it or feel overwhelmed because the topic you are referring to feels too complicated to explain just at this very moment, write a note to yourself in brackets and move on to the next paragraph. For example, "[include a brief review of the 1970s feminist movement here]." When you come back to your writing tomorrow, there's a good chance you'll feel ready to write about whatever you put in brackets.

Need a Morale Boost?
Start off writing in single space. When you have a few pages written, change your document to double space, and, voila! You will be impressed with how much you've accomplished so far.

Things to Do When You Don't Want to Write

Sometimes you just don't feel like writing. While as a general rule, it's better to maintain your discipline and try to push through and write anyway, there are times when that just doesn't work. After all you are a human being, not a robot. When that happens, you still don't need to abandon your writing project. It can be very fruitful to shift gears and do something else, especially if that something else is in support of your writing. What follows is a list of things you can do when you don't want to write.

Break Large Tasks Down into Small Ones
Most of the time, when people procrastinate, it's because the task in front of them feels too overwhelming. An excellent strategy is to take a large task and break it down into small, manageable chunks. So, for example, if the next thing you have to do is work on a section of your dissertation, but you're feeling that you just don't want to write, you can instead make a list of all the points you want to cover in that section, down to the smallest detail. That way, the next time you sit down to write, you can refer to your list and tackle one very manageable point at a time.

Work on Your References and Bibliography
When you don't feel like writing, it can feel soothing to occupy your mind with a task that doesn't require much thinking. Formatting your

references and bibliography is a great way to "veg out" while still using your writing time productively. It's boring and mindless, and you have to do it eventually, so you might as well do it now and feel good that you're being productive.

Check Your Citations
Checking your citations and putting them in the correct format is another way to make progress without overly taxing your brain. Make sure your quotes are accurate and that you've got the correct source, year, and page numbers.

Gather Your Research Materials
Go to the library to get that book you needed, or return the books you don't need. Research and print out, photocopy, or download some articles so you have them handy to read while you're on the train commuting to work or sitting in the park.

Clean Your Desk and Organize Your Files
Sitting down to a neat workplace can help clear your brain and make the prospect of writing more inviting. Take some time to clean up your desk and organize your files so you can more easily find what you're looking for.

Buy Your Office Supplies
Get those nice pens that you enjoy writing with, a notebook where you can jot down ideas as they come to you on the subway, a file folder to hold your stray papers.

Whatever you do, make sure you do something! You'll be surprised that the habit of getting something done every day, no matter how small, can be addictive. Of course, many of these tasks can also be used to procrastinate and avoid writing, so try to be honest with yourself, and do your best to bring yourself back to writing. If relevant, check out chapter 17 in this book about procrastination.

Finishing Your Incompletes

Your life doesn't stop just because you're in graduate school. Along the way, things happen: a family member becomes seriously ill; a spouse loses a job; a child is having trouble at school. There are times when you may need to put your academic work on hold in order to attend to other important aspects of your life. You might find that you have piled up one or more incompletes and are experiencing the unpleasant feeling that these incompletes are following you around like a storm cloud waiting to rain on you.

If your goal is to graduate, sooner or later, you will have to finish your incompletes so that you can receive a grade for your courses and move on to the next level in your program. Like most obligations that have been put on the back burner, they grow bigger and bigger in your imagination the longer you spend trying not to think about them. Perhaps adding to your anxiety about the prospect of facing your incompletes is the fear that your professors are getting more and more annoyed with you the more time has passed without you submitting your papers. The good news, however, is that the likelihood that your professors are thinking about you at all is very low. While your incompletes are looming large in your mind, they are not occupying the same position of importance in anyone else's. What follows is a brief list of suggestions for dealing with your incompletes.

Carve Out a Dedicated Time to Work on Them

If you are still taking classes, you will likely be busy fulfilling the current requirements for those classes and will not have much time left over for working on your incompletes from previous courses. If that's the case, it will be easiest for you to work on your incompletes during your upcoming school breaks. Take a look at your calendar and see when you will be off from school next. Then be deliberate about carving out times during your break that you can devote exclusively to working on your incompletes.

Break Down a Large Task into a Series of Small Ones

If you have several incompletes to work on, make a list of the papers you will need to write. The goal is not to think about them all as one huge and overwhelming task. Instead, you will be tackling them only one at a time.

Do What's Easiest First

Look at your list of papers due and determine which one feels easiest to work on. It may be the one with the shortest page requirement, the assignment for the class you liked best, or the topic you're most interested in. Set a goal of writing the paper that feels easiest to write first. Completing just one paper will give you a sense of accomplishment and reduce your tendency to procrastinate on finishing the rest.

Don't Go It Alone

As mentioned earlier, working on a long-term project such as a master's thesis or doctoral dissertation can feel extremely isolating. You no longer see your classmates on a daily basis and probably don't have the opportunity to hang out with your cohort in the student lounge the way you used to. During the dissertation phase, it's not an uncommon experience for graduate students to feel unmoored, disconnected from their department and from their peers. These feelings of disconnection and isolation can all too often lead to low morale and a sense that your project doesn't really matter.

One solution is to find other people who are working on their dissertation and schedule time to work together in parallel. Perhaps there's a person in your cohort, or a friend in a different department, who would make a good writing buddy. Making the commitment to another person to meet for regularly scheduled joint writing sessions will increase the likelihood that you will stay on track. If meeting in person is not possible, this can be done virtually on Zoom or another platform. These joint writing sessions have the added benefit of supplying you with a healthy dose of social interaction. After all, human beings are social animals. We need each other's company. After you finish your work session, you can have lunch or coffee together.

Some graduate school departments offer dissertation groups, in which students are encouraged to discuss their research with one another. If your department offers such a group, try it out. Getting together regularly with other people who are in the same situation can make you feel less alone, and talking with others about your work can help you clarify your ideas. If you prefer not to get together with people from your department, you can try forming your own dissertation group. All you need is one or two people who are willing to commit to meeting regularly. Another potential resource is your school's student counseling center, which may offer writing and dissertation groups, in addition to other academic counseling services. If your university has a writing center, check out what services they offer as well.

Don't Be Afraid to Ask for Help

A final piece of advice for those of you who are struggling to get the writing done: Don't be afraid to ask for help. If you are having difficulty finding time in your schedule to write, let your family members know what you need. Perhaps your partner can take over some of your child-care responsibilities or household chores. If you're making the final push to finish your dissertation but need a block of concentrated time to write, speak with your employer about taking a few days off from work. If you're feeling lost in your research and need some direction, schedule an appointment to meet with your advisor. The likelihood is that most of the people in your life are rooting for you to succeed and will be happy to help you if they can. But they can't help you unless you let them know what you need.

Takeaways for Students

- Whenever possible, choose a topic that interests you. It's much easier to write when you have a genuine interest in the subject you're writing about.
- Be strategic. If you will eventually be writing a thesis or dissertation, choose paper topics that are related to your main area of interest and that might be relevant to your larger project later on.
- Carve out a "sacred space" for writing. Think about where and when you work best and the minimum amount of time you need in order to be productive. Schedule this time into your calendar, taking the rest of your daily life into account. Do *not* expect to write all day, every day.

- If you're feeling overwhelmed by the task at hand, break it down into smaller tasks and tackle them one at a time.
- Be willing to make a mess! If you are blocked in your writing because you are afraid you don't sound smart enough or that your writing will not be perfect, be willing to be messy. Tip: When you write, imagine that you are teaching someone who knows nothing about your subject.

Suggestions for Administrators, Faculty, and Advisors

- If you are advising dissertations or master's theses, set up regular meetings with your advisees. How often these meetings occur is up to you, but I would recommend at least four meetings a year. Encourage them to get in touch with you if they're feeling stuck. Making yourself available to your advisees on a regular basis reduces the chances of a student falling through the cracks, and it lets them know that you are interested in them, their work, and their progress.
- If you are the chair of a department, consider offering a series of department workshops geared around writing the dissertation or thesis. These can include an initial workshop that outlines the dissertation process from start to finish: choosing a topic; choosing an advisor; forming a committee; writing and defending a proposal; conducting research; and preparing a defense. They can also include presentations by current students in various stages of the research and writing process, as well as presentations by graduates of the program who have completed their projects. You might also consider forming a department writing group, in which students can bring in their work for the group to read and comment on.
- If you are an advisor, don't assume that "no news is good news." If one of your students seems to have dropped off the face of the earth, touch base with them to see how they're doing. Keep in mind that they might be struggling with family or health issues that are interfering with their ability to progress academically.
- If a student has multiple incompletes, consider it a red flag—a sign that the student is having difficulty keeping up with their

academic work. Reach out to the student to get a sense of what's going on, and let them know that you are available to help. If your university counseling center offers academic services, referring the student to the counseling center can be an excellent way to help get them back on track.

Suggestions for Mental Health Professionals

- Keep in mind that a student's presenting problem of "I can't write" may be about far more than the need to develop good writing habits. Be careful not to launch too quickly into problem-solving mode. Spend some time getting to know the student as a person, as well as the larger context of the student's life. There may be other factors that are getting in the way of the student's ability to make progress in their writing.
- Encourage students to look into centers at their university that could help, such as student counseling and/or writing centers.
- If you work at a university counseling center, consider forming a dissertation or writing group in which students from various departments could participate. You will be amazed at how much students can benefit from sharing their experiences and strategies with peers.

~

CHAPTER SEVENTEEN

Taming the Tenacious Beast of Procrastination

Building a Bridge between Intention and Action

Jennifer Lee and Enid Gertmenian

Perhaps this sounds familiar to you . . .

I was running out of excuses. My adviser inquired about the status of my thesis, a draft of which was due in a few short weeks. This project cast a dark shadow that followed me wherever I went. In this shadow lurked the procrastination gremlins that taunted and teased me. The more I procrastinated, the louder and more punishing the gremlins grew. "How did you ever get into graduate school? If you can't buckle down and get to work, you're going to be eating ramen for the rest of your life." And when I mustered up enough energy to sit down at my computer, I suddenly had the urge to do something else that required my immediate attention. "How can I write in such a messy room? I need to organize my stuff and do laundry." And then the next, "I need to itemize my expenses right this very minute." And the next, "I'm going to watch an episode of *Game of Thrones*. It's an act of self-care and it will help me get motivated. Just one episode, I promise." These urges were just other procrastination gremlins in disguise. When they weren't berating me for not getting work done, they were coaxing me into thinking I was moving towards my goals when I was doing anything but. The dueling procrastination gremlins—the self-deprecating and the avoidant/self-indulgent ones threw me into a vicious cycle of despair, shame, and hopelessness. Hours had passed and I had nothing to show for my thesis except for an immaculate room, a perfectly balanced spreadsheet of my expenses, and bragging rights for binge-watching an entire season in one night. Of course, the gremlins picked up right where they left off the next morning and never seemed to let up.

For those who resonate with the pain, frustration, and humiliation of the procrastination cycle, we feel you. We write this chapter from experience—not just with the clinical work that we do with our clients, but from our own struggles with procrastination. We hope to illuminate the driving forces behind procrastination, offer some helpful tips on disengaging from the cycle, encourage you to harness your inner strength and knowledge, and build up your mastery so that you can get your work done. We won't, however, try to sell you snake oil and tell you that we have foolproof methods to eliminate procrastination because, in fact, procrastination is an inevitable part of the human condition. The problem of procrastination, which the Greeks called "akrasia," was a concept even Plato and Aristotle grappled with.[1] Armed with this understanding, we share some best practices to help you wrestle with the procrastination gremlins and approach your work with a sense of awareness and self-compassion.

The Prevalence of Procrastination: Join the Club

Procrastination has become such a common term that it has lost its heft as a very real psychological problem for many, especially graduate students. Procrastination isn't simply about a late paper, a missed class, or a pile of laundry bigger than your fridge. It is shown to have serious consequences on academic performance, degree completion, self-confidence, motivation, physical health, and mental well-being.[2]

Procrastination exists on a continuum. Everyone participates in it to one degree or another, but research shows that the prevalence rate of procrastination in Westernized countries is approximately 20 percent.[3] While a substantial portion of the general public struggles with this issue, rates of procrastination in higher learning institutions are astonishingly high, with as many as 80 to 95 percent of students identifying as procrastinators and approximately 50 percent identifying as chronic procrastinators.[4] Chronic procrastinators suffer even more acutely from their avoidance of work because the longer they put things off, the more significant the consequences are. People who suffer from this painful condition may stay in their room for weeks, neglect to take out the trash, and avoid all texts, calls, and emails. Overwhelmed, they go into a shutdown mode called "ostriching" with no exit plan and no connection to the outside world.

It's likely no surprise to you that procrastination has reached epidemic proportions in academic settings. As a graduate student, you're faced with extreme pressure to excel in a highly competitive environment, and you're expected to maintain self-discipline at all times while exercising humility as a constant learner. For many, procrastination is not just an occasional nuisance, but a crippling and demoralizing condition.

Defining the Pernicious Problem of Procrastination

Our understanding of procrastination has evolved over the years, but its definition has ultimately remained the same: delaying beginning or completing an intended course of action.[5] One of the most frustrating and baffling aspects of procrastination is the fundamental discrepancy between our intentions and behaviors. We intend to finish our qualifying paper, but we are unable to execute the task of writing. When our intentions are out of step with our actions, we experience emotional suffering.

Much like other behavioral health problems like depression and addiction, procrastination has long been seen as the result of character defects, such as laziness, irresponsibility, and moral weakness.[6] While that stigma unfortunately remains, procrastination is now understood as a more complex issue involving emotions, cognition, motivation, and behavior. In this chapter, we begin with the emotional impact of procrastination, since contemporary research is revealing procrastination to be primarily a problem of emotional dysregulation—an inability to manage and tolerate overwhelming feelings such as frustration, sadness, anxiety, and anger. Who hasn't felt emotionally dysregulated at some point in our academic careers? Are we the only ones who had the impulse to throw our computers out the window when we didn't know how to start a paper?

This focus on emotional dysregulation at the root of procrastination is a profound shift in our understanding of the condition. In a *New York Times* article, procrastination researcher Dr. Fuschia Sirois explained,

"People engage in this irrational cycle of chronic procrastination because of an inability to manage negative moods around a task."[7] Procrastination then acts as a short-term strategy to neutralize the feeling of being overwhelmed.[8] Rather than viewing procrastination as a personal failing or laziness, we can recognize it as an attempt—albeit an ineffective one—to regain stability, and thereby offset the additional suffering caused by self-criticism and shame.

A Holistic Approach to Procrastination

While other books on procrastination might focus on behavioral strategies to enhance your time management and organizational skills, we encourage you to approach your procrastination more holistically. It has been our experience that fundamentally changing procrastination patterns has more to do with the way you talk to yourself, the way you relate to your emotions, and the way you understand and utilize your motivation. Your ability to address these problems without falling into the trap of shame—an emotion that usually is the death knell for creative problem solving, initiative, and persistence—is essential to trying out new behaviors.

Working through Emotional Barriers

Shame and Self-Compassion

When you're stuck in the pitfall of procrastination, try practicing self-compassion. Why? Because shame is one of the most common emotions that procrastinators experience. First, it's important to point out the critical difference between guilt and shame, two emotions that often get conflated. When we experience guilt, we feel bad about the behavior we did because it wasn't aligned with our values. Usually, this leads us to rectify the situation and avoid the behavior in the future, allowing us to feel a sense of resolution and restored self-esteem. Shame, however, makes us feel as though the bad behavior we engaged in, which didn't align with our values, has now defined *who we are*. This is a crucial distinction because guilt can motivate us to change our behaviors since we believe we are still okay at our core, whereas shame erases all other aspects and reduces us to being a "bad person."

Practicing self-compassion decreases shame, allowing us to embrace a nonjudgmental stance where we can remain curious about our behaviors, act benevolently towards ourselves, and reignite our motivation to move forward. Studies have shown that practicing self-forgiveness increases our ability to regulate our emotions and experience more positive feelings, which allows us to accept responsibility for our actions, uphold a sense of integrity, make amends to ourselves, and ultimately give us the emotional strength to try again.[9]

Often, when we suggest the self-compassionate approach to our clients, they vehemently protest and explain that self-criticism is the only thing that kicks them into action. The underlying belief here is, "If I'm compassionate towards myself, I'll get really lazy and I'll just continue to make excuses for myself." To be fair, the drill sergeant approach may have worked for us at times, but in the long run, it's ineffective because it eventually causes a stronger desire to retreat. Lest you think self-forgiveness is merely "letting yourself off the hook," be forewarned. It takes a lot of fortitude to be good to yourself. Self-forgiveness requires rigorous honesty, taking responsibility for your actions, and a willingness to change your behavior patterns, steps that are a far cry from babying yourself.

You may be thinking, "Well, this self-compassion approach sounds like something I'd be willing to try, but what do I actually *do?*" Perhaps you're imagining self-forgiveness as extended self-hugs, repeating positive affirmations in the mirror, and drinking organic herbal tea while cuddling on your sofa. While those are not necessarily unhelpful practices, self-forgiveness requires a lot more than mere self-soothing. According to pioneers in the field, Kristen Neff and Chris Germer, self-compassion is composed of three main components: self-kindness, common humanity, and mindfulness.[10]

Self-Kindness

Self-kindness entails being caring towards ourselves when faced with perceived failures or inadequacies. In essence, this allows us to disengage from the grips of the harsh critic in our heads and cultivate a space of nonjudgmental acceptance and exploration where we can start to decouple our past actions with our sense of self.

One practical way to start is to imagine putting an amplifier to all of the self-critical thoughts that run through our minds and directing them outwards to a friend. We would be mortified at how accusatory, unforgiving, and unrelenting this would sound. To a friend, you would be more likely to listen attentively, be open and curious, and offer encouraging words. Verbalizing or writing down statements of self-kindness in your own voice can help enhance the effects of this practice.

Common Humanity

Common humanity refers to a sense of interconnectedness and the understanding that suffering is a shared human experience. Shame breeds in isolation, and its power can be mitigated once we expand our understanding of ourselves in the context of our communities. So how do we practice common humanity? First, you might remember evidence that procrastination is endemic for graduate students, so it's more likely than not that your peers are procrastinating as well. You might speak up about your struggles with trusted colleagues, who in turn might feel relieved that you started the conversation. When you practice common humanity, you acknowledge that pain is an inevitable part of life shared by all.

Mindfulness

Mindfulness means being aware of the present moment, allowing ourselves to sit with our experiences, without avoiding or overindulging, and creating the space to take a more balanced perspective. Often people say that they can't practice mindfulness because their minds are so distracted with what they need to do, what they didn't do, or just random thoughts like what they're planning for dinner. All of this is perfectly natural, so practice self-kindness and quietly let go of the expectation that you'll be able to sit in a zen state for hours. Be gentle with yourself and start with just a few minutes. Below we describe specific ways to practice mindfulness, especially when you're feeling overwhelmed and grappling with the urge to avoid an unpleasant task.

Increasing Awareness with Mindfulness

If emotional regulation issues are at the core of procrastination, the practice of mindfulness may help you move through difficult emotions surrounding a task. Through a nonjudgmental and receptive approach, we learn to recognize how strong emotions can cause us to react in predictable, self-defeating ways. The moment you recognize that you're procrastinating, ask yourself, "What are my feelings? What are my thoughts? What is happening in my body?" In essence, once we iden-tify these experiences, we create a space to *respond* rather than *react* in automatic pilot mode.[11]

Working with Thoughts

You might be consumed by particularly sticky thoughts: "I've dug myself into a hole and now I can't get out. It's impossible to finish all that I need to do. My situation is totally helpless." These thoughts might lead to more punishing thoughts and lead us down a dark hole where our only choice is to give up. In those moments, it might be helpful to look at your thoughts from a distance, as mental events pass-ing through the mind, for example, looking at our thoughts as if they were clouds passing through the sky or leaves falling from a tree (or a different metaphor that speaks to you). When we make this subtle shift—creating a space between ourselves and our thoughts and recog-nizing that "thoughts are just thoughts" and not who we are—it can have profound effects on the way that we feel.[12] Later on, we'll say more about how you can further work with some of these irrational thoughts.

Working with Emotions

When we are in the throes of a procrastination spiral, we might vaguely acknowledge that we're feeling frustrated and disappointed in ourselves, but we continue to disengage or engage in off-task activi-ties out of habit. When we are mindful of our emotions, we learn to recognize a feeling as it arises and not when we're in the midst of some consequential action. As we become more aware of the experience of shame, anger, or sadness, we can learn to be with these emotions in a more balanced way—finding the middle path where we're not pushing them away or overly identifying with them. In those moments, we can learn to acknowledge the feeling, become aware of our urge to retreat and procrastinate, and, hopefully, discover a different way forward.

Working with Body Sensations

Some people are adept at naming their feelings and identifying their thoughts, while others are more in tune with what is happening in their bodies. When you sense a strong feeling arising, try to locate the place in your body where you're holding that emotion. You might not realize you're feeling anxious until you notice that your shoulders are tense, you're clenching your jaw, and there is a hollow feeling in your stomach. If you bring full awareness to the sensations in your body, allowing them to be without needing or wanting them to be different than they are, you might notice that the experience shifts on its own. While our muscles might loosen and our breath might deepen, we might also notice that our emotions and thoughts don't have the same charge. By being present with all of our experiences, we can identify our urge to procrastinate, disengage from our old, damaging narratives, and open ourselves to new possibilities and behaviors (for more practices, see the section on mindfulness in chapter 3).

Bridging the Gap between Intention and Behavior

You set an intention to get on top of your work this semester, but you find yourself at the edge of a deep crevasse. You're looking beyond to the other side, to the sweet feeling of satisfaction you experience after having completed your work. But it feels completely out of your reach. The feeling of despondency makes you want to turn around and give up without even trying. Rest assured, there are different tools to help you bridge the gap between your intentions and behaviors, that is, taking action to execute your most important tasks.

Affirming Core Values

A newer form of psychotherapy, Acceptance and Commitment Therapy (ACT), has emphasized "core values" as an essential ingredient to making changes in our lives.[13] Identifying your core values might lead to a deeper sense of self-knowledge and can be a very powerful way to increase your motivation and self-respect. To clarify, core values are not the same as goals. A goal is an action you want to accomplish (e.g., learn to play the guitar, teach your daughter how to ride a bike); whereas core values are your north star, describing the person you want to be and how you want to live your life. If your goal is to obtain a PhD, your core values might include being a lifelong learner, researching a social issue for change, as well as having the status and prestige that goes along with earning that degree.

One way to start clarifying your personal values is to separate the values you have in different parts of your life—family, friends, school, personal, health, and community. One particularly useful tool is the "Bullseye Exercise,"[14] where you identify your values and place a mark on a bullseye indicating how far or how close you are to living in line with those values.[15] This can sometimes be a painful exercise if you feel as though you've strayed far from the center, like when you're procrastinating, which can entangle us in feelings of paralysis and isolation. However, looking at your core values can help you start problem solving and move you closer to being the person you want to be. We encourage you to be honest with yourself about what matters to *you*, rather than what you *think* you ought to aspire to.

On a more practical level, identifying your core values is a way to connect to the larger purpose of the (potentially annoying, seemingly pointless, or massively overwhelming) task in front of you. For example, you might be the kind of person who values finishing what you start and completing that literature review is a way to be aligned with that value. Maybe you want to be the kind of person who sets an example for your kids to persist in the face of struggles. Tackling statistics when it's incomprehensible is a way to start becoming that person. Writing down a reminder about why taking action matters on a deeper level and keeping it in your line of vision can help you persevere and ride out the fear, frustration, and boredom you might be feeling at the moment.

Doing Our Future Selves a Solid

When we rationalize delaying or avoiding our work, we're opting to relieve stress and painful emotions using the short-term strategy of procrastination. While we might immediately feel better, we avoid acknowledging (consciously or unconsciously) how putting off the task will affect us in the long run. Essentially, we end up throwing our future selves under the bus.

One way we do this is by idealizing our future self, fantasizing that in the abstract near future, we'll be imbued with more willpower to tackle a tedious task. You might stare down the barrel of a monstrous research paper and think, "Future me is going to have so much more interest and energy to get this done. She'll also probably be able to unload the dishwasher and clean up that pile of papers on her desk too." Connecting with your future self in a more realistic way is no easy task, especially when you are on a long vacation into the "dark playground"—a term coined by Tim Urban, a popular blogger, to describe the experience of guiltily frittering time away on seemingly meaningful distractions despite having more important work to do.[16] With a little creativity, there are several ways you can create strategies to rewire your brain to take care of future you, and in doing so, take care of current you. One client who was prone to snoozing created a video, which she set up to play as her morning alarm, reminding herself how much better she felt when she got out of bed on time. While getting up on time felt annoying for a short while, it ultimately helped her have a more productive day.

Precommitment, another helpful tool to connect to your future self, involves limiting your options so that you are more likely to follow through with your intended plan.[17] The more temptations you face and potential decisions to make, the more depleted and likely you'll succumb to procrastination. Precommitment in graduate school might be: promising to bring food to a study potluck knowing you'll be persona non grata if you don't show up; or committing to present at next month's journal club so that you'll have to prepare or else you'll be caught in the spotlight with nothing to say; or going to the library without your cell phone or computer so you're forced to focus on your reading materials.

Recognizing Rationalizations and Challenging Belief Systems

Procrastination is often frustrating, since we delay an intended task in spite of feeling worse off after delaying.[18] When we procrastinate, we act against our self-interest, knowing that down the road, we'll have to "pay the piper" for our temporary relief. Depending on our personality traits, emotional states, and values, we might use different explanations for our seemingly irrational behavior.

Many procrastinators report a feeling of inertia and sudden sleepiness when they consider taking action. You aren't sure how to get started and tell yourself that you need a "reset nap." For others, the experience is one of apathy. You can't see any value in this seemingly irrelevant task, so there's no point wasting time on it. Alternatively, some students anticipate that doing the work will bring up unmanageable feelings of fear and humiliation. Your rationalization might be that attempting to do the work will elicit your inadequacies, so it's better to hold off until you're feeling more resilient. Finally, a different sort of procrastinator might use a form of optimistic rationalization. You remind yourself that you've coasted by doing assignments at the last minute, so why bother changing now?

It's important to keep in mind that rationalizations often serve a protective function and develop for a reason. You might think of them as an over-reactive guard dog that may have protected you from feeling overwhelmed—and staved off the fear that more will be expected of you if you change, or the fear that you won't master the skills even if you try hard—but they are no longer working for you and allowing you to grow.

After becoming aware of your inner rationalizer, we invite you to challenge these statements in a way that feels authentic to you. Start by validating those thoughts and feelings, and then check the facts about the reality of the situation. For example, with inertia, you could conjure up a memory where day napping made you more productive. If you can, then it's not a rationalization. But if you can't, it's an opportunity to look at the evidence and be honest with yourself. Taking the stance of a realist rather than a pessimist or optimist can help diminish self-judgments and allow you to develop an alternative plan. To address apathy, you might start by validating your disenchantment or cynicism and then connect with your higher purpose for earning your degree and reframe the task to be more personally relevant to you. You don't need to feel confident or excited about responding to your rationalizations. In fact, you can expect to feel some fear, frustration, and insecurity that naturally arise from working in a new way. If you feel stuck, try imagining that part of you as a person in your life whom you care about. Start a dialogue, be curious, ask questions, and listen.

Acting Opposite

One of the most familiar tropes for procrastination is, "I need to be in the right mood to start writing." We wait for a bolt of lightning to jolt us into action or a magical wave of inspiration once our muse arrives, but the truth is, it might come too late or never at all. Mindfulness-Based Cognitive Therapy (MBCT), a program designed for individuals who suffer from depression, underscores the principle that "motivation works backwards."[19] The program helps individuals to momentarily suspend the belief that they need to feel better to leave their house and meet a friend for coffee. Through the practice of mindfulness, individuals learn to recognize how thoughts represent and distort their present moment awareness. If individuals who suffer from depression can do something activating, even though they might not like it or find it particularly pleasurable, they start to build momentum in small increments. We can think of procrastination in the same way. You might not have the luxury of waiting until the right mood hits, but if you do something (anything) work-related as a start, the motivation will likely build.

Another way to motivate backwards is to use a skill from Dialectical Behavioral Therapy (DBT) called "opposite action," where we can change our emotions by acting opposite to the emotion we're currently experiencing.[20] Let's say Talena is experiencing unjustified fear that she'll write a nonsensical paper, be an embarrassment to her professor, and ultimately fail the class. At this point she rationalizes, "It's safer to not work on it because it makes me too anxious." The goal of acting opposite is to go against the grain of the emotion, rather than marinating in it. When acting opposite, Talena may need to take a few minutes of deep breathing and then do anything related to making progress on her paper, such as make an appointment with her adviser or review her outline and research articles. When facing fear, remember phrases such as "approach don't avoid" and "do whatever you're afraid of over and over and over" until you build mastery. Remember that the alternative is avoidance, which won't improve things. By repeatedly moving through the feared situation, you realize that your emotions were giving inaccurate information about how catastrophic the situation would be. If you feel paralyzed, you might find it helpful to get into "zombie mode" by turning off your brain, engaging your muscles, and moving your body towards the activity before you have the time to talk yourself out of it.

Calling Out Pseudo-Efficiency

As you probably already know, procrastination doesn't just happen when you are in your pajamas bingeing on Netflix while your computer glares at you from across the room. While delaying a task is at the core of procrastination, it can also take other forms that are harder to spot, such as the phenomenon of "pseudo-efficiency," or as we call it, "procrastination with a top hat." Spending the entire afternoon organizing and inputting all of your research articles into EndNote may feel important in the moment, and in small doses it can provide the kindling to get started on a tough task. The problem arises when you are doing more preparation than actual work. This sort of "righteous delaying" can be especially easy to slip into if you have a perfectionistic style or obsessive tendencies.

So how do you know you're in pseudo-efficiency? As with all of the tools we've suggested, increasing your self-awareness is the first step in changing entrenched behaviors and reclaiming your time. Describe what you're doing and be honest with yourself, "I've spent the last hour formatting the methods section of my dissertation" or "I spent the entire afternoon downloading articles, but I'm getting inundated with information that's not relevant to my thesis." Sometimes, taking the extra step of actually vocalizing these thoughts aloud can diminish their power and break the pseudo-efficiency spell. Then ask yourself, "Am I avoiding something? Might there be a fear that I'm not fully acknowledging?" You might discover that you're dreading the next step because it requires more intellectual heavy lifting like a synthesis of your own ideas. Acknowledge that you're procrastinating and give yourself a time limit. If disengaging from these more gratifying tasks proves too challenging, consider using those tasks as a reward for completing the tedious ones.

The Perfectionistic Procrastinator

The procrastinator with perfectionistic tendencies holds strong to the belief and expectation that they must be perfect, and their work as an extension of themselves must be perfect as well. Being overly preoccupied with impression management, they typically need to present a flawless image of themselves and might be reluctant to seek help and otherwise challenge the perfect facade they are trying so desperately to control.[21]

Sung was crippled with perfectionistic tendencies, handing in his writing assignments late and some not at all. Worried about losing face with his professors, he often skipped class when assignments were due.

This created an even deeper hole, missing out on critical opportunities for class participation and pulling him farther behind on his academic work. For Sung, procrastination shrouded his fears of being imperfect. If he handed in something late, he expected to receive a grade penalty for tardiness, not because there was something fundamentally wrong with the quality of his work. While he could preserve his pristine self-image, he recognized the damaging cycle he created. The longer he delayed, the greater the grade penalty, and he might give up altogether. He would rather receive a zero for not trying rather than a failing grade after putting in some effort. He was stuck in this chronic loop, which bred an endless cycle of depression, anxiety, and hopelessness.

In counseling, Sung became aware of these underlying dynamics, learned to challenge his unproductive and entrenched beliefs, and slowly adopted a more flexible mindset, allowing for "good enough" work. With a looming deadline, this meant handing in a paper that was a page short of the minimum or with a few references missing. He also gave himself permission to reach out and share his struggles with his professors. As a second-generation Asian American, Sung grew up in a strict, authoritarian household where he learned to be deferential to and fearful of authority figures. He also felt pressured to excel and experienced the unrelenting judgment of not doing enough. While he believed his professors had a positive impression of him through his active class participation and passion for the subject, he worried that exposing his vulnerabilities would make him appear incompetent and inadequate. Although hesitant at first, Sung discovered that his professors were willing to help, offering to review his outlines and establish small goals for the remainder of the semester. Through these interactions, he discovered his self-agency and dismantled his worries of "not having it all together," especially in the eyes of those in power.

While the threat of falling back into his perfectionistic ways was ever present, Sung learned to utilize some work-arounds. Like Sung, you might find yourself completely paralyzed once you muster enough courage to even sit at your computer. In the film *Finding Forrester* by Gus Van Sant, William Forrester, a reclusive Pulitzer Prize–winning author, finds an unlikely mentee in Jamal Wallace, a young writing prodigy. William tells Jamal, "You must write your first draft with your heart. You rewrite with your head."[22] This might help distill the irrational belief for perfectionistic procrastinators that every sentence, as a first pass, needs to be perfect. Writing a first draft with your heart might mean putting down your ideas, no matter how ill formed or imperfect. It might be helpful to turn off the spelling/grammar checker in Word so that the squiggly line indicating an error doesn't distract and pull you out of first-draft mode. Writing from your heart might also mean giving yourself permission to be as messy as you can be. "Prescribing the symptom," a paradoxical psychological strategy, is where you engage in the very behavior you are trying to resolve. For the perfectionist, this might mean writing a very sloppy first draft filled with misspelling and grammatical errors and inserting a marker such as "(CITATION)" every time you're missing a reference. Once you have your first draft or really anything on the page, you can begin to "rewrite with your head" and engage the editor mindset to clean up your sentences and fill in missing information.

If you're still stuck looking at a blank document with the cursor blinking, daring you to write a less than perfect sentence, try yet another approach. In moments of paralysis, Sung was encouraged to record his nascent ideas about his paper into the audio recorder on his phone. He could do this while waiting in line at the grocery store or on the treadmill at the gym and then transcribe his audio notes when he got home. Remembering that motivation works backwards, he learned that it is easier to keep writing when you have something, anything, to work with. He discovered that once he started the writing process, it was easier to keep going.

For the perfectionistic procrastinator, pseudo-efficiency can some-times work as a mask to cover up perceived inadequacies. As the therapist for an executive-functioning skills group, I (Enid) finished writing the training manual but found myself tinkering with the for-matting for what seemed like hours and delayed printing it for as long as possible. My dithering concealed my self-consciousness about all of the grammatical errors I might have missed and my fears of presenting an unpolished manual to the members—some of whom were talented writers and copy editors. I imagined them thinking that I was a fraud to present myself as an expert on executive functioning. Given all I had studied about procrastination, I decided to own my shortcomings and model what my mentor calls "graceful ignorance." I let the group know that the manual was a work in progress and that my passion for the topic far outweighed my grammatical skills. When I enlisted their help to point out any errors, the members were overwhelmingly appreciative that I showed vulnerability and respected their contributions. Seeing me put forth imperfect work and asking for help, they were emboldened to do the same.

Enlisting Your Community and Asking for Help

Because of the shame that surrounds procrastination, it's easy to hide away and isolate ourselves, which only breeds more shame. When we find the courage to acknowledge suffering within ourselves and in the presence of others, we might discover that one of the most powerful antidotes to shame is recognizing our common humanity and tending to our connection to others.

After months of inertia on my research project and testing my adviser's patience, I (Jennifer) joined a six-week procrastination workshop specifically designed for graduate students. One philosophy student arrived with a meticulously prepared binder filled with color-coded notes on each theory and musing for his dissertation. Imprisoned by his binder, he couldn't make any substantial progress on his writing. One English literature student in her tenth year of studies was ABD (all but dissertation) and at risk of never earning her degree if she didn't defend within the next year. All of their stories were lamentable and relatable. Within the first session, we were paired with our "Taskmaster" (TM), someone who would keep us accountable to our work and help establish a timeframe for getting it done. I dreaded facing Janice, my TM and veteran workshop participant, during our daily check-ins, as I felt constantly ashamed of my lack of progress. With spring break around the corner, I sheepishly vowed that I would work on my project while out of town visiting family. My TM challenged this predictable tactic and encouraged me to stay home to write. After a reluctant surrender and with her uncompromising lead, I had a completed first draft by the end of the week. It was Janice's vital accountability that kept me on track and her redirection out of tough love that helped me disengage from the mental gymnastics of procrastination I was so entangled in.

If one is offered, consider joining a procrastination group or work-shop. The sense of solidarity with other struggling students can be a powerful remedy to shame. If you can't bring yourself to be part of such a group, you might consider enlisting support in other ways. You could invite your peers to a weekly study or writing group with a specific time and place to meet. The one caveat is to be mindful that you're not spending too much time socializing, lamenting about the amount of work you all have, and complaining about departmental politics. As with pseudo-efficiency, set a time limit. Group norms might allow for ten minutes of banter and then shifting to the real work of studying or writing.

Another way to stay accountable is to meet with your professor or thesis adviser to help you develop a timeline for assignments. Creating smaller deadlines (such as one for your outline, another for your first chapter, and so on) and receiving frequent feedback after each deadline have been shown to increase productivity.[23] We recognize that asking for help is easier said than done for most graduate students, especially if you have perfectionistic tendencies. Shame can be a powerful deter-rent, but you might be surprised at how liberating it feels to acknowl-edge that you need help.

In Closing

In this chapter, we hope that the vignettes we shared offered a sense of hope, solidarity, and validation. We imagine that you might see some of yourselves in these stories. We were there too. And just when we feel confident in our full recovery, those gremlins may resurface when faced with another unpleasant task. But the gremlins have aged a bit. Their caustic comments don't have as much bite, and their seductive ways designed to steer us away from actual work are less compelling. When we practice awareness, forgiveness, and compassion for ourselves, the gremlins retreat further into the shadows. Their echoes might still be there, but we can choose to pay attention to the new narrative that we've constructed for ourselves and courageously walk across the bridge from our intentions to action.

Takeaways for Students

- Practice self-acceptance and self-forgiveness and acknowledge a sense of shared experience and common humanity with those who also struggle with procrastination.
- When managing the urge to procrastinate, build your emotion regulation skills by becoming aware of your thoughts, feelings, and body sensations through the practice of mindfulness.
- Identify and affirm your core values so that you can align your behaviors to your ideals.
- Imagine your future self so that you can act in your current self's best interests.
- Notice irrational beliefs and rationalizations when they arise and challenge them to be more flexible and realistic.
- When you're feeling anxious and find yourself avoiding a task, try acting opposite.
- Become aware of the pitfalls of perfectionism and pseudo-efficiency.
- Connect with your community, ask for help, and join a procrastination workshop if one is available.

Suggestions for Faculty and Administrators

- If a student appears to be struggling with procrastination and fails to communicate with you about missed assignments, reach out and meet with them individually. This might be particularly helpful to perfectionistic procrastinators who tend to hide in the perceived safety of their exacting standards or self-doubting procrastinators who are too ashamed to ask for help out of fear of being judged.
- If a student falls far behind in their coursework, encourage them to seek individual counseling services on campus. In more severe cases, discuss the possibility of petitioning for a limited course load to help the student focus and build mastery in small increments.
- Be open-minded when you perceive students as "entitled, lazy, or irresponsible." These might be signs of underlying competence

issues, particularly in students with learning disabilities and/or ADHD.

- For large assignments and final projects, consider establishing interim deadlines throughout the semester.
- Offer procrastination groups on campus.

Suggestions for Mental Health Professionals

- For perfectionistic procrastinators, model a relaxed approach to home practice assignments.[24] Because of their exquisite sensitivity to negative evaluations from others, adopting a nonpunitive style may help them loosen their high self-standards.
- For more chronic procrastination issues, clients might need the personalized approach of individual therapy and concurrent group therapy.
- Consider recommending that the student engage the services of a one-on-one executive-functioning skills coach who can help them with accountability and problem solving so that you can focus on the more emotional aspects of the student's distress.

$\sim$

Notes

Chapter One

1. Jason S. Moser, Hans S. Schroder, Carrie Heeter, Tim P. Moran, and Yu Hao Lee, "Mind Your Errors: Evidence for a Neural Mechanism Linking Growth Mind-Set to Adaptive Posterror Adjustments," *Psychological Science* 22, no. 12 (October 2011): 1484–89.

2. Teresa Evans, Lindsay Bira, Jazmin Beltran Gastelum, L. Todd Weiss, and Nathan Vanderford, "Evidence for a Mental Health Crisis in Graduate Education," *Nature Biotechnology* 36 (March 2018): 282 84, https://doi.org/10.1038/nbt.4089.

3. David L. Brunsma, David G. Embrick, and Jean H Shin, "Graduate Students of Color: Race, Racism, and Mentoring in the White Waters of Academia," *Sociology of Race and Ethnicity* 3, no. 1 (January 2017): 1–13.

4. National Center for Education Statistics, "Fast Facts: Back to School Statistics," 2016, accessed March 12, 2019, https://nces.ed.gov/fastfacts/display.asp?id=372.

5. Evans et al., "Evidence for a Mental Health Crisis in Graduate Education," 282–84.

6. Sarah Ketchen Lipson, Sasha Zhou, Blake Wagner III, Katie Beck, and Daniel Eisenberg, "Major Differences: Variations in Undergraduate and Graduate Student Mental Health and Treatment Utilization across Academic Disciplines," *Journal of College Student Psychotherapy* 30, no. 1 (2016): 23–41.

7. Graduate Assembly, "Graduate Student Happiness & Well-Being Report," 2014, http://ga.berkeley.edu/wp-content/uploads/2015/04/wellbeingreport_2014.pdf.

8. Graduate Assembly, "Graduate Student Happiness & Well-Being Report."

9. Juliana Breines, "Graduate School and Mental Illness: Is There a Link?" *Psychology Today*, November 26, 2015, https://www.psychologytoday.com/us/blog/in-love-and-war/201511/graduate-school-and-mental-illness-is-there-link.

Chapter Two

1. "Michelle Obama: 'I Still Have Impostor Syndrome,'" BBC News, accessed August 19, 2019, https://www.bbc.com/news/uk-46434147.

2. Pauline Clance and Suzanne Imes, "The Impostor Phenomenon in High Achieving Women: Dynamics and Therapeutic Intervention," *Psychotherapy: Theory, Research and Practice* 15, no. 3 (Fall 1978): 241.

3. Joe Langford and Pauline Clance, "The Impostor Phenomenon: Recent Research Findings Regarding Dynamics, Personality and Family Patterns and Their Implications for Treatment," *Psychotherapy: Theory, Research and Practice* 30, no. 3 (Fall 1993): 495.

4. Pauline Clance and M. O'Toole, "The Impostor Phenomenon: An Internal Barrier to Empowerment and Achievement," *Women and Therapy* 6, no. 3 (1987): 51–64.

5. Langford and Clance, "The Impostor Phenomenon: Recent Research Findings," 495.

6. Malissa McLean and Jay Avella, "IP in Information Technology," *Journal of IT Management* 27, no. 4 (2016): 138–50.

7. Darlene G. Miller and Signe M. Kastberg, "Of Blue Collars and Ivory Towers: Women from Blue-Collar Backgrounds in Higher Education," *Roeper Review* 18, no. 1 (September 1995): 27–33.

8. Shannon McClain, Samuel T. Beasley, Bianca Jones, Olufunke Awosogba, Stacey Jackson, and Kevin Cokley, "An Examination of the Impact of Racial and Ethnic Identity, Impostor Feelings, and Minority Status Stress on the Mental Health of Black College Students," *Journal of Multicultural Counseling and Development* 44 (April 2016): 103–5.

9. Brian D. Smedley, Hector F. Myers, and Shelly P. Harrell, "Minority-status Stresses and the College Adjustment of Ethnic Minority Freshmen," *The Journal of Higher Education* 64, no. 4 (1993): 434–52.

10. Gregory M. Walton and Geoffrey L. Cohen, "A Question of Belonging: Race, Social Fit, and Achievement," *Journal of Personality and Social Psychology* 92, no. 1 (2007): 82.

11. Geoffrey L. Cohen and Claude M. Steele, "A Barrier of Mistrust: How Stereotypes Affect Cross-Race Mentoring," in *Improving Academic Achievement: Impact of Psychological Factors on Education*, ed. J. Aronson, 305–6 (Oxford: Academic Press, 2002).

12. McClain et al., "An Examination," 110–13.

13. Claude M. Steele and Jason Aronson, "Stereotype Threat and the Intellectual Test Performance of African Americans," *Journal of Personality and Social Psychology* 69, no. 5 (1995): 797–811.

14. Clance and Imes, "The Impostor Phenomenon in High Achieving Women," 242–43.

15. Heinz Kohut, *How Does Analysis Cure?* (Chicago: University of Chicago Press, 1984).

16. C. Bussoti, "The Impostor Phenomenon: Family Roles and Environment," PhD diss., Georgia State University, 1990.

17. Denise Castro, Rebecca Jones, and Hamid Mirsalimi, "Parentification and the Imposter Phenomenon: An Empirical Investigation," *The American Journal of Family Therapy* no. 3 (May–June 2004): 212.

18. Loretta Neal McGregor, Damon E. Gee, and K. Elizabeth Posey, "I Feel Like a Fraud and It Depresses Me: The Relation between the Imposter Phenomenon and Depression," *Social Behavior and Personality* 36, no. 1 (2008): 46–47.

19. Sabine M. Chrisman, W. A. Pieper, Pauline R. Clance, C. L. Holland, and Cheryl Glickauf-Hughes, "Validation of the Clance Impostor Phenomenon Scale," *Journal of Personality Assessment* 65, no. 3 (1995): 456–67.

20. S. Cowman and Joseph R. Ferrari, "'Am I For Real?' Predicting Imposter Tendencies from Self-handicapping and Affective Components," *Social Behavior and Personality: An International Journal* 30 (2002): 119–26.

21. Langford and Clance, "The Impostor Phenomenon: Recent Research Findings," 497.

22. M. E. H. Topping, "The Impostor Phenomenon: A Study of Its Construct Validity and Incidence in University Faculty Members," PhD diss., University of South Florida, 1983.

23. T. J. Prince, "The Imposter Phenomenon Revisted: A Validity Study of Clance's IP Scale," unpublished master's thesis, Georgia State University, 1989.

24. J. Langford, "The Need to Look Smart: The Impostor Phenomenon and Motivations on Learning," PhD diss., Georgia State University, 1990.

25. Carol S. Dweck, "Motivational Processes Affecting Learning," *American Psychologist* 41, no. 10 (1986): 1040–48.

26. Ted Thompson, Peggy Foreman, and Frances Martin, "Impostor Fears and Perfectionistic Concern over Mistakes," *Personality and Individual Differences* 29 (2000): 629–47.

27. B. Cromwell, N. Brown, J. Sanchez-Hucles, and F. L. Adair, "The Impostor Phenomenon and Personality Characteristics of High School Honor Students," *Social Behavior and Personality: An International Journal* 5 (1990): 563–73.

28. Cowman and Ferrari, "'Am I For Real?'" 119–26.

29. Jean Piaget, *Origins of Intelligence in the Child* (London: Routledge and Kegan Paul, 1936).

Chapter Four

1. US Department of Education, Institute of Education Sciences, National Center for Education Statistics, *Profile of Students in Graduate and First-Professional Education: 2007–08*, accessed July 5, 2019, https://nces.ed.gov/pubs2010/2010177.pdf.

2. Teal Burrell, "Dispelling Myths about Students with Disabilities," *American Psychological Association gradPSYCH Magazine* 13, no. 2 (April 2015): 28, https://www.apa.org/gradpsych/2015/04/dispelling-myths.

3. Teresa Evans, Lindsay Bira, Jazmin Beltran Gastelum, L. Todd Weiss, and Nathan Vanderford, "Evidence for a Mental Health Crisis in Graduate Education," *Nature Biotechnology* 36 (March 2018): 282, https://doi.org/10.1038/nbt.4089.

4. Ezra Smith and Zachary Brooks, *Graduate Student Mental Health 2015* (Tucson: National Association of Graduate-Professional Students and the Graduate Professional Student Council [GPSC], University of Arizona, August 2015), http://nagps.org/wordpress/wp-content/uploads/2015/06/NAGPS_Institute_mental_health_survey_report_2015.pdf.

5. Smith and Brooks, *Graduate Student Mental Health 2015*.

6. Evans et al., "Evidence for a Mental Health Crisis in Graduate Education," 282.

7. Colleen Flaherty, "Mental Health Crisis for Grad Students," *Inside Higher Ed*, March 6, 2018, https://www.insidehighered.com/news/2018/03/06/new-study-says-graduate-students-mental-health-crisis.

8. Graduate Assembly, "Graduate Student Happiness & Well-Being Report," 2014, http://ga.berkeley.edu/wp-content/uploads/2015/04/wellbeingreport_2014.pdf.

9. Jenny K. Hyun, Brian C. Quinn, and Temina Madon, "Graduate Student Mental Health: Needs Assessment and Utilization of Counseling Services," *Journal of College Student Development* 47, no. 3 (May/June 2006): 261.

10. Arielle F. Shanok, PhD, Deputy Director for Student Counseling Services at The Graduate Center, CUNY, personal communication, July 7, 2019.

11. The Jed Foundation, *Student Mental Health and the Law: A Resource for Institutions of Higher Education* (New York, 2008), http://www.jedfoundation.org/wp-content/uploads/2016/07/student-mental-health-and-the-law-jed-NEW.pdf.

12. All student examples have either had their identifying details disguised or changed to protect their confidentiality or are based on a composite of many different people.

13. Carl Straumsheim, "New Era for Disability Rights," *Inside Higher Ed*, November 7, 2016, https://www.insidehighered.com/news/2016/11/07/disability-rights-advocates-shift-strategies-ensure-equal-rights-digital-age.

14. Hyun, Quinn, and Madon, "Graduate Student Mental Health," 257.

15. Hyun, Quinn, and Madon, "Graduate Student Mental Health," 261.

16. Hyun, Quinn, and Madon, "Graduate Student Mental Health," 255.

17. Hyun, Quinn, and Madon, "Graduate Student Mental Health," 255.

Chapter Five

1. Sara Houshmand, Lisa B. Spanierman, and Romin W. Tafarodi, "Excluded and Avoided: Racial Microaggressions Targeting Asian International Students in Canada," *Cultural Diversity and Ethnic Minority Psychology* 20, no. 3 (July 2014): 377–88, https://doi.org/10.1037/a0035404.

2. Yuefang Zhou et al., "Theoretical Models of Culture Shock and Adaptation in International Students in Higher Education," *Studies in Higher Education* 33, no. 1 (May 2008): 63–75, https://doi.org/10.1080/03075070701794833.

3. Kenneth T. Wang et al., "Profiles of Acculturative Adjustment Patterns among Chinese International Students," *Journal of Counseling Psychology* 59, no. 3 (July 2012): 432, https://doi.org/10.1037/a0028532.

4. Ibid.

5. Sara Houshmand, Lisa B. Spanierman, and Romin W. Tafarodi, "Excluded and Avoided: Racial Microaggressions Targeting Asian International Students in Canada," *Cultural Diversity and Ethnic Minority Psychology* 20, no. 3 (July 2014): 384, https://doi.org/10.1037/a0035404.

6. Kenneth T. Wang et al., "Profiles of Acculturative Adjustment Patterns among Chinese International Students," *Journal of Counseling Psychology* 59, no. 3 (July 2012): 431–33, https://doi.org/10.1037/a0028532.

7. Jean Kesnold Mesidor and Kaye F. Sly, "Factors that Contribute to the Adjustment of International Students," *Journal of International Students* 6, no. 1 (January 2016): 272–73.

8. Osman Özturgut and Carole Murphy, "Literature vs. Practice: Challenges for International Students in the U.S.," *International Journal of Teaching and Learning in Higher Education* 22, no. 3 (2009): 381–82.

9. Blake Hendrickson, Devan Rosen, and R. Kelly Aune, "An Analysis of Friendship Networks, Social Connectedness, Homesickness, and Satisfaction Levels of International Students," *International Journal of Intercultural Relations* 35, no. 3 (May 2011): 290–91, https://doi.org/10.1016/j.ijintrel.2010.08.001.

Chapter Six

1. H. Okahana and E. Zhou, *Graduate Enrollment and Degrees: 2007 to 2017* (Washington, DC: Council of Graduate Schools, 2018).

2. Reid Wilson, "Census: More Americans Have College Degrees Than Ever Before," *The Hill*, April 3, 2017, https://thehill.com/homenews/state-watch/326995-census-more-americans-have-college-degrees-than-ever-before.

3. The graduate students presented in this chapter were created to highlight the examples of different group dynamics. Elements of the scenarios are based on real-life examples.

4. The family roles were created based on Carl Jung's archetypes: "The 12 Jungian Archetypes," Exploring Your Mind, January 26, 2019, https://exploringyourmind.com/twelve-jungian-archetypes/; and inspired from family roles listed on the following website: "Family Roles," Innerchange, 2020, https://www.innerchange.com/parents-resources/family-roles/.

5. W. C. Schutz, *FIRO: A Three-Dimensional Theory of Interpersonal Behavior* (New York: Holt, Rinehart, and Winston, 1958).

6. Ilene Morrison, "Discover Your Personality, 'FIRO-B™ Test Online,'" 2020, https://www.discoveryourpersonality.com/firo-b.html.

Chapter Seven

1. Derald Wing Sue, Christina M. Capodilupo, Gina C. Torino, Jennifer M. Bucceri, Aisha M. B. Holder, Kevin L. Nadal, and Marta Esquilin, "Racial Microaggresions in Everyday Life: Implications for Clinical Practice," *American Psychologist* 62 (2007): 273, https://dx.doi.org/10.1037/0003-066X.62.4.27.

2. Daniel G. Solórzano and Tara J. Yosso, "Critical Race Methodology: Counter-Storytelling as an Analytical Framework for Education Research," *Qualitative Inquiry* 8, no. 1 (2002): 32.

3. Ryan Evely Gildersleeve, Natasha N. Croom, and Philip L. Vasquez, "Am I Going Crazy?!: A Critical Race Analysis of Doctoral Education," *Equity & Excellence in Education* 44, no. 1 (2011): 102–6, https://dx.doi.org/10.1080/10665684.2011.539472.

4. Daniel G. Solórzano, Miguel Ceja, and Tara J. Yosso, "Critical Race Theory, Racial Microaggressions, and Campus Racial Climate: The Experiences of African American College Students," *Journal of Negro Education* 69, no ½ (Winter/Spring 2000): 70–71.

5. Erica Morales, "Beasting at the Battleground: Black Students Responding to Racial Microaggressions in Higher Education," *Journal of Diversity in Higher Education* (January 2020): 1, https://dx.doi.org/10.1037/dhe0000168.

6. Derald Wing Sue, Sarah Alsaidi, Michael N. Awad, Elizabeth Glaeser, Cassandra Z. Calle, and Narolyn Mendez, "Disarming Racial Microaggressions: Microintervention Strategies for Targets, White Allies, and Bystanders," *American Psychologist*, 74, no. 1 (2019): 134, https://dx.doi.org/10.1037/amp0000296.

7. Sue et al., "Disarming Racial Microaggresions," 134.

8. Sue et al., "Disarming Racial Microaggresions," 135.

9. Sue et al., "Disarming Racial Microaggresions," 138.

10. Sue et al., "Disarming Racial Microaggresions," 138.

11. Sue et al., "Disarming Racial Microaggresions," 139.

Chapter Eight

1. Xenia Hadjioannou, Nancy Rankie Shelton, Danling Fu, and Jiraporn Dhanarattigannon, "The Road to a Doctoral Degree: Co-travelers through a Perilous Passage," *College Student Journal* 41, no. 1 (2007).

2. Kimberle Crenshaw, "Mapping the Margins: Intersectionality, Identity Politics, and Violence against Women of Color," *Stan. L. Rev.* 43 (1990): 1241, doi:10.2307/1229039.

3. Nicola Curtin, Janet Malley, and Abigail J. Stewart, "Mentoring the Next Generation of Faculty: Supporting Academic Career Aspirations among Doctoral Students," *Research in Higher Education* 57, no. 6 (2016): 714–38.

4. M. Christopher Brown II, Guy L. Davis, and Shederick A. McClendon, "Mentoring Graduate Students of Color: Myths, Models, and Modes," *Peabody Journal of Education* 74, no. 2 (1999): 105–18.

5. Becky Wai-Ling Packard and N. L. Fortenberry, *Successful STEM Mentoring Initiatives for Underrepresented Students: A Research-based Guide for Faculty and Administrators* (Sterling, VA: Stylus Publishing, 2015).

6. Alan N. Miller, Shannon G. Taylor, and Arthur G. Bedeian, "Publish or Perish: Academic Life as Management Faculty Live It," *Career Development International* 16, no. 5 (2011): 422–45.

7. Miller, Taylor, and Bedeian, "Publish or Perish."

8. Adelbert H. Jenkins, "Individuality in Cultural Context: The Case for Psychological Agency," *Theory & Psychology* 11, no. 3 (2001): 347–62.

9. Daniel Solorzano, Miguel Ceja, and Tara Yosso, "Critical Race Theory, Racial Microaggressions, and Campus Racial Climate: The Experiences of African American College Students," *Journal of Negro Education* (2000): 60–73.

10. Richard J. Reddick and Michelle D. Young, "Mentoring Graduate Students of Color," *The SAGE Handbook of Mentoring and Coaching in Education* (2012): 412–29.

11. Edward Taylor and James Soto Antony, "Stereotype Threat Reduction and Wise Schooling: Towards the Successful Socialization of African American Doctoral Students in Education," *Journal of Negro Education* (2000): 184–98.

12. Vicki L. Baker and Lisa R. Lattuca, "Developmental Networks and Learning: Toward an Interdisciplinary Perspective on Identity Development during Doctoral Study," *Studies in Higher Education* 35, no. 7 (2010): 807–27.

13. W. Brad Johnson and Jennifer M. Huwe, *Getting Mentored in Graduate School* (Washington, DC: American Psychological Association, 2003).

14. Vicki L. Baker and Meghan J. Pifer, "The Role of Relationships in the Transition from Doctoral Student to Independent Scholar," *Studies in Continuing Education* 33, no. 1 (2011): 5–17.

15. Rowena Ortiz-Walters and Lucy L. Gilson, "Mentoring in Academia: An Examination of the Experiences of Protégés of Color," *Journal of Vocational Behavior* 67, no. 3 (2005): 459–75.

16. Nabil Hassan El-Ghoroury, Daniel I. Galper, Abere Sawaqdeh, and Lynn F. Bufka, "Stress, Coping, and Barriers to Wellness among Psychology Graduate Students," *Training and Education in Professional Psychology* 6, no. 2 (2012): 122.

17. Sheridan Center for Teaching and Learning, 2019, *Inclusive Mentoring*, https://www.brown.edu/sheridan/teaching-learning-resources/inclusive-teaching/inclusive-mentoring.

18. Baker and Pifer, "Role of Relationships."

Chapter Nine

1. Graduate Assembly, "Graduate Student Happiness and Well-Being Report," accessed December 1, 2018, http://ga.berkeley.edu/wpcontent/uploads/2015/04/wellbeingreport_2014.pdf.

2. Luke A. Williams, "Graduate Student Parents Face Steep Costs, Social Isolation," *The Crimson*, April 5, 2019, https://www.thecrimson.com/article/2019/4/5/student-parenthood-feature/.

3. Patricia A. H. Dyk, "Graduate Student Management of Family and Academic Roles," *Family Relations* 36, no. 3 (July 1987): 329–32.

4. Nicholas J. Beutell and Jeffrey H. Greenhaus, "Integration of Home and Nonhome Roles. Women's Conflict and Coping Behavior," *Journal of Applied Psychology* 68 (1980): 43–48.

5. D. L. Spar, *Wonder Women: Sex, Power and the Quest for Perfection* (New York: Macmillan Corporation, 2013).

6. Shawn Johansen, "Perspectives of a Graduate Student Father," *History Teacher: Issues of HigherEducation and Family Care* 29 (August 1996): 487–92.

7. Patrick J. Dillon, "Unbalanced: An Autoethnography of Fatherhood in Academe," *Journal of Family Communication* 12, no. 4 (October–December 2012): 284–99.

8. Amanda M. Kulp, "The Effects of Parenthood during Graduate School on PhD Recipients' Path to the Professoriate: A Focus on Motherhood," *New Directions for Higher Education* 176 (Winter 2016): 81–95.

9. Sheree L. Toth, Fred A. Rogosch, Jody Todd Manly, and Dante Cicchetti, "The Efficacy of Toddler-Parent Psychotherapy to Reorganize Attachment in the Young Offspring of Mothers with Major Depressive Disorder: A Randomized Preventive Trial," *Journal of Consulting and Clinical Psychology* 74, no. 6 (2006): 1006–16.

10. Graduate Assembly, "Graduate Student Happiness and Well-Being Report."

11. Claire Cain Miller, "Stressed, Tired, Rushed: A Portrait of the Modern Family," *New York Times (The UpShot)*, November 4, 2015, https://www.nytimes.com/2015/11/05/upshot/stressed-tired-rushed-a-portrait-of-the-modern-family.html.

12. Elrena Evans and Caroline Grant, *Mama, PhD: Women Write about Motherhood and Academic Life* (Piscataway, NJ: Rutgers University Press, 2008).

13. Donald W. Winnicot, *Playing and Reality* (London: Tavistock Publications Ltd., 1971).

14. Jenny K. Hyun, Brian C. Quinn, and Temina Madon, "Graduate Student Mental Health: Needs Assessment and Utilization of Counseling Services," *Journal of College Student Development* 47, no. 3 (May/June 2006): 247–66.

15. Jessica Smartt Guillon, "Scholar, Negated," in *Mama, PhD: Women Write about Motherhood and Academic Life*, ed. Elrena Evans and Caroline Grant (Piscataway, NJ: Rutgers University Press, 2008), 16–24.

16. Selma Fraiberg, Edna Adelson, and Vivian Shapiro, "Ghosts in the Nursery: A Psychoanalytic Approach to the Problems of Impaired Infant-Mother Relationships," in *Parent-Infant Psychodynamics: Wild Things, Mirrors and Ghosts*, ed. Leff J. Raphael, 87–117 (Philadelphia: Whurr Publishers, 2003).

17. Judith A. Myers-Walls, Larissa V. Frias, Kyong-Ah Kwon, Mei-Ju Meryl Ko, and Ting Lu, "Living Life in Two Worlds: Acculturative Stress among Asian International Graduate Student Parents and Spouses," *Journal of Comparative Family Studies* 42, no. 4 (2011): 455–78.

18. Myers-Walls et al., "Living Life in Two Worlds," 470.

Chapter Ten

1. Frank R. Dillon, Roger L. Worthington, and Bonnie Moradi, "Sexual Identity as a Universal Process," in *Handbook of Identity Theory and Research*, ed. Seth J. Schwartz, Koen Luyckx, and Vivian L. Vignoles, 649–70 (New York: Springer, 2011).

2. Gender identity and sexual identity are different. Because sexual orientation labels are based on one's gender identity and the genders of the people to whom one is attracted, the terms are related and somewhat interdependent. A transgender woman may be attracted only to men, so she is heterosexual. A cisgender woman who is attracted only to men is also heterosexual. A trans- or cisgender woman attracted to only women is lesbian; if she is attracted to people of all genders, she is pansexual.

3. Abbie E. Goldberg and Katherine Kuvalanka, "Transgender Graduate Students' Experiences in Higher Education: A Mixed-Methods Exploratory Study," *Journal of Diversity in Higher Education* 12, no. 1 (2019): 38.

4. Goldberg and Kuvalanka, "Transgender Graduate Students' Experiences in Higher Education."

5. Jodi L. Linley and David J. Nguyen, "LGBTQ Experiences in Curricular Contexts," *New Directions for Student Services* 152, no. 2015 (2015): 41–53; Jodi L. Linley, David Nguyen, G. Blue Brazelton, Brianna Becker, Kristen Renn, and Michael Woodford, "Faculty as Sources of Support for LGBTQ College Students," *College Teaching* 64, no. 2 (2016): 55–63.

6. Josh Keller, "Carnegie Mellon Course Dissects Statistics about Sexual Orientation," *Chronicle of Higher Education* (Washington, DC), February 9, 2007.

7. Dillon, Worthington, and Moradi, "Sexual Identity as a Universal Process."

8. Joan Hope, "Implement a Preferred Name Policy to Support Transgender Students," *The Successful Registrar* 16, no. 6 (2016): 7.

9. Genny Beemyn and Dot Brauer, "Trans-inclusive College Records: Meeting the Needs of an Increasingly Diverse US Student Population," *Transgender Studies Quarterly* 2, no. 3 (2015): 478–87; Z. Nicolazzo and Susan B. Marine, "'It Will Change If People Keep Talking': Trans* Students in College and University Housing," *Journal of College & University Student Housing* 42, no. 1 (2015).

10. Brett Beemyn, "Serving the Needs of Transgender College Students," *Journal of Gay & Lesbian Issues in Education* 1, no. 1 (2003): 33–50; Brett Genny Beemyn, "Making Campuses More Inclusive of Transgender Students," *Journal of Gay & Lesbian Issues in Education* 3, no. 1 (2005): 77–87; Z. Nicolazzo and Susan B. Marine, "'It Will Change If People Keep Talking'"; Kristie L. Seelman, "Transgender Individuals' Access to College Housing and Bathrooms: Findings from the National Transgender Discrimination Survey," *Journal of Gay & Lesbian Social Services* 26, no. 2 (2014): 186–206.

11. Abbie E. Goldberg and Katherine Kuvalanka, "Transgender Graduate Students' Experiences in Higher Education."

12. In some fields it is essential to gain lab or other research experience in one's discipline; an assistantship at the LGBT resource center might sound appealing, but students should check with advisors or trusted others before leaving funded positions in their department for an assistantship in an administrative unit of the university.

13. Sarah Brown, "'Heat Maps' Give Michigan State a New View of Campus Climate," *Chronicle of Higher Education*, October 23, 2016.

Chapter Eleven

1. The names of all trans grad students are pseudonyms. The interviews with the grad students were recorded, and quotes were confirmed with the speakers.

2. Abbie E. Goldberg, Genny Beemyn, and JuliAnna Z. Smith, "What Is Needed, What Is Valued: Trans Students' Perspectives on Trans-Inclusive Policies and Practices in Higher Education," *Journal of Educational and Psychological Consultation* 29, no. 1 (2019): 19.

3. Abbie E. Goldberg, "Higher Educational Experiences of Trans Binary and Nonbinary Graduate Students," in *Trans People in Higher Education*, ed. Genny Beemyn, 135–57 (Albany, NY: SUNY Press, 2019); Abbie E. Goldberg, JuliAnna Z. Smith, and Genny Beemyn, "Trans Activism and Advocacy

among Transgender Students in Higher Education: A Mixed Methods Study," *Journal of Diversity in Higher Education* 12, no. 1 (2019): 38–51.

4. Abbie E. Goldberg, Katherine A. Kuvalanka, Stephanie L. Budge, Madeline B. Benz, and JuliAnna Z. Smith, "Health Care Experiences of Transgender Binary and Nonbinary University Students," *Counseling Psychologist* (2019), https://doi.org/10.1177/0011000019827568.

5. Abbie E. Goldberg, Katherine Kuvalanka, and Kaitlin Black, "Trans Students Who Leave College: An Exploratory Study of Their Experiences of Gender Minority Stress," *Journal of College Student Development* (in press).

6. Harrington Park Press, "LGBTQ Professional Societies/Caucuses/SIG's," https://harringtonparkpress.com/lgbtq-professional-societies.

7. LGBTQ+ Physicists, http://lgbtphysicists.org; Spectra: The Association for LGBT Mathematicians, http://lgbtmath.org.

8. Alex Hanna, "Being Transgender on the Job Market," *Inside Higher Ed*, July 15, 2016, https://www.insidehighered.com/advice/2016/07/15/challenge-being-transgender-academic-job-market-essay.

9. Goldberg, Beemyn, and Smith, "What Is Needed, What Is Valued."

Chapter Twelve

1. Teresa M. Evans et al., "Evidence for a Mental Health Crisis in Graduate Education," *Nature Biotechnology* 36, no. 3 (March 2018): 282–84, doi: 10.1038/nbt.4089.

2. Andrea M. Zimmerman, "Navigating the Path to a Biomedical Science Career," *PLoS ONE* 13, no. 9 (September 2018): 18–20, https://doi.org/10.1371/journal.pone.0203783.

3. Zimmerman, "Navigating the Path to a Biomedical Science Career," 10–15.

4. Jonathan W. Yewdell, "How to Succeed in Science: A Concise Guide for Young Biomedical Scientists. Part I: Taking the Plunge," *Nature Reviews Molecular Cell Biology* 9, no. 5 (May 2008): 413–15, doi: 10.1038/nrm2389.

5. Evans et al., "Evidence for a Mental Health Crisis in Graduate Education," 283.

6. Ronald J. Daniels, "A Generation at Risk: Young Investigators and the Future of the Biomedical Workforce," *Proceedings of the National Academy of Sciences of the United States of America* 112, no. 2 (January 2015): 313–18, https://doi.org/10.1073/pnas.1418761112.

7. Zimmerman, "Navigating the Path to a Biomedical Science Career," 15–17.

8. Cynthia N. Fuhrmann et al., "Improving Graduate Education to Support a Branching Career Pipeline: Recommendations Based on a Survey of Doctoral Students in the Basic Biomedical Sciences," *CBE Life Sciences Education* 10, no. 3 (Fall 2011): 240, https://doi.org/10.1187/cbe.11-02-0013.

Chapter Thirteen

1. Chi-Ying Cheng et al., "Reaping the Rewards of Diversity: The Role of Identity Integration," *Social and Personality Psychology Compass* 2, no. 3 (2008): 1182–98, https://doi.org/10.1111/j.1751-9004.2008.00103.x.

2. Harold G. Koenig, "Research on Religion, Spirituality, and Mental Health: A Review," *Canadian Journal of Psychiatry* 54, no. 5 (2009): 283–91, https://doi.org/10.1177/070674370905400502.

3. Edward T. Hall, *Beyond Culture* (Garden City, NY: Anchor Press, 1976).

4. Patrick O'Keeffe, "A Sense of Belonging: Improving Student Retention," *College Student Journal* 47, no. 4 (2013): 605–13.

5. Emma Seppala, Timothy Rossomando, and James R. Doty, "Social Connection and Compassion: Important Predictors of Health and Well-Being," *Social Research: An International Quarterly* 80, no. 2 (2013): 411–30, doi: 10.1353/sor.2013.0027.

6. Debra Umberson and Jennifer Karas Montez, "Social Relationships and Health: A Flashpoint for Health Policy," *Journal of Health and Social Behavior* 51 (2010): S54–S66, doi:10.1177/0022146510383501.

7. O'Keeffe, "A Sense of Belonging," 605–13.

8. Nick Repak, "The Professor/Grad Relationship," Grad Resources, 2018, accessed June 9, 2019, http://gradresources.org/profgrad-relationships/.

Chapter Fifteen

1. Sam Dogen, "It Now Costs $350,000 a Year to Live a Middle-Class Lifestyle in a Big City—Here's a Sad Breakdown of Why," CNBC, accessed September 12, 2019, https://www.cnbc.com/2019/09/11/you-need-to-make-350000-a-year-to-live-a-middle-class-lifestyle-today-heres-why.html.

2. Lael Brainard, "Is the Middle Class within Reach for Middle Income Families?" Board of Governors of the Federal Reserve System, accessed November 20, 2019, https://www.federalreserve.gov/newsevents/speech/brainard20190510a.htm.

3. Megan Leonhardt, "62% Of Millennials Say They're Living Paycheck to Paycheck," CNBC, accessed September 12, 2019, https://www.cnbc

.com/2019/05/10/62-percent-of-millennials-say-they-are-living-paycheck-to-paycheck.html.

4. Abigail Hess, "New Study Finds That 36% of College Students Don't Have Enough to Eat," CNBC, April 6, 2018, https://www.cnbc.com/2018/04/06/new-study-finds-that-36-percent-of-college-students-dont-have-enough-to-eat.html.

5. Alia Wong, "Graduate School Can Have Terrible Effects on People's Mental Health," *The Atlantic*, accessed November 30, 2018, https://www.the-atlantic.com/education/archive/2018/11/anxiety-depression-mental-health-graduate-school/576769/.

6. Janice S. Lieberman, *Clinical Evolutions on the Superego, Body, and Gender in Psychoanalysis* (Abingdon, Oxon: Routledge, 2019).

7. Brenda Berger and Stephanie Newman, eds., *Money Talks: In Therapy, Society, and Life* (New York: Routledge, 2012).

Chapter Seventeen

1. George Ainslie, *Picoeconomics: The Strategic Interaction of Successive Motivational States within the Person* (Cambridge: Cambridge University Press, 1992), 29.

2. Carola Grunschel, Malte Schwinger, Ricarda Steinmayr, and Stefan Fries, "Effects of Using Motivational Regulation Strategies on Students' Academic Procrastination, Academic Performance, and Well-Being," *Learning and Individual Differences* 49 (2016): 166, https://doi.org/10.1016/j.lindif.2016.06.008.

3. Joseph R. Ferrari, Jean O'Callaghan, and Ian Newbegin, "Prevalence of Procrastination in the United States, United Kingdom, and Australia: Arousal and Avoidance Delays among Adults," *North American Journal of Psychology* 7, no. 1 (2005): 5.

4. Piers Steel, "The Nature of Procrastination: A Meta-Analytic and Theoretical Review of Quintessential Self-Regulatory Failure," *Psychological Bulletin* 133, no. 1 (2007): 65, https://doi.org/10.1037/0033-2909.133.1.65.

5. Steel, "The Nature of Procrastination," 66.

6. Joseph R. Ferrari, Judith L. Johnson, and William G. McCown, *Procrastination and Task Avoidance: Theory, Research, and Treatment*. The Plenum Series in Social/Clinical Psychology (New York: Plenum Press, 1995), 8–9, https://doi.org/10.1007/978-1-4899-0227-6.

7. Charlotte Lieberman, "Why You Procrastinate (It Has Nothing to Do with Self-Control)," *New York Times* (online), March 25, 2019, https://www

.nytimes.com/2019/03/25/smarter-living/why-you-procrastinate-it-has-nothing-to-do-with-self-control.html.

8. Fuschia Sirois and Timothy Pychyl, "Procrastination and the Priority of Short-Term Mood Regulation: Consequences for Future Self," *Social and Personality Psychology Compass* 7, no. 2 (2013): 115, https://doi.org/10.1111/spc3.12011.

9. Lucia Martinčeková and Robert D. Enright, "The Effects of Self-Forgiveness and Shame-Proneness on Procrastination: Exploring the Mediating Role of Affect," *Current Psychology: A Journal for Diverse Perspectives on Diverse Psychological Issues* (July 2018): 2, https://doi.org/10.1007/s12144-018-9926-3.

10. Kristin Neff and Christopher Germer, *The Mindful Self-Compassion Workbook: A Proven Way to Accept Yourself, Build Inner Strength, and Thrive* (New York: Guilford Press, 2018), 10–12.

11. Zindel V. Segal, J. Mark G. Williams, and John D. Teasdale, *Mindfulness-Based Cognitive Therapy for Depression*, 2nd ed. (New York: Guilford Press, 2013), 108–10.

12. Jon Kabat-Zinn, *Full Catastrophe Living: Using the Wisdom of Your Body and Mind to Face Stress, Pain, and Illness* (New York: Bantam Books, 2013), 66.

13. Steven C. Hayes, Kirk D. Strosahl, and Kelly G. Wilson, *Acceptance and Commitment Therapy: An Experiential Approach to Behavior Change* (New York: Guilford Press, 1999), 296.

14. Link to online worksheet: https://thehappinesstrap.com/upimages/Long_Bull%27s_Eye_Worksheet.pdf.

15. Tobias Lundgren, Jason B. Luoma, JoAnne Dahl, Kirk Strosahl, and Lennart Melin, "The Bull's-Eye Values Survey: A Psychometric Evaluation," *Cognitive and Behavioral Practice* 19, no. 4 (2012): 524–26, https://doi.org/10.1016/j.cbpra.2012.01.004.

16. Tim Urban, "Why Procrastinators Procrastinate," Wait But Why, October 20, 2013, accessed September 15, 2019, https://waitbutwhy.com/2013/10/why-procrastinators-procrastinate.html.

17. Jon Elster, *Ulysses Unbound: Studies in Rationality, Precommitment, and Constraints* (New York: Cambridge University Press, 2000), 1–7.

18. Steel, "The Nature of Procrastination," 66.

19. John D. Teasdale, J. Mark G. Williams, and Zindel V. Segal, *The Mindful Way Workbook: An 8-Week Program to Free Yourself from Depression and Emotional Distress* (New York: Guilford Press, 2014), 176.

20. Marsha M. Linehan, *DBT® Skills Training Manual*, 2nd ed. (New York: Guilford Press, 2015), 349.

21. Gordon L. Flett, Paul L. Hewitt, Richard A. Davis, and Simon B. Sherry, "Description and Counseling of the Perfectionistic Procrastinator,"

in *Counseling the Procrastinator in Academic Settings*, eds. Henri C. Schouwenburg, Clarry H. Lay, Timothy A. Pychyl, and Joseph R. Ferrari, 185, 189–90 (Washington, DC: American Psychological Association, 2004), http://dx.doi.org/10.1037/10808-013.

22. *Finding Forrester*, DVD, directed by Gus Van Sant (Culver City, CA: Sony Pictures Home Entertainment, 2001).

23. Dan Ariely and Klaus Wertenbroch, "Procrastination, Deadlines, and Performance: Self-Control by Precommitment," *Psychological Science* 13, no. 3 (2002): 223–24, https://doi.org/10.1111/1467-9280.00441.

24. Flett, Hewitt, Davis, and Sherry, "Description and Counseling of the Perfectionistic Procrastinator," 193–94.

Bibliography

Chapter One

Breines, Juliana. "Graduate School and Mental Illness: Is There a Link?" *Psychology Today*, November 26, 2015. https://www.psychologytoday.com/blog/in-love-and-war/201511/graduate-school-and-mental-illness-is-there-link.

Brunsma, David L., David G. Embrick, and Jean H. Shin. "Graduate Students of Color: Race, Racism, and Mentoring in the White Waters of Academia." *Sociology of Race and Ethnicity* 3, no. 1 (January 2017): 1–13.

Evans, Teresa, Lindsay Bira, Jazmin Beltran Gastelum, L. Todd Weiss, and Nathan Vanderford. "Evidence for a Mental Health Crisis in Graduate Education." *Nature Biotechnology* 36 (2018): 282–84. https://doi.org/10.1038/nbt.4089.

Graduate Assembly. "Graduate Student Happiness & Well-Being Report." 2014. http://ga.berkeley.edu/wp-content/uploads/2015/04/wellbeingreport_2014.pdf.

Lipson, Sarah Ketchen, Sasha Zhou, Blake Wagner III, Katie Beck, and Daniel Eisenberg. "Major Differences: Variations in Undergraduate and Graduate Student Mental Health and Treatment Utilization across Academic Disciplines." *Journal of College Student Psychotherapy* 30, no. 1 (2016): 23–41.

Maslen, Geoff. "Worldwide Student Numbers Forecast to Double by 2025." *University World News*, February 19, 2012. http://www.universityworldnews.com/article.php?story=20120216105739999.

Moser, Jason S., Hans S. Schroder, Carrie Heeter, Tim P. Moran, and Yu Hao Lee. "Mind Your Errors: Evidence for a Neural Mechanism Linking Growth Mind-Set to Adaptive Posterror Adjustments." *Psychological Science* 22, no. 12 (October 2011): 1484–89.

National Center for Education Statistics. "Fast Facts: Back to School Statistics." 2016. Accessed March 12, 2019. https://nces.ed.gov/fastfacts/display .asp?id=372.

Chapter Two

BBC News. "Michelle Obama: 'I Still Have Impostor Syndrome.'" Accessed August 19, 2019. https://www.bbc.com/news/uk-46434147.

Bussoti, C. "The Impostor Phenomenon: Family Roles and Environment." PhD diss., Georgia State University, 1990.

Castro, Denise, Rebecca Jones, and Hamid Mirsalimi. "Parentification and the Imposter Phenomenon: An Empirical Investigation." *The American Journal of Family Therapy*, no. 3 (May–June 2004): 205–16.

Chrisman, Sabine M., W. A. Pieper, Pauline R. Clance, C. L. Holland, and Cheryl Glickauf-Hughes. "Validation of the Clance Impostor Phenomenon Scale." *Journal of Personality Assessment* 65, no. 3 (1995): 456–67.

Clance, Pauline, and Suzanne Imes. "The Impostor Phenomenon in High Achieving Women: Dynamics and Therapeutic Intervention." *Psychotherapy: Theory, Research and Practice* 15, no. 3 (Fall 1978): 241–47.

Clance, Pauline, and Maureen O'Toole. "The Impostor Phenomenon: An Internal Barrier to Empowerment and Achievement." *Women and Therapy* 6, no. 3 (1987): 51–64.

Cohen, Geoffrey L., and Claude M. Steele. 2002. "A Barrier of Mistrust: How Stereotypes Affect Cross-Race Mentoring." In *Improving Academic Achievement: Impact of Psychological Factors on Education*, edited by J. Aronson, 303–27. Oxford: Academic Press.

Cowman, S., and Joseph R. Ferrari. "'Am I For Real?' Predicting Imposter Tendencies from Self-handicapping and Affective Components." *Social Behavior and Personality: An International Journal* 30 (2002): 119–26.

Cromwell, B., N. Brown, J. Sanchez-Hucles, and F. L. Adair. "The Impostor Phenomenon and Personality Characteristics of High School Honor Students." *Social Behavior and Personality: An International Journal* 5 (1990): 563–73.

Dweck, Carol S. "Motivational Processes Affecting Learning." *American Psychologist* 41, no. 10 (1986): 1040–48.

Kohut, Heinz. *How Does Analysis Cure?* Chicago: University of Chicago Press, 1984.

Langford, Joe. "The Need to Look Smart: The Impostor Phenomenon and Motivations on Learning." PhD diss., Georgia State University, 1990.

Langford, Joe, and Pauline Clance. "The Impostor Phenomenon: Recent Research Findings Regarding Dynamics, Personality and Family Patterns and Their Implications for Treatment." *Psychotherapy: Theory, Research and Practice* 30, no. 3 (Fall 1993): 495–501.

McClain, Shannon, Samuel T. Beasley, Bianca Jones, Olufunke Awosogba, Stacey Jackson, and Kevin Cokley. "An Examination of the Impact of Racial and Ethnic Identity, Impostor Feelings, and Minority Status Stress on the Mental Health of Black College Students." *Journal of Multicultural Counseling and Development* 44 (April 2016): 101–17.

McGregor, Loretta Neal, Damon E. Gee, and K. Elizabeth Posey. "I Feel Like a Fraud and It Depresses Me: The Relation between the Imposter Phenomenon and Depression." *Social Behavior and Personality* 36, no. 1 (2008): 43–48.

McLean, Malissa, and Jay Avella. "IP in Information Technology." *Journal of IT Management* 27, no. 4 (2016): 138–50.

Miller, Darlene G., and Signe M. Kastberg. "Of Blue Collars and Ivory Towers: Women from Blue-Collar Backgrounds in Higher Education." *Roeper Review* 18, no. 1 (September 1995): 27–33.

Piaget, Jean. *Origins of Intelligence in the Child.* London: Routledge and Kegan Paul, 1936.

Prince, T. J. "The Imposter Phenomenon Revisted: A Validity Study of Clance's IP Scale." Unpublished master's thesis, Georgia State University, 1989.

Smedley, Brian D., Hector F. Myers, and Shelly P. Harrell. "Minority-status Stresses and the College Adjustment of Ethnic Minority Freshmen." *The Journal of Higher Education* 64, no. 4 (1993): 434–52.

Steele, Claude M., and Jason Aronson. "Stereotype Threat and the Intellectual Test Performance of African Americans." *Journal of Personality and Social Psychology* 69, no. 5 (1995): 797–811.

Thompson, Ted, Peggy Foreman, and Frances Martin. "Impostor Fears and Perfectionistic Concern over Mistakes." *Personality and Individual Differences* 29 (2000): 629–47.

Topping, M. E. H. "The Impostor Phenomenon: A Study of Its Construct Validity and Incidence in University Faculty Members." PhD diss., University of South Florida, 1983.

Walton, Gregory M., and Geoffrey L. Cohen. "A Question of Belonging: Race, Social Fit, and Achievement." *Journal of Personality and Social Psychology* 92, no. 1 (2007): 82–96.

Chapter Four

Bell, Nathan. "Data Sources: Graduate Students with Disabilities." *Council of Graduate Schools*. July 1, 2011. https://cgsnet.org/data-sources-graduate-students-disabilities.

Breines, Juliana. "Graduate School and Mental Illness: Is There a Link?" *Psychology Today*, November 26, 2015. https://www.psychologytoday.com/blog/in-love-and-war/201511/graduate-school-and-mental-illness-is-there-link.

Burrell, Teal. "Dispelling Myths about Students with Disabilities." *American Psychological Association gradPSYCH Magazine* 13, no. 2 (April 2015): 28. https://www.apa.org/gradpsych/2015/04/dispelling-myths.

Cooper, Mary Ann. "Hidden Cost of Seeking Graduate Degrees: A Deadly Mental Health Crisis." *The Hispanic Outlook in Higher Education*, April 2019, 16–18. http://ezproxy.gc.cuny.edu/login?url=https://search.proquest.com/docview/2220172104?accountid=7287.

Davis, Ben. "Graduate School Success for Students with Disabilities: Scholarships, Support Resources, and Insight for Achieving an Advanced Degree." Accessed July 5, 2019. https://www.gograd.org/resources/students-with-disabilities/.

Evans, Teresa, Lindsay Bira, Jazmin Beltran Gastelum, L. Todd Weiss, and Nathan Vanderford. "Evidence for a Mental Health Crisis in Graduate Education." *Nature Biotechnology* 36 (2018): 282–84. https://doi.org/10.1038/nbt.4089.

Flaherty, Colleen. "Mental Health Crisis for Grad Students." *Inside Higher Ed*, March 6, 2018. https://www.insidehighered.com/news/2018/03/06/new-study-says-graduate-students-mental-health-crisis.

Graduate Assembly. "Graduate Student Happiness & Well-Being Report." Berkeley: University of California, 2014. http://ga.berkeley.edu/wp-content/uploads/2015/04/wellbeingreport_2014.pdf.

Hammer, Barbara. "A Brief Conversation with . . . Barbara Hammer: Provide Support to Graduate Students with Disabilities. Interview by Joan Hope." *Disability Compliance for Higher Education* 20, no 12 (July 2015): 2. doi:10.1002/dhe.30075.

Higby, Jeanne L., and Emily Goff, eds. *Pedagogy and Student Services for Institutional Transformation: Implementing Universal Design in Higher Education.* Minneapolis: University of Minnesota, 2008. https://files.eric.ed.gov/fulltext/ED503835.pdf.

Hyun, Jenny K., Brian C. Quinn, and Temina Madon. "Graduate Student Mental Health: Needs Assessment and Utilization of Counseling Services." *Journal of College Student Development* 47, no. 3 (May/June 2006): 247–66.

Jed Foundation. *Student Mental Health and the Law: A Resource for Institutions of Higher Education*. New York: The Jed Foundation, 2008. http://www.jed-foundation.org/wp-content/uploads/2016/07/student-mental-health-and-the-law-jed-NEW.pdf.

Kerschbaum, Stephanie L., Laura T. Eisenman, and James M. Jones. *Negotiating Disability: Disclosure and Higher Education*. Ann Arbor: University of Michigan Press, 2017.

Langin, Katie. "Amid Concerns about Grad Student Mental Health, One University Takes a Novel Approach." *American Association for the Advancement of Science*, July 11, 2019. https://www.sciencemag.org/careers/2019/07/amid-concerns-about-grad-student-mental-health-one-university-takes-novel-approach.

Lee, Shannon. "Mental Health in Grad School: Recognizing, Understanding & Overcoming Mental Health Issues in Grad School." Accessed July 2, 2019. https://www.gograd.org/resources/grad-student-mental-health/.

Lieberman, Mark. "Helping Institutions Reach Accessibility Goals." *Inside Higher Ed*, February 20, 2019. https://www.insidehighered.com/digital-learning/article/2019/02/20/guide-accessibility-practices-aims-help-institutions-develop.

Lipson, Sarah Ketchen, Sasha Zhou, Blake Wagner III, Katie Beck, and Daniel Eisenberg. "Major Differences: Variations in Undergraduate and Graduate Student Mental Health and Treatment Utilization across Academic Disciplines." *Journal of College Student Psychotherapy* 30, no. 1 (January 2016): 23–41. https://doi:10.1080/87568225.2016.1105657.

McCallister, Leslie, Kalah Wilson, and Joseph Baker. "An Examination of Graduate Students' Perceptions toward Students with Disabilities." *The Journal of Faculty Development* 28, no. 2 (May 2014): 19–26. http://ezproxy.gc.cuny.edu/login?url=https://search.proquest.com/docview/1673849349?accountid=7287.

Pain, Elisabeth. "Graduate Students Need More Mental Health Support, Study Highlights." *American Association for the Advancement of Science*, March 6, 2018. https://www.sciencemag.org/careers/2018/03/graduate-students-need-more-mental-health-support-new-study-highlights.

Perry, David. "How to Make Grad School More Humane." *Pacific Standard*, February 5, 2019. https://psmag.com/ideas/grad-school-continues-to-ignore-students-with-disabilities.

Smith, Ezra, and Zachary Brooks. *Graduate Student Mental Health 2015*. Tucson: National Association of Graduate-Professional Students and the Graduate Professional Student Council (GPSC), University of Arizona, August 2015. http://nagps.org/wordpress/wp-content/uploads/2015/06/NAGPS_Institute_mental_health_survey_report_2015.pdf.

Straumsheim, Carl. "New Era for Disability Rights." *Inside Higher Ed*, November 7, 2016. https://www.insidehighered.com/news/2016/11/07/disability-rights-advocates-shift-strategies-ensure-equal-rights-digital-age.

Tomar, David. "Grad School's Mental Health Crisis." *The Quad*, February 4, 2019. https://thebestschools.org/magazine/grad-school-mental-health-crisis/.

US Department of Education, Institute of Education Sciences, National Center for Education Statistics. *Profile of Students in Graduate and First-Professional Education: 2007–08.* Accessed July 5, 2019. https://nces.ed.gov/pubs2010/2010177.pdf.

Chapter Five

Hendrickson, Blake, Devan Rosen, and R. Kelly Aune. "An Analysis of Friendship Networks, Social Connectedness, Homesickness, and Satisfaction Levels of International Students." *International Journal of Intercultural Relations* 35, no. 3 (May 2011): 281–95. https://doi.org/10.1016/j.ijintrel.2010.08.001.

Houshmand, Sara, Lisa B. Spanierman, and Romin W. Tafarodi. "Excluded and Avoided: Racial Microaggressions Targeting Asian International Students in Canada." *Cultural Diversity and Ethnic Minority Psychology* 20, no. 3 (July 2014): 377–88. https://doi.org/10.1037/a0035404.

Mesidor, Jean Kesnold, and Kaye F. Sly. "Factors that Contribute to the Adjustment of International Students." *Journal of International Students* 6, no. 1 (January 2016): 262–82.

Özturgut, Osman, and Carole Murphy. "Literature vs. Practice: Challenges for International Students in the U.S." *International Journal of Teaching and Learning in Higher Education* 22, no. 3 (2009): 374–85.

Wang, Kenneth T., Puncky Paul Heppner, Chu-Chun Fu, Ran Zhao, Feihan Li, and Chih-Chun Chuang. "Profiles of Acculturative Adjustment Patterns among Chinese International Students." *Journal of Counseling Psychology* 59, no. 3 (July 2012): 424–36. https://doi.org/10.1037/a0028532.

Zhou, Yuefang, Divya Jindal-Snape, Keith Topping, and John Todman. "Theoretical Models of Culture Shock and Adaptation in International Students in Higher Education." *Studies in Higher Education* 33, no. 1 (May 2008): 63–75. https://doi.org/10.1080/03075070701794833.

Chapter Six

Exploring Your Mind. "The 12 Jungian Archetypes." January 26, 2019. https://exploringyourmind.com/twelve-jungian-archetypes/.

Innerchange. "Family Roles." 2020. https://www.innerchange.com/parents-resources/family-roles/.

Morrison, Ilene. "Discover Your Personality, 'FIRO-B Test Online.'" 2020. https://www.discoveryourpersonality.com/firo-b.html.

Okahana, H., and E. Zhou. *Graduate Enrollment and Degrees: 2007 to 2017.* Washington, DC: Council of Graduate Schools, 2018.

Schutz, W. C. *FIRO: A Three-Dimensional Theory of Interpersonal Behavior.* New York: Holt, Rinehart, and Winston, 1958.

Wilson, Reid. "Census: More Americans Have College Degrees Than Ever Before." *The Hill,* April 3, 2017. https://thehill.com/homenews/state-watch/326995-census-more-americans-have-college-degrees-than-ever-before.

Chapter Seven

Gildersleeve, Ryan Evely, Natasha N. Croom, and Philip L. Vasquez. "Am I Going Crazy?!: A Critical Race Analysis of Doctoral Education." *Equity & Excellence in Education* 44, no. 1 (2011): 102–6. https://dx.doi.org/10.1080/10665684.2011.539472.

Morales, Erica. "Beasting at the Battleground: Black Students Responding to Racial Microaggressions in Higher Education." *Journal of Diversity in Higher Education* (January 2020): 1–12. https://dx.doi.org/10.1037/dhe0000168.

Solórzano, Daniel G., and Tara J. Yosso. "Critical Race Methodology: Counter-Storytelling as an Analytical Framework for Education Research." *Qualitative Inquiry* 8, no. 1 (2002): 32.

Solórzano, Daniel G., Miguel Ceja, and Tara J. Yosso. "Critical Race Theory, Racial Microaggressions, and Campus Racial Climate: The Experiences of African American College Students." *Journal of Negro Education* 69 no. ½ (Winter/Spring 2000): 60–73.

Sue, Derald Wing, Sarah Alsaidi, Michael N. Awad, Elizabeth Glaeser, Cassandra Z. Calle, and Narolyn Mendez. "Disarming Racial Microaggressions: Microintervention Strategies for Targets, White Allies, and Bystanders." *American Psychologist* 74, no. 1 (2019): 128–42. https://dx.doi.org/10.1037/amp0000296.

Sue, Derald Wing, Christina. M Capodilupo, Gina C. Torino, Jennifer M. Bucceri, Aisha M. B. Holder, Kevin L. Nadal, and Marta Esquilin. "Racial Microaggresions in Everyday Life: Implications for Clinical Practice." *American Psychologist* 62 (2007): 273. https://dx.doi.org/10.1037/0003-066X.62.4.27.

Chapter Eight

Baker, Vicki L., and Lisa R. Lattuca. "Developmental Networks and Learning: Toward an Interdisciplinary Perspective on Identity Development during Doctoral Study." *Studies in Higher Education* 35, no. 7 (2010): 807–27.

Baker, Vicki L., and Meghan J. Pifer. "The Role of Relationships in the Transition from Doctoral Student to Independent Scholar." *Studies in Continuing Education* 33, no. 1 (2011): 5–17.

Brown II, M. Christopher, Guy L. Davis, and Shederick A. McClendon. "Mentoring Graduate Students of Color: Myths, Models, and Modes." *Peabody Journal of Education* 74, no. 2 (1999): 105–18.

Crenshaw, Kimberle. "Mapping the Margins: Intersectionality, Identity Politics, and Violence against Women of Color." *Stan. L. Rev.* 43 (1990): 1241. doi:10.2307/1229039.

Curtin, Nicola, Janet Malley, and Abigail J. Stewart. "Mentoring the Next Generation of Faculty: Supporting Academic Career Aspirations among Doctoral Students." *Research in Higher Education* 57, no. 6 (2016): 714–38.

El-Ghoroury, Nabil Hassan, Daniel I. Galper, Abere Sawaqdeh, and Lynn F. Bufka. "Stress, Coping, and Barriers to Wellness among Psychology Graduate Students." *Training and Education in Professional Psychology* 6, no. 2 (2012): 122.

Hadjioannou, Xenia, Nancy Rankie Shelton, Danling Fu, and Jiraporn Dhanarattigannon. "The Road to a Doctoral Degree: Co-travelers through a Perilous Passage." *College Student Journal* 41, no. 1 (2007).

Jenkins, Adelbert H. "Individuality in Cultural Context: The Case for Psychological Agency." *Theory & Psychology* 11, no. 3 (2001): 347–62.

Johnson, W. Brad, and Jennifer M. Huwe. *Getting Mentored in Graduate School.* Washington, DC: American Psychological Association, 2003.

Miller, Alan N., Shannon G. Taylor, and Arthur G. Bedeian. "Publish or Perish: Academic Life as Management Faculty Live It." *Career Development International* 16, no. 5 (2011): 422–45.

Ortiz-Walters, Rowena, and Lucy L. Gilson. "Mentoring in Academia: An Examination of the Experiences of Protégés of Color." *Journal of Vocational Behavior* 67, no. 3 (2005): 459–75.

Packard, Becky Wai-Ling, and N. L. Fortenberry. *Successful STEM Mentoring Initiatives for Underrepresented Students: A Research-based Guide for Faculty and Administrators.* Sterling, VA: Stylus Publishing, 2015.

Reddick, Richard J., and Michelle D. Young. "Mentoring Graduate Students of Color." *The SAGE Handbook of Mentoring and Coaching in Education* (2012): 412–29.

Sheridan Center for Teaching and Learning. 2019. *Inclusive Mentoring*. https://www.brown.edu/sheridan/teaching-learning-resources/inclusive-teaching/inclusive-mentoring.

Solorzano, Daniel, Miguel Ceja, and Tara Yosso. "Critical Race Theory, Racial Microaggressions, and Campus Racial Climate: The Experiences of African American College Students." *Journal of Negro Education* (2000): 60–73.

Taylor, Edward, and James Soto Antony. "Stereotype Threat Reduction and Wise Schooling: Towards the Successful Socialization of African American Doctoral Students in Education." *Journal of Negro Education* (2000): 184–98.

Chapter Nine

Beutell, Nicholas J., and Jeffrey H. Greenhaus. "Integration of Home and Non-home Roles: Women's Conflict and Coping Behavior." *Journal of Applied Psychology* 68 (1980): 43–48.

Dillon, Patrick J. "Unbalanced: An Autoethnography of Fatherhood in Academe." *Journal of Family Communication* 12, no. 4 (October–December 2012): 284–99.

Dyk, Patricia A. H. "Graduate Student Management of Family and Academic Roles." *Family Relations* 36, no. 3 (July 1987): 329–32.

Evans, Elrena, and Caroline Grant. *Mama, PhD: Women Write about Motherhood and Academic Life*. Piscataway, NJ: Rutgers University Press, 2008.

Fraiberg, Selma, Edna Adelson, and Vivian Shapiro. "Ghosts in the Nursery: A Psychoanalytic Approach to the Problems of Impaired Infant-Mother Relationships," in *Parent-Infant Psychodynamics: Wild Things, Mirrors and Ghosts*, edited by Leff J. Raphael, 87–117. Philadelphia: Whurr Publishers, 2003.

Graduate Assembly. "Graduate Student Happiness & Well-Being Report." http://ga.berkeley.edu/wp-content/uploads/2015/04/wellbeingreport_2014.pdf.

Guillon, Jessica Smartt. "Scholar, Negated," in *Mama, PhD: Women Write about Motherhood and Academic Life*, edited by Elrena Evans and Caroline Grant, 16–24. Piscataway, NJ: Rutgers University Press, 2008.

Hyun, Jenny K., Brian C. Quinn, and Temina Madon. "Graduate Student Mental Health: Needs Assessment and Utilization of Counseling Services." *Journal of College Student Development* 47, no. 3 (May/June 2006): 247–66.

Johansen, Shawn. "Perspectives of a Graduate Student Father." *History Teacher: Issues of Higher Education and Family Care* 29 (August 1996): 487–92.

Kulp, Amanda M. "The Effects of Parenthood during Graduate School on PhD Recipients' Path to the Professoriate: A Focus on Motherhood." *New Directions for Higher Education* 176 (Winter 2016): 81–95.

Miller, Claire Cain. "Stressed, Tired, Rushed: A Portrait of the Modern Family." *New York Times (The UpShot)*, November 4, 2015. https://www .nytimes.com/2015/11/05/upshot/stressed-tired-rushed-a-portrait-of-the-modern-family.html.

Myers-Walls, Judith A., Larissa V. Frias, Kyong-Ah Kwon, Mei-Ju Meryl Ko, and Ting Lu. "Living Life in Two Worlds: Acculturative Stress among Asian International Graduate Student Parents and Spouses." *Journal of Comparative Family Studies* 42, no. 4 (2011): 455–78.

Spar, D. L. *Wonder Women: Sex, Power and The Quest for Perfection.* New York: Macmillan Corporation, 2013.

Toth, Sheree L., Fred A. Rogosch, Jody Todd Manly, and Dante Cicchetti. "The Efficacy of Toddler-Parent Psychotherapy to Reorganize Attachment in the Young Offspring of Mothers with Major Depressive Disorder: A Randomized Preventive Trial." *Journal of Consulting and Clinical Psychology* 74, no. 6 (2006): 1006–16.

Williams, Luke A. "Graduate Student Parents Face Steep Costs, Social Isolation." *The Crimson*, April 5, 2019. https://www.thecrimson.com/article/2019/4/5/student-parenthood-feature/.

Winnicot, Donald W. *Playing and Reality.* London: Tavistock Publications Ltd., 1971.

Chapter Ten

Beemyn, Brett. "Serving the Needs of Transgender College Students." *Journal of Gay & Lesbian Issues in Education* 1, no. 1 (2003): 33–50.

Beemyn, Brett Genny. "Making Campuses More Inclusive of Transgender Students." *Journal of Gay & Lesbian Issues in Education* 3, no. 1 (2005): 77–87.

Beemyn, Genny, and Dot Brauer. "Trans-inclusive College Records: Meeting the Needs of an Increasingly Diverse US Student Population." *Transgender Studies Quarterly* 2, no. 3 (2015): 478–87.

Brown, Sarah. "'Heat Maps' Give Michigan State a New View of Campus Climate." *Chronicle of Higher Education*, October 23, 2016. https://www .chronicle.com/article/Heat-Maps-Give-Michigan/238112.

Dillon, Frank R., Roger L. Worthington, and Bonnie Moradi. "Sexual Identity as a Universal Process." In Seth J. Schwartz, Koen Luyckx, and Vivian L. Vignoles (eds.), *Handbook of Identity Theory and Research*, 649–70. New York: Springer, 2011.

Goldberg, Abbie E. "Higher Educational Experiences of Trans Binary and Nonbinary Graduate Students." *Trans People in Higher Education* (2019): 135.

Goldberg, Abbie E., and Katherine Kuvalanka. "Transgender Graduate Students' Experiences in Higher Education: A Mixed-Methods Exploratory Study." *Journal of Diversity in Higher Education* 12, no. 1 (2019): 38.

Hope, Joan. "Implement a Preferred Name Policy to Support Transgender Students." *The Successful Registrar* 16, no. 6 (2016): 7.

Hughes, Bryce E. "'Managing by Not Managing': How Gay Engineering Students Manage Sexual Orientation Identity." *Journal of College Student Development* 58, no. 3 (2017): 385–401.

Hughes, Bryce E. "Coming Out in STEM: Factors Affecting Retention of Sexual Minority STEM Students." *Science Advances* 4, no. 3 (2018): eaao6373.

Keller, Josh. "Carnegie Mellon Course Dissects Statistics about Sexual Orientation." *Chronicle of Higher Education* 53, no. 23 (2007).

Linley, Jodi L., and David J. Nguyen. "LGBTQ Experiences in Curricular Contexts." *New Directions for Student Services* 152, no. 2015 (2015): 41–53.

Linley, Jodi L., David Nguyen, G. Blue Brazelton, Brianna Becker, Kristen Renn, and Michael Woodford. "Faculty as Sources of Support for LGBTQ College Students." *College Teaching* 64, no. 2 (2016): 55–63.

Linley, Jodi L., Kristen A. Renn, and Michael R. Woodford. "Examining the Ecological Systems of LGBTQ STEM Majors." *Journal of Women and Minorities in Science and Engineering* 24, no. 1 (2018).

Nicolazzo, Z., and Susan B. Marine. "'It Will Change If People Keep Talking': Trans* Students in College and University Housing." *Journal of College & University Student Housing* 42, no. 1 (2015).

Pitcher, Erich N. *Being and Becoming Professionally Other: Identities, Voices, and Experiences of US Trans* Academics.* New York: Peter Lang Incorporated, International Academic Publishers, 2018.

Seelman, Kristie L. "Transgender Individuals' Access to College Housing and Bathrooms: Findings from the National Transgender Discrimination Survey." *Journal of Gay & Lesbian Social Services* 26, no. 2 (2014): 186–206.

Stout, Jane G., and Heather M. Wright. "Lesbian, Gay, Bisexual, Transgender, and Queer Students' Sense of Belonging in Computing: An Intersectional Approach." *Computing in Science & Engineering* 18, no. 3 (2016): 24–30.

Tillapaugh, Daniel, and D. Chase J. Catalano. "Structural Challenges Affecting the Experiences of Public University LGBT Services Graduate Assistants." *Journal of Diversity in Higher Education* 12, no. 2 (2019): 126.

Trenshaw, Kathryn F., Ashley Hetrick, Ramona F. Oswald, Sharra L. Vostral, and Michael C. Loui. "Lesbian, Gay, Bisexual, and Transgender Students in

Engineering: Climate and Perceptions." In *2013 IEEE Frontiers in Education Conference (FIE)*, 1238–40. IEEE, 2013.

Vaccaro, Annemarie. "Campus Microclimates for LGBT Faculty, Staff, and Students: An Exploration of the Intersections of Social Identity and Campus Roles." *Journal of Student Affairs Research and Practice* 49, no. 4 (2012): 429–46.

Woodford, Michael R., Jill M. Chonody, Alex Kulick, David J. Brennan, and Kristen Renn. "The LGBQ Microaggressions on Campus Scale: A Scale Development and Validation Study." *Journal of Homosexuality* 62, no. 12 (2015): 1660–87.

Yoder, Jeremy B., and Allison Mattheis. "Queer in STEM: Workplace Experiences Reported in a National Survey of LGBTQA Individuals in Science, Technology, Engineering, and Mathematics Careers." *Journal of Homosexuality* 63, no. 1 (2016): 1–27.

Chapter Eleven

Goldberg, Abbie E., Genny Beemyn, and JuliAnna Z. Smith. "What Is Needed, What Is Valued: Trans Students' Perspectives on Trans-Inclusive Policies and Practices in Higher Education." *Journal of Educational and Psychological Consultation* 29, no. 1 (2019): 19.

Goldberg, Abbie E. "Higher Educational Experiences of Trans Binary and Nonbinary Graduate Students," in *Trans People in Higher Education*, ed. Genny Beemyn, 135–57. Albany, NY: SUNY Press, 2019.

Goldberg, Abbie E., JuliAnna Z. Smith, and Genny Beemyn. "Trans Activism and Advocacy among Transgender Students in Higher Education: A Mixed Methods Study." *Journal of Diversity in Higher Education* 12, no. 1 (2019): 38–51.

Goldberg, Abbie E., Katherine A. Kuvalanka, Stephanie L. Budge, Madeline B. Benz, and JuliAnna Z. Smith. "Health Care Experiences of Transgender Binary and Nonbinary University Students." *Counseling Psychologist*, 2019. https://doi.org/10.1177/0011000019827568.

Goldberg, Abbie E., Katherine Kuvalanka, and Kaitlin Black. "Trans Students Who Leave College: An Exploratory Study of Their Experiences of Gender Minority Stress." *Journal of College Student Development* (in press).

Hanna, Alex. "Being Transgender on the Job Market." *Inside Higher Ed*, July 15, 2016. https://www.insidehighered.com/advice/2016/07/15/challenge-being-transgender-academic-job-market-essay.

Harrington Park Press. "LGBTQ Professional Societies/Caucuses/SIG's." https://harringtonparkpress.com/lgbtq-professional-societies.

LGBTQ+ Physicists. http://lgbtphysicists.org.
Spectra: The Association for LGBT Mathematicians. http://lgbtmath.org.

Chapter Twelve

Daniels, Ronald J. "A Generation at Risk: Young Investigators and the Future of the Biomedical Workforce." *Proceedings of the National Academy of Sciences of the United States of America* 112, no. 2 (January 2015): 313–18. https://doi.org/10.1073/pnas.1418761112.

Evans, Teresa M., Lindsay Bira, Jazmin Beltran Gastelum, L. Todd Weiss, and Nathan L. Vanderford. "Evidence for a Mental Health Crisis in Graduate Education." *Nature Biotechnology* 36, no. 3 (March 2018): 282–84. doi: 10.1038/nbt.4089.

Fuhrmann, Cynthia N., Dina Gould Halme, Patricia S. O'Sullivan, and Bill Lindstaedt. "Improving Graduate Education to Support a Branching Career Pipeline: Recommendations Based on a Survey of Doctoral Students in the Basic Biomedical Sciences." *CBE Life Sciences Education* 10, no. 3 (Fall 2011): 239–49. https://doi.org/10.1187/cbe.11-02-0013.

Yewdell, Jonathan W. "How to Succeed in Science: A Concise Guide for Young Biomedical Scientists. Part I: Taking the Plunge." *Nature Reviews Molecular Cell Biology* 9, no. 5 (May 2008): 413–16. doi: 10.1038/nrm2389.

Zimmerman, Andrea M. "Navigating the Path to a Biomedical Science Career." *PLoS ONE* 13, no 9 (September 2018): e0203783. https://doi.org/10.1371/journal.pone.0203783.

Chapter Thirteen

Cheng, Chi-Ying, Melissa Sanders, Jeffrey Sanchez-Burks, Kristine Molina, Fiona Lee, Emily Darling, and Yu Zhao. "Reaping the Rewards of Diversity: The Role of Identity Integration." *Social and Personality Psychology Compass* 2, no. 3 (2008): 1182–98. https://doi.org/10.1111/j.1751-9004.2008.00103.x.

Hall, Edward T. *Beyond Culture*. Garden City, NY: Anchor Press, 1976.

Koenig, Harold G. "Research on Religion, Spirituality, and Mental Health: A Review." *Canadian Journal of Psychiatry* 54, no. 5 (2009): 283–91. https://doi.org/10.1177/070674370905400502.

O'Keeffe, Patrick. "A Sense of Belonging: Improving Student Retention." *College Student Journal* 47, no. 4 (2013): 605–13. https://www.ingentaconnect.com/content/prin/csj/2013/00000047/00000004.

Repak, Nick. "The Professor/Grad Relationship." Grad Resources, 2018. Accessed June 9, 2019. http://gradresources.org/profgrad-relationships/.

Seppala, Emma, Timothy Rossomando, and James R. Doty. "Social Connection and Compassion: Important Predictors of Health and Well-Being." *Social Research: An International Quarterly* 80, no. 2 (2013): 411–30. doi: 10.1353/sor.2013.0027.

Umberson, Debra, and Jennifer Karas Montez. "Social Relationships and Health: A Flashpoint for Health Policy." *Journal of Health and Social Behavior* 51 (2010): S54–S66. doi:10.1177/0022146510383501.

Chapter Fifteen

Berger, Brenda, and Stephanie Newman, eds. *Money Talks: In Therapy, Society, and Life.* New York: Routledge, 2012.

Brainard, Lael. "Is the Middle Class within Reach for Middle Income Families?" Board of Governors of the Federal Reserve System, November 20, 2019. https://www.federalreserve.gov/newsevents/speech/brainard20190510a.htm.

Dogen, Sam. "It Now Costs $350,000 a Year to Live a Middle-Class Lifestyle in a Big City—Here's a Sad Breakdown of Why." CNBC, September 12, 2019. https://www.cnbc.com/2019/09/11/you-need-to-make-350000-a-year-to-live-a-middle-class-lifestyle-today-heres-why.html.

Flaherty, Colleen. "New Study Says Graduate Students' Mental Health Is a 'Crisis.'" March 6, 2018. https://www.insidehighered.com/news/2018/03/06/new-study-says-graduate-students-mental-health-crisis.

Hess, Abigail. "New Study Finds That 36% of College Students Don't Have Enough to Eat." CNBC, April 6, 2018. https://www.cnbc.com/2018/04/06/new-study-finds-that-36-percent-of-college-students-dont-have-enough-to-eat.html.

Leonhardt, Megan. "62% of Millennials Say They're Living Paycheck to Paycheck." https://www.cnbc.com/2019/05/10/62-percent-of-millennials-say-they-are-living-paycheck-to-paycheck.html.

Lieberman, Janice S. *Clinical Evolutions on the Superego, Body, and Gender in Psychoanalysis.* Abingdon, Oxon: Routledge, 2019.

Richardson, Jill. "There Is an Ugly War Being Waged against Poverty-Stricken Grad Students." Alternet.org, November 22, 2017. https://www.alternet.org/2017/11/washingtons-war-poor-grad-students/.

Wong, Alia. "Graduate School Can Have Terrible Effects on People's Mental Health." *The Atlantic,* November 30, 2018. https://www.theatlantic.com/education/archive/2018/11/anxiety-depression-mental-health-graduate-school/576769/.

Chapter Seventeen

Ainslie, George. *Picoeconomics: The Strategic Interaction of Successive Motivational States within the Person.* Cambridge: Cambridge University Press, 1992.

Ariely, Dan, and Klaus Wertenbroch. "Procrastination, Deadlines, and Performance: Self-Control by Precommitment." *Psychological Science* 13, no. 3 (2002): 219–24. https://doi.org/10.1111/1467-9280.00441.

Elster, Jon. *Ulysses Unbound: Studies in Rationality, Precommitment, and Constraints.* New York: Cambridge University Press, 2000.

Ferrari, Joseph R., Judith L. Johnson, and William G. McCown. *Procrastination and Task Avoidance: Theory, Research, and Treatment.* The Plenum Series in Social/Clinical Psychology. New York: Plenum Press, 1995. https://doi.org/10.1007/978-1-4899-0227-6.

Ferrari, Joseph. R., Jean O'Callaghan, and Ian Newbegin. "Prevalence of Procrastination in the United States, United Kingdom, and Australia: Arousal and Avoidance Delays among Adults." *North American Journal of Psychology* 7, no. 1 (2005): 1–6.

Finding Forrester. DVD. Directed by Gus Van Sant. Culver City, CA: Sony Pictures Home Entertainment, 2001.

Flett, Gordon L., Paul L. Hewitt, Richard A. Davis, and Simon B. Sherry. "Description and Counseling of the Perfectionistic Procrastinator." In *Counseling the Procrastinator in Academic Settings,* edited by Henri C. Schouwenburg, Clarry H. Lay, Timothy A. Pychyl, and Joseph R. Ferrari, 181–194. Washington, DC: American Psychological Association, 2004. http://dx.doi.org/10.1037/10808-013.

Grunschel, Carola, Malte Schwinger, Ricarda Steinmayr, and Stefan Fries. "Effects of Using Motivational Regulation Strategies on Students' Academic Procrastination, Academic Performance, and Well-Being." *Learning and Individual Differences* 49 (2016): 162–70. https://doi.org/10.1016/j.lindif.2016.06.008.

Hayes, Steven C., Kirk D. Strosahl, and Kelly G. Wilson. *Acceptance and Commitment Therapy: An Experiential Approach to Behavior Change.* New York: Guilford Press, 1999.

Kabat-Zinn, Jon. *Full Catastrophe Living: Using the Wisdom of Your Body and Mind to Face Stress, Pain, and Illness.* New York: Bantam Books, 2013.

Lieberman, Charlotte. "Why You Procrastinate (It Has Nothing to Do with Self-Control)." *New York Times* (online), March 25, 2019. https://www.nytimes.com/2019/03/25/smarter-living/why-you-procrastinate-it-has-nothing-to-do-with-self-control.html.

Linehan, Marsha M. *DBT® Skills Training Manual*. 2nd ed. New York: Guilford Press, 2015.

Lundgren, Tobias, Jason B. Luoma, JoAnne Dahl, Kirk Strosahl, and Lennart Melin. "The Bull's-Eye Values Survey: A Psychometric Evaluation." *Cognitive and Behavioral Practice* 19, no. 4 (2012): 518–26. https://doi.org/10.1016/j.cbpra.2012.01.004.

Martinčeková, Lucia, and Robert D. Enright. "The Effects of Self-Forgiveness and Shame-Proneness on Procrastination: Exploring the Mediating Role of Affect." *Current Psychology: A Journal for Diverse Perspectives on Diverse Psychological Issues* (July 2018): 1–10. https://doi.org/10.1007/s12144-018-9926-3.

Neff, Kristin, and Christopher Germer. *The Mindful Self-Compassion Workbook: A Proven Way to Accept Yourself, Build Inner Strength, and Thrive*. New York: Guilford Press, 2018.

Segal, Zindel V., J. Mark G. Williams, and John D. Teasdale. *Mindfulness-Based Cognitive Therapy for Depression*. 2nd ed. New York: Guilford Press, 2013.

Sirois, Fuschia, and Timothy Pychyl. "Procrastination and the Priority of Short-Term Mood Regulation: Consequences for Future Self." *Social and Personality Psychology Compass* 7, no. 2 (2013): 115–27. https://doi.org/10.1111/spc3.12011.

Steel, Piers. "The Nature of Procrastination: A Meta-Analytic and Theoretical Review of Quintessential Self-Regulatory Failure." *Psychological Bulletin* 133, no. 1 (2007): 65–94. https://doi.org/10.1037/0033-2909.133.1.65.

Teasdale, John D., J. Mark G. Williams, and Zindel V. Segal. *The Mindful Way Workbook: An 8-Week Program to Free Yourself from Depression and Emotional Distress*. New York: Guilford Press, 2014.

Urban, Tim. "Why Procrastinators Procrastinate." Wait But Why, October 20, 2013. Accessed September 15, 2019. https://waitbutwhy.com/2013/10/why-procrastinators-procrastinate.html.

Index

acceptance: balance between change and, 57–58; skills for determining level of, 58–59
Acceptance and Commitment Therapy (ACT), 320
ADA. *See* Americans with Disabilities Act
adaptability, 9
administrators: biomedical grad student suggestions for, 252; counseling services suggestions for, 87–88; disability services suggestions for, 88–89; financial aid suggestions for, 283–84; financial hardship suggestions for, 292; grad parent suggestions for, 197–98; group dynamic suggestions for, 135–36; impostor syndrome suggestions for, 49–50; international students suggestions for, 112–13; letter to, 1–2; LGBTQ+ student suggestions for,

211–13; mentorship suggestions for, 169–70; multicultural identity suggestions for, 266–67; procrastination suggestions for, 330–31; racial microaggressions suggestions for, 150–51; stress and anxiety of student suggestions for, 66–67; successful learning environment suggestions for, 29–30; trans grad student suggestions specifically for, 232–33; writing process suggestions for, 310–11
advisors: boundary setting with, 12; counseling services suggestions for, 87–88; disability services suggestions for, 88–89; dissertation and thesis topic help from, 299–300; grad parent suggestions for, 197–98; Grad Parent Triad regarding, 187–88; international student communication issues with, 99;

About the Editors
and Contributors

Editors

Arielle F. Shanok, PhD, is the deputy director at the Graduate Center, City University's Student Counseling Services, where she has helped graduate students to thrive for more than a decade. Dr. Shanok earned her PhD in clinical psychology at Teachers College, Columbia University, and her BA at Wesleyan University. She previously taught at Barnard College, Columbia University. Dr. Shanok has published book chapters and articles in peer-reviewed journals on a range of topics from psychotherapy effectiveness to gender and money in therapy to pregnant and parenting teen students. She has a small private practice in midtown Manhattan. Dr. Shanok provides consultations and counseling to graduate students in individual, couples, and group contexts integrating psychodynamic,

cognitive-behavioral, dialectical-behavioral, emotion-focused, and systems approaches. She also provides consultations to faculty. Dr. Shanok grew up in a multicultural, social justice–oriented family. Her approach is informed by compassion, multicultural humility, and a strength focus.

Nicole Benedicto Elden, PsyD, is assistant director at the Graduate Center of the City University of New York's Student Counseling Service. She has worked in various settings including college counseling centers; city, state, and research hospitals; government agencies; community centers; and nursing homes. Dr. Elden is a first-generation Filipina American who immigrated to the United States as a teenager. She is the first in her family to obtain a doctoral degree and is proud to have the opportunity to help and mentor graduate students through their journey, particularly one-and-a-half-generation immigrants and graduate student parents. Her therapeutic approach is integrative with a focus on multicultural humility. She has been trained in dynamic, interpersonal, supportive, cognitive-behavioral, and dialectical-behavioral therapies and family systems. She has been involved in research in psychotherapy techniques and graduate student development and supervision. Her interests include cross-cultural and minority identity formation, the immigration experience, couples and parenting, interpersonal and relationship issues, and adjustment to life transitions. She has presented on various topics throughout the years in many different settings. With this book she is very proud to add editor and author to her accomplishments.

Contributors

Kristan Baker, PsyD, is a New York State–licensed psychologist with more than twenty years of experience working with children/adolescents and their families and graduate students. Since 2003, she has worked as a clinical director, administrator, and clinician for MercyFirst, a nonprofit agency that serves clinically and diagnostically complex youth and their families. Her work focuses on addressing intergenerational trauma and community safety, which has allowed her to advocate for family treatment needs, community safety, and system changes. In addition, she has focused on training and supervising clinical and program staff, including graduate students, regarding trauma-informed interventions. She is a member of the Psychology Training Committee, responsible for overseeing the teaching and professional development of psychology interns and externs. Dr. Baker is currently transitioning to private practice to expand her trauma-focused work with adults and their families. Her doctorate in clinical psychology is from Long Island University, Post Campus, with training in cognitive-behavioral, trauma-focused cognitive-behavioral therapy (CBT), and dialectical-behavioral and psychodynamic theories.

Genny Beemyn, PhD, is director of the UMass Stonewall Center and coordinator of Campus Pride's Trans Policy Clearinghouse. They have published and spoken extensively on the experiences and needs of trans college students, including writing some of the first articles on the topic. Among the books they have authored are *A Queer Capital: A History of Gay Life in Washington, D.C.* and *The Lives of Transgender People*. Genny's most recent book is an anthology, *Trans People in Higher Education*. They are currently writing *Campus Queer: Addressing the Needs of LGBTQA+ College Students* and coediting *The Encyclopedia of Trans Studies*.

Michelle Chu-Camba, PsyD, is a New York State–licensed clinical psychologist in private practice. She specializes in working with young to middle-age adults, particularly graduate students and young professionals. Dr. Chu-Camba identifies as a therapist of color and incorporates a multicultural approach in her clinical work. She has extensive experience providing therapy to clients struggling with multicultural challenges, depression, anxiety, relationship concerns, low self-esteem, identity development, and women's issues. Prior to private practice, Dr. Chu-Camba worked in college counseling centers and community mental health clinics located in Philadelphia, Baltimore, and New York City. In addition to individual therapy, she enjoys facilitating training seminars for psychology trainees and behavioral health clinicians as well as psychoeducational workshops for community members. Dr. Chu-Camba received her PsyD in clinical psychology from La Salle University in Philadelphia. She also served as an adjunct professor, teaching Theories of Counseling and Psychotherapy.

Dr. Isabelle M. Elisha is associate director of the psychology programs at CUNY's School of Professional Studies. Her work focuses on cultural and contextual influences on children's and adolescents' developmental trajectories with a strong emphasis on the roles of race, ethnicity, gender, and socioeconomic status. Her current research examines young people's experiences, perceptions, and reasoning about civic and community engagement and their thinking about human rights. The goal of her work is to promote empirically based solutions that meaningfully address the negative impact of discrimination, inequality, and injustice on young people's well-being.

Enid Gertmenian, LCSW, is a psychotherapist in New York City. She received her undergraduate degree from Eugene Lang College, where she majored in psychology and literature. After coordinating several National Institute of Mental Health–funded research projects, she completed a graduate degree in social work at the Columbia University School of Social Work, focusing on mental health. Since 2008 she has been a faculty member at Columbia University Department of Psychiatry's Day Treatment Program and the Lieber Recovery Clinic. There, she developed a manualized group therapy treatment to address executive-functioning skills deficits. Group members work collaboratively to apply motivational theories to their own experiences to reach personal goals and better understand procrastination, avoidance, and perfectionism. With Columbia's Teach Recovery training center (www.teachrecovery.com), she developed a training program to help clinicians engage patients with executive dysfunction to turn their intentions into action. She enjoys working with small groups and individuals in her private practice.

Abbie E. Goldberg is professor in the Department of Psychology at Clark University in Worcester, Massachusetts. She received her PhD in clinical psychology from the University of Massachusetts Amherst. Her research examines diverse families, including lesbian- and gay-parent families and adoptive-parent families. A particular focus of her research is key life transitions (e.g., the transition to parenthood, the transition to kindergarten, the transition to divorce) for same-sex couples. She has also studied the experiences of transgender college students, families formed through reproductive technologies, and bisexual mothers partnered with men. She is the author of more than one hundred peer-reviewed articles and three books: *Gay Dads*; *Lesbian- and Gay-Parent Families*; and *Open Adoption and Diverse Families*. She is coeditor of *LGBTQ-Parent Families: Innovations in Research and Implications for Practice* (2nd ed.), coeditor of *LGBTQ Divorce and Relationship Dissolution*, editor of the *Encyclopedia of LGBTQ Studies*, as well as coeditor of the *Encyclopedia of Trans Studies*, which is in production. She has received research funding from the American Psychological Association, the Alfred P. Sloan Foundation, the Williams Institute, the Gay and Lesbian Medical Association, the Society for the Psychological Study of Social Issues, the National Institutes of Health, and the Spencer Foundation.

Vivi Wei-Chun Hua, PsyD, is a New York State–licensed psychologist. She received her doctorate at Ferkauf Graduate School of Psychology at Yeshiva University in Bronx, New York. Dr. Hua is the founder of Vivid World Psychology PLLC, whose mission is to empower individuals regardless of their race, ethnicity, gender, sexual orientation, country of origin, or disability to be their authentic selves and to break free of any fear, worry, or anxiety as a result of individual, societal, or systemic forces of oppression. Dr. Hua has extensive training and experiences working with individuals, couples, and families with diverse backgrounds. Originally from Taiwan, Dr. Hua is particularly insightful about the unique experiences and challenges of international students and is passionate about supporting them in achieving academic and personal success in the United States.

Dr. Juliana Karras-Jean Gilles is an incoming faculty member in San Francisco State University's Department of Psychology. She completed her postdoc in human development and psychology at the University of California, Los Angeles; PhD in developmental psychology at the Graduate Center, City University of New York; and MA in human development and social intervention at New York University. Her multimethod work centers inequality by using a structural lens to study the social development of children and adolescents in context, specifically inequality in civic development, the human rights of children, and ethnic-racial inequality across contexts. The goal of her work is to advance social justice through actionable science by generating empirical knowledge that researchers, practitioners, and policy makers can use to identify and rectify social systems that reproduce inequality in development.

Jennifer Lee, PhD, is a clinical psychologist who specializes in mindfulness-based practices and group dynamics. She serves as visiting assistant professor of psychology at Soka University in Southern California, where she teaches and advises undergraduate students. She has published in the areas of adolescent mental health and ethnic minority identity development and is coauthor of the book *Mindfulness-Based Cognitive Therapy for Anxious Children*. Jennifer has been actively involved with the group relations community for the past fifteen years, consulting at national and international conferences, business schools, and governmental organizations. She earned her undergraduate degree from Cornell University and her doctorate in clinical psychology from Teachers College, Columbia University.

Dr. Alice Mangan holds a PhD in clinical psychology from CUNY Graduate Center and a master's degree in special education from Bank Street College of Education. Formerly a member of the graduate faculty at Bank Street College of Education, Dr. Mangan has a private practice in New York City where she works clinically with adults, adolescents, and children as well as parents and families to provide consultation, assessment and evaluation, and psychotherapy services. Dr. Mangan is also a consulting psychologist at schools, companies, and start-ups and advises authors and editors of children's books. Dr. Mangan's research interests center on the relationships between schools and families and the influence of learning disabilities on the psychological and relational life of the child, parent, and family system. Dr. Mangan has a strong commitment to sensitively addressing concerns related to learning and learning disability, autism spectrum disorders, the interplay between disability and social, emotional, and psychological development, parenting and family life, and other crucial and intersecting dimensions of identity such as gender, sexuality, race, and ethnicity.

Stephanie Newman, PhD, FABP, is a psychologist-psychoanalyst, visiting scholar-clinical supervisor of doctoral candidates at Columbia University, faculty member at PANY, affiliated with the School of Medicine at NYU Institute, and a member of the American Psychoanalytic Association's Committee of Public Information. Dr. Newman has more than twenty years' experience providing insight-oriented talk therapy for those with anxiety, depression, and relationship, health, and workplace difficulties and frequently consults with parents on such issues as divorce and bullying. She is coeditor of *Money Talks*, author of *Mad Men on the Couch*, and a regular contributor to *Psychology Today* online. Her writing has appeared in outlets such as the *Washington Post*, the *Wall Street Journal*, and nbc.com, and she has recently published *Barbarians at the PTA*, a novel about teens, social media, and maternal identity. Dr. Newman recently gave the keynote speech on cyberbullying at the United Federation of Teacher's clinical appreciation day.

Dr. Adjoa Osei is a licensed clinical psychologist who received her doctorate from Long Island University, Post Campus, with a concentration in serious mental illness. Her dissertation focused on examining how Black clinical and counseling psychology doctoral students experienced navigating personal and professional relationships within their academic program. She was trained in both psychodynamic psychotherapy and cognitive-behavioral therapy, which she uses in her virtual private practice and in her private practice, located in Brooklyn, New York. She practices from a trauma-informed, culturally sensitive approach. Her private practice is founded on the perspective that identity is integral to therapeutic work and thus she views a person and their presenting problems within a cultural context.

Kristen A. Renn, PhD, is professor of higher, adult, and lifelong education at Michigan State University and serves as associate dean of undergraduate studies for student success research. With a background in student affairs administration, including inaugurating the role of LGBTQ resource provider at Brown University, she has for the last twenty years focused her research on the identities, experiences, and development of minoritized students in higher education. She is coprincipal investigator of the National Study of LGBTQ Student Success, a two-phase study of LGBTQ college students comprising a mixed-methods survey/interview phase and a four-year longitudinal interview study conducted with LGBTQ students.

Martin D. Ruck is professor of psychology and urban education at the Graduate Center of the City University of New York. His research examines the overall process of cognitive socialization—at the intersection of race, ethnicity, and class—in terms of children and adolescents' thinking about human rights, equity, and social justice. Much of his research has addressed how children and adolescents view their protection and participation rights across various cultural contexts. His work has appeared in journals such as *Applied Developmental Science, Child Development, Group Processes and Intergroup Relations, International Journal of Children's Rights, Journal of Adolescence, Journal of Applied Social Psychology, Journal of Early Adolescence, Journal of Educational Psychology, Journal of Research on Adolescence, Journal of Social Issues,* and *Journal of Youth and Adolescence.* He is currently a member of the editorial boards for *Human Development* and the *Journal of Social Issues* and is associate editor for *Developmental Psychology.* He is coeditor with Stacey S. Horn and Lynn S. Liben of the two-volume *Equity and Justice in Development Science* (2016). With Michele Peterson-Badali and Michael Freeman, he is coeditor of the *Handbook of Children's Rights: Global and Multidisciplinary Perspective* (2017). Currently, Dr. Ruck serves as senior advisor for diversity and inclusion to the president of the Graduate Center and is executive officer of the Office of Educational Opportunity and Diversity (EOD).

Phyllis Schulz, PhD, earned her doctorate in higher and postsecondary education from New York University. She has committed the last fourteen years of her career to supporting graduate education. In her current role as executive director of fellowships and financial aid at the Graduate Center, Dr. Schulz oversees all financial aid processes for the graduate school, the CUNY School of Journalism, and the CUNY School of Labor and Urban Studies. Prior to joining the Graduate Center, Dr. Schulz served as director of financial aid at New York University's School of Medicine. She has served on the editorial board of *Journal of Student Financial Aid* and as a member of the National Association of Student Financial Aid Administrator's Graduate and Professional Task Force.

Karen E. Starr, PsyD, is a clinical psychologist and psychoanalyst who teaches writing, conducts writing workshops, and provides one-on-one writing and dissertation consultations. She is adjunct clinical supervisor at the Student Counseling Service at the Graduate Center, City University of New York, where she supervises clinical psychology doctoral students providing academic consultations and short-term psychotherapy to graduate students. She was formerly visiting professor and staff psychologist at the Graduate Center. Dr. Starr is faculty and cochair of the Independent Track at the New York University Postdoctoral Program in Psychotherapy and Psychoanalysis, where she completed her psychoanalytic training and teaches the course *Writing Psychoanalytically* to doctoral-level mental health clinicians. She earned her doctorate in clinical psychology from Long Island University. Dr. Starr is the author of numerous journal articles and books, including *Repair of the Soul: Metaphors of Transformation in Jewish Mysticism and Psychoanalysis; A Psychotherapy for the People: Toward a Progressive Psychoanalysis;* and *Relational Psychoanalysis and Psychotherapy Integration.* She maintains a private practice in New York City and Great Neck, New York.

Dr. Inez Strama is a supervising clinical psychologist and certified group psychotherapist at the Student Counseling Service of the Graduate Center, CUNY. She works exclusively with master's- and doctoral-level graduate students in individual and group psychotherapy, as well as in training and clinical supervision. She has conducted research on identity formation, acculturation, and class mobility experiences of 1.5-generation immigrants and is committed to placing social justice, cultural humility, and intersectionality at the foreground of treatment. She is a practitioner of mindfulness meditation and an advocate of self-compassion as a radical act. Her loving partner and two cat children continue to teach, inspire, and amaze her. She would like to thank her former and current colleagues working in disability services for sharing their expertise as she was writing her chapter, namely Vincent Kiefner, PhD, Anna Riquier, LMHC, and Clare Wilson, PhD.

Dr. Lauren Wisely is a clinical psychologist in private practice specializing in the treatment of relationship issues, anxiety, and trauma. Lauren attended graduate school at the Long Island University's CW Post Clinical Psychology Doctoral Program. She has a private practice at Delaware Psychological Services (https://www.delawarepsychologicalservices.com/), where she treats children, teens, college students, and adult populations. She has extensive training and experience in psychodynamic, cognitive-behavioral, dialectical-behavioral, and trauma-focused psychotherapy. A travel and photography enthusiast, Lauren now resides in the quiet seaside town of Lewes, Delaware, with her husband, three children, and their menagerie of family pets.

Jess Zonana, M.D., is assistant professor of clinical psychiatry and spent ten years working as a therapist and psychiatrist for Weill Cornell Medical College's student mental health program, treating biomedical graduate students, medical students, and physician assistant students. She currently serves as chief of adult outpatient services in the Department of Psychiatry at New York-Presbyterian-Weill Cornell Medical Center, where she oversees outpatient clinical programming for the adult psychiatry residency training program. She also serves as medical director of the Weill Cornell Medicine Wellness Clinic, a free student-run mental health clinic serving queer and transgender populations in New York City.

CPSIA information can be obtained
at www.ICGtesting.com
Printed in the USA
BVHW031103030721
611032BV00002B/2